Deaf Worlds

In memory of Edith Maud Thatcher

Deaf Worlds

A study of integration, segregation and disability

Sally Sainsbury

with the assistance of Penny Lloyd-Evans

Hutchinson

London Melbourne Sydney Auckland Johannesburg

Hutchinson & Co. (Publishers) Ltd

An imprint of the Hutchinson Publishing Group

62–65 Chandos Place, London WC2N 4NW
and 51 Washington Street, Dover, New Hampshire 03820, USA

Hutchinson Publishing Group (Australia) Pty Ltd
16–22 Church Street, Hawthorn, Melbourne, Victoria 3122

Hutchinson Group (NZ) Ltd
32–34 View Road, PO Box 40–086, Glenfield, Auckland 10

Hutchinson Group (SA) (Pty) Ltd
PO Box 337, Bergvlei 2012, South Africa

First published 1986

© Sally Sainsbury and Penny Lloyd-Evans 1986

Set in 11/13 pt Compugraphic Baskerville by Colset Pte Ltd, Singapore

Printed and bound in Great Britain by
Anchor Brendon Ltd, Tiptree, Essex

British Library Cataloguing in Publication Data

Sainsbury, Sally
 Deaf worlds: a study of integration,
 segregation and disability.
 1. Deafness——Social aspects
 I. Title II. Lloyd-Evans, Penny
 362.4'2 HV2395

Library of Congress Catalog Card Number
 85–'30605

Contents

Acknowledgements

Many people have contributed to this book. In particular, we are grateful to all those deaf people living in private households, hostels, homes for the elderly and the deaf, and hospitals, who generously talked at length about their lives. Staff at every level in the local authorities, voluntary organizations, residential homes and hostels, and hospitals involved in the study, were helpful in talking about their work and those in their care, as well as in making arrangements for interviews. We owe them a considerable debt of gratitude.

We are also indebted to Ruth Griffiths, Bridget Atkinson, Doreen Young and Elizabeth Plumb for producing successive typescripts; to Thelma Sainsbury and Huw Rees for their helpful comments; and to colleagues in the Department of Social Science and Administration for their help and advice.

The fieldwork on which the book is based was carried out between 1979 and 1982: our thanks are due to the Social Science Research Council for funding this research.

Foreword

The historical neglect of deaf people is as disgraceful as it is perplexing. There can be no excuse for failing to give them the same care and consideration as is shown to those with other disabilities. Abundant evidence proves that severely deaf people suffer acutely from this discrimination.

Most people are ignorant of the problems of the deaf. Surprisingly, comparatively little has been written about deafness, yet this must be one of the most rewarding disabilities of all to study. It has a crucial effect on the quality of life, affecting speech, language, reading ability, educational attainment, employment prospects and social relationships. Studies which shed light on the difficulties of communication, the inevitable concomitants of deafness, help deaf people to shed their load.

Those who suffer the worst consequences of deafness are the profoundly deaf, born without hearing, or losing it very early in life. They struggle to acquire language, have little speech and in some cases only tenuous contact with the normal world.

By making a case study of profoundly deaf people in all kinds of settings, Sally Sainsbury has illuminated a scene hitherto shrouded in darkness. Deafness today is still often treated with derision rather than concern. But, as the case study reminds us, in the past it was treated with cruelty and even brutality. The discipline, beatings, isolation, frustration, desolation and despair in some institutions show, in an extreme form, what terrible penalties the innocent victims of deafness had to endure.

Conditions have improved somewhat today but the searchlight of this study confirms that there is still vast, unnecessary human suffering. What possible justification can there be for the staff of some hospitals making no effort to communicate beyond the basic necessities? Why should people guffaw like donkeys when the deaf attempt to communicate by signing? What sort of health authorities are they that permit such patients to be imprisoned in a callous and indifferent institution of silence?

Deaf people with a loving family are happily placed; and a loving spouse is a piece of human gold. Yet some deaf people are isolated within their own families. They can be separated from their nearest and dearest by the barriers of deafness, yet the appearance is one of apparent normality.

Institutional care varies according to the institution, but in most of them it is plagued by the difficulties of communication.

This basic problem, lying at the heart of deafness, can occasionally be solved by brilliant lip reading or excellent manual signing. But such a solution is extremely rare. The born deaf child cannot be expected to acquire the subtleties of language with the same easy facility of a hearing child. Manual signing can bridge the gap and it is evident that when using manual communication profoundly deaf people have no difficulty in communicating with each other. Unfortunately, this whole issue is bedevilled by the ancient controversy about manualism versus oralism.

The dogmatists of both sides leave much to answer for. Total communication is surely the only reasonable and intelligent way forward. Yet it is apparent from this study that the controversy which has shadowed deafness for so many decades is far from being solved.

There are no simple solutions and even modern developments like sub-titling of television cannot make a substantial contribution. The profoundly deaf are caught in a classic Catch 22 situation. Television, the greatest medium of communication ever known, places greater emphasis on the spoken word than is commonly assumed. Sub-titles, through Ceefax and Oracle, could interpret these words for profoundly deaf people. But they are largely poor because their handicap limits earning power. So they are unable to afford the modern development which would improve their knowledge and possibly enhance their prospects. And even if they could afford it, their poor reading ability would make comprehension of sub-titles difficult.

Progress will lie not on one front but on all of them. But some recommended forms of progress could turn out to be prescriptions for disaster. We need to consider carefully what are the objectives. The current fashionable aim is integration. Yet this is just a means to the over-riding end of making the lives of deaf people as happy and fulfilled as possible. In so far as integration helps to fulfil this it should be pursued. But we should recognize that there are dangers. Hearing people, who determine the life style of so many who are congenitally deaf, could provide a framework which creates the illusion rather than the reality of integration.

The profoundly deaf still suffer acute and sometimes unnecessary deprivation. They need the informal network of understanding family and friends, but they depend heavily on the formal network of specialized statutory and voluntary agencies. They desperately need to communicate and to take more responsibility for their own lives. All methods of communication need to be pursued, including the use of interpreters. Their selective and appropriate use can bridge the gap between the deaf and hearing worlds.

Deaf people also need a vast improvement in their education, training and employment opportunities. The sooner the public, policy makers and administrators accept these necessities, the better for the prospects of the deaf people concerned.

Above all, they need understanding from hearing people, appreciation of the gravity of their disability, and respect for their individual qualities which are unimpaired, except in the imagination of others.

The Rt Hon. Jack Ashley, CH, MP
July 1985

1 Introduction

I was born deaf – in Derbyshire, 1915. That's my home.

The doctor looked at my ears when I was little and said 'Can't cure'. I used to pour holy water in my ears when I was young. I had one brother and four sisters. My deafness caused a lot of problems when we were all playing together.

I went to a residential school for the deaf when I was four. The teachers all used sign. The staff were bad at this school. They beat us, threw things at us, hit our faces with things. I was often sick. For punishment the bold pupils were locked up in an empty room or they had to get up at five in the morning to do the washing. I will never forget it. And I was treated as stupid by my parents. I only ever had one holiday, and I was frightened and miserable. I moved to a day (deaf) school at the age of 12. In this school we were forbidden to use sign. I think teachers should sign and speak. They taught me baking, shoe repairing, carpentry and tailoring. They suggested I should go in for cabinet making when I left school.

From 1932 I was a cabinet maker, then in 1939 I went on war work as a machinist making generators and later fridges. They tried to bomb the factory. I remember pushing my bike into a field and watching the doodlebugs. My two boys were born about that time. In 1945 I went to work at the film studios. I made boats and special effects for film sets. Film work wasn't regular so I had lots of different jobs, shop fitter, machinist. I lost my thumb in a machine. There was always terrible union problems. I got regular full-time work until 1980 when I reached retirement age and went part-time as a cutter-moulder.

I've been to the Labour lots of times. They lost all my references and cards. I'm on their register of disabled, and I've seen the DRO* frequently. He's got me a number of jobs – I think he's done his best. He couldn't sign at all, never went with me to an interview or arranged for an interpreter. I got this job through the Labour. It's a firm of coachbuilders. It's best working with other deaf. One manager told me I was a quicker worker than the hearing. It depends on my health how long I stay in work. The best job was the exhibition work – the Motor Show, the Boat Show – lots of variety.

*Disablement Resettlement Officer.

I had my ears tested with modern equipment for the first time at the hospital in 1956. The doctor said 'Go and get yourself an aid.' I went again three years ago. I've got a National Health Service bodyworn aid. I don't wear it at work. They get mad and shout 'Why don't you put your aid on?' It helps a bit with lip reading. It's quiet, peaceful without it. I find it's too noisy at work for it. I made my own flashing doorbell, no other aids. I never use the telephone. My biggest difficulty as a deaf person is making lady friends. Watching people's mouths when we are talking makes me sleepy. It's hard reading newspapers – it's the words. Some I don't understand so I don't bother. I find it difficult to understand hearing people. But I'm very patient and calm. Deaf friends say, 'I've never seen you lose your temper.'

I've been married twice. My first wife died in 1970 and I remarried five years ago, but we divorced. They were both deaf. I like living on my own but I would like a lady friend. I have two sons; the eldest is 41 and has two daughters. I don't see a lot of them. When they were young I couldn't give them much help at school. I had to leave all that to the teachers and the grandparents. I didn't have any trouble understanding them though. We couldn't do much for them and we relied a lot on the grandparents. Still, they grew up very well.

I feel lonely without a lady around. I've got a friend near the South Coast – I don't spend much time here at home. I'd like to spend less time alone than I do. Sometimes I feel fed up.

Touch wood, I haven't had any accidents. I don't get nervous, but I would be more confident if I were hearing. I can use my voice. In an emergency I could call the neighbours downstairs. I don't get on with downstairs so I don't communicate with them. They haven't replaced the broken light bulb in the downstairs hall for more than a year. There are broken light switches down there and they leave the kitchen dirty. They're putting refuse in the back garden and encouraging the rats. With the hearing I try sign, gesture, finger-spelling, but mostly I have to use writing and I can't write very well. Sometimes I don't feel up to it. It's like a test of strength – I don't make the attempt, it's too much effort. Things would be different if I could hear. It takes longer to get things. I rely on others more. All my friends are deaf.

When people realise I'm deaf they're usually awkward. The neighbours chat and interpret a bit for me. I think they're understanding and sympathetic but they're still awkward. Life is different if you're not hearing because it's hard to find friends, know what's going on. I go to the pub, play bingo in the (deaf) clubs, shop and go visiting a lot. The hearing are different from the deaf and dumb. Most people can't understand what I'm saying. I feel different to the hearing. I've got a deaf friend living locally – just got married. I was a witness. If the hearing don't use sign it's difficult to lip read them. When you're communicating with the hearing you don't have easy talking.

I meet other deaf people in the clubs and when I go visiting. We use sign and speech and there's usually no difficulty. Me and my (deaf) friend talk

about everything – politics, sport. We usually have no difficulty understanding, but there are times when I can't understand – some of his signs are
funny because he's Irish. I see deaf friends once a week at least. At work we
talk about politics, taxes, etc. but that's always difficult because I have to rely
on speech. I'm not bothered if hearing people see me signing even though they
sometimes make jokes. I would never avoid trying to communicate with
hearing strangers but I always feel awkward.

The worst problem is with the housing: can't negotiate directly with the
council. I have to rely on my sister. It's difficult dealing with outsiders. I have
to write everything down. Sometimes I finger-spell, but very few know the
alphabet. I would like to see more of the social worker with the deaf: there are
always problems to clear up. Mr Green used to come but not now a long time.
I would like a visit – he talks when he comes, signs and finger-spells well.

I would like the deaf welfare to help to transfer me to Wandsworth. I don't
see anyone from the welfare. At the moment my sister is helping me. I've used
an interpreter when I've had to talk to the gas board and the council – usually
neighbours or my sister. When I had to deal with the police and the courts
over my car accident and the divorce I wanted an interpreter but I had to
manage on my own. I haven't been able to get satisfactory interpretation at
work or in dealing with the council. I feel a bit embarrassed having an interpreter present, but I appreciate the help. I usually have problems getting an
interpreter–can't get one now. If I want any information or advice I go to
hearing friends or relatives. Usually I manage to read and write letters, but if
they are complicated I go to my sister. Everything takes longer if you are deaf.
Getting the writing done at work takes longer and if I'm late with it I lose my
bonus. I want to live in South London with my sister. She's crippled with
arthritis. The council won't do anything for me only exchange.

I watch television, mostly football, sport. Never go to matches, not for a
long time. I go out plenty. I play bingo at three (deaf) clubs – Southend,
Luton – they have a bar, Ipswich. I used to go to hearing clubs occasionally
but not now. I don't read – not interested. I might visit seven or eight different
(deaf) clubs in the course of a year. We play games – cards, bingo, snooker,
dominoes, talk, sometimes I'm bored by too much gossip.

I drive my own car for holidays. I go with my deaf friend. We went to a
hotel in Scotland this year – can only afford one a year. Touring in the car is
the best kind of holiday. Went one day abroad – to Bologne – with my deaf
friend. I like holidays with the deaf, it's better with the deaf.

I never think about my situation much but there should be more help for the
deaf.

Deaf people go to work

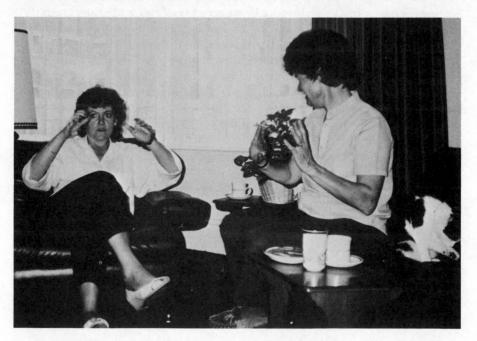

. . . enjoy the company of relatives and friends

. . . retire

. . . and live alone in old age . . . in a hearing world.

Few of us have any understanding or knowledge of the way of life of those deaf people for whom speech cannot be the normal method of communication. That this is so is not surprising. Many deaf people achieve little contact with the hearing: often, their communication with the hearing world, won with great difficulty, is restricted to interaction which is essential for day-to-day living. Written communication is limited, since literacy is difficult to achieve without speech. And to attain the most modest levels of understanding through lip-reading requires considerable powers of concentration and good eyesight. As a consequence, many deaf people are debarred from both our formal and informal information systems which rely predominantly on sound, or assume literacy. Yet among themselves deaf people communicate freely and effectively in their own manual or sign language, in which they achieve fluent and even poetic levels of expression. Therefore, for many deaf people, the deaf community, identified by the use of sign language, meets their most important personal requirements. Beyond that, only the contact with central and local government agencies, such as health, housing, social security and employment, where it is essential for achieving an acceptable framework for life, is pursued with determination. The informal conversational exchanges at the workplace, in shops or the neighbourhood, are regarded as peripheral and optional.

However, the lives of members of a community at once separate from the mainstream of our society yet largely invisible within it, are in themselves of interest. Furthermore, there should be concern that the hearing, who for the most part are unable to communicate with many deaf people except at the most basic level, dominate the allocation of provisions within the social services. How do doctors, psychiatrists, teachers, housing and employment authorities know how to deal appropriately with people dependent upon sign language? Our carelessness and ignorance conspire to ensure that many deaf people experience considerable deprivation and suffering.

Moreover, study of the deaf community offers an opportunity for some of the important principles which underlie social policy to be tested. In considering the distinction between normality and disability, how far may lives lived within the deaf community, yet which in all other essentials – such as attending school, going to work, raising a family and so on – appear to conform to the norms of our society, be regarded as normal? How far may policies designed to enable people to achieve the *appearance* of normality in these terms, be judged as successfully promoting normality? Much of the rhetoric of our social policy emphasizes the desirability of provisions which promote integration rather than segregation, and therefore insists on the superiority of policies designed to enable people to live 'in the community' rather than in residential or hospital settings. How far may those who live outside residential homes and hospitals, but within the deaf community, be regarded as integrated? Within the personal social services, the battle continues to rage as to the superiority of specialist or generic provision. Where substantial problems of communication exist, what are the appropriate policy responses? As we shall see, in seeking answers to such questions, considerable doubts may be raised about the general applicability of some of the major principles underlying social welfare provision.

Although in recent years there has been a growing interest in the deaf, particularly deaf children, and a body of literature has begun to accumulate which explores the role of communication problems in the development and education of the deaf child, little attention has been paid to the problems experienced by deaf adults.

Our interest was first aroused in 1978 by the discussions within voluntary bodies regarding the possibility of closing down the homes for the deaf. Specialist provision appeared to be outmoded at a time when there was widespread acceptance among policy-makers and caring agencies, both statutory and voluntary, that their objective should be the integration of all disabled people into the normal community. Yet there appeared to be much confusion about the nature of integration: some saw integration in terms of the abolition of specialist provision and the absorption of groups such as the deaf into the facilities provided for the hearing community (homes for the elderly, for example); others considered integration to be nothing short of everyone, other than those who required medical treatment in hospital, living in their own homes and enjoying a pattern of life which at least closely resembled that of normal people. But how appropriate is it to apply to deaf people the assumptions regarding integration which have commonly informed social policy discussion in recent years? To clarify this issue, we decided to talk to a group of deaf people who were reasonably easy to identify and whose impairment might be expected to create severe communication difficulties, namely profoundly prelingually deaf adults (hereafter, the deaf). In what senses are the lives of deaf people normal and to what extent does the degree of their normality depend upon whether they live in their own homes or in institutions? How far may a normal pattern of life be achieved within institutional settings and are there differences in this respect between institutions for the deaf (specialist institutions) and those which cater predominantly for the hearing (general or non-specialist institutions)?

To seek answers to such questions we decided to talk to deaf people living in a range of specialist and non-specialist institutions as well as private households.

Deaf people in private households provided evidence of how far and in what ways they were able to integrate with 'normal' people in the community, the degree to which they sought integration (or segregation) in the deaf community, and how far they were isolated by deafness. For comparison, those in residential care for the deaf explained what, if any, part they played in the life of the community outside the residential home among both deaf and hearing people. And those in hostels for the deaf showed how far people in half-way houses in practice occupy a middle ground in terms of engaging in normal daily activities with the hearing. Deaf people living in institutions not specifically for the deaf – residential accommodation for the elderly, and psychiatric and mental handicap hospitals – provided evidence about the degree to which they mixed with or engaged in activities with 'normal' people outside their specialist institution and the extent to which they were isolated from others, including staff, *within* that institution.

From the outset discussion of integration/segregation poses questions about the meanings to be attached to the term 'community', which has played a prominent part in debates about care in the post-war period and which has been yoked firmly to anti-institutionalism and arguments for desegregation. In what sense do those living in private households live 'in the community'? To what extent can each of the residential and hospital settings themselves be regarded as sufficient communities? Do they represent acceptable alternative ways of life for deaf people? What concept of community is fostered in therapeutic settings, such as hostels for the deaf where the objective is to return residents to the community?

Integration and engagement in a 'community' raised the questions of the degree to which in practice services promote integration or segregation and the practicability of adopting one or the other. How far is integration an objective of policy as far as staff are concerned? How far and in what ways is the policy implemented? The present study was structured to provide systematic evidence across a broader spectrum of services for a single client group than has been possible to date. Unlike much recent research which has focused on either community-based provision and services, or residential institutions and hospitals, it allows policy regarding 'integration' to be explored across a wide range of settings. How far can therapy achieve integration into either the normal or deaf communities for those in non-specialist institutions such as psychiatric and mental handicap hospitals? Do arrangements within specialist institutions promote integration with the normal community or the deaf community? To what degree do arrangements within half-way hostels for deaf people promote their integration into the local community, deaf and hearing? And how far does care in the community actively seek to *foster* the integration of deaf people with the normal community or with the deaf community outside residential care?

The possibility of substituting one type of service for another has been argued with increasing force in recent years but rarely on the basis of empirical data. Standard interviews with deaf people and staff across a broad spectrum of settings provide the opportunity for considering how far substitutability is possible for this particular group. Crucial to a discussion of substitutability is the identification of the factors which seem to determine where deaf people live. Studies of institutional care carried out in the late 1960s and early 1970s suggested that in terms of their need for care and treatment many people in institutions differed little from those living elsewhere. How far is this true of deaf people?

Then there was the question of the overlapping care provisions for the deaf made by the NHS, local authorities and voluntary organizations. Recent discussion of substitutability has focused on the necessity for flexibility of response to care provision. Increasingly, assessments of effectiveness both in terms of cost to the providing agency (but rarely to the informal network of family and neighbourbood) and client satisfaction have emphasized the necessity for co-ordinated multi-agency provision. To what extent does overlap between agencies ensure a flexible service for deaf people? What are the particular contributions made by genericism and specialization? Are specialist skills necessary within a generic social services department? What happens to the possibility of treatment/therapy for other conditions such as mental handicap or psychiatric illness where specialist skill in communicating with deaf people is absent? To consider such questions it was necessary to interview deaf people in settings provided by the NHS, local authorities and voluntary organizations.

Concern with substitutability has also increased interest in the balance between formal and informal networks of care. Government policy and much of the writing on community care and integration have emphasized the importance of informal networks. The present study provides an opportunity to explore not only how far the balance changes according to personal characteristics and to social circumstances but also according to setting.

A number of central issues arising from the approach adopted and the nature of the problems which deafness presented in carrying out the study, determined the plan of the book. First, considerable difficulties attach to the identification of the deaf. There is no universally accepted definition of profound prelingual deafness. Furthermore, little systematic evidence is available about the incidence and distribution of the deaf population. As a consequence, there is no handy source, such as there is for the blind (the Blind Register), from which a representative sample of deaf people might be drawn. In the event, it was decided to carry out a case study rather than to identify a representative sample of deaf people. Nor was it possible to choose representative institutions for inclusion in the study, and arbitrary choices had to be made on the basis of what little was known of the deaf populations of individual institutions (see Chapter 2).

Much of the experience of deaf people was attributable to the interplay between their disability and personal characteristics. It seemed appropriate, therefore, to provide an analysis of personal characteristics at the outset to inform subsequent discussion (see Chapter 3). But the central theme of the study was the impact of communication difficulties arising from severe hearing impairment on the daily lives of deaf people. How far was speech acquisition affected by hearing loss? Could deaf people compensate for their loss of hearing by developing lip-reading skills of a high order? What impact did deafness make on childhood and adolescence? How did it affect family relationships? (See Chapter 4.) All of the people interviewed experienced roughly equivalent degrees of hearing loss, yet they were found to be living in a wide range of settings – long-stay hospitals, hostels, homes and private households. Why should this be so? Was the determining factor the presence of an additional handicap such as a mental disorder or a physical impairment? (See Chapter 5.)

Then there was the question about the degree of normality achieved by deaf people in their day-to-day living. In what sense was there any difference in the type of integration achieved by those living in general institutions? Were there any differences between the settings in the degree to which deaf people were segregated from the hearing? How far did deaf people in the different settings vary in the extent of the choice they exercised in their personal lives, the autonomy they enjoyed in their use of personal space and the responsibilities they shouldered? (See Chapter 6.) Some of the criticism levelled at institutional care has focused on the absence of the kind of generational mix which is common in many households and most neighbourhoods. It has been argued that the segregation of long-stay hospital patients and residents of homes from the informal network of family, friends and neighbours, a network which constitutes the natural and normal care system, is a common effect of life in institutions. What variation was there between those living in the different settings in the part played by the informal network in their lives? How well did the strength of family relationships withstand the strain arising from severe communication difficulties? How was the position of the deaf person within the family affected? (See Chapter 7.)

In recent years it has become increasingly popular to argue that the formal network of services has grown too large, and that the professional and the specialist should give way to the volunteer. How did the deaf manage to operate the formal system of care? What role was played by specialists in their lives? Were the activities of specialists such that they could be readily replaced by volunteers? (See Chapter 8.) For most adults below the retirement age, normality is achieved in large measure through paid employment which ensures both status and financial independence. How successfully were deaf people educated and trained for work? What employment opportunities were available to them? How typical of our society in general were the financial rewards which they enjoyed? And how much economic independence did they experience? (See Chapter 9.) Finally, there is the question of leisure: how far did deaf people pursue the same activities as the hearing, and to what extent did they do so in the company of the hearing? (See Chapter 10.)

Considerable problems are involved in the presentation of case-study material where more than one case is involved. In such circumstances, especially when the cases concerned are markedly different, it must be assumed that a major objective is comparison. Yet it is common practice for material relating to each case to be presented separately, with the comparisons relegated to a concluding chapter. Such an approach ensures a thorough understanding of each case in turn. But when more than two or three cases are included, the reader who is interested in comparisons may well find it difficult to sustain impressions from one case to another, and indeed, may even be at a loss until the synthesis provided at the end. The purpose of the present study was avowedly one of comparison. The over-riding concern was to illuminate the lives of deaf people by considering the impact of their communication difficulties and how this varies according to living setting. The book is, therefore, written in terms of themes such as communication, education, health, work and personal relationships with family, friends and neighbours, as they are affected by communication difficulties. Each of the different living settings is discussed in relation to each theme. Inevitably, some of the clarity with which life in different settings is presented has been sacrificed. However, it is hoped that the loss is justified by a consequent increase in the strength of the portrayal of the experience of deafness, and how far and in what ways that experience differs according to setting.

As this is a case study, no claims are made that the experiences reported here are necessarily those of the deaf population in general, though evidence from other studies suggests that in certain important respects, such as communication skills and levels of literacy, those interviewed were, in fact, typical. However, in view of the nature of the study our conclusions must be tentative. From time to time it has seemed appropriate to provide information about the deaf people involved in the study as a group. It is not the intention to imply thereby that such information is in any way representative of all deaf people, or to confuse case study with survey material. In the absence of any systematic information about the deaf population there seemed to be advantage in aggregating the experiences of those in different settings, and for that purpose treating the whole group as a case before going on to make comparisons across the settings.

Whenever possible we have illustrated our discussion with the replies made by deaf people to our questions. Because British Sign Language is not signed English, we have not sought to reproduce exactly the written English equivalent of the individual signs used by deaf people, but have translated the sense of the total signed sentence. The way in which sign language is used is as idiosyncratic to an individual as is speech; but no attempt has been made to convey such particularity by adopting comparably distinctive speech patterns in the translation. However, some of the characteristics of signed communication, such as the repetition of a single word to give emphasis to a particular point, have been retained.

To preserve anonymity the names of the people and institutions involved in the study have been changed in the text.

2 Method

Where did deaf people live?

A major difficulty besetting any study of deaf people and the provisions made for them is the dearth of information about their number. Estimates of prelingual profound deafness in children vary between 0.8 and 1.5 per 1000 live births. And the distribution of profoundly deaf persons across the range of different types of care is unknown.[1]*

The voluntary nature of registration with local authorities[2] means that registers under-represent the total number of deaf people. Indeed there has been variation over time as well as between different local authorities in the number of deaf people registered as a proportion of the total population. Between 1959 and 1977, the number registered rose by a third. Deaf registrations were not alone in showing an increase: during the same period, registration of the hard of hearing, the blind and the general classes of the physically handicapped also rose. Perhaps it is significant that in each case the most substantial part of the increase is attributable to the rise in registration among persons over 65 years of age.[3] In part, then, increases in registration appear to be a function of rising numbers of elderly people and in part of the expansion of provision made by the personal social services which has encouraged disabled people in all categories to turn to those services for help. That registration with local authorities substantially understates the total numbers of deaf people in the population is suggested by the fact that the rate of registration of *all* deaf people is no greater than the estimated incidence of those who are prelingually profoundly deaf.[4] Furthermore, combined registration of deaf and hard of hearing people varies widely between local authorities. For example, among Inner London boroughs, Kensington and Chelsea registered 0.63 per 1000 population as deaf and hard of hearing in the year 1978–9 compared with 1.09 in Lambeth, 1.39 in Westminster, 2.15 in Lewisham, 2.43 in Islington and

*Superior figures refer to the Notes and references section beginning on p. 299

2.49 in Southwark. Similar disparities in registration rates are to be found among all categories of registering authorities.[5]

An ageing population is estimated to have had less impact on the number of those with 'very severe impairment' (that is, those unable 'to hear speech at all, even with amplification), compared with those with 'other impairments' defined as 'all other hearing defects down to and including difficulty in hearing in public places or in group conversation'.[6] But whatever the reason for the growth of registration over time it appears to be accepted that local authority registration seriously understates the prevalence of those in the 'very severe impairment' category.[7]

To some extent variation between local authorities in their rates of registration may reflect regional differences in the prevalence of hearing impairment. For example, prevalence in the northwest was nearly 40 per cent higher than the national average according to the 1947 national survey, while that in the southwest was substantially below the average. In comparison, it has been estimated that 'the registration rate in 1975 for the outer London area, for instance, was 40 per cent higher than the national average while the northwest was 20 per cent higher and the southwest 19 per cent higher'.[8]

Nevertheless, local authority registers offer a more reliable source of information for the prelingually profoundly deaf than for other categories of deaf people. It has been estimated that the deaf without speech appear 'to be fairly fully registered with a national rate of 0.31 per 1000 population compared with an average of 0.37 in the 1947 survey and about 0.40 in the 1975 estimate'.[9]

Local authority registers, then, were regarded as a suitable source from which to identify deaf people living in private households. As *all* profoundly prelingually deaf people in each institution were interviewed, so were all those registered and living in private households. The choice of local authority was dependent upon good practice, defined as the maintenance of a senior social worker with the deaf or an otherwise good staffing level. The selected London borough had for three years retained the services of one of the best qualified social workers with the deaf in the country who had been a pioneer in the field of deaf studies, and who had a broad interest in the field of deaf welfare. Nevertheless, in practice the borough concerned was considered to make provision at a level which was representative of areas reliant on a single specialist. At that time seventy-two persons over the age of 16 were registered in the borough as being deaf with speech, and eighty-one as being deaf without speech. From these two groups (mainly from the latter) fifty-two were identified as being prelingually deaf by the specialist social worker.

To balance this outer London borough a random sample of one in sixteen of those registered were interviewed in an inner London borough, which had recently updated its register and employed one qualified social worker with the deaf. The two London boroughs presented a contrast in terms of the voluntary contribution made to their deaf welfare provisions. In the case of the first, voluntary involvement in club and social work service provision was considerable; but in the second there was no major voluntary provision. The problems and responses of these boroughs were likely to be typical of those of cities, and to balance them all but two of those registered in a southern county area were interviewed. Here services for the deaf (including the social workers for the deaf) were provided by a voluntary association on an agency basis for the local authority. Thus the interviews with those living in private households – sixty-eight in all – were designed to reflect organizational differences in service provision and to include both metropolitan and non-metropolitan areas.

The three residential homes for the deaf illustrated a range of type of facility, geographical area, balance between the sexes, and size. However, they were all run by voluntary bodies, though all three had residents sponsored by local authorities. The small London home provided residence for eight women, mainly in middle and old age, in a converted Victorian house. It was close to facilities such as shops, entertainment and transport, and local authority welfare provision such as a day centre and the area team office.

The south of England home was run by the county's Association for the Deaf. The superintendent had overall responsibility for *all* deaf people in the area, and the Association employed social workers for the deaf on an agency basis for the local authority. There were eighteen residents, only four of whom were men, living in a converted large Victorian home in a comfortable residential area. Although the house was at the top of a steep hill, it was close to transport facilities and local authority social services were located nearby.

The west of England home was situated in a small country town near the Welsh border. It was run by the county's Association for the Deaf, but the Association used the social work services provided by the county council. There were fifteen women but only five men in residence, and they were housed in buildings which has been purpose-built as a preparatory school. Although the home was located near the centre of town in a comfortable residential area, and good public transport was available for mobile residents, access to shops and other facilities was difficult because of hills. And the home was more remote than the others from social service facilities for deaf people.

The five residential homes for the aged were run by local authorities. The first, in an outer London borough, provided beds for thirty-five elderly men and women in a large Victorian house in a middle-class residential area. Transport facilities were poor, making visits by friends and relatives and access to shops and entertainment difficult. The second home was in North Wales, and at least potentially offered a different approach to the care of elderly deaf people. It provided accommodation for thirty-six elderly men and women but included a new six-place unit for deaf people which allowed deaf residents the choice to integrate with hearing residents as much or as little as they wished. To provide a refuge for and to preserve the separate identity of the small group of deaf residents a separate kitchen and lounge were available. At the time however, only two deaf people were in residence because difficult decisions had to be taken regarding the removal of those who were in voluntary organization homes for the deaf outside county boundaries. Access for the elderly to transport, shops and other facilities was difficult, and steep hills posed problems for those with restricted mobility. The home was located in the estate manager's house in the grounds of a stately home; the local authority social services area team was housed nearby in converted stables.

In contrast, the third home was situated in an inner London borough and provided residence for sixty elderly men and women. Shops and a busy street market were a quarter of a mile away, while welfare facilities were nearby and the social worker for the deaf visited frequently. The fourth home was situated in a small south coast seaside town, half a mile from the promenade shops. Finally, a sheltered housing scheme for the elderly in an outer London borough provided self-contained one-room flats with kitchen and bathroom. It was staffed by a warden and two domestics who cleaned the communal areas such as the large lounge and entrance hall, as well as the flats of frail residents. There was easy access to day centre facilities and area social work teams, and although his office was 2 miles away, the social worker for the deaf was a frequent visitor.

The two hostels contrasted sharply in a number of ways. The first had been purpose-built a mile and a half away from all the facilities of an East Anglian city centre. It provided self-contained flatlets with shared baths for couples and single people, and three entirely self-contained cottages. The intention was to make accommodation of a variety of styles available to young deaf working people. A warden was present to provide maintenance and other types of help, but hostel staff had no avowed treatment aims. Local voluntary bodies and the local authority were involved in the provision of social work help for residents. The hostel was built largely by local Rotarians: residents paid an unsubsidized rent from their salaries or benefits. Although some services were available, residents were largely self-sufficient. Men predominated here: there were ten men and six women. Transport and access were easy and the location was ideally chosen for employment opportunites. Although the hostel backed on to a pleasantly wooded, middle-class residential area at the rear, it faced a busy main road and an industrial estate.

The primary objective of the second hostel was to accommodate and rehabilitate young ex-psychiatric patients. The hostel worked in conjunction with a nearby psychiatric hospital which had a special unit for the deaf, and was situated in a working-class area of a small north-western industrial town, near public transport, and one mile from a shopping centre. The hostel had been purpose-built as a joint project by two voluntary bodies. Accommodation was available for an equal number of male and female residents amounting to twenty-four in all. Full-time employment for residents was the first objective, since normality was defined largely in terms of holding a job. Social work help was provided by a voluntary organization, but the psychiatric supervision of residents was provided by the deaf unit of the psychiatric hospital of which most of the residents were out-patients or ex-patients. Local authority social workers with the deaf assumed no responsibility for residents. The residential costs of the hostel were met partly by payments from the local authority and partly by residents from their personal income.

No systematic evidence was available on which to base the choice of non-hospital residential care facilities available to deaf people. Individual institutions were selected to illustrate a variety of geographical settings, organization, objectives and practice in relation to the care of deaf people and in the case of non-specialist provision, their known presence.

However, systematic information was available both of the numbers and the ages of deaf people in hospitals for the mentally ill and mentally handicapped in 1971, following the study by the RADD of deaf people in psychiatric hospitals in the London area, and by the RNID in hospitals for the mentally ill and mentally handicapped in England and Wales in 1971.[10] The most important criterion for the selection of hospitals was an above-average population of deaf patients. The RNID study had shown that although there were as many as 1004 deaf people in psychiatric and mental handicap hospitals in England and Wales in 1971, on average the number in each hospital was small.[11] Another important consideration was the necessity for variation in both size of hospital and geographical location.

Of the four psychiatric hospitals included in the study, by far the largest, with rather more than 1500 beds, was situated in a village to the north-east of London. No special facilities were available for deaf people other than regular visits from the voluntary association for the deaf. The hospital was in a mixed residential area, half a mile from the nearest shops, and London Transport provided easy access by bus. The second hospital was located in a middle-class area of North London and offered care for 1130 in-patients. Access was difficult by public transport, and the hospital was remote from shops and other facilities. The local authority social worker with the deaf contributed the only specialist facilities for deaf patients. The third hospital, located in Essex, was remote from facilities such as shops and entertainment. It had 827 in-patients and included a rehabilitation unit for the deaf. The unit operated on a day basis, providing therapy for fourteen hearing-impaired out-patients and in-patients. Not all the hospital's profoundly deaf patients were in the care of the unit. A voluntary association worked closely with the hospital and a local authority social worker for the deaf visited on two or three occasions in the year. Finally, the smallest hospital, with 650 in-patients, was situated in a working-class area in the middle of a Midlands industrial town. As such, it was conveniently placed for transport, shops and other facilities. There were no special facilities for the deaf patients in the hospital, though a voluntary organization, funded by the local authority, provided a social worker for the deaf who maintained irregular contact.

The two hospitals for the mentally handicapped were both in the north of England. The smallest accommodated 192 patients: although it catered for both sexes there were only four women patients. It was located in a remote rural area, with an infrequent bus and a railway station a mile away. Special facilities for developing non-verbal communication were available to deaf patients. The local authority social worker for the deaf supported the hospital psychiatrist in establishing and running the hospital's Makaton workshop. The largest of the two hospitals for the mentally handicapped had 360 patients. Its facilities included a hospital school with special facilities for deaf children. Moreover, there was a sensory unit in the hospital which was intended to benefit some of the deaf as well as other patients. It was run by a nursing sister who had learnt and used Maketon. The hospital was situated in a rural setting about half a mile from a small market town which offered employment in light industry.

Defining profound deafness

Despite the increasing interest in disabled people in recent years both by those engaged in research and by policy-makers, problems of definition and measurement remain acute. A variety of definitions and assessment procedures operate even within the social security system. And even within each benefit scheme, allocation may be made according to a variety of principles or criteria which themselves reflect still other interpretations of the nature of disability.[12] In the absence of any agreed, overall definition of disability policy-makers and academics alike have responded in an *ad hoc* fashion to the problem.[13] It is not surprising, then, that considerable difficulties attach to the definition of profound prelingual deafness. No single standard and generally acceptable definition has yet been devised. The problem is twofold. First, there is the difficulty of defining what is meant by 'profound deafness'. And second, the definition of 'prelingual deafness' has to be established. Let us begin with profound deafness. No clinical assessments of deafness are required for registration with the local authority. Classification according to the categories 'deaf with speech', 'deaf without speech', 'hard of hearing' is left to the discretion of the social worker. However, particularly within the field of education and medicine, sophisticated measurements based on audiometric testing have become common. In recent years, audiologists have begun to make their assessments according to a wide range of criteria, including the reception and discrimination of speech, degree of decibel loss, as well as level of intelligence, emotional stability, age at the onset of deafness, and of speech and language development.[14] The most commonly conducted of the variety of audiometric tests in use are pure tone audiometry and speech hearing tests. The purpose of pure tone audiometry is to discover the degree of hearing loss at a variety of pitches of sound associated with the range of the human voice. Speech hearing tests are administered using a list of words each of which combines a variety of sounds at different frequencies or pitch.

In pure tone audiometry the receptivity of each ear to pure tones is tested at three or more points within the range of speech. To some extent decibel loss at individual points on the scale indicates the functional level of hearing at these points. Decibel loss is recorded for each ear separately on an audiogram. The overall assessment of an individual's hearing loss is established as the average of the addition of the decibel losses recorded at each point on the scale. It is clear that the precise meaning of such an assessment is ambiguous: people with high pitch loss, low pitch loss, and 'islands' of hearing may all produce an identical overall assessment of decibel loss and yet experience very different problems in the reception of speech.

Speech-hearing tests clarify the precise nature of the hearing difficulty to some extent. Even so, test conditions cannot reproduce the range of acoustics present in the everyday situations in which hearing is used. More complex and discriminating measures, therefore, may be required, particularly for educational purposes.[15]

Capacity to measure deafness has changed with technology over time, and measures remain ambiguous. But definitions and assessment of deafness have varied over time in response to changes in aids to hearing as well. Many of those who, because of current techniques of sound amplification, are identified today as hard of hearing would have been assessed as deaf even in the inter-war period. Variation over time in the definition of disability is not confined to deafness.[16]

Clinically defined blindness in practice covers a wide range of residual sight[17] and in a similar way, among those categorized as deaf there is a wide range of residual hearing. The proportion of deaf people without any residual hearing is in the region of 2 or 3 per cent. It is generally agreed that optimal use should be made of residual hearing by employing available audiological technology. The earliest reports of a powered hearing aid date from the year 1900. Eight years later technological development of hearing aids remained at a relatively primitive level, and as a consequence there was an ambivalent attitude to the degree to which a purely discriminating measure of deafness appeared to be appropriate even within the education system,[18] despite the importance attached to hearing in educational achievement since 1892. By 1910 all ambivalence had disappeared: 'Among the requirements of a satisfactory scheme of medical inspection is that of applying a hearing test to every child who is old enough to respond'.[19] However, it was not until the late 1920s that audiometry in the form of a gramophone audiometer was introduced into the school health services in London, Birmingham and Tottenham. Government interest in the problems of deaf children was aroused by the publication in 1932 of Fichioly's study of the deaf in England and Wales;[20] and a Committee of Inquiry was set up which reported in 1938.[21] The Second World War intervened to prevent the implementation of the Committee's recommendations, until the Education Act 1944 obliged local education authorities to identify and assess handicapped children, including those with defective hearing, from the age of 2 years.

It was in the early 1940s that pure tone audiometry began to replace gramophone audiometry, and from 1948 the Mednesco hearing aid became available free of charge under the new National Health Service. The developing emphasis on early diagnosis, auditory training, early education and audiological advances has meant that children who in earlier days would have been regarded and taught as deaf are now categorized as partially hearing. Some of those involved in the present study attended school before the First World War, others were educated in the inter-war period, while many were of school age in post-war Britain. Thus, depending upon their age, the deaf people discussed here differed widely in the range of audiological resources available to them in childhood. As a consequence, not only were they likely to differ substantially according to age group in degree of residual hearing, as well as within age groups, but also in terms of the degree to which they had been helped to exploit any residual hearing. There were differences between the age groups, even in the type of categorization to which they had been subjected. For it was not only the case that the older members of the group had been the subject of methods of audiometric testing and amplification which were primitive by today's standards, but that their classification as deaf was established by means of a functional assessment rather than by actual decibel loss. Even the terms of the classifications were different: in 1928, deaf people were classified for educational purposes as deaf-mutes, deaf semi-mutes, speaking deaf and partially deaf,[22] whereas the current categories are restricted to profoundly deaf and partially hearing.

Despite the technological developments both for the testing and amplification of hearing, even today, the functional impact of deafness may vary widely between people of identical assessments and the same age. If appropriately prescribed, hearing aids currently on the market may result in a gain of between 30 and as much as 60 decibels – at least as much as the difference necessary to enable some profoundly deaf people to discriminate speech. On the other hand, other profoundly deaf people with similar test results may derive no benefit from amplification because they have a different type of hearing loss. Furthermore, tolerance of amplification varies from person to person: some find the distress it causes so great that they are prepared to forego its apparent usefulness. The degree to which amplification can be used determines in part the extent to which a deaf person is able to participate in activities within the hearing community.

In Britain 'profound deafness' is recognized as the most severe category of deafness. The difficulties associated with measurement in general pose considerable problems for arriving at and operationalizing a definition of profound deafness. It is now common for decibel loss to be the main criterion by which assessment is made. Profound deafness is defined by some educationalists and researchers as a loss of 70 decibels and over.[23] But there is wide variation in functional capacity within a group of persons identified by such an assessment. Beyond a decibel loss of 70 and up to a loss of 106 speech discrimination with amplification diminishes and beyond 106 decibel loss it is unlikely that with a hearing aid of the usual range any speech sounds will be recognized. However, a decibel loss of 70 is by no means universally accepted as the threshold of profound deafness. It is equally common for a loss of over 85 or even 90 decibels to be required for an assessment of profound loss.

The limitations of definitions according to decibel loss have been recognized for some years. The actual decibel loss does not indicate whether the loss in question is conductive or sensory, whether it is uni-lateral or bilateral. As early as 1956 Goodhill evaluated deafness in terms of the way in which hearing loss interferes with communication.[24] It is only recently that this approach has been adopted more widely. Studies such as that of Kyle have shown a direct relationship between speech intelligibility and degree of deafness.[25] The importance of functional as opposed to decibel loss has been increasingly argued in recent years. It is now being stressed that in cases where the onset of deafness occurs at an early age, it is at least as important to assess the nature and degree of difficulties likely to be experienced in the acquisition of language and development of speech as it is to assess decibel loss, especially where the assessment is based on pure tone audiometry.

For the purposes of the present study a functional approach to the defini-tion of profound deafness was adopted. The reasons for the decision were threefold. First, it was apparent that because the age range of the people involved in the study was likely to span three generations, no standard audiometric test would have been applied to all of them. The criteria by which the profoundly deaf were to be identified, therefore, would have to be applied in the course of the study: no pre-existing assessment would be satisfactory. But assessment criteria would have to be such that they were easy to operationalize. Given the wide variety of settings in which inter-viewing was to take place and the time scale, satisfactory audiometric tests were out of the question. Finally, in view of the growing awareness of the limitations of assessment according to decibel loss and the increasing interest in functional approaches, it seemed reasonable to adopt the latter, which appeared to be peculiarly appropriate for a study designed to investi-gate integration.

Defining prelingual deafness

Previous studies have shown that disabilities which are congenital or which are acquired in early childhood make a substantially different impact on daily living to those which occur in later life. And these differences are particularly marked in the case of sensory disabilities.[26] Scott has explored the implications for the blind of reliance on the sighted for information required for social interaction.[27] The problems posed by deafness for per-sonality development and social functioning are certainly no less than those posed by blindness. It has been pointed out elsewhere that 'the most striking feature in any description of deaf persons is the insoluble dilemma that they are forced to live in a hearing world where the major part of the cognitive communication takes place orally'.[28]

Discussion of the importance of *congenital* deafness on later development has focused on speech reception which has been identified as crucial
to the development of speech acquisition. Di Vasiliu has argued that a
viable baby of, say, 30 weeks gestational age, hears after birth, and would
hear at that gestational age even if unborn.[29] Indeed, others have gone so
far as to state that 'the human foetus in utero and newborn babies can
discriminate speech like signals on the basis of frequency and intensity'.[30]
By the age of 4 weeks or so the normal infant discriminates and shows a
preference for the maternal voice.[31] The deaf infant, dependent upon visual
and tactile stimuli alone, takes longer to learn the significance of events
with aural cues. And as Lenneberg has argued, 'sensory deprivation is
multiplicative'.[32] It seems likely that the development of the deaf child will
depend heavily upon the non-aural stimuli provided.

The development of speech is crucial in a society in which the
predominant form of interpersonal communication is oral. In recent years
there has been increasing speculation that receptive language heard in the
early months of an infant's life is a positive influence on the future development of language.[33] Indeed, Lenneberg goes so far as to refer to the
biological time locked function of language learning which can never be
regained once its time is past.[34] The first few years of life have been shown
to be crucial for cognitive language development,[35] which has been shown
to operate on a continuum from earliest interaction with those upon whom
the infant is dependent. Soon after birth the infant is able to interpret and
respond to the stimuli of which he or she is aware. For the normally hearing
child, communication develops quickly thereafter towards language
proper. By the age of 6 months, babble takes on the recognizable quality of
the surrounding language. Thus, American and Chinese babies can be
differentiated by the sounds they make, other features apart.[36] It is at this
point, when communication in the normal child is developing rapidly, that
a decline in the development of communication skills has been noted in
hearing impaired infants.[37] From this age the hearing child's language
develops rapidly and by the age of 12 months normal children utter sounds
in clear imitation of words. It has been shown that by the age of 24 months
the child may have a vocabulary of fifty spoken words, and by the age of 3
years, the 'grammatical complexity of utterances is roughly that of collo-
quial adult language' and a vocabulary of between 1000 and 2000 words
has been acquired.[38] In comparison, the typical deaf child has a vocabulary
of fewer than twenty-nine words at the age of 4 years, while an unusually
bright deaf child will have acquired 200 words.[39]

Hearing impairment not only affects the development of vocabulary in
young children, it also affects the quality of speech. Kyle was able to

identify ranges of hearing loss from an evaluation of speech.[40] In Britain, studies have shown widespread speech difficulties among children with little residual hearing. For example, two studies carried out by the Department of Education and Science found that of children with an 80 decibel loss or more, 33 per cent and 23 per cent respectively were assessed as having unintelligible speech.[41] Conrad's recent work supports the existence of the relationship between decibel loss and speech intelligibility, but suggests that the DES studies seriously underestimated the proportion of severely hearing-impaired children involved. He found that in the range of 71 to 90 decibel loss almost a third (31.4 pr cent) of children had speech which was 'no better than barely intelligible, while at a decibel loss of 91 and above, almost three-quarters (73.5 per cent) of children had speech which was no better than barely intelligible'.[42]

The impact of slow language development on the educational achievements of deaf children is understandably immense. Both Conrad[43] and Rodda[44] have suggested that educational achievement is low, held back by protracted difficulties in language development and associated problems. Indeed, half of the deaf school-leaving population fail to achieve sufficient language comprehension to enable them to read a tabloid newspaper with any real grasp of its meaning.[45]

It is not surprising, then, that sign language is widely adopted among those whose hearing is severely impaired, particularly when deafness is congenital or when onset occurs in early childhood. Signs are as visibly distinctive as the speech sounds of English are phonologically distinctive.[46] Moreover, 'the gross movements of simple signing are almost certainly easier for children to form than are the precise articulations of speech and follow naturally from the gestural behaviour common to all infants'.[47] And it must not be assumed that sign is necessarily inferior or less effective than speech: it has been shown that internal sign is quite as efficient as internal speech.[48] Sign language develops whenever deaf people gather together in groups. As early as 1900, the necessity for sign language and its sophistication were already recognized.[49] Yet in England, sign language has been viewed unfavourably by those responsible for the education of the deaf.[50] Only in recent years has this point of view been challenged in Britain. Conrad has shown that early signing cannot be said to impair subsequent skill in English, and that at the very least it provides an enviable and otherwise unattainable vocabulary.[51]

Thus for those with severe hearing impairment from birth or early childhood the main medium of communication with other deaf people is sign language. But sign language cannot be used in the course of interaction with the hearing community. In cases where everyday use of amplification is not helpful, lip-reading is the common method of receptive communication with the hearing world. Yet lip-reading skills are not easily developed. It has been estimated that about 40 per cent of children in special schools for the deaf fall into the category where no usable speech will be heard,[52] but the vocabulary of such children is usually very limited, and a deaf person can lip-read at best only those words which he knows. Lip-reading tests of deaf and hearing youngsters seem to show that deaf children benefit very marginally from all the educational effort put into the practice of lip-reading.[53]

The crucial difference, then, between those who are born with severely impaired hearing or who acquire it in early childhood, and those who become deaf in later life, is that for the former, speech development normally will be severely limited, and as a consequence, sign language will be relied upon for communication with deaf people and lip-reading with all its limitations for receptive communication with the hearing world.

At what age of onset may the division be drawn between those who are prelingually and those who are post-lingually deaf? Like all other definitional problems related to deafness, that of prelingual deafness is the subject of considerable controversy, and as a consequence, no generally acceptable standard definition exists.

Indeed, even the importance of the division between pre-and post-lingual deafness is not universally regarded as necessarily the most crucial: others are those between congenital and non-congenital and between prevocational and post-vocational deafness. But in practice none of these terms can be used without qualification. At first glance, the terms congenital and non-congenital deafness appear to be the least arbitrary of the classifications in general use.[54] But it is difficult to know whether a hearing loss is present at birth, since a loss may be partial, unilateral and/or limited to a narrow frequency range. Such deafness is difficult to detect by the methods currently available for neo-natal screening. Furthermore, factors present at the time of birth may result in the loss of hearing, but may not be manifest until some time after birth. The division between pre-and post-vocational deafness is open to wide interpretation. It was regarded as crucial in the 1970 National Census of the Deaf Population of the United States where the prevocationally deaf were defined as 'those people who could not hear and understand speech and who had lost (or never had) that ability prior to 19 years of age'.[55] Nevertheless, many accept that the importance attached to the age of onset of deafness is associated with the implications for speech and language development. But the definition of prelingual deafness, despite the importance attached to it, remains arbitrary.

Conventions about the significant age-range when deafness makes its most far-reaching impact on development have changed over time. When the US Bureau of the Census conducted its last decennial study of the incidence of deafness in 1930, all of those who had become deaf before the age of 8 years were included in the category of prelingually deaf persons.[56] Recently, however, there has been a marked trend towards defining the prelingually deaf in terms of very early ages of onset. To a large extent this change is attributable to technological advances which have eased the difficulties associated with diagnosis, and developments such as the establishment of the 'at risk' register. Such innovations have increased public and professional awareness of the symptoms and causes of deafness and as a consequence there has been a reduction in the delay between onset and diagnosis.

The driving force behind the move towards early diagnosis has been a growing recognition of the importance of developing appropriate programmes of aural rehabilitation as early as possible, but there is still no agreement as to the precise division between prelingual and post-lingual deafness.[57] Recent empirical studies have drawn the dividing line variously between 18 months and 3 years as the latest age of onset. For example, Fundudis, Kolvin and Garside concluded that their small sample of deaf school-age children could 'be included in the category of "prelingual deafness" as the deafness almost always had an onset before the age of three years'.[58] On the other hand, in a recent study of seventy-five deaf adolescents the prelingually deaf were regarded as only those for whom the onset of deafness had occurred before the age of 2 years.[59] In contrast, Meadows defined the prelingually deaf as those for whom onset had occurred by the age of 18 months.[60] In a recent study of deaf and partially hearing persons in Devon mental handicap hospitals, reliance was placed entirely upon assessments and categorizations made by hospital staff.[61] And in 1973, an Irish study classified respondents as 'profoundly deaf' when they had 'no useful hearing, and were born deaf or lost their hearing before the development of speech'.[62]

In practical terms, reluctance to specify an age by which the division between pre- and post-lingual deafness may be defined reflects a realistic appreciation of the shortcomings of such an approach, especially where an early age is chosen. The difficulties of diagnosis are most acute in infants and small children, whose response to auditory stimulus is difficult to interpret without the use of highly specialized monitoring equipment. Deafness which is present at birth may not be detected for some time. Both parents and professionals sometimes misinterpret an infant's reaction to stimulus which appears to be unusual: it is all too easy to attribute such reaction to late development or mental retardation. Thus delay between onset and diagnosis is still common. Indeed, of 22,000 children studied in the US known to have been born deaf, fewer than half had been diagnosed as deaf by their third birthday.[63]

Moreover, it is increasingly argued that even modern audiometric tests are not sufficient on their own. Tests of hearing, it is now argued, are most useful when they are made within the total context of the life of the individual being assessed.[64] It is not surprising, given the difficulties of early diagnosis, that many profoundly prelingually deaf people were consigned to hospitals as congenital mental defects in the first quarter of this century. Lack of speech or indecipherable noises and heedlessness were enough to consign a child to the closed wards.

Perhaps it is understandable in view of the difficulties of ascertaining both degree of early loss of hearing and age at onset that it is becoming common for functional criteria to be used for the assessment of profound prelingual deafness. In the case of children, Liben has defined the profoundly prelingually deaf as 'generally those who cannot function normally in settings, such as education and social settings in the hearing community rather than those with any (specific) hearing loss at all. That is they are people who have profound pre-lingual hearing losses that are not eliminated through amplification and are, therefore, people who require special education, special service, and so on'.[65] Functional definitions have been in use within the education system since the end of the Second World War. For example, a Ministry of Education Circular issued in 1945, and revised in 1953 and 1959, classified deaf children as 'those who require educational methods suitable for pupils with little or no naturally acquired speech or language'.

A high proportion of those involved in the present study were born before the introduction of modern techniques for the diagnosis of profound prelingual deafness. As a consequence, to rely on age at the point of diagnosis as the age of onset was judged to be inappropriate. Therefore, a functional approach was adopted to the definition of prelingual deafness as well as to profound deafness. An age limit which was more generous than those adopted in some recent studies was included more as a guide than as a strict criterion of definiton, but in practice none of those interviewed exceeded the age limit, though delays between onset and diagnosis appeared to be common, especially among people in the older age groups.

In the event, therefore, it was decided to define profound prelingual deafness as that which rendered the hearing-impaired person where onset of deafness occurred before the age of 4 years, unable to hear sounds from which speech might be developed through the use of hearing alone either aided or unaided; that is, people who lacked appreciation of sound within the intensity ranges usually associated with communication. An additional advantage of adopting such a definition was that in practice it corresponded roughly with the category 'deaf without speech' on local authority registers from which the names of those living in private households were drawn: it is common in the literature for the terms prelingually deaf and profoundly deaf to be used interchangeably.

The selection of people for interview

To be interviewed those identified as deaf had to be resident within the setting. During the pilot study, it emerged that non-residents differed substantially from resident populations in range of activities and relationships available to them. Second, only those deaf people who had reached their sixteenth birthday were interviewed. The objective of the study was to focus on adults, that is, on those who in the normal way were not legally dependent and for whom choice associated with autonomy over day-to-day living would be a usual expectation. Third, deaf people in institutional settings such as homes, hostels and hospitals, were interviewed only if staff were sure that a long interview would cause no ill-effects. Thus a few ailing elderly people and a few who were in an acute phase of mental illness were excluded from the interview and observation.

Operationalizing the definition of 'profound' deafness

Having defined profound deafness in functional terms it was necessary to devise criteria by which the definition could be operationalized and the people to be included in the study identified. The criteria chosen were those used in 1970 by Schein *et al.*[66] The basis of the test was self-assessment of functional ability to hear according to seven descriptions of different thresholds of hearing. The Schein study showed that each description equated with a range of decibel loss. Only those who identified their hearing threshold with one of three of the descriptions below were included in the present study:

1 'Can hear a loud sound only', which Schein had shown to have a decibel loss equivalent of 109 decibels.
2 'Can usually tell one loud noise from another', where the equivalent decibel loss had been shown to be within the range 98.6 and 109 decibels.
3 'Can usually tell the sound of speech from other sounds and noises'.

Thus the threshold of profound deafness was defined as that point at which sounds would be identified as speech sounds, but would not be discriminated one from another. As in the study for which the scale was devised, respondents described their capacity to hear in their customary hearing state, amplified or non-amplified.

Operationalizing the definition of 'prelingual' deafness

The reluctance to define the term 'prelingual' in terms of years and months reflects the known variation between children in their development. It has also been suggested that children achieve their cognitive 'milestones' at different rates.[67] However, Lenneberg has argued that the complexity of language and syntactical structure is within the grasp of the normal 3 year old[68] Nevertheless, the delays in diagnosis likely to have been experienced by those born before the Second World War determined the adoption of an age limit of 4 years for the onset of deafness, but even this limit was used as a guide only. The pilot study had shown that some elderly respondents, despite being informative in all other respects, were uncertain about their age at the onset of deafness, which they tended to describe in terms such as: 'well before going to school'; 'I remember something happening when I was very little'; 'after my youngest sister was born, I remember her crying, etc.'; 'I was very ill in bed and the curtains were closed. I was hot and the Doctor came'. Those born before 1930 were included if their speech development had been severely restricted and if they communicated largely by sign, gesture or in writing.

The identification of deaf people

All of the hospitals provided a list of hearing-impaired patients before interviewing was due to begin, but it was clear at the outset that these lists all represented an underestimation in view of the total number of patients, and the proportion who were aged. Previous research had indicated that such factors were important in determining the number of deaf patients.[69] Thus the lists had to be augmented by information from other sources.

Supplementary information was sought from hospital records. Whereas all hospitals had centrally-kept information about their patients, only two recorded details of hearing impairment.

Once the records had been searched, ward staff were approached for information. Each ward was visited to determine whether those who had been identified as deaf met the criteria by which profound prelingual deafness had been defined, and to search for further patients who had not been identified either on the hospital lists or in the central records. It was striking that when two or more qualified nurses were available to provide information on a ward, they rarely identified the same patients as deaf or hard of hearing. Substantial omissions from the original hospital lists were found not only of hard of hearing patients but also of profoundly prelingually deaf patients.

, In the case of people living in private households and residential accommodation for the elderly, identification was based on local authority registers of the deaf. Outside London, names and addresses were divulged by the voluntary organizations' social worker for the deaf who was responsible for local authority provision in the area. In the London boroughs lists were compiled in consultation with the social worker for the deaf. A letter was sent to the individuals and families concerned in which the purpose of the project was explained. A visit was made at each adddress and the hearing-impairment test was applied as a sifting procedure. The interview took place either then, or at a time for which an appointment was made.

In the hostel for the young working deaf a list of residents was provided by the warden and letters of explanation and times for appointments were sent to residents before the arrival of the interviewer who resided in the hostel throughout. Residents of the half-way psychiatric hostel were introduced by the warden to the interviewer, who explained the nature of the study: each resident was given an explanatory letter.

The same approach was adopted in the three residential homes for the deaf where no difficulties were encountered in identifying and making contact with deaf people.

The response

Altogether 182 people were identified as deaf of whom 175 were interviewed, giving a response rate of 96 per cent.

	Identified as deaf	*Interviewed*
Living in own home	71	67
Local authority Part III accommodation for the elderly	5	5
Living in hostels	35	33
Homes for the deaf	34	33
Psychiatric hospitals	27	27
Mental handicap hospitals	10	10
All	182	175

The high response rate appeared to be a tribute to the great interest in the project shown by the deaf people, who were keen to see their disability more widely understood by the hearing and were full of ideas for expanding the scope of the study.

The quality of the evidence

Reluctance or inability to provide evidence

It was understandable that most of the people interviewed required an explanation of the significance of some questions, particularly those relating to financial circumstances. For a minority, mainly those in the older age groups, the difficulty remained and, as a consequence, it will be found that some of the discussion regarding personal and household income is based on information from a smaller number of people than might have been expected.

Those residing in hospitals, local authority and voluntary homes and hostels were often unable to give full details of their personal circumstances, especially their financial affairs. In part, their lack of knowledge was attributable to the administrative arrangements made in some institutions, to problems of communication between hearing and deaf persons, and to the rapid changes in benefit levels in recent years. Thus many patients and residents suggested that information about personal finances be sought from wardens, matrons or ward staff, not because they wished to avoid disclosure but because they considered that these were the only sources of precise information. A similar difficulty arose with questions concerning treatment.

Communication difficulties

There was a small category of respondents whose powers of communication were so limited that it was impossible to rely on interview alone. They were mainly patients in hospitals for the mentally handicapped though they included a few aged long-term patients in psychiatric hospitals. In the main, such people were limited to a minimal and idiosyncratic communication code of iconic gestures and mime. In such cases, basic information was sought from other sources.

During the pilot stage of the study it emerged that communication could be seen in terms of a multi-dimensional continuum. For example, receptive skills did not necessarily relate closely to expressive skills. In instances where skill in either expressive or receptive communication was limited it was sometimes possible for a third party who was known to and trusted by the deaf person to interpret questions or the response. Interviews were most successful where an understanding by the interviewer and the deaf person about their respective range of skills was achieved quickly and a common ground sustained throughout the interview. This was most commonly achieved in private households and hostels where there was a more uniform use of signs and more accurate finger-spelling than in the hospitals and residential homes. It was distressing to interview manually communicating hospital patients whose proficiency had clearly deteriorated from prolonged isolation from other deaf people. Although eager to respond, they experienced great difficulty in recalling the signs quickly and finger-spelling accurately. There was a great sense of pride among deaf people in their performance of manual communication, and especially in their ability to acquire difficult vocabulary and to finger-spell accurately. Some elderly confused people experienced periods of lucidity during which they realized how much they had lost of their earlier command of language.

Variation in attitudes towards communication helped to determine differences between settings in ability to communicate which affected the interviews. Because their use was not encouraged in some settings, communication skills had declined: isolation from other deaf people compounded the problem. In psychiatric hospitals where the deaf comprised only a small proportion of the total number of patients, distinctions were made between patients with different types of mental illness but not between the deaf and the hearing. For staff, deafness was usually no more than an irritant which forced a divergence from routine: whereas normally nurses could rely on a call to bath, bed, meals, and so on, a deaf person often had to be fetched. In contrast, in special residential homes and hostels where deafness was seen as the primary reason for admission, other conditions, such as physical dependence, poor communication or mental illness, were often regarded as a consequence of deafness and staff accepted and compensated for communication handicap as a matter of course. Although the manual communication skills of staff in specialist residential homes and hostels were often no greater than those displayed by hospital staff, communication and their approach to it was flexible. Hence, communication was a first objective, and as a consequence staff had developed skills of clear speech and a feeling for the tone of voice which would facilitate receptive communication on the part of residents. Whereas hospital staff appeared to be diffident and indeed even embarrassed to be seen using unaccustomed modes of communication with deaf people, such as clear articulation and gestures, staff in special residential homes and hostels used a wide range of communication methods without self-consciousness or hesitation.

Some hospital staff were embarrassed to see evidence of communication skills displayed by deaf people for the first time during interviews: the implications for treatment and rehabilitation were clear. Some regarded attempts at communication as foolish, and considered that it was more sensible to acquire information from staff. Others, however, were impressed by the sight of sign language in operation and sought advice about the treatment of deaf people in general. Still others appeared to gain derisive satisfaction from crude displays of gesture and mime by deaf patients. Time and again deaf people were called upon to give displays of what was regarded as their oddest communication behaviour. Not only were opportunities for deaf patients to practise their communication skills limited, and the importance of their association with other deaf people in this respect not appreciated, their communication was observed to be widely misinterpreted by staff.

In view of the limited communication skills of some deaf people it seemed appropriate to identify additional sources of information, of which the most important were observation and staff.

Observation

Most of those with very severe communication problems were in hospitals or homes and it was possible to observe them in special units, in occupational therapy, undertaking chores, at meal times and during leisure periods. On average, between ten and fifteen hours were spent in observation before an interview, whenever severe communication difficulties were anticipated. In two cases observation was a major source of information because communication proved to be impossible: the first was a blind–deaf woman who was without communication, and who was cared for in a high dependency ward of a mental handicap hospital, for whom even the unaccustomed touch of a hand seemed to be disturbing, and produced frenzied clapping which was not a show of approval but of insecurity; the other case concerned a severely handicapped young man who had no voluntary movement.

A methodological issue was raised by the approach described here. For those in residential institutions and hospitals information was obtained both by interview and by observation. These two methods are complementary but qualitatively different. Moreover, the reliance placed on one rather than the other varied according to the deaf person's communication ability.

Staff

Almost without exception staff appeared to be keen to provide information about individual deaf people as well as the institution in general. Despite the pressures resulting from low staffing levels they were prepared to spend anything up to several hours discussing individuals in their care. On the whole, long-standing staff had a wide knowledge of deaf people's background, characteristics, preferences and skills. Because many patients in mental handicap and psychiatric hospitals were unable to provide full information about themselves, a great deal of reliance was placed on staff to provide what would otherwise have been missed. However, such information was not invariably accurate: details on record pertaining to one patient were sometimes found to have been ascribed to another in conversation. Therefore, checks were made with written records.

Variation between the settings in the quality of evidence

Both observation and the interviews reflected a genuine difference between people in the various care settings in relation to the range of their daily activities, but such differences in no way represented capacity to engage in activities: many hospital patients had a wider frame of reference than was true of residents of specialist homes, for example, when they assessed their capacity to participate in daily activities. None of the residents of specialist homes had access to as many rehabilitation facilities as did the medium and low dependency patients in the hospitals. Only very high dependency patients and those who were physically unwell in the hospitals remained on the ward for all their daily activities. In contrast, no regular daily activities were provided outside any of the homes visited. Domestic tasks performed in the homes could be compared with patients' performance of domestic chores on the ward. But in terms of recreational activities, comparisons were difficult. One home provided weekly sessions for selected patients at a local club for handicapped people, but over the four weeks of observation and interviews lack of transport and unsuitable weather reduced attendance at the club to two sessions. To a large extent such variation represented actual differences in the range of experiences available to deaf people, but this was not entirely true in all cases, and certainly did not represent the *potential* for activity among them.

Many of the activities of those living in hostels and private households, such as work and social engagements, were usually beyond the range of observation. Observation in general was intended only to augment what was provided by the interview, and assumed importance only when acute communication difficulties limited the information provided by interview. For the most part those living at home and in hostels had no difficulty in describing their activities.

The second factor which caused variation in the quality of information between settings was the difference in the range of staff available to provide information. In residential homes and hostels, there were only a relatively small number of staff, whereas a wide range of settings existed within the hospitals, each with its own specialist staff.

The third related factor concerned staff attitudes to the study. Staff differed in their knowledge of deaf people in their care. Thus the warden of one hostel who encouraged independence in residents had little to add to interviews, and considered those who took part in the study well able to account for themselves. In contrast, the warden of the other hostel adopted a far more protective attitude towards residents despite the fact that the majority were young and employed. In two homes for the deaf matrons proved to have only basic biographical details about residents and were dismissive of those in their care. They were free with statements such as: 'They've nothing in their heads', 'They're subnormal', 'I shouldn't believe a word they say', 'Take them with a pinch of salt.'

Where deaf people were not living in private households, the attitudes of staff could be of crucial importance in determining the success of interviews. In some cases their hostility to the interviews was considerable and may have affected the quality of the material collected. On the other hand, in a home run by a husband and wife, the attitude was one of encouragement, a factor which was especially important when time and persistence were required to interview those with severe communication problems. In two homes for the deaf where antagonism was most marked, communication with residents in general was undervalued and disbelief in the possibility of communication was at its strongest. One matron remarked of an elderly woman 'If her own daughter can't communicate with her how can I believe you have been able to?'

It was common for those working in specialist residential homes to 'humourously' urge residents to 'behave themselves' during interviews, to be careful what they said, not to say too much, not to let the side down, and so on. It is possible that such admonitions were taken seriously by deaf people and affected the freedom with which questions were answered. In contrast, nursing staff in hospitals, perhaps because they were used to patients being interviewed by consultants and social workers, gave straightforward encouragement to patients who had agreed to be interviewed. They automatically allocated a sideroom for interview purposes and the door remained shut until the session was terminated. Thus hospital interviews were more relaxed than many of those carried out in specialist residential institutions, where interruptions were frequent.

Even in private households interviews were conducted in widely differing conditions which may have affected the outcome. For example, relatives were present during some but not all of the interviews.

It may be that the advantages and disadvantages of the various settings for interview purposes had the effect of evening out their impact on the quality of evidence collected. While deaf people in hospitals were unable to practise communication skills, those in specialist residential homes could do so at least among themselves; on the other hand, the conditions in which interviews were carried out in hospitals encouraged free expression of opinions, whereas this was by no means always true of specialist residential homes.

Communication in interviews

How reliable were the interviews carried out with deaf people? What confidence can be placed on the receptive and expressive communication of both interviewer and respondent?

Despite the growing number of studies concerned with hearing impairment in recent years, there is little discussion in the literature about the mechanics of conducting interviews with deaf people. For example, a recent study based on interviews with deaf adolescents, while in other respects invaluable, offers no indication of some of the uncertainties which may arise in the course of interviewing. Only the competence of the interviewers in sign language is mentioned.[70] An exception in this respect was the study of the young, adult, hearing-impaired population of Ireland.[71] Here the relationship between interviewer and respondent is explored, but there is no discussion of difficulties of communication during interviews, and there is no discussion of the possible impact of communication skills on the interview as a method of data collection.

Yet it seems that whenever communication difficulty exists, even where skilled interviewers are used, the possibilities of misunderstanding and misrepresentation are multiplied. It seems important to explore the *nature* of these difficulties, therefore, even if no overall assessment of their impact on the data collected can be made. Communication is a two-way process, and the capacity of a hearing interviewer to communicate in sign language, for example, must be an important factor in determining the outcome of an interview.

As far as possible interviews were conducted by the communication method in which deaf persons conversed most easily – in the majority of cases British Sign Language. The hearing interviewer had acquired considerable proficiency in sign language, but, not having the benefit of deaf parents had not, therefore, been exposed to sign from childhood. During interviews it was necessary sometimes to control the flow of language and ask for a repeat, either because the flow of sign was too fast or because specialized signs were used. Just as hearing people verbalize in different ways – in terms of style, speed and pitch – so deaf people develop idiosyncracies. The degree to which sign is grammatical depends upon the situation. For example, more grammatical sign may be used at a formal meeting or in communication with hearing persons than when relaxing with family or friends, especially when everyone communicates manually. Furthermore, there are differences of dialect. In the course of the study, as many as twenty signs were encountered for the first time, most of which appeared to be native to the locality.

Capacity to sign in itself acts as a passport to the deaf world. If the deaf person answered the door the reaction was usually one of consternation: a stranger had to be dealt with. But as soon as the interviewer began to sign, she was invited into the house before an explanation for the visit had been given. The assumption was that those using sign language must be either a friend or an official. It was generally the receipt of language which caused difficulty both for the deaf person and the interviewer. At the outset the interviewer adopted signed and spoken communication. Deaf people responded in a variety of ways, but usually with sign, finger-spelling and lip patterns, and frequently using the voice as well. During the early exchanges, some elements of communication were adjusted to facilitate mutual understanding. For example, it was common for deaf people to reduce their rate of finger-spelling and sign and to sustain the established speed thereafter. However, there were exceptions. Some elderly and isolated people responded with a rush of signs, as they gave expression to emotions which had been pent up, often for many years. And it was not always easy to restrain the flow which had been unleashed.

Little use was made of the written word during interviews, though it was necessary sometimes for proper names, place names and the names of employers. In the case of finger-spelling there were inevitable mistakes which caused confusion. Concentration was crucial to accurate communication, but after about an hour and a half it was noticeable that tiredness reduced concentration. If during the next half hour concentration improved, as was usually the case, the interview was completed in one session.

Voice played an important role in communication. Efficiency in the use of voice and lip patterns by deaf people directly affected comprehension of their signed communication. The use of voice ranged from clear enunciation of every word to none at all. And the interviewee's comprehension of voice ranged from perfect understanding of spoken words to virtual incomprehension. Mutual comprehension took place most rapidly when voice and sign were used simultaneously. In a few cases, sign language as an accompaniment to voice receded as the interview progressed. In time, both the quality of the voice and concentration deteriorated, and either a request was made for a resumption of signed voice, or the session was brought to a temporary halt. It was more usual, however, for voice to be accompanied by signs and finger-spelling at the beginning of an interview, and for the voice to shrink gradually to a whisper or disappear entirely: lip patterns alone remained as a support to signs and finger-spelling. In such cases, comprehension remained swift and concentration was not over-strained. Even so, that there was strain on both parties is undeniable. And in the circumstances it is remarkable that no deaf people attempted to terminate an interview prematurely, or refused to participate in a second session where this was needed.

Some of the problems associated with interviewing, therefore, were related to the wide variety of communication methods adopted by deaf people. The variety of communication skills and variations in the levels of skills encountered was a reflection of the lack of uniformity which prevails in the teaching of communication to the deaf. However, among those who are born deaf, or who become deaf in early childhood, the majority experience an initial emphasis on oral communication. Parents often do not realize initially that a child is deaf. After diagnosis doctors, social workers and peripatetic teachers of the deaf usually advise oral communication for fear of reducing the child's motivation to learn to lip-read and later to speak. Deaf children may begin to attend school at the early age of 18 months and once within the formal education system they usually experience primarily oral communication. The University of Manchester training school for teachers of the deaf, which has dominated special education for deaf people, maintains a purely oralist approach to communication. However, in the last decade, other colleges of education have developed more flexible attitudes and are prepared to consider the merits of different forms of manualism. The method by which a child is taught – whether oral or manual, or a combination of the two – depends upon the school attended.

However, while at school, whatever the efforts of parents and teachers, deaf children are exposed to a form of sign language which has some relationship with adult sign language. Schoolchildren produce a language for themselves – 'school-signs'. Certain signs identify the school-leaver as the product of a particular school. Signs used at school may be a combination of 'home' signs, the signs used by adult deaf people with whom the children have had contact, signs created by the children themselves within the school environment and those used by teachers.

In schools where pure oralism is no longer adopted, a child may be exposed to a wide range of communication methods, including different types of signing systems. For example, teachers may use signs from the Paget Gorman or British Sign Language vocabularies, the speech adjustments of the cued speech system or the Danish Mouth Hand.

It is not surprising then, that the products of deaf schools exhibit a wide variety of communication systems. On leaving school, deaf youngsters usually turn to the adult deaf community for the social and intellectual stimulus which they cannot easily acquire among the hearing. But even within the deaf community they are hampered by poor communication skills – school signs, a limited vocabulary and inadequate finger-spelling ability. Nor is it clear where they should place the emphasis in improving their communication skills – whether on oralism to promote their chances of training and employment in the hearing community, or on sign communication to improve their relationship with the deaf community within which the special facilities for the deaf are provided. The choice has to be faced at the point when the deaf person leaves the security of the school routine.

In practice, the communication system of most adult deaf people is a combination of oral and manual skills, and this, for the most part, was reflected in the interviews. The precise combination used by any one person was dependent upon a number of factors including the type of communication adopted within the family, communication within the school, educational method and the degree to which the deaf person chose to participate in the hearing or deaf communities. Prevailing communication norms in particular locations are important too: for example, in some areas, especially in Scotland, finger-spelling is more important than in others; and location may determine the amount of lip pattern used in combination with signs and finger-spelling.

Interviews reflected the full variety of skills in communication which might be anticipated from the current education system. Among the younger age group – those under 30 years of age – some school signs were still in use, and communication was more enthusiastically oral, including a greater use of mime and gesture not formally associated with British Sign Language than was true of the conversation of older people. In addition, they used a greater range of skills, and made a greater use of hearing aids than other people. Younger people appeared to experience no greater problems of receptive communication though the range of skills used to communicate with them was wider than for older people, and they had greater difficulty in understanding how the questions applied to them.

Only two interviews were conducted orally. In one an elderly woman spoke grammatically but clearly in a monotone. She refused to wear a hearing aid, had poor lip-reading skills, and rejected signs, though she clearly understood more easily when the occasional sign was used. The second involved an 84-year-old woman with rapidly failing eye-sight. She had attended an ordinary school where she was endlessly punished for inattention, and her hearing loss remained undiagnosed until the age of 11 or 12, shortly before she left school. Although she was unable to derive much benefit from her body-worn hearing aid, she had a tin box full of old batteries which she kept in the hope that they would recharge themselves: whenever communication problems arose she got the box out and tried another battery. Much of her retirement had been devoted to the welfare of the deaf–blind: she was proficient in deaf–blind manual communication, but despite her own failing vision, could not accept that such a skill would be useful as a practical aid to her own communication with hearing people.

The number of misunderstandings which occurred during interviews with oral deaf people far outstripped those where manual communication was employed. Indeed, the time required to obtain comparable amounts of information was much greater where deaf people insisted on using oral rather than other methods of communication: interviews were most efficient and relaxed when it was possible to combine manual skills (signs, finger-spelling and occasional gesture) and oral skills.

Staff in one psychiatric and two mental handicap hospitals were making some use of Makaton, but otherwise little British Sign Language or finger-spelling was encountered in communication between hospital staff and patients, or even between patients. At hospitals other than those using Makaton, deaf patients had not been made known to each other, and therefore were isolated in terms of communication. A number of them had been in institutions since childhood and had not been exposed to the forms of sign language generally in use among the deaf population. None had intelligible speech; their lip-reading was minimal, and they were unused to all but the most basic mimed communication. Most of the factual information about such patients was obtained from records, conversation with hospital staff, and observation. Others, having been in hospital and without access to signed communication for many years, had difficulty in recalling, and subsequently using, finger-spelling and conventional signs.

On average, interviews were completed within four hours. A higher proportion of the interviews carried out in institutional settings were incomplete than was true of those conducted in private households. In all settings it was necessary to have regard to emotional and other stress signals during interviews, and these were least frequently displayed in private households.

In fact, there was a greater range of response in institutional settings generally than in private households. On the one hand, a few elderly and confused people made little response, but others were so effusive that the interview took eight hours to complete.

Observation

Observation played an important part in augmenting the information made available through interviews by deaf people living in hospitals, hostels and residential homes for the deaf. The interviewer became a part of the community for between a month and six weeks and was able to observe informally the interaction of deaf people with staff and other residents, their leisure pursuits, their social skills, and their range of communication skills. The hostel in which deaf people lived independently in self-contained flatlets provided the least opportunity for observation: here, interviewing conditions closely resembled those which obtained in private households, but the communal television lounge was used regularly by about 80 per cent of residents. In observation it was always possible to see in operation an extension of the range and increase in the fluidity of communication skills beyond those displayed during the interviews.

Hospital staff were too busy either to intrude on periods of observation or to be bothered by them. It was easy, therefore, to sit among the serried ranks of institutionalized comfy chairs, warm, a little sticky and faintly dettolized, and listen to the whisper of the support tights, the screamed orders, the crash of crockery on the bouncing tea trolley as the milk and sugar went simultaneously into the urn along with the tea.

Staff interviews

As many as 300 staff contributed informally to the study, while long formal interviews were conducted with forty-two and shorter interviews with another 100 members of staff.

Selection of staff for interview

Hospitals

Staff were selected for interview from a range of disciplines and at different levels of seniority, while most had some responsibility for the treatment and care of deaf people. They included staff nurses, charge nurses, SSENs and SENs. Interviews were also carried out with ancilliary staff – occupational therapists, social workers, the head teacher of a hospital school as well as

nursing assistants and student nurses. In all, seventeen long formal interviews were conducted in hospitals, and in addition there were fifty shorter
interviews.

Residential homes and hostels

Long formal interviews were conducted with staff who had responsibility
for running homes and hostels; but all other staff were interviewed as well,
except for the night staff at one of the specialist residential homes. In all,
thirteen long interviews were conducted in residential homes, and seven in
hostels. In addition, there was a total of fifty short interviews.

Community staff

In all, four long interviews were conducted with those having overall
responsibility for the care of deaf people living in private households. These
included three local authority social workers for the deaf employed by the
London boroughs, and one social worker for the deaf employed by the
voluntary organization with responsibility for *all* services for the deaf,
including residential care in the county involved in the study. In addition
there were shorter interviews with two social workers for the deaf.

Duration of interviews

It was rare for long interviews to be completed in a single session. In some
instances they took as many as four sessions of between half an hour and an
hour and a half to complete.

Despite the repeated emphasis on under-staffing, in specialist homes and
hostels for the deaf, staff were more accessible for interview than those
working in hospitals. Much of the interviewing in specialist institutions
was conducted in the evenings and at weekends, when there appeared to be
a considerable reduction in the pressure of work. In contrast, in the hospitals, evenings were a busy time for nurses. Activities units had usually
closed by 5 p.m., and the full complement of patients was normally on the
wards in the evening, to be bathed, supervised and so on. At the weekends
the staffing levels were reduced even further on the wards, and the occupational and industrial therapy departments closed. Although the leisure
social centres and patients' clubs usually remained open on Saturdays, and
sometimes on Sundays as well, the diminished number of ward staff had to
cope with a greater number of patients at weekends than was normal. For
the most part, ward staff interviewing was confined to the relatively quiet
periods of weekday mornings and afternoons. Many said how much they
relished the attention of senior staff which research projects attracted to
their wards: research projects offered staff at all levels the opportunity to

express their views in a way that they were not often able to do even at their own nursing and interdisciplinary meetings.

Social workers with the deaf managed to continue an interrupted interview. Much of their work took place during the evenings and at weekends. Of all the staff interviewed, they were most at leisure during the day.

In all, long interviews with staff took between two and six hours to complete and on average lasted for four hours. In comparison, short interviews were completed in anything from twenty minutes to one and a half hours, the average length being an hour.

Quality and type of evidence obtained

Although standard information was collected from all staff, considerable flexibility was essential to allow for appropriate variation in emphasis, depending upon the particular role of an individual. For example, staff varied in their type of contact with and knowledge of deaf people. The cook in the residential home, for instance, had far more day-to-day contact with deaf residents who co-operated with her on a formal rota for kitchen chores, than a senior nurisng officer with responsibility for three or four deaf patients, whose contact was usually second hand, through senior ward staff. On the other hand, questions relating to policy-making, the delegation of responsibility and so on, were very much the province of the senior nursing officer, but baffling to the cook. Similarly, local authority social workers for the deaf were preoccupied by the relationship between local authorities and the voluntary associations which run residential homes for the deaf and visit hospitals. Social workers for the deaf were usually the mediators between services and interpreters for the deaf in their dealings with government, local authority and voluntary agencies. Different themes, then, dominated the interviews, depending upon the nature of the care provided for deaf people by individual members of staff.

3 Personal characteristics

Much of the experience of deaf people was determined by the interaction of their personal characteristics with hearing impairment. In succeeding chapters questions explored will include whether the impact of deafness varied between men and women; whether there are differences in the perceptions of deafness depending upon age, marital status, employment, social class; and whether the experiences of deaf people living with their families differed from those who lived alone or in institutions, with deaf people or hearing people; and the effect of additional handicaps on those with severe hearing impairment. Thus analysis of personal characteristics provides a framework for subsequent discussion.

The age range of deaf people was wide – from 16 to 84 years – the majority being below retirement age. Indeed, a little more than a third (35 per cent) were below the age of 40 while rather more than a quarter (27 per cent) were aged between 40 and 59. In all, two-fifths were aged 60 or more. The age distribution was a reflection of the settings in which they lived rather than the age structure of the deaf population as a whole. There were marked differences between the settings in the relative youth and age of their deaf population. Only among those living in private households were there representatives of the whole age range. Whereas those in hostels and mental handicap hospitals included people below the age of 20 but no one in their eighties, in psychiatric hospitals and residential homes for the deaf the youngest people were in their twenties and the oldest in their eighties. Only in local authority residential homes for the elderly, where all but one of the deaf people was aged 70 and over, was the age range narrow. However, although for the most part each setting exhibited a wide age range, there were marked differences between settings in the relative youth and age of their populations. Thus among those living in private households roughly equal proportions were below the age of 40, aged 41 to 59 years, and 60 years and over. However, those living in the hostels were predominantly young: there more than two-thirds were below the age of 40 and only a little more than a tenth were aged 60 years or more. The youthful predominated in the mental handicap hospitals too: almost two-thirds were below the age of 40. In contrast, in the residential homes for the deaf, less than a tenth were below the age of 40, whereas almost two-thirds were above retirement age. In psychiatric hospitals, where almost three-quarters were above retirement age, the predominance of the elderly was even more marked.

Rather more women (54 per cent) than men were involved in the study, and these proportions were found among those living in their own homes. But in other settings the sexes were distributed differently. In psychiatric hospitals equal numbers of men and women were interviewed, but in the mental handicap hospitals less than a third of deaf people were women. Men also predominated in both the hostels and local authority residential homes for the elderly where almost two-thirds of deaf people were men. In contrast, in the residential homes for the deaf as many as four-fifths of the residents were women. As a group, women tended to be rather older than the men: whereas a little more than two-fifths of the women were above retirement age, this was true of less than a third of the men. However, a higher proportion of men than women were in middle age, but the sexes were evenly balanced in the younger age group.

Despite the wide age range and the predominance of people below retirement age, the vast majority of deaf people (two thirds) were single. Only a little less than a fifth (18 per cent) were married. But almost as many again (16 per cent) had been married, the majority of these being widowed – almost a tenth of deaf people – while only 4 per cent were divorced and 2 per cent separated. A third of deaf persons, then, had experienced married life. It seems likely that marital status was a function of the setting in which deaf people lived. None of those in local authority homes for the elderly, residential homes for the deaf, or the hospitals were married. Research has consistently shown a disproportionate number of single people and those whose marriages have been broken by death, divorce or separation among those in long-term residential and hospital care.[1]

Perhaps it is not surprising, then, that of deaf people in long-term residential and hospital care, as many as four-fifths were single, while a seventh were widowed, rather less than a tenth were divorced, and the remainder were separated. The hostels, too, catered predominantly for the single: a little more than four-fifths of hostel residents were single, and only one was married, though a further sixth reported marriages which had ended in divorce or separation. Only among those living in their own homes was there a substantial proportion (a little more than two-fifths) of married people: indeed the majority (more than three-fifths) had some experience of married life. Thus only in private households were single people in a minority. Overall then, deaf people were predominantly single and this was markedly true of all settings, except private households. It was striking that all but three of the married deaf people living in private households had a deaf spouse.

The majority of those in private households lived with someone else: only a fifth lived alone. Although a tenth lived in relatively large households with five, six or seven other people, the majority lived in three or four-person households. The most common type of household was one in which the deaf person lived with a spouse. Rather more than two-fifths did so, half of them with children as well. Almost a quarter of those living at home were younger deaf people who lived with their parents. Another fifth lived with siblings, in many cases in the parental home. About a third of those living with siblings were older married persons. For the most part those who lived with at least one other person at home had someone else in the household who was deaf. Thus of those living in two or more person households, a little more than two-fifths lived with other deaf people, while a third lived with a mixture of deaf and hearing: only a little more than a third found themselves the sole deaf person in a hearing household.

Of course, a high proportion of married people had sought a deaf spouse, but a number had close relatives who were deaf. How far was this true, not just for people living in their own homes, but for those living in other settings as well? Information was available for 85 per cent about all members of the immediate family, that is, parents, grandparents, children and grandchildren, siblings, aunts, uncles and first cousins. In all, a fifth reported hearing impairment among them: 4 per cent had at least one deaf parent, and more than half of these said that both parents were deaf; but deafness was more common among siblings – almost a fifth of those with siblings reported at least one who was deaf, and of these two-fifths had more than one, while a sixth reported three or more deaf siblings. Almost a fifth reported that they had at least one deaf aunt, uncle or first cousin. Thus, as many as two-fifths of deaf people had one or more close relative who suffered severe hearing impairment. Other studies have drawn attention to the tendency for hearing impairment to be present in more than one member of the family. For example, an Irish study indicated that those who are born deaf are more likely than other hearing-impaired people to have deaf relatives. Deaf people involved in the present study seem to have been typical too, in that most such relatives were of the same generation. In Ireland it was found that as many as 72 per cent of deaf relatives were of the same generation, as many as 22 per cent having reported hearing-impaired siblings.[2]

A substantial minority then, of deaf people were brought up in families already familiar with the problems associated with deafness. The presence of more than one deaf person in a family raises the question of the possibility of hereditary factors in causing deafness. Eicholz cites the London County Council review of cases, 1919–28, which found that of all cases of congenital deafness, about 21 per cent appeared to be due to hereditary factors.[3] In Conrad's study of deaf school children, apart from genetic causes, the single most common cause of deafness was rhesus incompatibility which accounted for 6 per cent of his cases, followed by maternal rubella and premature birth.[4] Hereditary causes of deafness are ascribed to those who have one or both parents deaf and/or at least one deaf sibling if rhesus incompatibility is not present. In the United States, Gentile and Rambin concluded that of the 30,000 deaf children for whom they had data, 30 per cent had a hereditary hearing loss[5] compared with the 27 per cent in Conrad's study of British deaf children.[6] However others have suggested that these studies understate the hereditary causes of hearing loss. Among the causes of non-hereditary deafness, Fraser ascribed 30 per cent to perinatal factors.

However, the cause of deafness is often difficult to establish. For example, it remained unidentified for as many as 42 per cent of children in Conrad's study[7] and this was consistent with the findings of other studies, except those of Fisch, who was able to establish cause of deafness in as many as 75 per cent of cases, though recent rubella epidemics may explain this high proportion.[8] Difficulties in identifying the cause of hearing impairment often arises when there is a considerable lapse of time between the onset of deafness and its diagnosis. This is often the case when deafness is present at birth or occurs in early infancy when the symptoms are easily confused with those of other handicaps. It was difficult to establish the cause of deafness for a high proportion of deaf persons interviewed. In all as many as 57 per cent reported that they had no idea of the cause of their hearing loss. Even when deaf people gave the cause of their impairment with some confidence it was often the case that the information had to be treated with circumspection. This was not because the self-reporting of the condition is inherently unreliable: recent research suggests that self-reporting of clinical conditions is surprisingly accurate.[9]

The difficulty arose because it was far from certain that the real cause of deafness had been conveyed to the deaf person, or alternatively, that they had correctly understood what had been conveyed. For example, it was striking that only one person reported rubella as a cause of deafness, yet a further eight associated the origin of their condition with measles in infancy or very early childhood. Again, a surprisingly high proportion who were able to provide a cause for their deafness attributed it to an accident such as a fall in infancy or early childhood – a little less than a fifth in fact. In such cases it was difficult to determine whether such accounts accurately identified cause of deafness, or were explanations provided when the demand for information required an easily understandable, easily conveyed fiction, or whether deaf people merely associated their condition with an early unpleasant memory.

It seemed likely that, in all, about two-thirds of those who gave a cause for their deafness – only a quarter of all deaf people – did so accurately. In most of these cases there was either a parent or another hearing relative, or other evidence available to corroborate the deaf person's report. That the proportion was so low compared with other studies is not surprising: both Conrad and Fisch were dealing with children for whom parents were available to provide evidence, whereas the present study was confined to adults, many of whom were in old age and all but the youngest of whom had not benefited from the screening and diagnostic procedures which have become available, particularly since the Second World War.

Cause of deafness may have repercussions on the socialization process. As in other studies, the most common causes of deafness were genetic in origin. This was true of a little more than a third of those for whom satisfactory explanations for deafness were available. Recent research has suggested that children with deafness of genetic origin are likely to achieve more highly on non-verbal IQ tests and in language acquisition than children with non-genetic deafness.[10] Furthermore, the deaf children of deaf parents suffer less disruption to their socialization process as a result of their hearing impairment than the children of hearing parents. It seems to be the case that the cause of deafness influences the way in which parents respond to their children. Where the causes are genetic, parents have less tendency towards over-protectiveness, and guilt feelings which affect the degree of empathy they feel for their children. Among the non-genetic causes of deafness, meningitis was the most common, accounting for as many as a quarter of the people for whom a satisfactory explanation of deafness was available, while for another seventh deafness was attributed to damage at or before birth. No other single cause was responsible for the deafness of a substantial category of people. Thus four people attributed their deafness to spasticity; one person was born without eardrums; in two cases, deafness was attributed to prematurity of birth; there appeared to be only one case pf rhesus incompatibility; two people suffered from Whandenberg Syndrome, and another two blamed mastoids, while one gave diptheria as the cause.

Some causes of deafness, especially maternal rubella, are incontrovertibly linked with the presence of additional handicaps. Whatever the difficulty of establishing *cause* of deafness, one-third of the deaf interviewed had at least one additional handicap as well. Additional handicaps not only present difficulties in themselves, they may also interact with deafness to create still greater communication problems for the deaf person. Poor visual acuity or involuntary movement of the head may seriously impede attempts to lip-read, while involuntary movement of the hands may reduce skill in signing and finger-spelling. In all, 5 per cent of deaf people were blind or partially sighted, while a little more than a tenth had other physical handicaps which reduced manual dexterity or capacity to focus attention visually for any length of time. There were other handicaps which also affected communication: as many as one-fifth of deaf people were clinically defined as mentally ill, and 5 per cent as mentally handicapped.

Inevitably the problems of the majority of handicapped included an intensification of the difficulties of communication. In all, as many as a tenth of deaf people had two or more handicaps in addition to deafness, the majority of whom were in hospitals, though some were in residential homes for the deaf.

The social class setting within and from which deaf people sought to grapple with communication and other problems was predominantly working class. But a large minority were hard to assign to any social class – a fifth in all. For the most part these were people who had been resident in hospitals or, less commonly, in special homes for many years, who had never worked, and who, having lost contact with their origins, were unaware of their family employment history. In general, the social class distribution of deaf people reflected the job opportunities and training available to them.[11] As many as 69 per cent were or had been unskilled manual workers (social class V) and another 19 per cent skilled manual workers (social class IV). Only a tenth were, or had been, in clerical jobs (social class III). In social class terms, then, the experience of the deaf differed substantially from that of the population in general, where, in comparison, only 8.4 per cent belonged to social class V, 18 per cent to social class IV, but as many as 50 per cent to social class III.[12]

For two-fifths of deaf people, social class reflected past rather than present employment, since they were above retirement age. But not all of those of retirement age had actually given up work: two were in full-time and six in part-time work. Nor were all those of working age in employment, training or education: only two-thirds were currently occupied. Of these, the vast majority, amounting to half of those of employable age, were in full-time employment, while another 8 per cent worked part time, and 5 per cent were in full-time further education. In addition there were five who attended a Day Centre.

In all, then, almost three-fifths of those interviewed below retirement age were in paid employment, and of these a little more than three-quarters were in open employment: only two were self-employed. The remainder worked in sheltered conditions either in hospitals or in sheltered workshops run by local authorities or Remploy.

4 Communication

Interest in sign language has developed from two distinct points of view. On the one hand there has been debate about the role of sign and gesture in the development of spoken language, and on the other, discussion has focused on the nature of sign language itself.

A sophisticated discussion on the origins of language has been conducted for more than 2000 years.[1] Throughout this period, the role and nature of sign language in the development of spoken language has been a major issue in the controversy.[2]. For example, it has been argued that sign language is not a phenomenon of recent origin, although the rigorous analysis of sign language as it is used by deaf populations dates only from the last quarter of the present century.[3]

In reviewing the theories concerning the origins of language proposed during the past four centuries, Hewes points out that in the majority of cases it is assumed that the use of gesture preceded or was concomitant with the development of speech.[4]

For example, in the mid eighteenth century the Abbé de Condillac argued that the early use of speech may have been simply to draw attention to gestural use of the hands. At the beginning of this century, the psychologist Wundt suggested that sign language is 'a natural product of the drive to express'.[5] In the 1930s Maud Jousse criticized studies which he considered misleadingly ascribed pre-eminence to sound and speech and instead asserted the importance of gesture.[6]

Recently other theorists have supported the importance of the role of sign. Le Roi Gourlain has suggested that some examples of prehistoric art in Europe represent the manual gestures of communication[7] and Critchley has supported the thesis that in the development of language, manual gesture preceded 'mouth gesture'.[8]

Today, manual systems of communication, both contrived and natural, occur in a wide variety of settings – in everyday communication, the theatre of mime, conducting traffic or music, religious ritual, as well as in the homes, clubs, schools and other institutions for the deaf, the deaf–

blind, the mentally handicapped, and in the rehabilitation of stroke victims. It is now widely assumed that among the deaf 'natural' signing develops without the necessity for formal learning. It is argued that rather as a hearing infant begins to develop a style of communication in keeping with prevailing social norms, so deaf populations adopt communication methods which are adjusted to their predominantly visual/motor, as opposed to aural/oral, abilities. It has been observed that all deaf populations invent signed communication, but there has been considerable debate as to whether this constitutes language.[9]

In modern linguistics a distinction has been made between language and speech, and speech has been regarded as subordinate to language. Thus language has been established as a distinct entity with a structure which can be studied in its own right.[10] Hockett has attempted to define the properties of language,[11] and several of those which he has identified are common to natural signed communication, though in addition signed communication has properties peculiar to itself such as simultaneity and bimodality.[12]

An aspect of the recent study of natural signed communication as language has been the growing interest in Diglossia. In 1959 Ferguson identified different forms of expression when language was used by the same speaker in different situations.[13] Stokoe developed the theory and used it to explain the different uses made of signed communication.[14] More recently, Deuchar has analysed British Sign Language in terms of Diglossia, and concluded that 'high' and 'low' uses of sign language may be identified, 'high' being used when deaf people are engaged in communicating with officials, and when hearing people are present, and 'low' being used in relaxed domestic or social situations when communicaton is between natural signing deaf people who are using signs as the primary method of communicaton.[15] Cicourel has remarked upon the feature of 'code-switching' in the use of 'high' and 'low' variations in signed communication observed in two London schools among deaf children.[16]

Such studies seem to indicate the continued existence of a sign system – 'high' – which takes its lead from conventional British usage in spoken language, and the normal language of the deaf – 'low' – which concedes far less to the demands of English grammar but has characteristics such as syntax of its own. Stokoe, Casterline and Croneberg have sought to demonstrate that American Sign Language is a language with its own morphology, semantics and syntax.[17] Tervoort has suggested that the communication of the deaf features two codes: that which is related to the prevailing language of the country in which the deaf live, and that developed consequent to the primarily visual perception which the deaf have in their surroundings.[18]

In Britain, sign language incorporates a considerable amount of finger-spelling, and as a consequence British Sign Language is less vernacular than its American counterpart. Conrad has suggested that manual language in Britain is a 'pidgin sign language which is neither pure vernacular nor an exact form of signed English. It borrows freely from both and from finger spelling'.[19] If this is so, it may represent only a stage in the development of British Sign Language. Protagonists of signed communication as a language in its own right assume that sign language, like any other, is in the process of development, and they appear to be supported by analysis of Israeli sign language, the complexity of which may be accounted for by the recent establishment of the state and the wide variety of ethnic backgrounds of its population. Perhaps signed communication in Britain is less well developed than its American counterpart and this may be due to the differences in the status of sign language in the two countries. Whereas there are several substantial dictionaries of American Sign Language,[20] there are only three slight works which collect together a relatively small number of British signs.[21] But the differences between signed communication in Britain and America are not solely to be explained in terms of different stages of development. There are fundamental differences of grammar and syntax between the two, quite apart from the dissimilarity of the signs employed.[22] The signing deaf of different nations are not mutually comprehensible when using their native sign system.[23]

It might be expected that the growing interest in sign language in recent years would make an impact on educationalists and the education of deaf children. In England and Wales, some educationalists in training colleges for teachers of the deaf continue to argue the oral case. They stress the poverty of British Sign Language as a communication system and reject the evidence of recent research that native competence may affect positively the deaf child's ability to learn spoken language. At Gallaudet College, the centre for higher and further education for the deaf in Washington, only those who have achieved fluency in American Sign Language are recruited to the staff, but in Britain there are few facilities for deaf students in higher or further education, and only a small number of interpreters who are fluent in British Sign Language.

Brennan and Hayhurst have argued that 'Many of the fears about using BSL in schools can be directly related to insufficient knowledge about the nature and function of BSL as the normal language of the deaf community.'[24] In reviewing the oral–manual controversy in this country, Conrad has sought to refute the criticism that BSL does not follow the grammatical rules of English[25] by adopting Brennan's argument that other languages do not conform to English rules of grammar either.[26] However, since the Lewis Committee conceded that manual communication might be appropriate to the education of some deaf children[27] a greater readiness to consider the possibilities of manualism as an adjunct to oral teaching methods has developed.

The oral basis of education for deaf children was firmly established in the 1930s when audiological advances improved the possibility of success in teaching speech, and predominantly manual methods in the classroom gave way to oralism. In the last decade the manualism against which oralists under the aegis of the University of Manchester Department of Audiology and Education of the Deaf crusaded, and which for almost half a century has been dismissed outright in many schools for the deaf, is now being tested and increasingly adopted.

As evaluation of communication methods used in schools and other small studies proliferate, teachers are increasingly willing to consider the possibilities of manualism. However, no detailed information is available about the number of schools in the United Kingdom in which the different methods of communication are utilized – Paget Gorman, Signed English, Cued Speech, the Rochester Method (finger-spelling and spoken English), and Total Communication. And there has been no survey of the skills in and attitudes to the different communication methods of classroom teachers. However, more than half the schools for the deaf in Scotland, including the largest schools, have adopted Total Communication and the Scottish Centre for the Education of the Deaf[28] now includes manual/visual communication as an essential part of the training course.[29]

In England, where the oral tradition is more firmly entrenched, many schools have begun to use Total Communication. The experiments being undertaken in such schools in the development of communication in teaching techniques are now attracting considerable interest, and a number of research projects have been initiated.

Communication and education

Inevitably, education plays a crucial role in determining the communication skills of deaf people. The intensity of the exposure to a given system or combination of systems of communication experienced by deaf people within the education system is the function not only of prolonged contact with formal education – by statute, deaf children may begin attendance at school from the age of 2 years – but also of the residential nature of much of the special schooling available to the deaf. In the case of the people interviewed, schooling was typically prolonged and residential. About half had attended residential schools while a further seventh had attended a combination of residential and day schools for the deaf: only a seventh had experience solely of day schools for the deaf, while a further five people had attended day schools for the deaf and maladjusted. The remainder, numbering thirty-three in all, had attended a variety of schools (in thirteen cases, hospital schools) for the hearing, for the most part before the Second World War.

The pattern of communication method by which instruction had taken place at school reflected the age structure of the group involved in the study rather than the methods of communication currently adopted within the education system for the deaf. Thus rather more than half (54 per cent) reported that signing had been the primary method of communication used at school. For a little more than a quarter communication had been predominantly oral, while for a little more than a tenth, a combination of oral and signed communication had been used at school. Among those who were under the age of 30 the majority had received education in schools or units for the deaf and had been instructed primarily by oral methods. The remaining 8 per cent who had attended either a hospital school or no school at all had been excluded from systematic and prolonged exposure to any dominant method of communication.

Current use of voice

Two factors in the use of voice were considered: the frequency with which the voice was used and the comprehensibility of the speech produced. Despite the preponderance of deaf people whose primary method of communication at school had been manual, as many as three-fifths usually or always used voice when communicating with the hearing. In contrast, only a fifth reported that they never used voice, and the same proportion did so only occasionally.

There was a clear relationship between an oralist education and the use of voice, though education by no means determined the degree to which speech was used. All of those who had been educated at a hearing school or in a deaf unit in a hearing school, and as many as four-fifths of those who attended schools in which the primary method of communication was oral, always or usually used voice compared with only a minority (two-fifths) of those educated primarily in sign. However, an even smaller minority of those educated in schools in which a mixture of communication methods were in operation, including sign and oralism, made use of speech, and indeed deaf people from these and primarily signing schools were the most likely *never* to use speech. Furthermore, there appeared to be some relationship between the number of years spent at school and the degree to which speech was used: the longer their exposure to education, the greater the likelihood that deaf people would use speech.

There were variations between settings in the degree to which voice was used in communication with the hearing. Speech was most common among those in private households, hostels or residential homes for the deaf. Among those living in private households, the vast majority – all but a fifth, in fact – usually or always used speech in communication, while this was true of half of those in hostels, and almost half of the residents of the special homes for the deaf. In contrast, voice was rarely, if ever, used by the residents of the homes for the elderly and hospital patients.

Confidence in the use of voice

The force driving educationalists in Britain to adopt a hostile attitude towards British Sign Language has been the conviction that the objective of special education for the deaf must be their integration into the hearing community which can be achieved only through the development of speech. In fact confidence about the intelligibility of their spoken language was not great among deaf people. Only a little less than a tenth considered that among their hearing intimates their spoken language was always intelligible, while between two-fifths and half considered that their speech was usually comprehended by those whom they knew well. However, more than a third assessed their spoken language as being only sometimes if ever comprehensible even to those with whom they were intimate.

The confidence of deaf people in the comprehensibility of their speech to hearing people who knew them well was highest among those living in private households, of whom as many as three-quarters assumed their speech to be usually or always intelligible. Elsewhere, the proportion of whom this was true varied between one-third and a half. Hostel residents alone challenged those living in private households in the confidence with which they used speech. In general, they had not been cut off for substantial periods of time in a relatively closed institution. In contrast, among the good oralists who were confident about the comprehensibility of their speech most were elderly people who had attended school before the advent of oralism, and who had lived in a deaf community where there was little need to communicate orally. A high proportion of those in psychiatric hospitals were patients of long standing of whom only basic communication was required. Furthermore, most, like the residents of the homes for the elderly, had been of educable age before the domination of oralism. Few of the mentally handicapped had received speech training, and in some cases the clinical condition itself prevented the production of comprehensible speech.

The barrier to integration with the hearing created by difficulties of communication were not in evidence in relation to the deaf community. In all, two-thirds of deaf people regularly met others outside their setting who were deaf. In communication with the deaf community, the influence of the education system was rarely apparent.

Only one person communicated with other deaf people orally: in the main, communication was maintained by the utilization of a combination of different methods, including lip-reading, finger-spelling, signs, mime and facial expression, that is, total communication, while a further tenth relied upon a combination of oral and signed or written communication. For the vast majority, communication with the wider deaf community presented no problems at all: a little more than four-fifths reported no communication difficulty, and the remainder would admit to experiencing only some difficulty.

Use of voice and child-rearing problems

The achievement of normality in terms of communication method may have consequences which belie the actual level of communication achieved by such means. For example, there appeared to be a strong relationship between the use of voice and child-rearing problems. Unfortunately the numbers involved were small and only the most tentative conclusions can be drawn: only a fifth of deaf people were parents, but the greater their use of voice, the less likely they were to experience child-rearing problems. Parents themselves expressed the view that their children came to an understanding of parental deafness at an early age. Stories of a hearing child's manipulation of his parents, especially where the child adopted the role of interpreter, were told by a number of deaf parents as well as by social workers with the deaf. Some of the frustration experienced by the hearing children of deaf parents was evident even in the interviews: most children were fascinated by the response of hearing strangers to their noise and clatter.

It may be that the achievement of 'normal' communication methods resulted in greater and more effective communication with the mainstream of society and therefore a better understanding of child-rearing practices; or perhaps the use of voice enabled parents to achieve better communication with their usually hearing children than was true of those who used voice infrequently if at all. Or it may be simply that ability to use voice engendered a feeling of normality which created confidence in dealing with both family and other relationships. There was certainly evidence that among those parents who rarely or never used voice there was considerable misunderstanding as to what types of child behaviour constituted a problem, stemming largely from a failure to appreciate the expectations of the 'normal' community and a lack of confidence in relating to others, particularly those who were hearing.

Oralism on the whole created a confidence in dealing with the mainstream of society which those who rarely or never used voice lacked. And this was true of the confidence required to perform a wide range of activities – to drive, to seek a better job, to go further afield on holiday, take more responsibility both inside and outside the home – within the deaf as well as the hearing communities. In marriages between 'oral' and non-oral deaf people it was the oral deaf spouse, regardless of sex, who took the initiative in domestic and social situations. And in the deaf clubs, the oral deaf dominated organization on the grounds that they had a better grasp of committee procedure and other administrative skills.

Comprehensibility of voice

Despite the criticisms which have been levelled at the insistence on oralism by educationalists in this country there appeared to be a positive relationship between the acquisition and use of speech on the one hand, and capacity to lip-read on the other. The less deaf people were accustomed to using voice in communication the greater the extent to which they were likely to admit difficulty in lip-reading. But how intelligible was the speech of deaf people? An eight point scale was devised for assessment of voice comprehensibility with a score of 1 representing total or immediate comprehensibility and a score of 8 indicating total unintelligibility.

Of course, such a scale is neither standard nor objective. It was unlikely either that assessments were held constant across all interviews or that they were reproducable. Only a tenth of deaf people achieved a score of 1 or 2, indicating immediately intelligible speech, and in all as many as half had speech which could be understood with moderate, little or no difficulty. Nevertheless, a fifth, scoring 5 or 6, were understood only with considerable difficulty, while as many as a third (score 7 or 8) were understood only with the greatest difficulty or not at all.[30] It is likely that a far higher rate of unintelligibility would have been recorded by an assessor unused to communicating with deaf people. Markides has shown that when assessing the recorded spontaneous speech of deaf children, teachers of the deaf understood 31 per cent, but lay people understood only 19 per cent. Furthermore, subjective assessments of the kind attempted here have been found to overestimate the degree of speech intelligibility of deaf people.[31] Moreover, it has long been recognized that, regardless of familiarity with such speech, individuals differ enormously in their ability to understand a deaf person's speech.

A further difficulty in making an assessment was that speech varied between individuals not only in terms of quality, but also in quantity. Except for oral persons who used speech consistently, there were some who used no speech at all, and others whose use of speech lay somewhere between these extremes. Apart from the complete oralists, and those who never used speech, deaf people usually made their maximum concession to a hearing interviewer at the beginning of the interview by using as much speech as possible. As the interview progressed it was usual for both the amount and volume of speech to diminish, as the interviewer became familiar with the manual system and lip patterns of the deaf person. Therefore, an assessment was designed to reflect both quality and quantity of speech on the following scale:

1   Easily comprehensible speech used constantly throughout the interview, usually without accompanying signs.
2   Usually comprehensible and constantly used speech.
3   Speech comprehended with some difficulty, not necessarily grammatical, and not used constantly throughout interview.
4   Speech often difficult to understand, frequent repeats necessary if not supported by signs; speech often used, but ungrammatically, and usually consisting of only key words in a sentence.
5   Occasional words used to support signed language, usually comprehensible after initial period of adjustment to voice.
6   Few words used, very difficult to comprehend even after adjustment to voice.
7   Little speech used, and that incomprehensible.
8   No attempt at speech.

The fact that half of deaf people scored 5 or more when assessed by someone familiar with deaf speech suggests far less facility for speech than is apparent when the factor of comprehensibility alone is taken into account.

Facility for spoken English was not necessarily dependent upon exposure to an oral education system: present skills were no guide to past achievement. Most of those who scored 6 or 7 on the assessment were the residents of hostels and special homes for the deaf, and hospital patients, some of whom were young enough to have been exposed to the oralist education system, and had in the past communicated by means of signs supported by speech. Those in hospitals and hostels rarely used their voice skills regularly and as a consequence their performance had declined.

Others, particularly in the homes, were older, and had attended school at a time when no provision was made for speech training. Still others were too ill to use the skills they once had, or had received no education or systematic training in communication: all who scored 8 belonged to this category.

Furthermore, two-fifths of those who scored 1 on the assessment owed their speech skills not to the education system, but to the remarkable perseverance of their parents:

Mrs Bosely, aged 74, said 'I sat on my mother's knee every evening while she taught me to read the Bible aloud – a chapter a night! When I got to school (which was residential) the teachers were astonished at my speech.' At the time of interview both her command of spoken English and her articulation were impressive.

In other cases, easily comprehensible speech among those too old to have experienced oral education in special schools was attributed to attendance at hearing schools. Thus two women in their seventies who declared themselves to have been profoundly deaf since birth or very early childhood, had been educated at normal, hearing schools.

Mrs Aves said 'I was slapped through schools. I think, because I couldn't hear, my behaviour gave the impression of disobedience or laziness.' She had learned to read at school, continued to read voraciously until in old age her sight failed her, and was an enthusiastic conversationalist. Her speech was clear despite a crackly quality in her voice. However, comprehensible voice in her case was no aid to receptive communication: little of her lip-reading skill remained as she had acquired a severe visual impairment in old age.

There were other instances in which an oralist education, despite ensuring clarity of speech, did not necessarily aid receptive communication.

Mr Owen always used voice, and was easily comprehensible. He had been privately educated at a hearing school. However, he was a poor lip-reader, which restricted his communication with hearing people, and his communication with other deaf people was equally restricted because he found it impossible to use finger-spelling, despite his exposure in recent years to the manual alphabet.

Those who had been educated outside the United Kingdom usually had poor oral skills or limited English. For most of their education, the three deaf people born in Ireland had communicated manually: their use of voice was negligible, though they formed clear lip patterns which were usually comprehensible. Two of the three Indians had been brought up and educated in Gujerati-speaking communities but had managed to learn to lipread in English well, though they did not speak clearly in English; the other, however, had developed speech only in Gujerati.

Mr Singh, aged 46, a type-setter with the highest earned income among the deaf people interviewed, had very poor lip-reading and speech in English and conversed entirely in Gujerati while his wife acted as interpreter. However, he read and wrote in English very skilfully.

The difficulties encountered by those of non-English origin were sometimes cruel.

Mr Kenton, aged 19, had been born in Cyprus of Greek parents but was educated in England at an oral school. Doctors in this country had advised that he should learn to lip-read only English – to attempt Greek as well would be confusing. However, the parents had achieved only a basic grasp of English, therefore the mother could not understand her son at all and the father had only limited comprehension. Ironically, Mr Kenton had achieved fluent spoken English, and lip-read well. He relied almost entirely on his older sister to act as interpreter between himself and his family.

Many of those with at most moderate oral skills but whose preferred method of communication was manual, lived in situations in which they were forced into oralism most of the time and therefore usually achieved a low level of communication. This was particularly true of patients in psychiatric hospitals where staff were not familiar with manual communication.

A number of those in mental handicap hospitals attempted vocalization, but only two achieved any comprehensible speech and there were no staff with non-verbal communication skills. On the other hand, there were some with poor expressive communication, whose receptive communication appeared to be good.

Mr Jones, who lived in a mental handicap hospital, never used speech and indeed rarely used expressive communication at all; but he lip-read well, appeared to be aware of the significance of events and seemed to exercise choice over the way his environment was ordered.

Half of those in mental handicap hospitals achieved little expressive communication either by voice or manually.

Voice and contact with friends and relatives

Deaf people were clear that familiarity was important to voice intelligibility. Despite the fact that the majority always or usually used voice in communication, there was even less confidence that their speech could be understood by hearing strangers than by hearing persons who knew them well. Indeed, only three considered that they were always intelligible to hearing strangers, while a fifth thought that this was usually so. The vast majority who communicated with strangers by voice – two-thirds – considered that in such encounters they were comprehensible only sometimes. Those few who thought that their speech was always intelligible to strangers, not surprisingly lived in private households or hostels. But even in these settings where strangers were not likely to be encountered, confidence about comprehensibility was low. Only two-fifths of those in private households and a third of hostel residents reported that strangers usually or always understood their spoken communication, while this was true of a sixth of the residents of special homes for the deaf. All of those in the hospitals, and the vast majority of deaf people in other settings found that strangers rarely if ever understood their speech.

It was not surprising, then, that a little more than a fifth of deaf people avoided communication with hearing strangers whenever possible, and this was most marked among those who were least confident of the comprehensibility of their speech. Whereas only a minority of those in private households (a sixth) and hostels (a quarter) avoided meeting strangers, this was true of between half and three-quarters of those in other settings. Thus the lack of confidence in the comprehensibility of their speech which was so disproportionately prevalent among people in relatively closed settings, reinforced their isolation from new contacts.

Yet the very use of speech itself regardless of its comprehensibility appeared to be important in determining whether contact was maintained with members of the family outside the setting. The more deaf people used speech, the more likely they were to have seen at least one member of the family living outside the household within the previous twelve months. Of course, to some extent the maintenance of contact with relatives is to be explained in terms of the settings alone. Those who were most likely to use voice in communication lived in private households and perhaps it was to be expected that they would maintain closer links with relatives than those living elsewhere. Nevertheless, it was striking that whatever the setting the less speech was used the more likely the deaf person was to be cut off from contact with family outside the home.

By no means all of those who used voice to communicate with hearing strangers necessarily did so at home. Many lived with other deaf as well as hearing people. Oralism with the hearing outside the household was clearly an indication of confidence in sustaining relationships beyond the immediate circle of intimates, but oralism in the household was likely to be the mark of the true oralist, who insisted on speech despite the capacity to and opportunity for other members of the household to learn sign. It was not oralism as such which determined whether the deaf maintained contact with relatives living outside the household, but a willingness to use speech in support of sign beyond the setting.

Reluctance or inability to use voice had a tendency to restrict the contacts of deaf people to those within the household and a small circle of hearing friends at most. Contact with the hearing world outside the home tended to be shunned by those who relied on signed communication, to the point of seeing little of relatives, and even losing contact with them. Not surprisingly, those deaf people most likely to achieve that hallmark of normality and integration – employment – were those who used voice in communicating with hearing persons outside the home. Indeed, the greater the frequency with which voice was used, the greater the likelihood that deaf people of working age would be employed.

Voice and the need for interpretation

Often the degree of normality achieved by deaf people was limited by dependence on interpreters when dealing with the hearing world, though oralists were less likely than others to require such help. Indeed, the less deaf people used speech, the more likely they were to have depended upon an interpreter at some time. All but one of those who never used voice had required an interpreter. Moreover, the degree to which interpretation was required varied with the frequency with which speech was used.[32] Almost half of those who never used voice belonged to the most dependent category who required interpretation in six or more of ten standard situations, though few oralists did so.

Hearing aids

The use of voice, then, signified an attempt to grapple with the hearing community on its own terms. And the more persistent deaf people were in using speech, the greater the likelihood that they would maintain links with and engage in the activities of the hearing world. Perhaps it was not surprising that those who were most committed to integration into the general community by their determined use of speech were also those who were most likely to attempt to maximize their hearing by employing technical aids. In fact, a little more than half of those who always used voice and two-fifths of those who usually did so when communicating with hearing people, had a hearing aid. But the majority of the deaf people – 54 per cent – had *never* owned an aid, and the less voice was used the less likely they were to have one. It cannot be assumed that those who always used speech and possessed an aid necessarily suffered from less of a decibel loss than other deaf people: often the use of hearing aids was an indication of a strong motivation to maximize the level of oral/aural interchange with both the deaf and hearing worlds. Nearly all of those below the age of 30, who had been educated in deaf schools or units for the hearing-impaired by oral methods, were numbered among such people.

Use of speech and relationships within institutions

The development of speech appeared to help those living in residential homes and hospitals to establish close relationships with staff. In general there was little contact between staff and deaf residents or patients beyond the formalities and instructions required to ensure that the establishments were well run. Relationships which went beyond this to include communication on a friendly basis usually involved good oralists. However, even among those who consistently used voice, only a small minority – a seventh – actually established such a relationship. Indeed, the less voice was used, the less likely deaf people were to establish a friendly relationship with a member of staff.

But the use of voice alone was not in itself enough: comprehensibility was essential if staff were to bother to move beyond a formal and minimal relationship with deaf people. Those who were assessed as having the greatest friendly contact with members of staff were always or usually understood by hearing intimates when using speech. Even where a level of friendship with staff was established by a deaf person which was average for the hospital or home in general, the importance of voice comprehensibility was still marked. Deaf people who achieved little or no friendly contact with members of staff were predominantly those whose speech was fitfully if ever intelligible to hearing people who knew them well.

Yet most staff in practice understood little of what deaf residents and patients said to them. More than half admitted that they understood only some, and a quarter only a little, of what deaf people said.

A woman who worked at a residential home for the deaf in the West Country said: 'I can sometimes pick up bits, but a lot of it's guesswork.'

No member of staff felt that they understood all the speech of deaf people, though a quarter considered that they probably understood most of what was said.

An SEN who worked in a special unit for the deaf at a psychiatric hospital said, 'I understand most of what is said. 'I'm quite well attuned to it now. Speech has to be encouraged.'

Of course, the quality of the voice is important in determining the comprehensibility of speech. However, only a third of staff admitted to finding the voices of deaf people 'off-putting'. It was odd that most of these worked in special homes or hostels for the deaf, or were specialist social workers accustomed to the speech of deaf people. Perhaps those who worked closely with the deaf were too inhibited to report their true feelings; or perhaps the greater exposure to a wide variety of deaf people in the homes and hostels where it was the norm for deaf residents to communicate reduced toleration overall. Because the residents of homes and hostels were used to communicating, they had few inhibitions about conversing with staff, while the 'family atmosphere' encouraged the use of voice with little regard to pitch or volume.

Lip-reading

In the interest of cognitive development it is crucial that the deaf child comes to an early understanding of the importance of lip movements. Although the deaf child receives the visual stimulus received by a hearing child from lip movements the aural stimulus is different and dependent upon type and degree of hearing loss. Moreover, lip movements in terms of language are often ambiguous. The hearing person can discriminate between speech sounds which look alike on the lips, whereas the deaf person often has a choice of translation of lip movement. In practice, however, unless brought up in a signing environment, deaf children are unlikely to begin to make much linguistic progress until they go to school. By then, their hearing counterparts usually have a substantial vocabulary.

Even in the intense oral environment of school, the greater the decibel loss from which the child suffers, the less language he or she is likely to know, and the less likely he or she is to be able to lip-read the language which is known.[33] Recent studies have emphasized the unreliability of communication through the medium of lip-reading. Even the best lip-readers, including the hard of hearing, experience difficulties. Conrad found no significant difference in lip-reading success between deaf and hearing children despite the emphasis placed on the acquisition of lip-reading skills in the education of deaf youngsters.[34]

Others have found that only 9 per cent of profoundly deaf school-leavers have speech and lip-reading skills which enable them to talk easily with hearing people, while as many as 16 per cent are totally unable to do so.[35] Tests of deaf adults have shown that it is unusual for even the most gifted lip-readers to understand word for word more than 80 per cent of a conversation.[36]

No attempt was made in the present study to assess objectively lip-reading ability. But deaf people were asked to assess the nature of the problems they experienced and the ease with which they lip-read in a variety of situations. They displayed even less confidence in their lip-reading skills than in the intelligibility of their speech. None considered that they were able to lip-read members of the hearing community with ease. As many as three-quarters reported some difficulty in lip-reading, while a fifth experienced very great difficulty and 5 per cent were unable to lip-read at all. It is likely that most had learnt to reduce the necessity to lip-read to occasions and subjects which they knew they could comprehend reasonably successfully. Thus self-assessments of skill in lip-reading were probably based on deliberately narrowed communication requirements.

There appeared to be agreement about the degree of ease or difficulty experienced in lip-reading a given individual such as a newscaster on television. All kinds of factors were reported as affecting the lip-reading performance, including clarity and speed of lip patterns, the fall of light, distractions such as shadows near the speaker, smoke in the room, the visibility of the mouth or tongue of the speaker, rings catching the light, heavily patterned clothes in bright colours and the movement of the hands around the face. Both sexes reported that it was easier to lip-read women than men. Most found it easier to lip-read when they were relaxed and unhurried, and when the speaker was sympathetic – anyone who cared enough to make themselves understood, would be understood.

To discriminate levels of lip-reading skills in terms of both degree of difficulty and the frequency with which it was experienced, deaf people rated themselves on a nine point scale ranging from 0 = never experienced any difficulty, to 8 = never able to lip-read. No one claimed never to have experienced difficulty in lip-reading, but a tenth said that usually they had no difficulty (score: 2) and about the same proportion reported some difficulty sometimes (score: 3). But the majority experienced at least some difficulty. Indeed, as many as two-thirds of deaf people could be described as having at least substantial difficulties in lip-reading (score: 5 or more), and a small minority (6 per cent) said that they could not lip-read at all.

However, those who achieved even a modest competence at lip-reading found that their ability enabled them to maintain relationships with the hearing more easily than those who lip-read only with very great difficulty or not at all. For example, those who lip-read 'with some difficulty' maintained closer links with relatives outside the household than did those with poor or no lip-reading ability: indeed the greater the difficulty in lip-reading the less likely were contacts with relatives to be maintained.

The speedy establishment of a good relationship based on easy communication with staff who frequently changed as a result of the shift system and the high staff turnover was essential for those in institutional establishments. Good lip-reading skills were required to establish even a modest relationship with staff. All of those who established a good relationship with two or more staff members were among the most skilled lip-readers. Only among those who achieved minimal relationships with staff did poor lip-readers predominate.

The failure to master the skills of lip-reading, then, could have serious consequences in cutting deaf people off from their families, and reducing the capacity of those in institutional settings to establish friendly relationships with staff.

So far expressive and receptive communication have been considered separately, but in practice, communication is a two-way process. How well did deaf people combine speech with lip-reading skills? In all, only a little less than half managed to combine frequent use of voice with reasonable lip-reading skills; more than a third always or usually used voice and lip-read with some difficulty, while a fifth either made extensive use of voice, or achieved a reasonable level of lip-reading skill. The remainder – over a quarter – used voice rarely, if at all, but varied in the ease with which they managed to lip-read. Only 5 per cent not only never employed speech in communication but could not lip-read either. Overall, then, lip-reading was more widespread than speech. Thus, some kind of receptive communication with the hearing community was available to most deaf people but the possibility of expressive communication was less common. Yet ability to use speech and the capacity to lip-read appeared to be related: in general, good lip-readers made frequent use of voice when communicating with hearing people, but there were many exceptions.

Manual communication

So far the discussion has concentrated on the communication methods required of the deaf by society at large. But manual communication is the language of the deaf community. It has been established that between 70,000 and 80,000 people in the United Kingdom communicate manually; sign is the primary method of communication for one person in every 2000 of the population.[37]

Face-to-face communication between normal hearing people does not rely exclusively on spoken language: body stance, facial expression and miming elaborate the stark meaning of words. Individuals vary in the degree to which they accommodate such 'informal' methods of communication. It is a feature of communication among signing deaf people that they rely more heavily on informal communication than hearing members of the community.[38]

The content of sign language

Any discussion of sign language requires an explanation of its composition. In physical terms, the 'signs' of British Sign Language, that is, those which are accepted by all or a large part of the adult deaf signing population are performed using hand and upper limb configurations which usually bear an accepted relationship to the upper trunk, head and face. Stokoe has emphasized the importance of the principal dimensions involved in American Sign Language.[39]

Perhaps because a number of dictionaries of American Sign Language have been compiled, it is easier to identify an accepted ASL sign than one belonging to British Sign Language. Thus in BSL the distinction between a 'sign' and a 'gesture' sometimes cannot be drawn. It seems reasonable to regard manual communication as being based on a continuum of signs from manual gestures which are idiosyncratic to one individual or to many, iconic or pantomime signs, which may also be in use by the hearing population to what Stokoe has identified as the 'arbitrary' signs – signs assigned to meanings without obvious symbolism.

Wundt categorized sign in the early years of this century,[40] and Stokoe, apparently independently, devised a similar classification in the early 1960s. According to the classification, *pantomime signs* are those which are usually applied to verbs, and which imitate the action to be represented with hands or fingers. Then there are *imitative signs*. For example, the sign representing a hat is made by defining the type of hat with the hands above and around the top of the head. *Metonymic signs* are those which abstract one feature of the object to be represented by the sign: thus a bird is signed by representing the opening and closing of the beak with the thumb and index finger. Then there are *indicative signs*, which simply involve pointing to the object in question, or an object similar to that which requires identification. *Initial dez* involves the first letter of the word being finger-spelled. For example, 'm' finger-spelled represents 'mother', 'f' is finger-spelled to represent 'father'. Sometimes the first letter is incorporated into a more involved sign. An example is the sign for 'family' in which the finger-spelled letter 'f' (index and second fingers of both hands are held together crossed) is held and moved horizontally in a clockwise circular fashion. *Name signs* are like proper nouns in English. For example, a person may be represented by the identification of distinguishing features, or signs may be used to represent the elements of a name.

Syntax

Early in this century, Wundt's studies suggested that the syntactical system of sign language was less highly developed in Britain than in the United States.[41] Sign language is sometimes said to be telegraphic: the syntax is not obvious, but it is beginning to emerge as a result of current research.[42] Wundt argued that 'where word ordering is not restrained by arbitrary rules, the words emerge in accordance with the general psychological principle of the successive apperception of features as a whole according to the degree of their effect on cognition'.

Two features of the syntax of sign are particularly salient: first, that natural sign language tends to follow the principle of strongest emphasis; second, syntax seems to be governed by the convention that a sign must be intelligible alone or through a sign preceding it. Despite the omission of function words such as 'if' and 'because', with obvious implications for syntax, the deaf avoid ambiguity without resorting to gesture or mime. It has been found that inflections such as those used in spoken or written English, which are conveyed by the use of suffixes, prefixes, tenses, additions to verb stems, preverbs to nouns, may also be conveyed by parts of a sign. But inflection is also achieved by other means, most commonly by using additional signs: for example 'he went' is conveyed by signing 'he go before', 'trees' are signified by signing many trees, some trees – trees trees (trees) etc.

Wundt's theory, that signs have types of grammatical identity as 'objects, properties and conditions' continues to be accepted today. But recent research has drawn attention to the frequency with which a sign may represent both 'condition' and 'object': an example is that the identical sign is used to represent the verb 'to sew' and the noun 'tailor'.[43]

Similarities and differences between signed and spoken communication

Signed and spoken languages have a number of features in common. These were initially identified by Hockett, and later revised by Hockett and Altman,[44] and include: specialization (both words and signs are only signals); semanticity (signs and words have specific meanings); arbitrariness (there is no physical relationship between many words and many signs and the objects they represent, though there are many signs that physically represent or represent elements of the objects they represent); discreteness (lack of continuity between the elements of a sign); displacement (both words and signs can describe events beyond present place and time); productivity (new ideas can be uttered and comprehended using words or signs); quality of patterning (elements of sign and word order can be ordered differently to mean different things); traditional transmission (both words and signs are learned naturally, that is, without formal education).

However, there are a number of features of sign language that do not occur in spoken language, including simultaneity of signing (two signs can be produced simultaneously), timing (the rate at which signs are produced is used to qualify or modify the meaning of a sign or group of signs) and expansiveness of signs (the language of signs can be contained physically within a small space, though exaggeration is acceptable, and often occurs when mime is included with elements of sign language).

Gesture

Gesture, which played an important part in communication for many deaf people, may be defined as manual communication which is not used as part of, or in conjunction with Deaf Blind Manual, British Sign Language, or finger-spelling. A few of those in institutions resorted to gesture as their primary method of communication with hearing people, either because they themselves had no formal knowledge of BSL, and little comprehensible speech, or because hearing people failed to understand their formal signed communication. Most of them were patients in mental handicap or psychiatric hospitals, although a small minority of the residents of homes and hostels for the deaf also used gesture. But deaf people were not the only ones to use gesture: a high proportion of staff in residential and hospital settings were observed to use gesture in conjunction with speech rather than signs associated with BSL. Indeed, some staff had no knowledge of the existence of a body of conventional signs used by the adult deaf population.

The dividing line between formal BSL and gesture is often far from clear. Even for those who are acquainted with the manual language of the deaf, it is difficult to identify a BSL sign as such: signs vary regionally and no comprehensive dictionary has as yet been compiled. At present, there are no widely agreed criteria by which BSL signs may be identified. Furthermore, many BSL signs are iconic or ideographic, and are readily accepted as meaningful gesture by the hearing as well as by the deaf community. Like BSL, the intelligibility of gesture depends upon the context in which it is delivered; and, however favourable the context, some gestures, such as the manneristic behaviour of some mentally ill people, may defy interpretation.

Both deaf and hearing people employed some gesture in communication, most of which was appropriate and comprehensible in context. But it was clear from observation and report that in practice much expressed communication between staff and residents or patients was misunderstood or only partly understood. Many members of staff not only failed to understand the communication of deaf people in their charge, but in addition themselves lacked the means to communicate with patients and residents. Indeed, few had given serious thought to the limited nature of the communication which they achieved with deaf people primarily through the medium of gesture: the private code developed between the two groups over the years enabled both parties to respond quickly to routine communication but was totally inadequate for non-routine situations. Often in cases where deaf people had at their disposal a complex method of manual communication such as BSL, they did not have the flexibility or skill to use it in a way in which staff would comprehend. For just as it may take a deaf child a number of years to realize that the soundless movement of mouth, tongue and lips represents communication so some staff are unaware that the apparently meaningless movements of hands and fingers represented the primary means of communication available to a deaf person.

Facial expression and body stance

Even more than gesture, facial expression is used in daily communication, both signed and spoken. Tonal inflections are denied to deaf people. Instead, the deaf rely more heavily than the hearing on facial expression, posture, and variations in the speed of signing and finger-spelling to add a further dimension to their communication. Rather than simply recount an event, the deaf person often acts it out, frequently adopting the role of each of the participants in the history. Such reconstructions can be surprisingly vivid, even at crowded social gatherings, such as sitting in a pub over a pint. Stories may gain rather than lose from their lack of words. The 'tone' of the story is usually clearly apparent: there is rarely any doubt about the attitude of the deaf person to the story being recounted – whether it is one of happiness or embarrassment, frustration or relief – even if the watcher appears mid-story. Many deaf people had a marvellous range of facial expression. Recent studies suggest that aspects of facial expression have a significance beyond mime: brow movements comprise a component of the grammar of sign language.[45] Lip movements, too, other than lip patterning of voiced or unvoiced words, like other non-manual elements, have been found to play a significant role in American Sign Language.[46]

Facial expression, however, was not restricted to use as a support for manual communication. There are deaf people who rely almost entirely on facial expression for communication. This was true of one person whose gestural code seemed to be secondary to his facial expression and was limited to pointing. Warmth, trust, longing for affection were expressed by seeking to hold the hand of and gazing at a member of staff.

Body stance is often used by deaf people deliberately to support signed or gestural communication. But for many hospital patients and some residents of homes for the deaf, this particular dimension of sign was restricted by poor posture – stooped shoulders, and bowed head – acquired through long years of institutional living, accident or illness.

Makaton

In recent years attempts have been made to devise a method of manual communication which is more systematic than gesture, but less complex than BSL, in the hope that it would improve the communication skills of those identified as subnormal, both deaf and hearing. The Makaton vocabulary derives from British Sign Language. Sets of signs chosen for ease of reproduction are taught in stages which have been structured 'according to the usefulness of the concepts' represented by the signs[47] and are intended to be accompanied by speech. Pilot schemes produced encouraging results, and in a survey of sign and symbol systems in use in special schools to which almost half of the ESN(S) schools responded in 1979, four-fifths reported that they had a signing programme, the majority using a BSL system, usually based on the Makaton vocabulary,[48] while most of the remainder (a fifth) used an adaptation of the Paget Gorman Signing System. The survey suggested that in recent years there had been an increase in the use of sign systems in schools, but how far Makaton is in use as a method of day-to-day communication is open to question: in only 46 per cent of ESN(S) community schools and 38 per cent of ESN(S) hospital schools was it used as a method of communication between classmates and friends, and the systems were used by an even smaller proportion of parents.

The adoption of Makaton appeared to have positive effects beyond any improvement which took place in communication. In hospital school programmes of up to two terms duration the average child learned to use and understand between one and five signs. However, in comparison with children who had taken part in Paget Gorman Sign System programmes lasting a comparable period, those attending classes in the BSL(M) system showed an increased understanding of speech of 42 per cent, while their use of speech rose by 100 per cent; substantial improvements were also recorded in articulation, interest in classroom tasks, academic skills, classroom behaviour and behaviour in other settings. But the crucial factor appeared to be not the use of Makaton but the skill of the teacher and the enthusiasm engendered in teachers by the Makaton programmes.[49] Others, such as Kyle and Woll[50] however, have suggested that language development in the long term may be retarded. Observation of the use made of Makaton by deaf adults for the present study suggested that in so far as it is an aid to the acquisition of vocabulary it is successful, but its success as a tool for encouraging conversational exchanges is more doubtful. Deaf people taking part in Makaton programmes usually reverted almost immediately to their natural gestural codes once the pressure of the classroom to exhibit Makaton signs was removed, particularly where the prevailing communication was oral.

Finger-spelling

Finger-spelling is used as an adjunct to sign language when there is no sign available to represent a word of spoken language: it is a direct translation of the word, each letter being spelled out in sign. While the majority of alphabet systems employ one hand, the British manual alphabet employs both hands, though a few English deaf schools have adopted the one-handed Rochester method.

The oral basis of deaf education is stronger in English than in American schools, and finger-spelling in British schools has been more acceptable than the use of signs since its use can conform closely to the English language. As a consequence of the greater educational emphasis on the use of finger-spelling and the apparent poverty of the formal classroom use of signs in Britain compared with the United States, finger-spelling is a more pronounced element in the communication of the deaf here. The relative poverty of signed as opposed to spoken language may be illustrated from the fact that whereas the projected dictionary of British Sign Language will contain between 2000 and 3000 morphemes, ASL is estimated to contain 3000 while contemporary English vocabulary contains as many as 750,000 elements.

The obvious implication of finger-spelling is that the deaf person using it is literate. The capacity of the deaf interviewed to use finger-spelling varied widely. Some had not achieved any facility in finger-spelling while others had a small vocabulary of finger-spelled words and attempted others which they spelled wrongly or abandoned part-way. However, the majority of those in private households and homes for the deaf showed evidence of good finger-spelling ability. Given the prominent role played by finger-spelling in BSL, it is clear that where there is little or no proficiency in finger-spelling, manual communication may be seriously limited. However, signed conversation between deaf people containing little or no finger-spelling may be observed which appears to be entirely effective.

Deaf–Blind Manual

Perhaps the most severely deprived of communication were those with two sensory impairments – the deaf–blind. A manual sign system depending

upon touch has been devised for communication with such persons –
Deaf–Blind Manual Language (DBM). Communication is achieved by
touching the palm or fingers of the blind person's hand: each finger tip of
the deaf–blind person is used to represent a vowel, starting at 'a' with the
thumb.

In many cases, deaf–blind persons lose their sight after the onset of
deafness, and can usually respond to DBM by using sign language, and
even speech, in communication with sighted people. Those who become
blind and deaf after the acquisition of literary skills often learn to receive
communication by means of the inscription of large block capitals in their
palms by the index finger of the communicator. Even some blind people
who lose their hearing before the acquisition of language are forced to learn
to communicate in this manner because the hearing–sighted person finds
it convenient.

A deaf–blind patient in a psychiatric hospital received limited and spasmodic
communication from staff who used this method in preference to the faster and
less confusing DBM in which the patient performed adeptly when he
communicated with his hearing–sighted mother.

For those who are born deaf and blind, communication poses such enormous problems that often in the past no attempt has been made to provide
them with a communication system.

A deaf woman who had been born without eyes was assumed to be subnormal
and her parents had been persuaded to send her to a mental handicap hospital.
Here, there was no record of a psychological assessment, or attempts to train
her to care for herself or to communicate. Now in her mid-forties, she was
inaccessible and solitary, immobile most of the time in a bent, seated position.
She was totally dependent on staff for feeding, dressing, bathing and going to
the lavatory.

The usage of manual communication

The ways in which, and the degree to which, British Sign Language was
used by deaf people varied both within and between settings.

Deaf people living in private households

All of those living in private households had at least some knowledge of
BSL. The three most oral people encountered relied on speech and lip-
reading or writing in preference to using signs and finger-spelling; they
mixed with hearing rather than deaf people socially. Even they, however,
had a knowledge of signs and peripheral contact with the deaf community.
Their speech was always intelligible, and whenever they experienced

difficulty in lip-reading all three resorted to the use of signs, though they found finger-spelling difficult to recall. The two eldest had devoted many years to voluntary work with the deaf–blind, and both mentioned their skills in Deaf–Blind Manual Language. Another oralist, whose literacy was of a high standard, had poor lip-reading and speech.

Another oralist group had left school within the last ten years, all but one of whom viewed the use of manual communication with disdain: they were prepared to resort to manualism only when intractable problems of communication arose. Their lip-reading and general understanding was poor, yet they were unable to compensate by adopting manual communication because they were not well versed in conventional BSL and had limited finger-spelling. Interviews with the small minority of youngsters who had attended signing schools were more lively and relaxed than those with their young oralist counterparts, though their articulation was less good. Another oralist group were in their late twenties and early thirties. Though they did not use signs in the presence of relatives they communicated by the simultaneous use of signs and speech accompanied by some finger-spelling during interview. None of them felt part of the deaf community, and their version of BSL was of a high diglossic variety, and incorporated more finger-spelling than was usual among older deaf people. A much larger category of people than the pure oralist, were those (nine-tenths) who used BSL in household and social communication but who struck a balance at interview between the use of manual and oral skills. A number of such people encouraged the use of sign by the interviewer to support their lip-reading, but preferred to reply to questions orally.

Then there were signers who used little or no voice at interview – a sixth of those in private households. Although some signed in a low diglossia clearly, most approximated more closely than usual to grammatical spoken English. A small minority rushed on at their normal speed in telegraphic and idiosyncratic BSL, making requests for frequent repeats inevitable. The largest group, a third of those living in private households, regarded themselves as equally oral and manual. In general, their speech and comprehension of speech were good, and communication with them was easy and relaxed. Most had contact with both the deaf and the hearing communities, and as a consequence were ready to compromise on the use of oral and manual skills. Their use of BSL changed with the nature of the questions. Formal questions on serious subjects were answered in speech supported by signs and occasional finger-spelling. But they relaxed when confronted by less demanding and more light-hearted questions, and couched their answers in a more telegraphic and idiosyncratic BSL which had much in common with the signed communication used among native signers.

BSL in psychiatric hospitals

Communication with a small minority of psychiatric patients (four) was primarily oral with strong BSL and finger-spelling support. However, an elderly woman who had spent thirty years in hospital communicated well in speech and sign, but was very nervous about using manual skills which had lain dormant for many years. Another small group (six) communicated adequately in BSL, using some speech in support, though some had to retrieve their BSL skills from long years of neglect. Indeed, inability to recall the letters of the manual alphabet led one man to write one or two word responses. However a deaf–blind man who had been sighted and fluent in BSL prior to admission, now communicated, without speech, by means of block capitals drawn by his index finger on his palm or the palm of his listener. Despite the ease with which communication could be achieved by this method, ward staff rarely took advantage of it. When they communicated it was only to pass on messages about hospital routine – for example, a 'B' would be drawn on his palm, meaning 'time for bath'.

Others (five) had lost BSL communication skills either as a result of illness, or neglect. Having lost contact with the social network and family members with whom their communication had been developed and practised, they had remained unrecognized by local voluntary organizations for the deaf, and were now unable to communicate except by means of a basic code of gesture which had been devised by and was therefore only recognizable to a few members of staff within the ward.

Others (about a seventh) had never developed a system of communication other than ideographic gesture devised to serve the needs of hospital routine, and rarely capable of elaboration beyond that. For a small minority, communication was even more restricted:

One deaf woman with cataracts communicated only by touch; she had no speech, and being illiterate, the only contact she could make with staff was by self-mutilation, facial expression and touch. According to the ward sister, she had had no communication of any sort with other patients for several years.

Manual communication in mental handicap hospitals

The number of deaf people in mental handicap hospitals was too small for generalizations to be made about their communication skills, the range of which was wide. To illustrate the spectrum of skills exhibited the communication method adopted by a number of patients will be indicated. It was difficult to know what impact long years of hospitalization had made on the methods of communication adopted: poverty of early case history made it difficult to determine the level of achievement attained prior to admission. Yet communication was often the crucial factor in determining whether patients were assigned to 'high' or 'low' dependency wards: a number of deaf patients who were rated as 'low dependency' in terms of task performance were nevertheless found in 'high dependency' wards: they were unable to communicate orally or manually with members of staff.

Of the ten patients concerned three had used BSL to some extent before their admission to hospital; another had oral skills which must have been developed before his admission in late middle age. Of these, one patient was on a high dependency ward and did not communicate by speech, writing or BSL with staff: she rarely responded to speech or gesture and was considered to be highly dependent and difficult. She had an unassessed visual impairment – conical cornea – which probably impeded lip-reading as well as reception of sign or gesture. The second was a young man who had been educated orally at a Rudolf Steiner school where he had achieved a modest degree of literacy, and an introduction to finger-spelling and some signs. Neither ward staff nor the occupational therapy staff were aware of these communication skills: they used clear speech and gesture, to which he responded with his own gesture system without voice. In the third case, staff did not recognize the gestures of a visually impaired deaf woman as BSL, nor did they respond to her written attempts to communicate. She communicated fluently using BSL signs, finger-spelling, writing, and a few partly-voiced words. She was on a 'medium-high dependency' long-stay ward, and was reported to have very little communication with other patients. Her visual impairment was probably responsible for her difficulties in lip-reading and perceiving gesture: when she was visited some time after an operation to remove one of her cataracts, communication was much easier despite her weeping eyes.

Not all patients were willing to use their communication skills with staff. For example, a middle-aged man who functioned well on a 'low dependency' ward and was known to communicate with other patients by speech was unwilling to look at staff and therefore was restricted in the degree to which he could lip-read, and communicated in muttered, indistinct speech. Moreover, he made no use of his Makaton vocabulary outside the classroom. In contrast, on the same ward another young man had devised his own system of gestures on which he had superimposed a small vocabulary of Makaton. Finally, in a 'medium-high dependency' ward a man, whose physical and sensory impairment rather than his mental handicap accounted for his high degree of dependency, was keen to learn at the Makaton class, but did not use it naturally outside class, and in his case, the signs were not reinforced by ward staff. He communicated by gesture and used his voice, very audibly but totally unintelligibly.

However, some deaf patients appeared to have almost no means of communication.

A deaf–blind woman who had entered hospital at an early age, had received no schooling or voice training. She had been introduced to neither a symbol nor a sign system, and was unable to communicate in any way other than by acquiescence or resistance to touch, by minimal facial expression, and hand clapping. Although she had little communication with staff, and indeed, resisted their attempts to undertake care tasks on her behalf other than feeding and bathing, she was able to distinguish between staff and patients, and permitted some patients to lay their heads on her lap or lean against her.

Two young adults continued to attend the hospital school and were there-fore still in a position to acquire or extend their communication capacity. One suffered from constant *petit mal* fits, and perhaps occular dystrophy as well: frequent facial grimacing and limb movements made it impossible to distinguish between involuntary movement and expressive communi-cation. The other was physically handicapped and had had minimal experience of formal education until the previous year: he appeared to comprehend Makaton signs used in class and could be persuaded to identify a few objects by sign, but on the ward where Makaton was not reinforced he relied on facial expression and pointing to achieve communication.

Where it was possible for patients to make the acquaintance of deaf people outside the hospitals, systematic communication could be learned without the benefit of formal education.

Mr Butler, aged 30, who had lived in hospital since early childhood and appeared to have had little communication training, had learned BSL signs when adult at a deaf club. He was receptive to speech, BSL and BSL(M), but used neither sign nor speech in response, though he occasionally communicated by gesture. He appeared to understand but took little active part in the Makaton classes.

The manual communication of residents of local authority homes for the elderly

British Sign Language had been the primary method of communication for four out of five deaf people in local authority homes for the elderly before they took up residence there. Two of them accompanied their BSL with speech, while another used minimal speech with BSL. Another resident used speech (which was unintelligible to staff and other residents) only in times of great stress: her mental illness had entailed the loss of sign and finger-spelling skills which created enormous difficulties in communicating with staff and fellow residents. The fifth person produced easily compre-hensible speech, but communication was difficult because of his poor lip-reading skills which were deteriorating as his sight failed and it was now difficult for him to read newsprint or even large and well formed hand-writing. As a consequence he had very little communication with staff and other residents.

The manual communication of those in hostels

The two hostels did not differ markedly in terms of the capacity of their residents to communicate despite their different objectives. However, the range of communication skills was greater in the psychiatric half-way hostel. A number of residents of the psychiatric hostel had lived in hospitals since adolescence and on admission had only limited literacy skills and virtually no manual skills either, though since then they had developed skills in BSL, literacy and speech.

Miss Probert who was admitted recently had arrived from her foster home. She had been treated as mentally handicapped and taken into the care of the local authority soon after birth: only at the age of 14 was she diagnosed as deaf and accepted by a residential school for the deaf where speech and BSL training enabled her to communicate at a basic level. After three months at the hostel she appeared to be thriving in the manualist environment.

In contrast, Mr Murdoch aged 44 had poor communication: he used primarily gesture and some speech and BSL signs but lacked finger-spelling and signing fluency. He did not easily understand other deaf residents, nor they him, but he was able to lip-read the staff a little, and incorporated a good deal of mime and natural gesture into his conversation.

All other hostel residents under 30 used some form of BSL communication, had some literacy skills and were thus able to finger-spell. In all, about one-third used very little voice, but the majority of those under 30 articu-lated as well as those in the same age group in private households, though their lip-reading skills were generally less pronounced, and they under-stood questions less readily.

Oralists were in a minority in both hostels: there were three in the psychiatric hostel, and one in the ordinary hostel, all of whom had some knowledge of BSL and finger-spelling, while one was fluent in the use of manual skills. In contrast, one resident of the ordinary hostel was barely literate and accompanied his BSL signs with copious gesture and mime. He found lip-reading difficult, and although he was slow to comprehend questions, once he grasped the meaning his answers were wonderfully comprehensive, not to say long-winded.

Manual communication – conclusion

The majority of the residents of hostels, homes for the elderly and the deaf, and those in private households communicated with hearing people by a combination of speech, lip-reading, writing and gesture. During the interview they communicated in BSL, accompanied by a varying degree of finger-spelling and speech; but among themselves the medium of communication was fluent BSL and finger-spelling.

Almost all of them, as well as a fifth of hospital patients, were able to adjust their mode of communication to suit the needs of the person with whom they were communicating – whether this was a staff member, unskilled in sign language, a stranger or friend from the deaf or hearing community, a relative, a fellow patient or resident. If communication were to be maintained on a wide basis, enormous flexibility in the use of methods of communication was required of deaf people, and for the most part they met the challenge.

However, communication difficulties sometimes led to serious misunderstanding. Some hospital patients were misunderstood because their efforts at communication were not recognized as such, and as a consequence staff adopted inappropriate behaviour towards them. Similar misunderstandings occurred in residential homes for the deaf, where the mental capacities of some residents were severely underestimated because their communication code was not understood by staff: but here at least residents were able to console themselves to some extent by finding sympathy and solace in the company of others with whom communication was possible – a consolation not available for the most part to deaf hospital patients who were usually marooned in isolation among hearing people.

Isolation resulting from communication difficulties was most marked among hospital patients and the residents of local authority homes for the elderly. The residents in the homes expressed their sense of isolation in a hearing community, but none wished to move into a home for the deaf, primarily because such a move would take them from the familiar environment of the home and its neighbourhood. In contrast, all of the hospital patients reported that they felt isolated and as many as were able to express themselves wished to move to a deaf community: for them isolation was not offset by a high standard of care in the hospital or attachment to the neighbourhood.

The widespread need to communicate by a method so demonstrably different from that of the mainstream of society presented for a minority an enormous hurdle to communication. For a few – 5 per cent – to be observed signing by the hearing caused enormous embarrassment and no more. But for another 12 per cent, that embarrassment became so acute that they stopped signing. Nevertheless, for the majority of deaf people communication was so essential that they carried on regardless of the impression they made on and the ridicule of hearing onlookers. A little more than two-thirds of deaf people said that jokes had been made at their expense when signing, by hearing people. However, the frequency with which ridicule was encountered varied substantially according to setting. It was not surprising to find that those who had most contact with the hearing community were most likely to encounter ridicule. Thus a majority of those in private households (three-quarters) and hostels (two-thirds) said that jokes had been made about their signed communication.

Literacy

In view of the large finger-spelling component in BSL literacy was crucial to deaf people even in their communication with members of the deaf community. Furthermore, because of the limitations of lip-reading, writing was often important to correct misunderstandings. And because verbal communication was so difficult, deaf people had to be able to read in order to acquire the information which hearing people obtained simply by listening. A superficial understanding of events was gained from subtitled TV news programmes, tabloid newspapers and information processed or translated by services for the deaf. Untitled TV programmes were of little help because of the difficulty of lip-reading. Those who were confident approached the general advice-giving services – CABs, police, doctor, town hall – and did so pen in hand. Literacy, then, was important for the deaf: writing was a vital tool for communicating with the hearing, and reading was critical for the acquisition of information.

Unhappily, it is far from easy for deaf people to achieve good literacy skills. Recent research suggests that deaf school-leavers are retarded by between six and seven years in their reading age compared with hearing children.[51] Indeed, it has been argued that as many as half of all deaf school-leavers have a reading age of only 9 years, and the other half do not even achieve that level of reading skill.[52] Nor is retardation in respect of reading confined to British deaf children. Similar patterns of achievement have been found in America.[53] While it is clear that, as Conrad points out, there is a relationship between reading ability and intelligence,[54] levels of intelligence and degrees of deafness also have an impact on reading ability. To a considerable extent, then, a high level of intelligence can compensate for a high degree of hearing impairment and offset the damage done to reading ability.[55]

For the purposes of the present study, no precise definition or measurement of literacy was devised, but an attempt at a broad assessment of literacy skills was made which relied heavily on self-reporting. A six point functional measure was based on the way in which deaf people responded to aspects of daily life in terms of communication:

1   Managed their own household affairs and did not require assistance in comprehending official letters or writing to officials.
2   Felt confident of their skills but occasionally required non-specialist advice to confirm their understanding of correspondence or a situation.
3   Usually sought advice but could manage to initiate correspondence or construct their own responses to correspondence.
4   Always referred correspondence to a hearing person.
5   Relied on non-specialists but had some understanding of writing and reading skills.
6   Always referred to specialists and were illiterate in the sense that they could not understand tabloid newspapers and were unable to devise letters of any description except by copying word for word.

Self-reporting and evaluation of finger-spelling were used to produce an assessment which would approximate to that of the six-point scale. Of course, the younger people interviewed who lived with their parents were not managing a household, but most of them had already had contact with the DHSS or the Department of Employment.

There were differences in the overall levels of literacy of people in the different settings. Among those living in private households all but two showed that they had some literacy skills, but only five were completely self-sufficient. By far the largest category – more than half – could manage their official correspondence without help but felt the need to seek advice or reassurance from time to time (score 2).

Most married couples where both partners were deaf discussed official matters and wrote official letters together. However, where one partner to a marriage was hearing, it was the hearing spouse who usually undertook domestic arrangements and official correspondence. Hearing spouses complained that they were overburdened by the responsibility, that the deaf partner did not have a realistic understanding of the family's financial situation or the negotiations involved in procuring a grant for a child's further education, in arranging mortgages, or even holidays. Even so, they preferred to handle family affairs themselves rather than explain the ramifications to their deaf partners.

Whatever their level of literacy, deaf people of all ages relied heavily on the help of hearing relatives, especially parents, children, brothers and sisters. Those who were elderly, widowed, single or childless relied most heavily on voluntary and statutory services. Several of those with poor oral skills and minimal literacy were heavily dependent upon the services of the local authority social worker for the deaf, and in his absence reluctantly had recourse to voluntary service advisers to the deaf or 'the Town Hall'.

A high level of literacy (score 1 or 2) was general among persons living in local authority accommodation for the elderly. Though hostel residents had some degree of literacy, by and large, only a third achieved a score of 1 or 2: as many as half relied on others to write letters of a formal nature for them (score 3 or 4), while the remainder were barely literate and never wrote letters. A similar pattern emerged in the homes for the deaf where as many as half of the residents did not attempt to express themselves using the written word, and as many as three-fifths required assistance with correspondence.

It was in mental handicap hospitals that literacy proved to be most rare. Only a fifth of deaf patients were known to have some minimal ability to read and write. Thus the maximum literacy score achieved by the deaf in mental handicap hospitals was 4. Mentally ill deaf patients presented a striking contrast: almost half had some useful literacy skills and achieved a score of 2 or 3, while another two gave evidence of minimal skills. However, on the whole, literate psychiatric hospital patients of all kinds confined the exercise of their ability to finger-spelling and reading; all but a tenth of them never expressed themselves in the written word.

A high level of literacy was not common, then, among deaf people. In the light of other studies, perhaps it was not surprising that only 7 per cent of them gave evidence of a good level of ability and never required help from others in either reading or writing. On the other hand, a substantial minority – a third in all – were sufficiently literate to feel confident of their skills, and only occasionally required help from specialists to confirm their understanding of correspondence or a situation. Almost as many (28 per cent) had acquired modest skills: while they usually sought advice they could initiate correspondence or construct their own response to correspondence. However, almost a third of the deaf were barely, if at all, literate, at most able to make some attempt at writing, but always referring correspondence to hearing people for advice (8 per cent) and at worst, being unable to devise letters of any description except by copying word for word (13 per cent).

Problems of communication

It is clear that for all but a minority of deaf people communication in every medium presented considerable hazards. How successful did they consider themselves to be in communicating inside and outside the home?

At home

In view of the much greater ease with which the majority of deaf people felt able to communicate in sign or total communication it seemed likely that their most profound communication would be with other deaf people, particularly those with whom they lived. In fact, almost two-thirds lived with at least one other deaf person with whom total communication was the most commonly used medium of conversation. In addition, a tiny minority used sign alone. The remainder (a fifth) used either gesture or sign, or a combination of speech and writing, or speech and sign. Thus, sign played a dominant role in communication between deaf people. The vast majority – three-quarters – found their chosen method of communication entirely satisfactory, and for most of the others it worked moderately well. In all, 15 per cent said that they had some difficulty in conversing with the deaf people with whom they lived, and, for a tenth, communication proved to be impossible. Of course, communication depended as much on the receptive skills of others as on the expressive skills of the persons interviewed. For this reason alone, it was impossible for anyone to achieve a consistent level of success, even with the same person over time. However, those who claimed to have no difficulty appeared to achieve a high level of consistency: indeed, the greater the difficulty experienced in communication, the greater the likelihood of variation in the level of success achieved.

A nine-point scale was devised to reflect the degree of difficulty experienced by deaf people in communicating with others in the household who were deaf.

1   No difficulty ever.
2   No difficulty usually.
3   No difficulty sometimes.
4   Some difficulty sometimes.
5   Some difficulty usually.
6   Some difficulty always.
7   Cannot communicate sometimes.
8   Cannot communicate usually.
9   Cannot communicate always.

At the level of daily chat the vast majority rated themselves as achieving a high level of success when communicating at home with others who were deaf: as many as four-fifths had, at most, some difficulty sometimes. Thus, only a fifth scored 5 or more according to the self-assessment, while only a little more than 1 per cent found communication impossible with other deaf people.

What degree of difficulty was encountered when deaf people attempted to communicate at a higher level of complexity than that of daily chat? How far did they ever discuss subjects such as the state of the country, politics, the economy, sport or religion? In fact, a substantial minority (a little more than two-fifths) never did so. Such discussion was most common in hostels, and homes for the deaf, where more than three-fifths claimed to indulge in such communication, while in contrast, almost half of the deaf people living in private households, and, perhaps less surprisingly, the majority of hospital patients (three-quarters) did so.

With what degree of ease were such subjects discussed? A surprisingly high proportion of deaf people (70 per cent) claimed to experience little or no difficulty, and another 13 per cent experienced difficulty only sometimes.

Many of the difficulties encountered in discussing topics of a demanding nature were reported to be 'just the same as when you are chatting about nothing much', but of a greater intensity. In addition, however, it was clear that conversations concerning the more complex issues of life were more demanding of the communication skills of all the parties involved, and therefore revealed the weaknesses in the communication techniques being used. To a large extent these weaknesses were perceived as short-comings in the communication skills of those with whom deaf people were accustomed to converse. It was a common complaint, especially among oralists, that few of those with whom they lived, particularly manualists, were able to attain their own level of discourse.

Mrs Simpson, now in retirement, was an oralist most of whose social activities involved people in the hearing community. However, her husband depended entirely upon manual communication. His social activities involved only the deaf community. Not only did they move very largely in separate social circles – he found it difficult to communicate with the hearing, and she with the signing deaf – but they also found it difficult to communicate with each other except at a relatively superficial level.

In other cases manualists found it difficult to converse on complex matters with those who relied heavily on silent speech. Others, particularly manualists who had difficulty in lip-reading, found the content of their conversation constrained by their reliance on the written word. Those with poor sight, too, found it difficult not only to lip-read, but also to follow manual signs, while deaf people with arthritic upper limbs often produced ambiguous signs. Not all difficulties owed their origin directly to com-munication problems as such. For example, there were some residents of homes for the deaf who considered that the major obstacle to the enjoyment of a wide-ranging conversation was the superiority of their own general

knowledge over that of other residents. A small minority found it difficult
to comprehend any but the simplest conversational exchanges. Then there
were other deaf people who found the behavioural characteristics of those
with whom they lived distracting and unhelpful in prolonged communication.

Mr Timpson said of his deaf wife: 'When we get into a conversation she gets
very excited and signs much too fast.'

Of course, many were not confined to conversation with the deaf alone.
Almost four-fifths lived with at least one hearing person and in only one
case was there no communication between them. The remainder employed
a wide variety of communication skills in order to maintain a dialogue with
hearing people in the household. Although a tiny minority – 3 per cent –
relied entirely on sign or a combination of sign and the written word, much
more common was the combination of sign and gesture employed by a little
more than a tenth of those who lived with hearing people, while about the
same proportion, as oralists, were able to communicate in the same medium
as the hearing. But by far the largest proportion of deaf people – as many
as two-thirds in fact – adopted a combination of oralism, the written word,
sign and gesture in their attempt to communicate with the hearing persons
around them.

But at what level and with what degree of ease was communication
achieved between deaf people and the hearing with whom they lived? In a
substantial minority of cases, deaf people estimated that communication
was achieved with considerable ease if they confined exchanges to the level
of daily chat: as many as three-fifths experienced difficulty only sometimes
at most. But the remainder found that even at the level of daily chat
communication with the hearing people around them usually proved to be
difficult, and indeed, for almost a fifth, impossible. It was striking that
those who experienced greatest difficulty lived in local authority homes for
the elderly, or hospitals. In terms of day-to-day chat, then, communication
with the hearing was considerably less successful than with deaf people.
To that extent, those who lived *only* with hearing people were at a
disadvantage.

The limited role played by the hearing in the household as sources of
communication was exemplified by their failure to offer the deaf substantial opportunities to engage in conversation beyond that of day-to-day chat.
As many as two-thirds of deaf people never attempted to discuss subjects
such as politics, religion or sport, for example, with hearing people. Of the
minority of those who made the attempt, only about a quarter did so with
ease, while more than half considered that such communication was almost

always fraught with difficulties. It was striking that those who attempted more sophisticated conversation than daily chat were largely confined to those living in private households, hostels or homes for the deaf – settings where hearing people were most likely to be able to respond.

Deaf people who regarded their own communication problems as the major source of difficulty were in a minority: little less than a third regarded the effects of deafness as the major obstacle to conversation. Of those who did so, a deaf–blind woman considered it unreasonable to expect more than minimal communication with hearing people, given the dimensions of her disability. Others found laborious communication which relied largely on the written word.

Mrs Jones said 'It's not just that I have to write it down. I'm very slow at writing.'

Half of those who engaged in conversation with hearing people in the household blamed their limited lip-reading skill.

Mr Levitt said 'Lip-reading some staff here is difficult.'

Mr Morris said 'I'm a good lip-reader, but I need repeats.'

However, as many as a quarter of those who encountered difficulty in such communication argued that the main problem was the attitude of the hearing people with whom they lived rather than their own deafness.

Mr Green said 'The hearing don't bother with the deaf.'

Mr Levitt retorted 'The hearing don't show any interest in us.'

Most hearing people were regarded as too impatient for satisfactory conversation to be possible.

Lack of signing skills on the part of the hearing were commonly blamed for communication difficulties by those living in private households, hospitals, and residential homes.

A hospital patient, Mr Green said 'I can't talk to anyone here: the staff don't know sign.'

Where the hearing people were disposed to be patient, and attempt communication, their lack of skill prevented real progress. Generally the conversational link with the hearing was minimal.

Mr Levitt, a hospital patient, said 'The only hearing person I can speak to here is the occupational therapy lady.'

However, for a small minority, primarily those in hospitals and residential homes, the problem lay in the physical or mental defects of fellow patients and residents.

Mr Gough, who was in a mental handicap hospital, said 'Other people here have only very limited conversation.'

Mr Ruskin, who was a psychiatric patient said 'You can't converse with them – it's their mental condition.'

But there were deaf people living in private households who encountered similar difficulties.

Mr Cross said of his mother 'I can't lip read her because she stutters.'

For the majority of deaf people, then, conversation tended to be superficial and any ventures beyond daily chat to be fraught with difficulties. How far were deaf people able to compensate with satisfactory conversation outside the home?

Outside the home

There proved to be fewer opportunities for conversation with those outside than inside the home. As many as a third had no conversational contact with other deaf people outside the household, and had no alternatives to the limited conversational opportunites of the home. Compared with those used at home the type and range of communication skills employed to communicate with deaf people outside the household displayed less emphasis on gesture and sign, perhaps because deaf people sought to converse socially with members of the deaf community whose communi-cation skills most nearly matched their own. Indeed the ease with which they engaged in such communication supported this interpretation: only four reported any difficulty. For the vast majority – four-fifths in fact – little difficulty was usually if ever experienced in communication at the level of daily chat, and the remainder reported only occasional diffi-culties. Furthermore, deaf people were more likely to communicate at a more complex level with members of the deaf community outside rather than inside the home: two-thirds did so, most of whom lived in private households, hostels and homes for the deaf. The difficulties associated with such an enterprise appeared to be less marked when embarked upon out-side rather than inside the household: only occasional difficulties were admitted and these were often associated with the different or superior communication skills of the other deaf person.

Mr Green said: 'Some people sometimes use unfamiliar signs.'

Mrs Ogmore said: 'Some people sign too fast – I can't keep up.'

 Some signing deaf people found it difficult to communicate with the oral deaf. The problems of unfamiliar signs and oralism were often attributed to 'a different educational background'. When more complex topics than those of daily chat were attempted, additional problems could arise which were associated not with communication skills as such, but with understanding the *content* of the topic under discussion. However, in general, conversations with deaf people outside the home were regarded as presenting little or no difficulty.

Communication outside the household was by no means restricted to other members of the deaf community. All but a fifth of deaf people talked to the hearing as well, usually in a combination of speech, writing, sign and gesture, though a further tenth relied primarily on the written word, while almost as many used gesture or a combination of sign and gesture; only 3 per cent communicated entirely orally. For the most part, then, a battery of communication methods was used. How successful did deaf people consider such methods to be? Whereas communication with the deaf proved to be easier with those outside than inside the home, the reverse was true regarding hearing people. It must be assumed that whereas members of the deaf community were chosen for the compatibility of their communication, communication was most assured with hearing people with whom the deaf person was familiar. Thus less than a fifth of those who conversed with hearing people outside the household did so with little or no difficulty even at the level of ordinary daily chat, while for as many as a third, communication usually proceeded with difficulty and a small minority (4 per cent) found it rarely if ever possible. Those who were most likely to make the attempt lived in private households, homes for the deaf, and – surprisingly – homes for the elderly. However, the latter, together with hospital patients, were most likely to experience great difficulty in communicating with hearing people outside the household.

Given the difficulties experienced during the interviews perhaps it is not surprising that rather less than half of the deaf people (44 per cent) made any attempt to converse at a more complex level with the hearing. Yet among those who did so, a majority (almost three-quarters) encountered at most only occasional difficulty. It was striking that those who were prepared to attempt to converse beyond the level of daily chat lived in private households, hostels, and homes for the deaf.

The major obstacle to communication was generally held to be the impatience of the hearing.

Mr Grey said 'It takes a long time to achieve communication between the deaf and the hearing. It doesn't matter as much to them as to me if they fail to communicate with me.'

Difficulties were also attributed to ignorance of the communication of the deaf.

Mrs Jones said 'Hearing people talk too fast.'

Others complained of the tendency of the hearing to shout when conversing with the deaf. It often appeared that the hearing had no appreciation of the prerequisites of lip-reading.

Mrs Smith said 'They use too long words.'

Mr Nixon explained 'They have unclear lips: they don't know how to speak properly.'

There were complaints that beards were both a distraction from and an obstacle to communication, while regional accents also caused confusion. The failure of the hearing to develop communication skills suitable for conversing with the deaf was rarely blamed; far more commonly raised (by between a quarter and a third) were their own shortcomings. Some reported that their difficulties originated in poor eye sight which restricted lip-reading skills while others blamed their poor speech.

Observed communication problems

So far, problems of communication have been considered only in terms of the perceptions of deaf people themselves. How far did these perceptions correspond to those of the interviewer? It was possible to observe 60 per cent of deaf people at home. A greater variety of communication method was observed than was reported by deaf people. For example, 3 per cent were observed to use a mixture of speech and gesture; 2 per cent employed speech and finger-spelling, while 3 per cent appeared to depend upon silent speech and finger-spelling, and 8 per cent on sign and finger-spelling. The numbers involved in each case were small, but none had categorized their language medium with other deaf people in these ways. Furthermore, there appeared to be substantial differences in the proportion of those who reported the use of, and those who were observed to use, sign and total communication. Whereas the majority of deaf people claimed to use total communication when conversing with other deaf people in the household, only a tenth were observed to do so. In contrast, the majority (54 per cent) were seen to use sign but only 3 per cent reported that they did so. Such discrepancies may reflect differences of definition, for example, of signed and total communication. Furthermore, some deaf people have been unsure about the nature of the different categories of communication method. And, of course, there is the possibility that the observed exchanges were not typical.

Observed conversation between the deaf and hearing members of the household revealed further discrepancies between the two assessments. For example, substantially more deaf people were observed to rely on sign alone, and on gesture, than appeared to be the case from their own reports, and there was correspondingly less dependence on gesture and sign, and on speech accompanied by writing, sign or gesture. Again, definitional problems and the questionable typicality of observed exchanges may be responsible at least in part for such discrepancies.

In contrast, little difference emerged between reported and observed assessments of the difficulties involved in conversing with members of the household: observation suggested that a small minority (about a tenth) overestimated the degree of ease with which they conversed at home at the level of daily chat, and this applied to conversation with deaf as well as hearing people. However, it appeared that as many as two-fifths of deaf people were over-optimistic about the ease with which they communicated with others, deaf and hearing, on the more complex topics such as politics and sport, but they were largely confined to those who claimed to experience no difficulty. The degree of discrepancy was not marked, though its scale was surprisingly large. Furthermore, it must be remembered that the opportunities for observing complex conversational exchanges were more limited than for those which were simpler, and perhaps observed conversations were not representative of such exchanges in general. However, the performance of deaf people during the interviews tended to lend support to the observed rather than the reported assessment.

The non-typicality of observed exchanges and the definitional problems associated with assessments may explain discrepancies which emerged between observed and reported assessments, but they may also arise from a genuine misapprehension on the part of deaf people of the degree of difficulty involved in complex communication, a misapprehension which arose from their partial comprehension determined by the limitations of their powers of communication.

Communication and dependence

Most deaf people, then, communicated in comfort only with the hearing people they knew well. When they went beyond the confines of the household, they found great difficulty in understanding unfamiliar areas of conversation. A combination of poor lip-reading and limited general knowledge made explanations difficult to understand. Even with other deaf people they were happier when communicating with those whom they knew well. Manualists sought to converse only with other manualists, and even then experienced difficulties with unfamiliar signs. The result was a desire to cling to those with whom they were familiar even among the deaf population.

Mrs Roberts summed up a common attitude when she said 'Friends know the best way to chat.'

It was pointed out by Mr Thompson, that even the communication of straightforward information is 'hard in my case. Both of us have to be very patient. It all has to be written down.'

So overwhelming were the problems posed by communication that more than half – 52 per cent – considered them to be the greatest difficulties they faced. For a small minority the sheer lack of communication, the absence of anyone to talk to, was the first concern.

Mrs Habant, aged 76, who lived alone, said 'I have no one to talk to for days on end. I'm all alone with the television, and I can't understand that.'

But for the majority the problems resolved themselves around one of understanding. First there was the difficulty of making themselves understood by the hearing.

Mr Selsby, who lived on his own said 'It's the frustration of having to deal with the hearing, of making yourself understood.'

Miss Argus, who lived with her blind mother, said 'The greatest problem is trying to communicate with strangers. It takes time and it's very difficult. The deaf and the hearing live in different worlds.'

Equally important were the difficulties involved in understanding the hearing.

Mr Himsworth said 'The great difficulty is understanding right – making sure you've understood correctly when dealing with bureaucracy. It's a great problem knowing what you get told which is rubbish, and what is really the law.'

Miss Watson said 'It's hard to understand what's going on. I don't know how bad I have to get before I should go to a doctor.'

Mrs Jones said 'The great problem is the bad speech of the hearing, it makes understanding very difficult. And you have to avoid being upset by things you don't understand.'

Severe hearing impairment substantially reduced the powers of those of ordinary intelligence to comprehend the hearing world beyond their homes.

Mr Smith explained 'The great difficulty for me is understanding official letters.'

When removed from the safety of home and the small circle of friends and relatives with whom they were able to converse, and forced into an alien and hearing environment, the result was usually bewilderment:

Mrs Hopkins, who lived in a residential home for the deaf, said 'I can't talk to the hearing easily. I've had a bad time in three hospitals. I used to be frightened.'

Even acquiring basic information about the operation of the residential homes for the deaf seemed to be a problem for some.

Mrs Faulkner preferred to write to the social worker with the deaf in the area from which she had been admitted and whom she had known well, rather than approach the Matron about a health problem she had begun to experience since admission.

Mrs Mornson said 'They don't tell us where we are going. We get up in the morning and then after breakfast they (the warden and his wife) say "We are going out for the day. Everybody in the bus, quick, ten minutes." '

The difficulty involved in achieving understanding in a hearing world manifested itself for some primarily in terms of obtaining information about the external environment.

Mr Forster, who lived with his hearing parents and deaf wife, said, 'You find out the news later than everyone else, and that's true of all areas of life. I depend upon the subtitles on TV: they should give us a free licence. Ceefax is too expensive.'

Most deaf people, however, were more concerned to obtain information about their immediate environment than to keep abreast of current affairs.

Miss Harris, who lived with retired hearing parents, said 'It's easier to get information if you're hearing. I don't know what's going on at work: I get to feeling lonely when the other women are talking gossip. But at least I'm not depressed like my dear friend who lives alone.'

But for others the barrier to information frustrated their attempts to understand how to make decisions for themselves.

Mrs Glending, who lived on her own, said 'You never get a full understanding of what to do for yourself or anything else, you can't communicate your feelings or take your own major decisions without asking.'

Miss Swanley, who was a patient in a psychiatric hospital, said 'I'm not happy. I can't talk to change situations.'

As a consequence many bore the burden of almost intolerable frustration.

A member of the care staff in a local authority home for the elderly said 'Poor Mrs Franklin, she trembles with the frustration of not being able to explain why she's upset.'

Much frustration arose from the difficulties of securing the help of intermediaries with the hearing world.

Miss Rose, a single parent with two hearing children, said 'I need others to help, and they are either not interested or impatient. It's difficult to understand about medical problems, and bringing up the children, and the coil.'

Mr Forester said 'I can't negotiate directly with the Council, I have to rely on the welfare and my son.'

Dependence on intermediaries outside the informal network, other than social workers for the deaf, could create a sense of obligation: a charitable relationship was considered to exist between the deaf person and those who adopted the interpreter's role.

Mr Fox said 'The problem is talking with the hearing. I don't want charity.'

The role of a dependent appeared to give the right to the hearing to take control:

Mrs Jackson explained, 'Because I can't understand, the greatest problem is being dictated to by others as if I were a child or a young person. And this is true not just at work but even in my leisure pursuits.'

Miss Cox said, 'Because I find lip-reading difficult everyone treats me as if I'm mental.'

Mr Douglas summed up the common experience of those in hospitals:
'Because you can't communicate, you miss out on friends and experiences. You don't understand what's going on or what will happen next. There's not much reading and little talk, and everyone pushes you around. You have to work hard for very little pay, and you have no chance to make your own decisions.'

Dependence on interpreters to explain the hearing world was widespread. No one had managed to live without interpretation, if only to a minimal extent, in the course of their adult lives. The need for interpretation from time to time did not necessarily lead to a *feeling* of dependence. And the degree to which deaf people perceived themselves as being dependent varied according to setting. Perceived dependency on interpretation of the hearing world by others was least apparent among those living in private households and homes for the elderly, but even among them the majority considered themselves to be dependent in this respect.

That feelings of dependency were not necessarily related to actual use of intepretation is reflected in the fact that only 6 per cent of deaf people considered that they did not need to have the services of an interpreter available to them, and even they admitted to having used such services on occasion. In ten standard situations involving the police, the courts, the general practitioner, the hospital, the children's school and clinic, the family planning clinic, the council and work, only five deaf people had never required an interpreter. Although a little under a half required interpretation in only one or two of these situations, a substantial minority (a third) proved to be highly dependent requiring help in all of them. For example, it was striking that more than two-thirds of deaf people required interpretation whenever they saw their general practitioner.

The most important source of help for those who required interpretation was the informal network of family and friends, both deaf and hearing. As many as a third of deaf people used relatives as interpreters, while almost a quarter depended upon deaf friends and 16 per cent had used the services of hearing friends. Of the formal network of service provision, the specialist services for the deaf, perhaps understandably, proved to be the most important source of help. Almost half of deaf people had been helped at some time by the social worker for the deaf, while a fifth had received the aid of a voluntary organization for the deaf. Interpretation, in the sense of explanation of a puzzling fact of contemporary life, had also been provided for small minorities of deaf people by the CAB, the police station, a community advice centre, general practitioners, and non-specialist social workers. Interpretation was defined broadly by deaf people to include not only the translation of spoken English but also explanations of the environment – for example, of official documents – by hearing officials. In general, however, the deaf sought out those members of the public with whom they were most likely to communicate easily.

In view of the heavy dependence on relatives for help with interpretation, it was ironic that those who relied on others for interpretation were least likely to be in close contact with their families. Indeed, the more reliant deaf people were on others for intepretation the less likely they were to have seen a relative within the previous month, and the more likely they were not to have seen a member of the family for more than three years.

The availability of help with interpretation varied enormously. There were a few – only five in all – who required interpretation but for whom no help was available. And as many as a third were dependent upon a single category of help – usually, family or friends. But for as many as half help was available from two or three sources, and a small number had a wealth of help at their disposal – from family, friends (both hearing and deaf), the social worker for the deaf, voluntary agencies for the deaf, and local authority social workers.

In succeeding chapters the effects of dependence on interpretation on health, family life, friendship, income and so on, will be explored in some detail. But it is crucial to consider in the context of communication some of the broad issues which have emerged in recent years in respect of interpretation for members of the deaf population.

Interpretation

Interpretation is a universal requirement, but the needs of the deaf are substantially more intense than those of the generality of hearing people. The interpretation of the environment by the individual commences at birth, if not before. Child and adult do not have identical communication codes. Infants receive messages from all the senses, from which they learn about the world within and outside them. Their parents mediate on their behalf with the environment at large. They make assumptions about an infant's physical and emotional needs based on their own experience and interpret and respond to his or her inarticulate cries and immature movement, until the child learns to give increasingly acceptable signals and to provide for his or her own needs.[56] However, in many cases, parental skills do not include familiarity with the craft necessary to socialize hearing-impaired children in such a way as to help them reach the interactional milestones of normally hearing children at a similar age. In this, deaf parents of deaf children have a natural advantage over hearing parents: they usually have native sign language, confidence in their ability to communicate with other hearing-impaired people, their personal childhood experiences and perhaps the experiences and resources of other deaf parents of both hearing and hearing-impaired children.[57]

Society assumes normality of the non-observable characteristics of the newborn in all but the few who are labelled 'at risk'. Awareness of substantial hearing defects may be awakened only after a prolonged period of non-response to aural stimuli. Even when hearing loss has been diagnosed parents are unsure of the immediate implications of deafness for communication, and receive insufficient counselling to awaken them to the difficulties the future will bring.[58] One of the consequences of society's present management of the child with a profound hearing loss is that 'deaf children do, in fact, possess a set of rules which frequently deviate from those of Standard English'.[59] It has been observed that social workers, using combined oral and manual methods of communication, are in a position to communicate more effectively with deaf youngsters than parents using combination of speech and *ad hoc* gesture. Yet 'in the case of deaf children social and behavioural education cannot begin until effective parent/child communication is established'.[60]

At a desperately frustrating period in life – namely, adolescence – when a deaf person's ability to communicate is several years behind that of hearing peers, he is removed from a secure communication environment – the deaf school or unit – and expected to integrate into a hearing environment in employment. It was not surprising that several young deaf people who had not long left full-time education maintained contact with one or more teachers. Just as most adult members of the hearing community develop a comfortable medium for communication and thereafter rarely consider how they manage it, so too deaf people achieved a range of communication skills, at least as great, which habit enabled them to manipulate and adjust to different situations. They relied on a range of people who acted as intermediaries between the hearing world and themselves whom they appeared to accept as a normal part of their communication pattern. But deaf people rarely admitted their dependence though they did admit the frustrations involved in arranging for interpretation. There was frustration, too, when hearing people gave a brief précis of a conversation after talking together at length, and appeared to make decisions on behalf of the deaf person, without consultation, or ignored requests for further information.

In general, deaf people preferred an interpreter who understood what it was like to be deaf, who was familiar with and proficient in manual skills. Often the first comment deaf people made on specialist social workers concerned their communication skills, and assessments of professionalism were formed accordingly.

There appeared to be a continuum of interpretation from informal to formal, from interpretation in everyday situations, perhaps by one deaf person for another to the rigours of the court of law, one example of a setting where the necessity for simultaneous interpreting arose.[61] The process and difficulties of simultaneous interpreting are discussed in some detail by P. Jones.[62] who draws parallels with foreign language interpreting.[63] Kyle and Jones[64] describe the difficulties of an experiment on HTV which included interpreting for a deaf target audience with the process of receiving information in 'headline' form on screen, and the development of signed communication methods which may be understood by deaf viewers. Local deaf people reported that they would have liked the signing to go on longer and all said they watched the programme because of the appearance of the interpreter. In the present study, most deaf people deliberately watched subtitled programmes (many enjoyed foreign films) but nearly all mentioned the difficult vocabulary of subtitles and would have preferred them to stay on screen longer. Signed interpretation posed no such problems.

The importance of the role of the interpreter in the life of the deaf child, adolescent and adult in formal and informal situations was recognized in the ACSHIP report of 1977. The survey found that all but one of the local authorities responding provided an interpretation service for deaf people, in both formal and informal settings. The report noted that 'an interpretation service is not synonymous with social work support' and 'very often a deaf person's communication needs can be met by a volunteer but these are in short supply'.[65]

It was clear from the present study that while volunteers are everywhere in evidence helping the deaf in everyday situations, there seem to be few available to function in formal situations. Although there was little evidence of difficulty for those living in private households in contacting interpreters for many situations, there were others where interpretation would have eased communication and promoted a clearer understanding for the deaf person.

The degree to which deaf people achieve integration in the hearing community must be determined, in part, by the availability of interpreters for every facet of life.

Time

The overall effect of communication difficulties was not merely to impede and restrict understanding and create dependence on interpreters but also to prolong the time taken to get things done. In all, as many as 52 per cent of deaf people reported that things took longer because they were deaf. Even for oralists, simply understanding what was being said to them took time.

Mr Johnson said 'It's repeat, repeat.'

But manualists dealing with the hearing often found receptive communication even more laborious.

Mrs Glending said 'It takes a long time to write things down, but it's quick to speak.'

Dependence on the combination of the written word and unclear speech often made communication a protracted business.

Mrs Hunsworth said 'I either have to write letters – I can do that on my own – or I have to talk very slowly and clearly to be understood.'

Inability to use the telephone was seen to be a major factor in protracting the communication process.

Mr Brown said 'It's slow making arrangements to see people – no phone, always no phone.'

Mrs Bosely said 'I have to go to see people or write.'

Many deaf people found the hearing world reluctant to reply to their letters.

Mr Varley said 'Speech is difficult, and I never get a reply to my letters.'

And even when a letter was received, it never seemed to be the end of the matter.

Mr Fox said 'It takes me three letters to get something done instead of one telephone call.'

Acquiring the ground rules for action was often a prolonged process.

Miss Robertson said 'Finding out about things takes a long time; I wait, wait.'

Because of the communication problem so much more information had to be deliberately acquired by deaf than hearing people.

Mrs Swale said 'There's so much explaining, talking – to get things done.'

Mrs Denton said 'It's the writing in shops and asking directions that takes the time.'

Mrs Green summed up the experience of many deaf people when she said 'What takes time is talking, getting things done. News comes through other people, messages – it takes a long time to get sorted out.'

5 Health, handicaps and the care setting

What determined whether deaf people lived in private households, homes for the deaf or elderly, hostels, or hospitals for the mentally disordered? On the face of it, the overriding factor should have been physical or mental capacity. According to current community care policy, only those diagnosed as requiring hospital treatment or unable to manage in their homes with the aid of domiciliary social service provision should be in any kind of residential accommodation. Yet other studies have shown that for the aged and mentally disordered, social factors – the death of a spouse, or the loss of a home – are crucial in determining entry into hospital or residental care.[1] Furthermore, it has been suggested that hospitals for the mentally disordered have proved to be convenient for the 'dumping' of deaf people whose only handicap is difficulty with communication.[2] How far, and in what ways, did the deaf people living in private households differ from those in other settings?

Why live here?

At the outset it became clear that residence in a hostel, home or hospital was no temporary, short-term feature of life. Yet those living in private households had little experience of institutional life. On average, hospital patients had lived about half their lives in such settings while residents of homes for the deaf had spent on average a quarter of their lives in institutions of one sort or another; and there was little variation around the mean. But there were marked differences between the hostels: residents of the half-way psychiatric hostel had on average lived in institutions for as much as 37 per cent of their lives, compared with only 4 per cent for those in the hostel for the young working deaf. In general, deaf people living in homes for the elderly were tasting institutional life for the first time: they had entered residential care only in frail old age, and on average had spent only 7 per cent of their lives in institutions. What marked out those with long experience of institutional life from other members of the deaf population?

It was striking that almost half of those in hospitals, homes for the deaf and the psychiatric half-way hostel had arrived there from some other institutional setting. Thus experience of more than one institutional setting was not uncommon. To some extent, this high proportion of transfers between institutions is to be explained by the role of the half-way psychiatric hostel, which offered places to deaf patients in local psychiatric hospitals: only an eighth of residents had arrived from the parental home, and none from the marital home. It was striking that no hospital patients and less than a tenth of the residents of homes for the deaf had transferrred from the marital home, though a substantial proportion (two-thirds and almost half respectively) had come from institutions. In contrast all but one of the residents of homes for the elderly had moved from the marital home.

Most transfers from other institutions (two-thirds) were from psychiatric hospitals, and appeared to be part of the process of running down long-stay hospitals in favour of 'community care'. Although a little more than half of those who had moved from psychiatric hospitals now found themselves in hostels, and therefore could be argued to be half-way to living in the community, more than a quarter had transferred to residential homes for the deaf. Moreover, such movement appeared to be largely restricted to the patients of psychiatric hospitals: only four had transferred from subnormality hospitals.

By and large, it was a family crisis which disrupted lives and precipitated entry into institutional settings. For most of those in homes for the deaf, communication difficulties became overwhelming only when the family home was broken by death, or when family carers could no longer cope. In all, a third of residents were there because they were unable to manage alone after the death of a household member.

Mr Johnstone, aged 71, said 'I've only been here a couple of years. My mother died, and I couldn't manage money.'

Miss Rickmansworth, aged 68, said 'I lived with my sister, and then she died. I've got another sister but her house is too small.'.

Another third were in homes for the deaf because of the increasing frailty of relatives with whom they had lived.

Miss Greene, aged 54, said 'I had to come here last year: my mother is getting too old to manage.'

Most of the remainder (almost a third) had transferred from psychiatric hospitals.

Mr Squire, aged 57, had spent more than half his life in institutions, having entered a psychiatric hospital at the age of 23.

Miss Glynn, aged 29, who had entered hospital at the age of 3, had recently been discharged after spending six months in a special psychiatric unit for the deaf.

The crucial factors which precipitated entry into homes for the deaf were, then, the destruction by death or handicap of informal caring networks, and the absence of suitable alternatives for those discharged from mental hospitals.

Similarly, social factors, especially the loss of the family home through the death of a spouse or redevelopment, rather than incapacity for self-care despite an average age of almost 80, propelled deaf people into homes for the elderly. Only two of the residents of the hostel for the young working deaf had moved there to take advantage of employment opportunites.

Mr Gregory, 19, said 'I was unemployed and there was no work in the village, so I came here to work.'

In contrast a third had arrived after separation or divorce while two had taken up residence after discharge from psychiatric hospitals, and another did so when the pressures of independent living became too great.

Miss Valery said 'I got the rent into arrears, and then there was a fire. I just couldn't cope with my own flat.'

One resident had been in search of a deaf community.

Mr Wright said 'There aren't any deaf in Great Yarmouth. It's better here.'

Even at the half-way psychiatric hostel, where the bulk of residents had transferred from hospitals, as many as a quarter had arrived after the disruption of the family network of care through frailty or death.

Disruption of the family's caring system tended to precipitate entry into hospitals too. As many as half of the hospital patients were there because families could no longer provide care for them. By no means all patients were mentally disordered.

Mr Frances had been sent from home as a child because he was illegitimate: as consequence, he had spent more than four-fifths of his 76 years in large institutions.

Mr Jones had entered hospital at the age of 12 (he was now 32) when his mother developed TB and could no longer care for him.

Mr Goad, age 36, had entered hospital at the age of 16 when his mother had a new baby and considered that she would be unable to look after both of them.

In the main deaf people had entered hospitals not because of mental disorder, but because there was nowhere else for them to go.

Miss Redde was sent to a Sunshine Home at age of 2. As she was deaf and blind, the double handicap proved too much for the voluntary homes to manage and her parents sought her admission to a mental handicap hospital: now aged 57 she had spent all but her first two years in institutional care.

To what extent were the deaf introduced to their current setting by those who were both familiar with their mode of communication and able to interpret the nature of their new environment? In all, a little more than half of those in institutional settings had been accompanied on their admission by someone who was either familiar with them and their method of communication or who was skilled at interpreting for the deaf – a relative, social worker with the deaf, or a member of staff from their former residential setting. The remainder, however, had not been so fortunate. Almost half had been accompanied by a representative of the local authority social services department (or the old welfare department), members of the ambulance team or a nurse with whom they were unable to converse, while 3 per cent had come on their own, and had to make sense of their new environment without the aid of interpretation.

Additional handicaps

The importance of the breakdown in family support in determining entry into residential and hospital care seemed to suggest that the presence of handicaps in addition to severe hearing loss could be a contributory factor in the process. How prevalent were additional handicaps and to what extent were these concentrated in hostels, homes and hospitals?

As many as 30 per cent of deaf people had additional handicaps, and although it was true that the vast majority were to be found in residential homes and hospitals, a little more than a seventh were living in private households. Indeed, a surprisingly large minority of those in private households and hostels (a ninth) had at least one additional handicap, but the proportion was highest among those in other settings – about half of those in homes for the deaf and four-fifths of the people in homes for the elderly and hospitals. However, perhaps the surprise should be that some hospital patients and residents of homes had no handicaps other than deafness. How did such a situation arise?

Mental illness, from which as many as a fifth of the deaf appeared to suffer, was by far the most common secondary handicap; in comparison, only 5 per cent had a formally diagnosed mental handicap. For a tiny minority – 5 per cent – deafness was accompanied by blindness, or partial sight. Epileptics accounted for 6 per cent, while 11 per cent suffered from other physically handicapping conditions. Almost a tenth of deaf people had more than one additional handicap; the majority of these were in hospitals, although there were a few in the homes for the deaf.

In only one hospital were medical and nursing staff familiar with the effects on behaviour of hearing loss. Perhaps it was not surprising, therefore, that sometimes the effects of deafness were confused with mental disorder. Two young hospital patients appeared to have been diagnosed as mentally handicapped because of poor communication skills, even though neither of them had encountered teaching designed to develop such skills. In one case, diagnostic testing had been assigned to a ward sister who had been baffled by the communication problem, and tests remained incomplete and inconclusive. Recently both patients had been introduced to signed communication and were beginning to respond to tuition. In the homes for the deaf, too, there were instances in which residents were labelled as mentally disordered for exhibiting behaviour determined by communication difficulties. And, of course, some deaf people had been admitted to hospital because they had nowhere else to go. In all, about a fifth of hospital patients appeared to have no mental disorder. Tempowski *et al.* have drawn attention to the ease with which a wrong diagnosis may be made in the case of prelingually deaf people.[3] And Williams has ascribed the consignment of deaf people to long-term incarceration in mental handicap hospitals to a dearth of alternative provision, particularly for male adolescents in the past, and misdiagnosis of more recently admitted younger people.[4]

In part, cases of misdiagnosis may arise because mental handicap and deafness share common origins, such as the rubella virus, certain genetic determinants and environmental factors – for example, trauma and toxins.[5]

To emphasize difficulties of diagnosis is not to minimize the problem of mental handicap in the deaf population. Denmark has argued that because some of the factors associated with prelingual deafness, such as meningitis and pre-natal rubella, have frequently been found to result in some degree of brain damage, 'There is a high incidence of mental handicap amongst the hearing impaired and a high incidence of hearing impairment amongst the mentally retarded.'[6] Furthermore, it has been suggested that prelingual deafness, particularly, has in itself the effect of retarding social competence:[7] 'This rather than maladjustment is their psychological handicap.'[8]

The deprivations associated with hearing impairment which have the effect of retarding maturity have been described by Kennedy: 'The actions of the adult are frequently inexplicable and the child must obey for no apparent reason. The amount of foreign control exerted in an entirely autocratic way by hearing people at this stage and throughout ensuing stages is not conducive to the development of self-esteem.'[9]

Thus misdiagnosis is explained by a wide range of factors. First, there is the absence of routine audiological tests in hospitals, and therefore a failure to identify those consigned (wrongly) to custodial care before the Second World War. Second, there is the possibility of misdiagnosis even today because deafness and mental subnormality share common origins. Third, because mental retardation and deafness have common origins, a disproportionate number of deaf people *are* mentally handicapped, and therefore mental handicap may be too readily assumed to be present as well. And finally, many deaf people may display socially retarded behaviour, because communication difficulties have impeded social development. The enormity of misdiagnosis lies in the average length of time deaf patients had spent in hospitals. Others have drawn attention to the fact that 'once admitted, deaf and physically handicapped people tend to remain for longer periods (than hearing persons) and become custodial cases'.[10] The high proportion of people identified as suffering from mental illness is not surprising. Research has suggested that communication difficulties are likely to predispose deaf people to mental illness.[11] And indeed, Basilier has argued that communication difficulties give rise to 'surdophrenia', a mental illness specific to the deaf: sufferers 'are invariably immature, egocentric, labile or explosive personalities. Their language, oral skills, general knowledge, educational achievements and work records are usually unsatisfactory; they may have disturbed family relationships and are poorly integrated into society'.[12]

Degree of disability

As much additional handicap was concentrated in institutional settings it seemed likely that incapacity for daily activities determined whether a family could continue to care for a deaf person. Incapacity was measured in functional terms,[13] deaf people being asked if they had any problems with having an overall wash, tying a good knot in string, running to catch a bus, going up and down stairs, doing the shopping and carrying a full bag in each hand, doing heavy housework like cleaning floors and windows, preparing and cooking a hot meal, making a cup of tea, washing up, washing and ironing clothes, stripping and making a bed. For difficulty in performing a task, a score of 1 was awarded, and a score of 2 where the task was impossible. The total score of each person provided a measure of incapacity.

In fact, a substantial minority (a third) experienced no difficulty whatever with any of the activities, though six deaf people were unable to perform any of them. However, the majority were incapacitated, a surprisingly high proportion of them severely so. As many as 20 per cent were assessed as slightly incapacitated (score: 1 to 4) but almost a third were severely or very severely incapacitated, while as many as a fifth suffered from very severe incapacity (score: 15 or more).

Comparison across the settings suggested that degree of dependence arising from incapacity for daily activities was an important factor in determining entry into residential or hospital care. In general those with little or no incapacity lived in private households or hostels, while the severely incapacitated lived in the homes and hospitals. Thus between half and three-fifths of deaf people in private households and hostels had no incapacity at all, while another quarter were only slightly incapacitated. In contrast, deaf people with little or no incapacity were in a minority among those living in homes for the deaf, but as many as two-thirds were severely or very severely incapacitated. The vast majority of hospital patients (between three-quarters and four-fifths) were incapacitated. And the deaf people in homes for the elderly were the most incapacitated of all. Yet even among the hospital patients, a small minority (a sixth) were slightly if at all incapacitated, and there were a few with severe incapacity even among those living in private households and hostels.

Although incapacity was not necessarily a guide to dependence on others, difficulty may have a cumulative effect, and individual tasks completed with great difficulty unaided become impossible when part of the demanding daily routine.[14] In fact, dependence was widespread: rather more than half were dependent on someone else for at least one of the activities included in the measure of incapacity. And although it is true that a substantial minority – 17 per cent – were dependent for only one or two activities, as many as a third were dependent for five or more. Indeed, a quarter of deaf people relied upon others for aid with as many as seven or more activities. In general, those in the homes and hospitals were more dependent than the deaf people in private households or hostels. In fact, more than two-thirds of those living in private households and three-quarters of hostel residents were not dependent in any way. In contrast, most of those in other settings were substantially dependent on the help of others. Indeed, between two-thirds and four-fifths of those in homes and hospitals required help with between five and nine of the activities included on the measure of incapacity. But dependence was by no means necessarily a precondition for entry into residential or hospital care: even among those in private households and hostels there was a small minority who were moderately or severely dependent, while a small minority of those in other settings reported only slight or moderate dependence.

Health

How far did health problems create sustained dependence on health services? What impact did communication difficulties make on perceptions for the need for and assumptions about the nature of treatment?

For the most part, deaf people considered that they enjoyed good health: almost half of them (46 per cent) 'always felt well enough to do the cleaning and get out to see friends and do the shopping', while another quarter reported that this was true most of the time. But a tenth felt well enough to engage in such activities only occasionally, while as many as a fifth never felt well enough to do so. Poor health and its consequent restrictions on activities was by no means confined to hospital patients, though it was associated with the presence of additional handicaps, incapacity, and dependence. Therefore it was not surprising that all but two of the deaf living in private households and all but an eighth of hostel residents felt well all or most of the time. In contrast, this was true of a little less than half of those in homes for the deaf, about a fifth of hospital patients, and all of the residents of homes for the elderly. Although ill health was largely confined to those who were severely or very severely incapacitated, this was not invariably the case; indeed, a little more than a fifth of such people reported that they always or almost always enjoyed good health. In contrast, a small minority of those with no incapacity at all considered that they suffered from poor health.

Of course, although such subjective perceptions of health were made with reference to standard functional criteria, they were arrived at within the context of considerable communication difficulties. Use of medical services proved to be ineffective as a measure of health worries, because communication difficulties created uncertainty as to the purposes of medical services. A large minority of deaf people living in private households or hostels (40 per cent) were unsure about the circumstances in which they should visit their general practitioner. In fact, more than half of deaf people had seen their general practitioner only once or not at all in the previous twelve months, while in contrast a tenth had paid between six and twelve visits. The distortions created by communication difficulties were present, too, at the point of consultation. To reduce the possibility of misunderstanding, as many as two-thirds of deaf people always took an interpreter when they visited their general practitioner, but the remainder depended entirely upon their own communication resources. Where there was no interpreter, communication was sought by a combination of the spoken and written word, but 8 per cent relied entirely on speech and lip-reading, and 6 per cent on writing. In such circumstances, the possibility of confusion was considerable.

Medication provided on a regular basis was the usual reason for attending the general practitioner's surgery more than three times in the course of a year. As many as half of the deaf were using some form of medication, which for a fifth was provided for 'nerves': the majority of these people, but by no means all, lived in psychiatric hospitals or the psychiatric half-way hostel. And a further 3 per cent required medication to control epilepsy.

However, medication and visits to a general practitioner were a last resort for many deaf people. It was striking that 'trouble with nerves' was far more widespread than use of medication for 'nerves'. Indeed, almost two-thirds complained that they 'suffered from nerves' to the point where they often felt fed up, worried or upset, were unable to face work or mix socially, became short-tempered with people, were liable to weep, found it impossible to concentrate, or slept badly.[15] It is true that for most the trouble was slight and posed few problems. However, for a fifth, the trouble was substantial, creating problems with three or more of the listed activities.

One condition which affected deaf people's sense of well-being remains to be considered – namely, tinnitus. A substantial minority of deaf people – 22 per cent – suffered from noises in the ears. In most cases the problem was regarded as slight, but even at this level it was upsetting. However, a sixth considered their problem to be moderate or severe, and acknowledged it to be worrying.

Despite a general feeling of well-being almost a third of deaf people reported that they required additional, mainly health, services.

Audiology tests and hearing aids

How far did deafness itself lead to contact with health services, particularly through audiological tests and the provision of hearing aids? More than a quarter (28 per cent) of deaf people could not recall an audiological test. And many of the tests reported had taken place long ago, when techniques and hearing aids were considerably less sophisticated than they are today: as many as a quarter had been tested over twenty years ago, while only a little more than a tenth (13 per cent) had been tested within the previous three years.

Perhaps, then, it is not surprising that a majority (57 per cent) had never had a hearing aid. For the most part, those for whom an aid had been prescribed still possessed one, and most of those in use (four fifths) were provided by the NHS. Although a substantial minority of aid users subscribed to the critical opinion of NHS aids which has been widely reported in recent years, the majority (three fifths) considered their NHS product to be satisfactory. Indeed, satisfaction was considerably less widespread among the small number of users of privately acquired aids. Possession of an aid did not always signify its use: a fifth of aid owners did not use one. It was striking that those living in private households, hostels, and homes for the deaf were the least likely to bother to use their aids, presumably because they lived in social contexts which were the most sympathetic to communication without speech.

Yet aid ownership was most widespread among those whose communication skills appeared to predispose them to communicate with the wider community of hearing people – those who always or usually used voice. However, the absence of a hearing aid did not necessarily imply a lack of willingness to improve communication or shyness about communicating. As many as half of those without one wanted a consultation for assessment for an aid.

In general, then, the prescription of hearing aids was even less likely than audiological tests to bring deaf people to the notice of medical services. Moreover, aids tended to reinforce the communication skills of those who were most proficient at lip-reading.

Autonomy

A major feature of the impact of severe hearing loss was dependence on the mediating role of others and a consequent loss of autonomy over the management of daily living. The presence of an additional handicap or health problems requiring sustained intervention by medical services could modify independence still further. To what extent was the degree of autonomy enjoyed by deaf people determined by the type of setting in which they resided? And how far were encroachments on autonomy justified by care provision? Some studies have sought to describe the impact of institutions on daily life in terms of the organizational imperatives and have argued that institutions are organized in the interests of carers rather than those receiving care:[16] actual autonomy has been measured against arbitrarily devised standards of personal autonomy.[17]

Others have been concerned through organizational studies to devise methods of management within institutional settings which maximize opportunities for individual choice among patients or residents.[18] The purpose of the present study was to consider how far, despite severe hearing loss, deaf people in each setting achieved self-determination in the management of their lives. It may be objected that such comparisons are unfair because hospitals require a' more restrictive regime to create a suitable environment for the provision of care and treatment. To some extent this may be true, but deaf people with mental disorders were to be found in all settings, while some of those in hospitals had been misdiagnosed and were only deaf. Dependence arising from secondary handicaps was also to be found in all settings. A further objective was to consider how far institutional settings provided specialist care which responded to the specific needs of deaf people and which was not available to those in private households.

Tiredness, depression, and a feeling of being 'fed up' were widespread, but for the majority (three-quarters), such feelings occurred only sometimes. Furthermore, the greater their incapacity, the more frequently and the more likely were deaf people to experience these feelings. Perhaps because of greater incapacity and dependence, and consequent loss of autonomy in daily living, feelings of depression, tiredness and so on were most pervasive and acute among those living in residential homes and hospitals.

One factor of life in residential homes and hospitals which was identified as important was enforced inactivity – having to sit or stand, inactive, for long periods of the day. A substantial minority of deaf people (a little more than a quarter) reported long periods of inactivity each day. However, there was wide disparity between the different settings in this respect. Whereas only 4 per cent of those in private households claimed to sit or stand inactive for long periods of the day, as many as half of the residents of homes of the deaf and the elderly did so.

Perhaps inactivity was inevitable among the dependent populations of the residential homes. Yet homes differed considerably: much appeared to depend upon the care regime adopted rather than degree of dependency among residents. Homes which were comparable in terms of numbers of residents and their degree of dependence, differed sixfold in the proportion of those complaining of inactivity. However, it was among hospital patients that long periods of inactivity were most frequently reported: between three-fifths and two-thirds of patients said that they had to sit or stand, inactive, for long periods of the day. Again, there was evidence to suggest that care regime rather than dependence accounted for the differences between hospitals: for example, the existence of a deaf unit in one hospital reduced the possibility of inactivity there. But generally, differences between hospitals were small.

Of course, inactivity was most usual among those who stayed in for all or nearly all of the day. Incapacity and dependence influenced the degree to which deaf people usually stayed at home, but more than a third of those with no incapacity and most of the slightly incapacitated remained at home for most of the day, while a tenth of the severely incapacitated usually went out. Thus neither deafness nor dependence inevitably restricted activities largely to the home. Nor was it true that only those in institutional settings remained at home most of the time. There were some in private households who, though without incapacity, chose to stay at home; but they were rarely inactive for long periods: unfettered by an externally imposed care regime, they were able to keep busy.

Loneliness was held to contribute towards depression and tiredness. Only a tiny minority often felt lonely, but as many as two-thirds did so sometimes. Although loneliness was pervasive across the settings, it was only among those living in private households where the majority reported never feeling lonely. Nevertheless there were substantial differences in this respect between individual institutions within each setting. There appeared to be some relationship between loneliness and the availability of other deaf people for conversation: deaf people were less likely to feel lonely in homes for the deaf than in other institutions, while loneliness was most pronounced among residents of homes for the elderly, who were isolated in their deafness. Loneliness appeared to have little to do with age: young people were as liable to feel lonely as were those in their middle years, or the elderly.

Treatment and care

To what extent was the loss of autonomy justified by the standard of treatment and/or care provided in the hospitals, hostels, and homes for the deaf and elderly?

Among the general population misunderstandings about deafness are widespread. It is common for the hearing to assume that when talking to someone who is deaf or hard of hearing they should raise their voices or shout and though it is generally known that deaf people use their hands more in conversation than hearing people, few relate this to the use of language.[19] And these misunderstandings are reflected in service provision, particularly of a residential nature where assessment is a priority. Denmark has argued that:

In an institutional setting the deaf and partially hearing often represent a
hidden minority group: and little priority is given to this aspect of their
handicap even though impaired hearing has serious consequences for everyday
living and long term resident management affecting assessment, treatment and
rehabilitation.[20]

Although 'communication is a pre-requisite for psychiatric diagnosis and treatment'[21] there is a failure to understand the importance of the *impact* of deafness on development in the treatment setting:[22] yet such understanding is crucial in the assessment of the mentally disordered. Denmark and Warren have pointed out that in psychiatric diagnosis, an understanding of the 'general psychopathology and the psychological and psychiatric implications of deafness' is not enough: 'facility in manual communication methods' is crucial. Even then, they warn, 'the poor language ability of many of the prelingually and profoundly deaf makes diagnosis extremely complex and time-consuming'.[23] In the case of psychological assessment, there is a complex relationship between deafness and intelligence:

Failure to develop speech because of deafness is often mistakenly regarded as due to intellectual retardation; on the other hand, the poor language development of the deaf child must have some retarding effect upon intellectual development.[24]

Not only is there a dearth of suitable tools for assessment, but considerable communication difficulties arise in administering the tests available, while the use of appropriate test materials is crucial.[25]

There appears to be a widespread lack of knowledge about deafness and sign language among professionals engaged in treating and caring for deaf people. Psychiatric diagnosis is usually carried out without reference to the impact of deafness on behaviour, knowledge of manual language, or appropriate testing programmes. In the case of mental handicap, deaf people tend to be found in higher dependency units, despite showing no significant differences in comparison with other patients in terms of WAIS performance, IQ means, social competence or dependency ratings. Assessment depends upon the attitude of staff.[26] In the course of the present study it emerged that in all hospitals there was a tendency for deaf people to be assigned to wards where most patients were incontinent and/or dependent by reason of physical disability or the severity of mental disorder even though most of them were neither incontinent nor physically dependent. Communication difficulties associated with severe hearing loss were perceived by staff as severe maladaptive functioning which warranted treatment with high dependency patients. Only at the half-way psychiatric hostel and psychiatric hospital with its own deaf unit was audiological, psychiatric and psychological assessment undertaken automatically, by those familiar with the effects of hearing loss and with a knowledge of sign language. Elsewhere, audiological testing was rarely a part of the assessment process, and there was little opportunity for assessment by those with a knowledge of manual language.

Appropriate care, of course, depends upon accurate assessment. And the skills required for appropriate therapy and care are largely those required for diagnosis – an understanding of the impact of deafness on development and behaviour, and the ability to communicate with the deaf. Cornforth and Woods[27] have argued for treatment and care under the guidance of psychiatrists with an understanding of and a capacity to communicate directly with deaf people.[28] In setting up their own deaf unit, Denmark and Warren found that it was essential for nurses, too, to acquire skills in communication with the deaf.[29]

However, special hospital units for the deaf remain the exception rather than the rule: usually treatment is undertaken on the principle of integration rather than speciality. How far were communication skills restricted to specialist institutions, or institutions with specialist units?

Most of those in charge of providing care and treatment reported a shortfall in trained staff. Despite complaints in the past decade about high staff turnover, most staff were of long standing: almost two-thirds of them had worked in their present setting for more than five years, while as many as a quarter had done so for more than ten years. Furthermore, the majority were experienced workers: almost two-thirds had undertaken such work for at least five years. For the most part, then, continuity was combined with experience in the provision of care.

To what extent did staff add a qualification especially for working with the deaf to their long experience? In institutions for the deaf, staff were least likely to be qualified. None of those working in homes were qualified in deaf welfare and in two there were no qualified staff at all. However, in the unit for the deaf in North Wales the matron was a qualified social worker and was closely supported by a social worker with the deaf. The only qualified hostel worker was a nurse with a degree in education. In contrast, those responsible for the welfare of deaf people in private households were all qualified, either as social workers for the deaf or in deaf welfare. None of those caring for deaf people living in homes for the elderly had qualifications. Of the institutions, only the hospitals employed qualified staff on a large scale. Although nursing qualifications predominated there were also occupational therapists and educationalists, but no one with qualifications for work with the deaf.

Although as many as two-thirds of all staff interviewed had been offered the opportunity to develop their skills in communicating with the deaf, usually on an informal basis, only a fifth of staff in homes for the deaf had done so. It was common for work experience to be regarded as sufficient for developing communication skills, though one worker had acquired some facility in communication by attending a deaf club, and in another home two workers had bought a book on sign language at their own expense in order to improve their communication with deaf residents. In the hostels for the deaf, only one worker (at the psychiatric half-way hostel) had attended a communication course; others had relied on contact with residents to develop communication skills. In contrast, the two people employed at the Welsh deaf unit had been provided with in-service training including tuition in communication. Although two-fifths of hospital staff, most of them in hospitals for the mentally handicapped, had endeavoured to improve their communication skills, the majority had done so in Makaton classes designed to improve skill in communicating with mentally handicapped patients in general, though two employees in the psychiatric hospital unit for the deaf had attended formal courses specifically in communication with the deaf.

In all, then, only a quarter of staff interviewed had attended a formal course which included some instruction in manual communication, and most of these were social workers with the deaf. However, about a quarter of staff, mainly those employed by hospitals, had had the opportunity to attend communication classes but only half had taken up the offer. The majority considered such a course would be of little benefit in their work, or that time could not be spared for attendance.

For the most part, then, little qualified skill was available in the residential care of the deaf. In hospitals, nursing skills predominated, though a minority of those in mental handicap hospitals had attended Makaton classes, while those working in the deaf unit of a psychiatric hospital had acquired formal skills in manual communication. In contrast, those living in private households were the responsibility of qualified social workers with good communication skills. Perhaps it is not surprising then that such persons were the least likely to feel lonely, depressed and fed-up.

Among hospital staff occupational therapists often had most knowledge and understanding of deafness and sign language, but by no means all deaf patients attended occupational therapy, and those who did not tended to be confined to long-stay wards where they were offered no opportunities for communication or occupation. Indeed, this was true for a third of patients in mental handicap hospitals, and a quarter of those in psychiatric hospitals. The remainder had been assessed as being incapable of benefiting from attendance. In all, then, a fifth of the deaf hospital patients were deprived not only of activity, but also of communication with staff who understood them. And with one exception they were isolated among hearing patients, whereas occupational therapy often included the company of other deaf patients. Contact with other deaf people was denied to those living in homes for the elderly and hospital patients who engaged in no activity off the ward. Perhaps it is small wonder, then, that these two groups were the most likely to be lonely and depressed. For those in other settings, there was, if nothing else the consolation of the company of other deaf people with whom they could communicate.

Yet the hospitals and the half-way hostel had a therapeutic function, which involved the development of the capacity to exercise autonomy in daily life. How important to progress was the fitful availability of persons with whom they could communicate? Many have suggested that staff with little understanding of the nature of the impact of deafness and no skill in communication may misinterpret the behaviour of deaf people and treat them inappropriately: behavioural responses to deafness are 'often misinterpreted by nurses and psychiatrists alike as psychotic behaviour'.[30] Lengthy observation revealed cases in which attempts by patients to communicate manually, and even in writing, were dismissed as disturbed behaviour by staff. Furthermore, other studies have emphasized the importance of communication to 'the development of emotional stability in psychologically disturbed deaf patients'.[31] Deprivation of opportunities for communication is not uncommon and, as a consequence, nor is isolation, which frequently gives rise to desperation and frustration.[32] That communication is important to the development and progress of deaf patients has been emphasized by Denmark and Warren.[33] Indeed, Cornforth and Woods go further: the simulation of security created by the provision of 'board and lodging' leads patient and staff to assume, in the absence of communication, that understanding has been achieved.[34]

If training specifically in the needs of the deaf was uncommon even in specialist homes and hostels, to what extent were standards and methods in care practice maintained and developed by contact with specialist professional groups operating outside the work environment? In fact, institutions differed widely in the degree to which staff were involved in the work of outside professional specialist groups. It was striking that those with formal qualifications in deaf welfare or who had attended courses to develop communication skills were the most likely to be involved with such groups. Staff in specialist facilities for the deaf rarely had contact with relevant professional groups outside. Only in one of the homes were close contacts maintained with specialist statutory and voluntary agencies. Although staff at the half-way psychiatric hostel had minimal outside contact, they benefited from association with the deaf unit at the local hospital, while the warden of the hostel for the young working deaf maintained outside contacts which enabled her to keep abreast of current thinking in relation to care and deafness, and the social worker with overall responsibility for the hostel was active in regional and national associations for the deaf. In the North Wales deaf unit one member of staff was involved in training programmes for which she acted as CSS course tutor, while the social worker for the deaf was involved in the work of three national organizations concerned with the welfare of the deaf. Yet on balance, specialist institutions and specialist facilities within general institutions were more likely than others to have members of staff engaged in regular discussion with outside specialists concerned with severe hearing loss. For staff of local authority homes for the elderly the only contact with a specialist interested in deafness was the occasional visit of the local authority social worker for the deaf. In contrast, the hospital with the deaf unit had one staff member who participated in two organizations concerned with the care and understanding of the deaf. In other hospitals, although social workers, occupational therapists, and heads of hospital schools attended their own professional meetings there was no contact with groups specifically interested in deafness. However, all social workers for the deaf were deeply involved in the activities of groups, both local authority and voluntary, professionally interested in the deaf.

In general, training in care, qualifications in deaf welfare and participation in discussion with groups of outside professionals if they existed at all were confined to one or two of the more senior members of staff. It was invariably pointed out that the problem was not merely one of untrained but also of too few staff. Staff shortages reduced the likelihood of acquiring trained staff: it was difficult to second staff to training courses. And the process of training was regarded as a challenging experience for all involved. A charge nurse in a psychiatric hospital said,'We've lost our trainees. It's not just the numbers we miss, it's the stimulation.'

Yet the insularity of most staff was combined with considerable power over the way in which the lives of deaf residents and patients were ordered. In each institution a few key members of staff were responsible for client review, the evaluation of care practice, creating contacts with outside organizations, determining – either on their own initiative or in conjunction with senior staff to whom they were immediately responsible, the overall objectives of care, and, except in the case of two of the hospitals, whom to admit at the point of referral. Their considerable autonomy created resentment among others involved in care. A care attendant in the south of England home said, 'I feel there should be far more sharing.' Yet staff attitudes are important in determining the type and level of care provided, and are themselves related to the degree to which staff feel they are consulted when important decisions are made regarding patients.[35]

The autonomy of senior staff in daily contact with residents or patients was considerable in the sense that they were in a position, if not to formulate, then to interpret care objectives and to distribute resources within their allocation. Although none of them took decisions which involved capital expenditure, their discretion in the matter of expenses varied widely. While most hospital staff referred any expenditure to those responsible for resource allocation, in one hospital where funds were available at ward level discretion was exercised in the case of expenditure of less than £50; whereas the warden of one hostel had discretion over expenditure except for 'large (unspecified) amounts of money', in the other hostel no such discretion was allowed. Similarly, while some homes and local authority social workers for the deaf exercised discretion in expenditure up to £100, others did not.

The autonomy of staff was rarely challenged by the necessity to accommodate the perspectives of those operating in other settings. Only occasionally was the advice of outside organizations sought. Indeed, the hostels and one of the homes for the deaf appeared to be immune to outside advice. In another home, the advice of the local hospital was sometimes sought, and in two others, that of the RNID or the local authority social worker for the deaf. In the hospitals, ward staff or occupational therapists occasionally sought advice, but they had to do so through senior staff. Those running homes for the elderly were intermittently in touch with RADD or RNID. Overall, then, staff were usually free to pursue their own preferred patterns of care with little outside advice to suggest alternatives. And this was true even where the institutions took local authority sponsored residents. All of the homes and hostels had residents sponsored by local authorities, but the referring social worker usually maintained only minimal contact. Indeed, the matron of the London home for the deaf declared herself to be 'not concerned' to maintain such contact. Only in the south of England home was the involvement of social workers encouraged: the warden said

I always try to make sure that they keep in contact with the social workers who were present when they were admitted. If the social worker doesn't continue to show interest I pass the name of the person concerned over to our local social services department and they are pretty involved.

Thus even where a local authority was financially responsible there was little sustained contact between the relevant social services department and deaf residents.

Care and communication

How did staff, despite their lack of training and insulation from alternative patterns of care, manage to provide a therapeutic environment in hospitals and the psychiatric hostel, and a comfortable home in residential settings?

Although largely untrained for the purpose, staff were accustomed to care for the deaf: the hospitals, homes and hostels had deaf populations which they both expected and regarded as normal. Non-specialist institutions imposed no limitation on the numbers of deaf people they admittted as a proportion of their total populations. Admission policy appeared to reflect no disquiet about the suitability of the care provided. Indeed, a charge nurse in a mental handicap hospital and a senior nursing officer in a psychiatric hospital were alone in questioning the wisdom of admitting deaf people.

Moreover, for the most part, staff did not consider the stay of deaf people as short-term. In the homes for the deaf, residents were regarded as being here 'forever', 'indefinitely', 'permanently', or 'for life'. Even in the hostels, no time limit was imposed on length of stay. And hospital patients were said to be 'here until they die', 'long term', 'here for as long as they live'. Staff assumed, then, that it was normal for them to provide care for deaf people usually extending over many years. Moreover, in the non-specialist institutions it was assumed that care would be unbroken by contact with deaf people from outside the institution: only those in the deaf unit of a psychiatric hospital had their routine occasionally disturbed by deaf visitors. And even in the specialist institutions, deaf visitors, though expected, were rare. Thus, to a considerable degree, care was long term, and likely to insulate those receiving it from communication with deaf people outside the institution.

Generally, staff were aware that most deaf people in their care used some kind of sign communication, though few of them understood this or the speech used by a minority of deaf people. Difficulty in comprehending the deaf was not confined to staff in non-specialist institutions: there was considerable variation in this respect between the homes for the deaf.

In the south of England home, the matron said 'I sometimes pick out bits', and the deputy matron said 'I do a lot of guess work.' The cook said 'Most of the time I can't understand them at all' –

an experience which was shared by other domestic staff there. But in the west of England home, some degree of comprehension was sometimes achieved.

The matron said 'I understand some of what they say', while a care attendant said 'It's a mixture: sometimes I understand.'

In contrast, hostel staff appeared to understand most of what was said to them.

The warden of the hostel for the young working deaf said 'I understand all that they say to me', and the deputy warden of the psychiatric half-way hostel said

'I understand most of what the deaf say', while a care assistant said 'the four who are best at speaking, I find it easy to recognize what they say'.

Despite the difficulties encountered by staff in comprehending the speech of deaf people, all considered speech to be the desirable form of communication. Staff at the Welsh unit, and social workers for the deaf, alone were clear that manualism did not signify mental retardation.

A London social worker said 'It's to do with the schools they went to, and the advice given to their parents.'

The superiority of speech was made explicit by the warden of the hostel for the young working deaf:

'It's better to be oral to be nearer the hearing.'

But usually such assumptions were implicit in the attitudes expressed towards manualism.

A senior nursing officer in a psychiatric hospital, when commenting on the lack of speech of some deaf patients, said, 'We are often dealing with very neglected people.'

Few criticized the deaf for relying on sign, but lack of speech was usually attributed to faulty upbringing.

In the south of England home, a member of the domestic staff said, 'It stems from the way they were looked after when they were small, I think.'

At the psychiatric hostel, however, staff considered degree of hearing loss to affect speech development:

A care attendant said, 'It depends on their degree of hearing and their background.'

For the most part, then, the deaf were pitied for their use of what was generally regarded as an inferior method of communication, and there was little understanding of the reasons for reliance on sign.

What did staff consider their purpose in working with deaf patients and residents to be? In the case of hospital nurses 'health' was their first priority. Only at the psychiatric hospital with a deaf unit was there any consideration of the implications of profound hearing loss for care.

The occupational therapist said, 'I see my role as being to improve the quality of their lives by achieving understanding through communication.'

But even here, ward staff who lacked suitable communication skills were unable to reinforce the work of the unit.

Referring to a patient who attended the unit, a charge nurse said 'I don't really see myself as doing more than providing basic care: Alf is hardly on the ward.'

Deaf patients assessed as unsuitable for attending the unit spent all their time on wards where the major concern of staff was the provision of basic care.

In other hospitals, staff emphasized that care objectives were the same for all patients, without realizing the specific problems posed by deafness.

A charge nurse in a London hospital said 'They are not treated any differently from the hearing: the aim is to rid them all of the effects of the old labelling.' A senior nursing officer observed that the purpose with the deaf was 'the same as for all mentally ill patients – to rehabilitate them and return them to the community'.

Similarly, staff in mental handicap hospitals considered their function in caring for all patients to be 'to assess, rehabilitate and discharge'. An occupational therapist saw her role as being 'to make the most of their abilities', but failed to recognize that deafness created particular difficulties for achieving this end. Although two occupational therapists made a special effort to communicate with deaf patients, elsewhere, except in hospital schools, it was assumed that the deaf could be treated like anyone else.

A sister on a high dependency ward said 'I don't think their care requires us to do anything additional to our normal duties.'

Nursing staff did not consider that treatment or training should involve the development of communication skills: the emphasis was on the provision of physical care. And this was also true of the other non-specialist institutions, the local authority homes for the elderly.

On the whole, the specialist institutions for the deaf presented a greater awareness than general institutions of the role of communication in the care of deaf people. But even in homes for the deaf, communication was not necessarily a primary consideration. In the south of England home, the matron's main concern was 'to provide a happy home life', based on physical comfort. The deputy matron wanted 'to see residents happy and comfortable'. No one mentioned the importance of communication.

A variety of reasons underlay the stress placed on communication in other homes. In the London home communication was regarded as essential to the smooth running of the home.

The matron said 'We see our aim as trying to communicate. If you don't, they can't find out the routine. It's important for keeping everything here on an even keel.'

In contrast, communication as a prerequisite for maintaining mental agility was stressed in the west of England home:

'Communication is important because we must keep the new ideas turning over.'

But the emphasis on communication was greatest in the North Wales deaf unit where staff were regarded as 'interpreters, and as arbitrators between the deaf and the hearing'. In both hostels, the encouragement of a sense of security, and the ability to understand and live a normal life, were regarded as being major objectives of care. But the recognition of the importance of communication to these processes was implicit rather than explicit.

In general, then, it was in the specialist facilities and units that the importance of communication to treatment or care was appreciated. Deaf people living in private households had at their disposal social workers who regarded communication as central to their work. Indeed, most social workers reported conflict between demand for interpretation and their wish to practise casework.

One working in London said 'Ideally I see myself as a social worker but my skills in communication enable me to do casework with the deaf. Mostly I interpret.'

How did the members of staff communicate to achieve their care objectives with deaf residents and patients? Apart from social workers for the deaf, about a quarter of the staff had a full understanding of and could communicate in BSL, while another seven had some knowledge of what was involved in total communication. But overall, the most common method of conversing with the deaf was by means of a combination of gesture, basic intuitive signs and finger-spelling, and speech. Those who had or were acquiring skills in BSL, were largely concentrated in the specialist facilities. Thus, all of the homes and hostels for the deaf had at least one member of staff who was fluent in BSL, and with the exception of the hostel for the young working deaf at least one other member of staff who was acquiring these skills. In all, about a third of the staff in the homes for the deaf had already acquired, or were in the process of acquiring, a knowledge of BSL, and this was true of more than a quarter of hostel staff. In the general institutions, the only staff with a proficiency in BSL were to be found in the deaf unit of the psychiatric hospital. In the mental handicap hospitals a few staff members were learning and regularly using Makaton, but elsewhere there was no one with BSL skills, there were no organized classes in communication, and in two cases there were no regular visits from a social worker for the deaf.

Deaf residents and patients were required to make sense of a wide variety of communication methods employed by their carers. In the London home the matron used speech, sign and finger-spelling; the care assistant employed sign, the written word, speech and finger-spelling; while the cook relied on speech augmented by the occasional gesture. In the west of England home the matron used high diglossic BSL, while the deputy matron used a combination of gesture, speech, some signs and the written word. The superintendent of the hostel for the young working deaf communicated in BSL, and the warden used speech and the written word.

A similar range of communication method was utilized by staff in the deaf unit of the psychiatric hospital where the senior nursing officer employed signs whereas the occupational therapist used a combination of signs, speech, finger-spelling and mime, and a nurse had devised her own system of speech, finger-spelling and writing. Only in the psychiatric half-way hostel was anything like a standardized communication system in operation, involving total communication.

In the hospitals and the homes for the elderly, the range of communication methods and the code employed by staff was far more restricted than in specialist institutions. In one psychiatric hospital, to communicate with deaf patients one charge nurse used speech and occasional signs, another used gesture, a third employed basic sign, while the sister communicated in a mixture of speech and gesture. Some variation in this communication pattern had been established in the mental handicap hospitals where a few members of staff had been introduced to Makaton. Despite the low proportion of staff who were fluent in sign language, and the limited communication code employed by the majority, a surprisingly high proportion – between a third and a half – were satisfied with the level of their communication skills.

In practice considerable use was made of oral communication. Whatever their communication skills, the vast majority (all but two) used speech, though predominantly in conjunction with other methods. Despite their heavy reliance on speech, few staff mentioned the importance and problems of lip-reading in communicating with deaf people. On observation, none of the oral or near-oral members of staff seemed concerned to raise the level of their verbal discourse with patients and residents above the basic and routine, except the warden of the hostel for the young working deaf who dealt with the practicalities of the full daily lives of residents in speech, and writing, frequently at length, and with great success according to the residents. Of course, where staff lacked or had only basic skills in manual communication (the majority), deaf people were reliant on lip-reading for information.

How did deaf people perceive the communication of staff? In the homes for the deaf, residents were generally accepting, though sometimes highly critical of attempts by staff to communicate with them. In the London and west of England homes all residents agreed that the main methods of communication used by staff were sign in the case of matron, and speech by everyone else. But a quarter were disparaging about the communication skills of staff. In London, even the matron was criticized:

One woman said 'She *tries* to sign', while another said, 'She *thinks* she signs.' And another resident claimed that communication was so difficult that 'the staff have to write'.

Generally, residents complained of the standard of finger-spelling, and resented the practice of being shouted at rather than spoken to by staff. Often communication proved to be so difficult that staff found it easier not to talk to residents. However, these criticisms were not prevalent in the south of England home, even though staff were not more likely than those elsewhere to be able to sign fluently.

One man said 'Some staff have good sign and finger-spelling', while another considered the speech used in the home to be easily lip-read.

Other residents commented on the fact that staff responded to their speech. Even here, though, speech was perceived as being the main medium of communication.

The hostels presented a contrast in terms of communication. In the hostel for the young working deaf, where staff had little systematic knowledge of sign, residents perceived speech and the written word to dominate communication; however, in the psychiatric half-way hostel where staff considered it important to acquire a systematic knowledge of sign, residents acknowledged the effort of staff to communicate manually, though even here speech was perceived to be the dominant mode of communication.

Although the dominance of speech was marked in all but one of the specialist institutions, there were members of staff with whom deaf patients could communicate in sign language and finger-spelling. But in the non-specialist institutions this was rarely the case. Speech – usually shouted – combined with some gesture and occasionally the written word were seen by deaf people in homes for the elderly as the major mode of communication. Only in the deaf units of the Welsh home and a psychiatric hospital was any concesssion possible to the communication needs of the deaf. And in the hospital unit itself there were only two signers among the staff, and therefore speech was important even here.

One patient said 'It's speech on the ward, and sign and speech in the unit.'

Patients in the unit regarded the dominant mode of communication between themselves and the staff as a combination of speech, sign and gesture. In other hospitals, deaf people considered speech and gesture to be the only means of communication employed by staff, though staff occasionally wrote messages.

As one patient said 'It's all speech, they don't use signs.'

Although some members of staff in hospitals for the mentally handicapped had acquired some skill in Makaton, it was at best employed as one of a number of communication methods. Only a third of patients in subnormality hospitals mentioned that staff used signs: most described the normal mode of communication as 'speech and gesture'.

Speech, then, the communication medium of the hearing community, was perceived by deaf people in all institutions to be crucial, even where staff had acquired facility in sign language. It was all the more striking, therefore, that there was so little appreciation of the difficulties involved in lip-reading. Writing, too, the other communication medium of the hearing world, played an important role in creating understanding between staff and deaf people. In seemed likely, in view of the difficulties involved in lip-reading speech, the generally low level of literacy among deaf people, the limitations of sign language used by staff, their heavy reliance on gesture, and even touch in some cases, that only a basic, restricted communication was possible between staff and deaf people. Moreover, the opportunities for misunderstanding appeared to be endless. How far were staff conscious of communication problems as barriers to the achievement of care objectives?

On the whole, staff in institutions with an overtly therapeutic intent were most conscious of the limitations on their work. Generally, in specialist institutions, where staff were most likely to have achieved some knowledge of BSL, care objectives were modest. Indeed some staff argued that this was realistic because the problems created by deafness 'make change almost impossible'. A care assistant in the London home considered that the rarity of conversational exchange between staff and residents produced a home 'like a closed order'.

The matron of the west of England home said 'They have such a limited background because of the communication problem that we try to ensure that the objectives are not too high for their potential: I'm wary of accidents.'

But not all homes set their expectations deliberately low. The matron of the south of England home said 'It takes so long to get through to them, and we have to teach so often by example.' And the deputy matron agreed that tremendous problems arose 'because of difficulty in understanding'.

In the hostels and the deaf unit of a psychiatric hospital, staff adopted a simplified approach.

The superintendent of the hostel for the young working deaf said 'You have to tell them what to do, *not* why.' A care assistant in the half-way psychiatric hostel said 'You have to be careful not to overload them. If it goes wrong, it knocks them for six, and then they revert.' In the deaf unit of the psychiatric hospital, the occupational therapist said 'It all takes much longer because they are deaf: you have to keep going over things', and the senior nursing officer explained 'What you can do is limited because you have to start from the basis that they are deaf.'

In other hospitals staff were divided about the importance of hearing impairment as a major problem in treatment: some assumed that there was no difference between hearing and deaf patients – treatment and care difficulties resulted from the mental condition only.

A charge nurse in a psychiatric hospital said 'Communication is the problem: it's not knowing what's going on', whereas another charge nurse in the same hospital argued that 'Communication can be a problem, but the problem is much more the mental illness and the personality.'

For social workers with the deaf, there was no communication problem. As trusted interpreters, they saw themselves overcoming the consequences of hearing loss, enabling deaf people to appreciate the full implications of interpreted conversations and situations.

A London social worker explained, 'The problem lies in their immaturity. Because of the simplified view of life which they have because they are deaf, they are terribly lacking in worldly wisdom.' While another observed, 'Their picture of life is necessarily simplified. They see things in black and white. For them, there are no shades of grey.'

The crude communication system available to most deaf people and staff seemed likely to limit the nature and frequency of conversational exchanges. In practice specialist and non-specialist settings differed little in terms of the frequency with which staff conversed with deaf patients and residents, though there were sharp differences between institutions. Although staff in all but one of the homes for the deaf reported frequent conversations with residents, these claims were refuted by residents.

A resident of the west of England home said 'We have a chat sometimes, but not to sit down', and a resident of the south of England home declared 'There's not much talk really, we don't have the opportunity.'

Most residents wanted more opportunities to talk with staff, if only to air grievances.

Staff at the half-way psychiatric hostel reported frequent or daily conversations but residents differed widely in their reports of the frequency and degree of relaxation of their conversations with staff. A minority (a quarter) reported that staff chatted only occasionally.

One resident said 'They don't chat much but they often tease me.' Others agreed that staff conversed frequently with them. A young woman said 'They are often in the lounge. They sit down by the table and have a chat', and another resident said 'We are very good friends with the staff. They are often in the lounge.' But another said 'The staff are friendly but they don't sit down with us much', and a young man agreed: 'They chat frequently, but not sitting.'

In the hostel for the young working deaf, while most residents agreed that the warden was accessible and frequently stopped to chat they insisted that such conversations were invariably brief.

A young man said 'She will stand for a few minutes in the corridor and chat.'

Only general settings with specialist facilities provided opportunities for conversation with staff. Of staff in homes for the elderly, only those of the North Wales deaf unit considered communication to be a crucial part of care, but even here, only limited conversation was possible.

The warden said 'I try whenever possible, but my skills aren't up to much yet.'

Elsewhere, little attempt was made to converse with deaf residents, who complained of loneliness and isolation.

Mr Lipp said 'I have a chat twice a week when a particular care assistant comes in. I find it lonely.' Mr Wilson said 'The only way I can have a chat is by writing usually, and they don't often do that.'

Similarly in the hospitals, only the staff of the deaf unit attempted to converse daily with deaf patients. But no regular conversation took place with ward staff. In other psychiatric hospitals, patients rarely conversed with the medical or nursing staff, who themselves reported only occasional exchanges. But patients attending occupational therapy enjoyed an added bonus.

As one patient said 'No chats with nurses, but the occupational therapy lady is friendly.'

But for patients without access to occupational therapy there was little opportunity to talk to staff.

One patient said 'We can't chat because the nurses do not understand sign.'

A similar pattern emerged in the mental handicap hospitals, where none of the nursing staff claimed to talk to deaf patients:

A nurse said 'It's not possible to discuss anything with them.'

Only occupational therapy and Makaton classes provided opportunities for conversation on a regular basis with staff who regarded such activity as essential to their work. And deaf patients were clear that conversations with staff were associated solely with these activities.

One patient said 'I don't talk to the nurses on the ward, but I chat to them in Sister Lucas's unit.'

In general, then, conversation between staff and deaf people was common only in those institutions in which staff, or a particular category of staff, considered communication to be essential to care objectives. Thus, in the hospitals, communication was highly regarded in the deaf unit, occupational therapy departments and schoolrooms, but not on the wards. On the whole, deaf people substantiated staff reports of conversational exchanges but generally perceived them to be less extensive and relaxed than staff reports suggested.

It was in the scope of conversational exchanges, rather than their frequency, that a clear difference in practice emerged between specialist and general facilities. In specialist facilities, only staff in the London home for the deaf failed to attempt to discuss topics beyond those associated with the daily routine of the institution, such as sport, religion, politics, personal relationships, and so on. Among general institutions, only staff in the psychiatric hospital deaf unit covered a full range of broad topics, though it was done only with great difficulty. Elsewhere no attempt was made to converse with deaf people at a level beyond that required by the daily routine: anything more was declared to be impossible except in one psychiatric hospital where a nurse said that she attempted to talk to deaf patients about personal relationships. Of course, diffferences in practice were largely a reflection of the differences in communication skills between care staff: only in specialist facilities and institutions did they have the skill to tackle broad topics of conversation with deaf people.

Despite the limited understanding of the effects of severe hearing impairment, difficulties of communiction, and the restricted nature of conversational exchanges, it was widely believed that deaf people used their handicap to manipulate situations to their own advantage. Indeed, all but a fifth of staff considered that hearing loss conferred the power of manipulation. Although this belief was held by a majority of those working in institutions, it was less pervasive in specialist institutions and facilities than in other settings including private households.

A belief that deafness conferred the power of manipulation predominated among staff who considered that deaf people were dependent upon them, but there was disagreement as to the *nature* of that dependence. Staff in specialist facilities emphasized the physical nature of the dependence while those employed in general facilities took a broader view. Some nurses considered that subjection to a hospital regime was itself a form of dependence.

One nurse said 'Just conforming is dependence.' A hospital occupational therapist said 'Mostly they know what to do – that's dependence.' Another said 'They are dependent on us for everything, including sensitivity', and a charge nurse in a psychiatric hospital said 'We are seen as a mother figure.'

Thus, in specialist institutions, where some skill in signed communication was most widespread, dependence was seen in terms of providing physical comforts. But in general institutions where few understood deafness, dependence was considered to encompass all aspects of life, placing deaf people in the role of small children.

In view of the acute problems and limited nature of the communication achieved with deaf people by most carers, how did staff know when they had succeeded in their objectives? Some, usually in specialist institutions or units, adopted a client-centred approach to success, and were reluctant to generalize about it at all.

The warden of the psychiatric half-way hostel said 'Success is relative – it always varies with the individual', and the warden of the hostel for the young working deaf said 'I try to help to solve individual problems – I'm not worried about success.'

But others tended to emphasize the importance of achieving communication and understanding.

The deputy warden of the psychiatric hostel said 'Success is getting over some initial difficulties and communicating with each other'. At the deaf unit in the psychiatric hospital the senior nursing officer said 'You know you're getting somewhere when you see the gradual development of awareness.'

In non-therapeutic facilities, however, staff emphasized the importance of a friendly atmosphere.

A care assistant in the London home said 'You know you have succeeded when they treat you as a friend.' In the west of England home, the deputy matron said 'Success is everyone feeling comfortable with everyone else.' But the warden of the North Wales deaf unit declared 'I succeed when I get feedback from the deaf telling me what they really think. We make them too dependent and we do it in the interests of a stuff-shirted organization.'

For others, especially those in general facilities, success was seen in terms of conformity to the regime.

A senior nursing officer said 'You are succeeding if you get through and you get co-operation', and a charge nurse in a mental handicap hospital said 'Success is in co-operation.'

The dividing line between the two categories of response was often narrow: a happy home benefited staff as much as residents. Nor were client and institution centred responses a monopoly of any single type of setting.

A care assistant in the west of England home said 'You succeed when he does what you want and he's happy about it.' But a nurse in a mental handicap hospital said 'You can *see* achievement – in improved function, and better relationships and communication.'

Moreover, those in therapeutic specialist facilities sometimes adopted the cosy atmosphere approach to success while occasionally staff in non-therapeutic specialist institutions perceived success in terms of communication and understanding:

A worker in the hostel for the young working deaf said 'You know you have succeeded when you see the light of understanding dawning on someone's face.'

Social workers for the deaf viewed success in terms of eliciting 'normal' responses from deaf people.

A London social worker stressed her interpreting role, and said 'Problem-solving leads to improved functioning.' Another saw normality in the rejection of a dependent role: 'You know you have succeeded when they start to pay for the drinks.' But a social worker in Wales was impressed by the resilient individualism of the deaf: 'I defy anyone to "succeed" wholly with the deaf.'

Almost all (seven-eights) were confident that the care they provided was entirely to the advantage of deaf people. In the homes for the elderly, the advantages were seen to be the care available there. In the specialist institutions, however, the opportunities for friendship and conversation with others employing sign language were considered advantageous.

The matron of the south of England home said 'They have so much in common and they can talk together.'

However, some staff raised the possibility of friendly communicating groups of deaf people precluding the necessity for the establishment of relationship with the wider hearing community.

The sub-warden of the hostel for the young working deaf observed 'This kind of provision has advantages and disadvantages. The communication – yes, that's an advantage. But while they're here there's no reason for them to integrate into the community.'

Furthermore, some social workers considered it a disadvantage that so many staff were trained in neither care nor communication.

Communication and care in practice

How far in practice did deaf people enjoy a homely atmosphere, friendly relationships with fellow signers, understanding, and so on? Their confidence suggested that staff were in a position to facilitate such developments in the homes, hostels and hospitals. Yet, the daily routine of care was conducted in a limited and crude communication medium. Other studies have stressed that the receptive skills of the deaf who rely on gesture alone are inferior to those who understand speech.[36] For the most part staff blamed the rarity of widely ranging conversations on the failure of deaf people to acquire suitable skills of understanding and communication.

A charge nurse said 'It's impossible to discuss matters such as personal relationships with the deaf: you have to gear all conversation to their capabilities'. And a care assistant declared 'There are not many deaf you can talk to about things like politics, religion or sport.'

Only a minority understood the deaf.

The warden of a hostel said 'You can have a good chat with them, they're always interested', and a care attendant in a home said 'They know how to bring things down simple.'

Staff sought to explain their communication difficulties by emphasizing the failures of the deaf rather than their own dependence on speech. Where deaf people were labelled as mentally disordered it was often assumed that it was part of the condition to resist or fail to develop communication.

The deputy warden of a hostel said 'If we can't get through, they're usually mentally confused.'

Others blamed their difficulties on deaf people's lack of communication skills and general knowledge. Even those with some skill in sign usually ascribed their communication difficulties to the nature of the deaf person's mode of communication. Thus, some staff complained of the unfamiliar signs used by the deaf, while others complained of their speed in finger-spelling. It was striking that no one mentioned that the deaf might have difficulty in lip-reading staff.

Yet the majority (more than four-fifths) of those with at least some knowledge of sign recognized that there was a different quality to the communication between deaf people compared with that which involved staff. Almost all commented on the speed of finger-spelling and sign used by many deaf people among themselves, but only two noticed that the nature of the sign language used between deaf people differed from that used in conversation with the hearing.

A nurse said 'It's just that deaf patients have short-cuts they can take with sign', and a member of staff of the west of England home for the deaf said 'They have quick signs: they use short bastard signs.'

Recognition that among themselves deaf people conversed with speed and ease was the only indication of staff sensitivity to and appreciation of the communication skills of the deaf. Observation of conversational exchanges over at least three weeks in each institution revealed only a few instances in which the communication of the deaf was received by staff with the consideration and courtesy which was automatically shown to the hearing. In the homes for the deaf, for example, staff showed little capacity for receptive communication, often brushing aside or adopting a patronizing attitude towards attempts at conversation by residents. On the whole, 'conversation' initiated by staff tended to be a series of dogmatic assertions with which residents were expected to agree without elaboration.

Observation showed that the communication of the deaf was most widely misunderstood in general settings, where staff were unaware of the difficulties involved in lip-reading, and, as a consequence, failed to attach importance to ensuring that the visual acuity of deaf patients was maximized by regular eye tests and changes of glasses where necessary, or by appropriate forms of eye treatment. Hospital staff made no distinction between deaf and hearing patients. Even the provision of a specialist facility within a general institution by no means guaranteed sensitivity and understanding for the deaf – or even common courtesy. Frequently staff exhibited poor communication skills, and made fun of the communication difficulties of the deaf people with whom they were conversing.

From systematic observation an attempt was made to assess the ease with which staff communicated with the deaf. Assessment was based on communication events, each consisting of at least three exchanges, according to the eight-point scale adopted for assessing the communication skills of deaf people (see Chapter 4). Communication was considered at two levels – ability for ordinary daily chat and for broader, more abstract themes. Astonishingly, more than a quarter of staff were not seen to communicate with deaf people in the course of three weeks, observation, while the majority (more than two-thirds) were not involved in a discussion of the more abstract themes such as sport, politics, religion and so on. Understandably, the chances of communication at the more sophisticated level were greatest in specialist facilities, especially those with therapeutic objectives, but this was true of conversation generally. However, in all institutions there were some staff who were not observed to engage in any conversation with deaf residents and patients. And the most skilled communicators frequently experienced some difficulty in understanding even ordinary daily chat while almost a fifth were observed to be unable to communicate even at this basic level. Although most of the skilled communicators worked in specialist institutions, the poorest communicators were to be found as frequently in specialist as in general institutions.

Usually staff who attempted the more sophisticated level of communication were observed to do so only with the greatest of difficulty. Indeed, apart from the social workers with the deaf, only three members of staff showed substantial skill at this level.

Interpretation

As few members of staff could communicate with deaf people at a level above that of the basic and routine with reasonable ease, it was unlikely that care objectives, especially those with therapeutic objectives dependent upon communication, could be achieved without interpretation.

Although staff in the homes and hostels for the deaf reported that interpreters always attended meetings involving hearing and deaf people, observation suggested that members of staff 'interpreted' for residents by speaking on their behalf. In the homes, little of the hearing side of the conversation was explained to the deaf: certainly there was no attempt at simultaneous or even a full translation. But hostel staff were observed to provide an account of the hearing side of the conversation which was close to a full interpretation, and made a conscious effort to involve deaf persons in the conversation. Of the general institutions, only the psychiatric hospital with a deaf unit claimed to offer the services of an interpreter. However, meetings which concerned deaf people usually excluded them. In other hospitals it was admitted that there was either no or only occasional provision for interpretation.

Thus institutions relied largely on their own resources for interpretation: where no one with suitable skills was employed, no provision was made.

But it must be remembered that even those most skilled in communication had difficulty in communicating beyond the basic and routine. Perhaps it is not surprising, then, that few attempted to provide a full translation of the speech of hearing people for the deaf in their care.

Despite the confidence in their own capacity to provide interpretation a substantial minority of staff (two-fifths) in all settings conceded that there had been instances when an interpreter would have been helpful. Although it was generally agreed that such instances were rare in practice, those occasions were likely to recur at frequent intervals. Although some saw the necessity for an interpreter only in unusually difficult circumstances, for instance, to counsel a deaf resident on the subject of marriage, others clearly saw a central role for an interpreter.

A care assistant said 'We need an interpreter day to day here.' And another agreed: 'I sometimes have to stop because we can't understand each other – it helps to have someone to hear and sign.'

Interpretation was considered desirable to ensure the smooth day-do-day running of the institution. But there were staff in therapeutic institutions who suggested that interpreters should have a central role in treatment.

An occupational therapist said 'An interpreter would be necessary in assessment', while a charge nurse said 'We need one for group situations. There is a delusion that the deaf are competent to participate in groups with hearing patients and staff without an interpreter.'

The strong desire for the regular services of an interpreter expressed by a large minority of staff contrasted with the satisfaction of the majority in their existing resources. Yet most – almost two-thirds – admitted that interpreters had been brought in to help in difficult situations.

The deaf as part of the residential or treatment group

The sparing use made of interpreters reflected the dearth of persons with suitable skills. It has been argued that 'the lack of trained interpreters for deaf people at every level in their adult life has led to an extreme isolation from the hearing community'.[37] Certainly, to a considerable degree, staff perceived deaf people as isolated, a group among themselves, separate from the hearing community.

Despite their general lack of communication skills, staff readily attributed distinctive characteristics to conversational exchanges between deaf people. As many as half considered that the conversational range of the deaf was narrower and less sophisticated than that of the hearing.

The warden of a hostel said 'There are constant disagreements over little things; they're very groupy and they get upset easily', and a care attendant in the other hostel said 'Their conversation is narrower in content and expression.'

Such opinions were strongly endorsed by hospital staff, among whom communication skills were rarest.

A nurse said 'There's a lot of basic conversation', and another observed 'The deaf are less concerned about world events.'

Of course, in the closed world of the hospital, where there was comparatively little stimulation, where drugs were in extensive use and mental disorders were assumed, conversation *was* relatively narrow. But the view was applied to all deaf people. However, it was striking that although it was found in every other care setting this was not a view held by skilled communicators in the homes for the deaf.

About a quarter of staff, predominantly those with good communication skills, considered that there was little difference between the conversation of the deaf and hearing.

The matron of a home for the deaf said 'There's as much discussion as between the members of any group', while the warden of the North Wales deaf unit said 'The conversations they have are much the same as ours.' And the occupational therapist of a hospital deaf unit said 'The older ones talk with great wisdom.'

Indeed, staff who were most skilled in communication were the least dogmatic about the nature of conversation between deaf people.

The warden of the south of England home for the deaf said 'I find it fascinating, but I don't really know what's going on.'

Within institutions, the deaf were perceived as forming groups bound by a common communication system.

The matron of the London home said 'They form very good relationships – close-knit, very friendly', and the matron of the west of England home said 'They're like families, except that they stick together more.'

Only the social workers for the deaf introduced a note of dissent.

One said 'They're not significantly different from the hearing.' And another considered that there was 'Suspicion between the generations.'

The experience of social workers was not restricted to institutional settings: for deaf people living in private households, with their wide choice of companions, the communication bond had less force than for those living in institutions. And where choice existed it could be exercised in forming and dissolving groups: perhaps outside institutions ties were weaker because the communication bond was not so powerful.

The relationship between prelingually deaf and hard of hearing people was used to illustrate the strength of the communication bond. Only a fifth of staff considered that good relationships existed between the deaf and hard of hearing. The distinction between the two groups appeared to be marked among hospital patients.

A charge nurse said 'At times the prelinguals have some conversation with the hard of hearing, but mostly there's no contact at all.'

Indeed, it was suggested that there was considerable resentment between them.

A social worker for the deaf said 'There's no relationship between the two groups because the hard of hearing rely on the normal means of communication.'

It was surprising to find that despite the importance widely attached to communication method a majority of staff in every setting considered that relationships between the deaf and hearing were good. In institutional settings, both general and specialist, the relationship was discussed in terms of that between deaf residents or patients and hearing staff.

The matron of the London home for the deaf said 'We've got common interests, a common goal, and we act together as a small group.' A social worker for the deaf said 'We've got an excellent working relationship', while a charge nurse said 'We have a very good relationship with the more permanent patients.' Only once was reference made to hearing patients: a nurse said 'Sometimes the deaf form quite strong relationships with hearing patients.'

However, as many as a third of the staff insisted that relationships between the deaf and the hearing were difficult. Those working in specialist institutions confined their observation to themselves and the deaf.

A deputy matron of a home for the deaf said 'We're different. They put themselves above us.'

But elsewhere there was a greater readiness to consider the relationship between deaf and hearing residents or patients.

A hospital therapist said 'In general, they're very cautious with each other.'

Social workers saw the communication barrier as creating a gulf between the two groups.

One said of those in private households 'They tend to be distant with each other', while another said 'The relationship is poor. They tend to mistrust each other.'

In general, then, only when the hearing were identified solely as staff was a favourable view of the relationship between deaf and hearing adopted.

Yet the vast majority of staff (a little more than four-fifths) and all of those in general institutions considered that they consciously attempted to help those in their care to understand each other. Only in the specialist homes, hostels and units were doubts expressed about such efforts: those with most knowldge of deaf people were least sure of their capacity to create understanding between hearing and deaf residents and patients. Where any formal measures were taken at all, the primary method of promoting understanding appeared to be group meetings between residents or patients and staff. An exception was the London home for the deaf where staff considered that relationships were satisfactory without such measures. In most cases an interpreter was present at meetings, though interpretation on these as on most other occasions was provided internally.

A care assistant said 'Matron interprets if necessary.'

However, in one psychiatric hospital it was admittted that group meetings took place at which no one could interpret for the deaf.

A charge nurse observed 'The deaf don't get much out of it', and a senior nursing officer said 'The deaf don't participate much.'

Elsewhere, the results of group meetings were considered to be positive. In the hostels residents and staff talked through the difficulties of living together.

The sub-warden of the hostel for the young working deaf said 'It helps to get rid of a lot of stress and bad feeling', while a care assistant in the psychiatric half-way hostel said 'We talk out problems – get things sorted out.' The superintendent of the west of England home considered that meetings were useful in promoting 'the interchange of ideas', while a senior nursing officer in the hospital deaf unit observed 'Our regular structured meetings create a better understanding and help to improve communciation.'

The strength of the communication bond raised fears that deaf people could become removed from the routine activities of the hearing community, but the availability of opportunities to practise the social skills required for participation in such activities varied between institutions. Specialist institutions largely relied on residents going outside the institution to participate in 'normal' activities. In the homes, staff assumed the ambulant would go shopping. The only opportunity for the deaf non-ambulant to mix with people outside was the fortnightly transportation on Sunday morning to the local deaf club. In the south of England home staff were particularly conscious of the little they offered.

The deputy matron said 'We don't do very much in that line. There's only the Committee bazaar.'

In the hostels, residents practised social skills at work.

The warden of the hostel for the young working deaf said 'They get plenty of opportunity. They lead very independent lives, and they can have visitors whenever they want them.'

Formal provision to enhance social skills tended to be restricted to specialist facilities within general institutions. The aim of the North Wales deaf unit was to integrate residents into the life of the hearing home, to encourage them to attend clubs, to invite friends in, and to preserve independence by encouraging the use of the kitchen especially when entertaining. A well developed programme had been established in the psychiatric hospital with the deaf unit. Although little was available elsewhere in the hospital, those attending the unit daily enjoyed a wide range of group activities including shopping and outings. Similar opportunities were available in one of the mental handicap hospitals for patients attending the rehabilitation unit. But in other hospitals, as a charge nurse admitted

'Apart from craft in the occupational therapy department, all we've got is the ward routine.'

More widely used than specially devised programmes to teach or maintain social skills was the expectation that deaf people would contribute to the day-to-day running of the institution. In every setting deaf people were expected to help with a variety of daily tasks, which usually included cleaning, making beds, laying tables, washing up and tidying, and sometimes helping with the preparation of food, gardening and maintenance.

As long ago as 1962 Townsend argued the value of such activity for ensuring residents a role[38] and thus avoiding institutionalization. In the case of the deaf there was some disagreement among staff even within the same institution as to the purpose of such activity. Although senior staff emphasized the therapeutic objectives, some admitted that, in view of staff shortages, the help of residents or patients was required for reasons of economy as well as therapy. All domestic and junior staff were clear that staff shortage alone accounted for the involvement of residents or patients. In the homes for the deaf, the help provided by residents appeared to be less systematized than in other settings.

Often in the last two decades, the acquisition and exercise of a range of skills required for an independent life has been identified as therapeutic, especially when undertaken on a reciprocal basis and from choice.[39] However, though choice was sometimes exercised, participation in the daily running of institutions was never justified by staff in terms of reciprocity, and because of the division of labour involved, helping with chores on the whole offered little opportunity for the exercise of autonomy. Moreover, the communication barrier largely precluded the understanding of deafness required to achieve therapeutic objectives. All staff were clear that the deaf achieved least when they were isolated among the hearing: it was not surprising, then, that an eighth admitted that their institutions did not provide a satisfactory context for the treatment of the deaf.

Yet there was some evidence of imaginative understanding of what it was like to be deaf: the acquisition of information was the problem most commonly associated with deafness.

The deputy warden of a hostel said 'It's lack of information: it means they can't understand everyday things.'

Another widely held view (by almost a third of care staff) was that frustration arising from the difficulties of communication was common among the deaf.

A senior nursing officer observed 'There's a lot of frustration because of the inability to communicate. They need an outlet for self-expression.'

A range of other difficulties were identified by a small number of staff. For example, a few considered that the problems of the deaf were the same as those of the hearing but were intensified by hearing loss.

A social worker for the deaf said 'Their problems are no different from anyone else's, but they're exacerbated by lack of information and communication problems.'

Others raised the difficulty associated with dependence on others.

A charge nurse said 'Time is their problem. They are dependent on others who don't realise the importance of speedy assistance.'

Still others argued that the biggest problem faced by the deaf was the failure of the hearing to understand them.

A deputy warden of a home for the deaf said 'They can't make others understand what is happening, why they are upset.'

And a few considered isolation and boredom to be intractable problems.

A charge nurse in a mental handicap hospital said 'Psychologically they are at a disadvantage because they are cut off, unable to communicate.' A care assistant in one hostel said 'The problem is being different, not part of the community or family. They must get bitter and depressed.'

Thus, the deaf were seen as having to struggle to make themselves understood and to understand what was going on around them.

The officer in charge of a deaf unit said 'Here they suffer from the inability to communicate adequately. We are all learning a difficult skill together.'

A few perceived the problem of the deaf in terms of the demands of the institutional routine.

A care assitant in a hospital said, 'The difficulty that comes up is explaining to them what you want.'

But others were more concerned about the difficulties deaf people faced in benefiting from standard treatment procedures.

An occupational therapist in a mental handicap hospital said 'You can never be sure how much they grasp of the purposes of what we ask them to do, etc.'

Only occasionally were the problems of the deaf seen in broader terms than the immediate purposes of the institution.

A social worker attached to a home for the deaf said 'They have immense problems here. It's difficult to get them to understand about their rights and to understand administrative procedures which are a normal part of everyday life. And they have terrible emotional problems.'

Not surprisingly almost all staff considered that it was especially difficult to work with deaf residents or patients. In many cases, the problem was finding the time to explain adequately: some staff admitted that they resorted to issuing commands without explanation. And the communication barrier often subverted therapeutic objectives.

A charge nurse in a psychiatric hospital said of one patient, 'There's no possibility of in-depth exchange. He can't communicate his wants, and we can't assess what needs to be done.'

The sheer exhaustion of trying to communicate in a unfamiliar medium was a common complaint.

The matron of a home for the deaf said 'Just understanding them sometimes – communication takes time. There's the constant strain of concentration when you're trying to communicate. It's very wearing.'

Deaf people often failed to appreciate the stress on those who cared for them.

The deputy warden of a hostel said 'They don't accept you're tired when you have worked an eighteen hour day.'

Perhaps it was this behaviour which was sometimes interpreted as self-ishness. A social worker for the deaf, drawing on her experience of deaf people in all settings explained

'Communication difficulties have given their lives a narrow aspect which leads to unrealistic expectations of others.'

Another social worker identified the cause of unrealistic expectations in a particular aspect of learning failure:

'They don't learn easily to relate procedure and appropriate behaviour in one situation to another situation.'

Despite the difficulties involved, almost all staff derived satisfaction from working with deaf people.

A matron of a home for the deaf was an exception. 'I find it frustrating and boring: I'm not a deaf fanatic. But there are aspects of the running of the home which compensate for working with the deaf.'

Sometimes satisfaction arose from involvement in the development of specialist provision.

The warden of the North Wales deaf unit said 'I'm thrilled with the status – that we've been chosen for the unit – and there's the satisfaction of creating a happy home here.'

Others were gratified by aspects of the caring process.

A domestic in a home for the deaf said 'They respond to your friendship, it's good to get to know them', and a care assistant in a hostel said 'In all kinds of ways they pay you back – just being accepted makes you feel great.'

Thus, specialist staff were rewarded by the reciprocity involved in the caring relationship. And social workers for the deaf considered that the attractions of their work went beyond a reciprocating relationship to include an interest in the communication process.

In contrast, non-specialist staff tended to concentrate on characteristics which distinguished the deaf from the hearing and which they found attractive.

A charge nurse said 'The deaf are a bit more grateful than other patients.'

In general, then, staff were well disposed to deaf people. Furthermore, almost all were confident that, despite communication difficulties, deaf residents or patients understood the objectives of care. Moreover, staff were convinced that they knew enough about the deaf people in their care to be sure that appropriate treatment and care regimes were being followed. Most (all but an eighth) who were in day-to-day contact with deaf people claimed substantial knowledge of them – their family background, employment history, health, and leisure interests – and had access to their files.

A major distinguishing feature of those in residential and hospital care was that they were more likely than those in private households to have secondary handicapping conditions and to be more incapacitated. How far were institutional settings equipped to care for such people? Only the London home and the hostel for the young working deaf had no nursing care available on the premises, though only the home had severely incapacitated or elderly residents. Furthermore, there were staff on call in all institutions at night, and in the hostel for the young working deaf there were bell links with the warden in case of emergency. Indeed, the vast majority of staff – all but a tenth – considered that the deaf people in their care had adequate help with their physical difficulties. Typical exceptions were the deputy matron of the south of England home for the deaf who required a hoist and bath aids for residents with substantial incapacity, and the senior nursing officer in the deaf unit of a psychiatric hospital who wanted transport between the wards and the unit for physically dependent deaf patients who were prevented from attending, especially in bad weather.

Apart from involving deaf people in the daily chores of homes and hospitals, few institutions provided rehabilitation facilities to help deaf people participate in life outside the institution. The expectation was that residents and patients would remain permanently in the homes and hospitals, an expectation which was reflected in the lack of any psychiatric, social, or vocational assessment. Exceptions were the North Wales deaf unit and the half-way psychiatric hostel, but only in the deaf unit of a psychiatric hospital was the rehabilitation ethos strongly reinforced by the team and adopted for patients of all ages. Elsewhere, even in this hospital, staff shortages precluded any attempt at *consistent* rehabilitation. Vocational or industrial training facilities and/or vocational placement services were available to all only in the hostels, and the deaf unit of the psychiatric hospital.

Although staff were confident that they offered suitable care to deaf people, there was a widespread demand for specialist provision in all general institutions. Where some specialist facilities already existed, staff called for greater use of specialist staff throughout, while staff in all hospitals considered that it was essential to utilize existing facilities for the deaf in the community, especially information resources. Moreover, individual hospitals had their own requirements.

In the hospital deaf unit, an occupational therapist said 'We need funds for an enlarged unit. If the deaf come to us it means that they can't attend industrial therapy. But it's impossible to do industrial therapy on the unit because of lack of space and the geography of the hospital.' In another hospital a nurse said 'We need talks on deafness for the whole hospital. And there should be more informed social work involvement in what we do.' A hospital occupational therapist said, 'We need more help in preparing Makaton classes and there should be more support all round in providing specialist facilities.'

In the homes for the deaf, the main concern was to improve staffing levels. Little importance was attached to specialization and qualification though there was support for a regime requiring deaf people to do more for themselves, especially domestic chores, and engage in a greater range of activity, including employment. In contrast, social workers for the deaf were convinced of the necessity for specialist trained staff in the homes particularly those trained for residential work with the elderly deaf, as well as occupational therapists, and the provision of greater support from specialist social workers.

Hostel staff argued for more hostel provision, and were anxious to improve staffing levels, and engage specialists, particularly in casework and literacy. For those living in private households, social workers for the deaf advocated greater specialist provision within the general framework of services – particularly in further education, apprenticeship, training and casework.

The need for greater specialist provision was substantiated by the failure of staff in all institutional settings to appreciate the importance of residual hearing: there was no urgent demand for a wider use of audiological testing, nor any concern about the maintenance of hearing aids, about which a substantial minority (two-fifths) knew little. However, the majority of qualified hospital staff and of senior staff in the homes and hostels were able to diagnose and mend a minor fault in a hearing aid: usually the information had been 'picked up' from experience or the DHSS booklet of instructions.

The deputy warden of a home for the deaf said 'You get plenty of bloody practice at it here.'

Furthermore, in most institutions spares for hearing aids were kept on the premises. Surprisingly, the exceptions were specialist institutions – the hostel for the young working deaf and the west of England home for the deaf. In contrast, two homes and a hostel had leads for body-worn aids and tubing for post aurals. All social workers for the deaf had a stock of batteries, leads, tubing and (unofficially) spare NHS aids, while a psychiatric hospital had spare ear moulds as well.

Nevertheless, in some institutions, key staff caring for deaf people had not been provided with basic information about hearing aids. For example, ward nursing staff did not realize that whistling meant that the ear mould did not fit properly and therefore the aid was largely ineffective, or that ear moulds should be replaced from time to time as the outer ear changes shape with age or with changes in weight.

All institutions had established a special relationship with their local NHS hearing clinic, yet in general, staff had little idea as to how long repairs to aids normally took. And even within institutions, staff varied in their knowledge of procedures at NHS hearing clinics. For example, in a mental handicap hospital, school staff, but not those of the back wards, were knowledgeable about clinic procedures. Thus, the efficiency with which deaf people were dealt by clinics was dependent on which wards they were in, and which units they attended.

Most staff were sceptical of the usefulness of hearing aids to the deaf people in their care. As a consequence, little attention was paid to the use of aids, particularly in specialist institutions: in the half-way psychiatric hostel and the homes for the deaf staff were unable to provide accurate information on the numbers of residents with hearing aids.

The lack of faith in the efficiency of hearing aids was demonstrated when matrons of two of the homes for the deaf declared that none of their residents would benefit from an aid, an assessment contradicted by social workers, who visited regularly. In other institutions most staff had never considered who might benefit from an aid. It was thought in mental handicap hospitals that there were no patients able to use an aid.

A nurse, one of whose patients, according to his file and his own report, had used an aid at school said 'We can't give them hearing aids: they would eat them.'

Of course, there are other aids to communication which anyone caring for deaf people might be expected to monitor. To lip-read effectively, sight is important and the periodic testing of visual acuity and the issue of suitable glasses where they are required, as well as the removal of cataracts when appropriate, may increase lip-reading skills. Communication, though, is a two-way process, and it is important for deaf people to speak with as little distortion as possible: false teeth, where they are required, should be a first priority, and speech therapy is advantageous.

In many institutions arrangements had been made to ensure physical well-being. All institutions used the services of general practitioners and dentists and with the exception of two mental handicap hospitals, opticians as well. However, only the mental handicap hospitals retained speech therapists, and physiotherapists were available only at two psychiatric hospitals, a home for the deaf, one hostel and the North Wales deaf unit. Thus, a framework of provision for monitoring physical efficiency was available in institutional settings, physiotherapy was available to a substantial minority, but speech therapy to only a tiny minority.

However, in practice staff revealed little interest in or appreciation of the importance of physical well-being. Neglect was marked in the homes for the deaf, particularly regarding aids to vision, false teeth and hearing aids. In all the homes and one hostel, residents showed broken false teeth, spectacles, and hearing aids, and privately acquired aids for which they had been unable to locate batteries in local shops.

Miss Nixon, who lived in a home for the deaf, was a keen embroiderer, but one of the lenses and an arm of her spectacles were broken. She held her spectacles on with one hand, put them down and made her stitch where she thought it should be, causing derision among staff.

Although staff invariably responded fully when cases of broken teeth, spectacles and hearing aids were reported after interviews, residents found senior staff remote and hesitated to seek their help themselves.

The pattern of neglect was repeated in general institutions. In mental handicap hospitals, spectacles were rarely provided for those with impaired vision.

A sister said 'We wouldn't give them spectacles: we've never tried them.'

Nor were false teeth replaced, because patients were said to exchange them for cigarettes. Furthermore, it had not occurred to nursing staff that the removal of cataracts would enhance the ability of deaf patients to lip-read as well as engage in therapeutic activities. Perhaps it is not surprising, in view of the widespread neglect of basic items such as teeth and spectacles, that speech therapy was so little in evidence.

While it is true that there were instances in which the deaf living in private households reported broken false teeth, spectacles or hearing aids, these were isolated examples and were not typical of the group as a whole. Generally, the care for which deaf people gave up their independence constituted no more than the provision of shelter, food and warmth. Even in the hospitals, staff failed to perceived health problems.

Mr Greens, a psychiatric patient, suffered great pain which was not relieved because he had 'given up trying to communicate with the staff'.

Except where deaf people gained access to educational or occupational provision, there was little opportunity to engage in therapeutic activity, other than daily chores. In the mental handicap hospitals, patients on low dependency wards, to whom occupational therapy was available five days a week, worked ferociously hard when set a task, but were unable to see to what end. But no such activity was available on high dependency wards where mutilation was frequent and those who became excitable with frustration were cuddled by staff. Indeed, 'loving', as it was called, was the major event: patients, regardless of age, trooped up to be given their ten-minute cuddle each day.

A nurse observed 'It's all you can do with them: you can't get any activities organized – staffing levels are unpredictable day to day, and we're always short.'

In the homes, of course, the purpose was to recreate the conditions of an ordinary home. To that end, block treatment with regard to health checks was avoided.

One matron said 'I don't have the doctor in regularly. I think the doctor bothers them.'

Yet appointments with health services were made by staff, not residents. Only in the half-way psychiatric hostel was the health of residents kept under thorough review. In addition to liaison with the local hospital's Department of Psychology for the Deaf, general practitioner, dentist, optician and audiologist arrangements were well established and used. But even here where staff made conspicuous efforts to be approachable, the reliability of the system could be jeopardized by the reluctance of deaf people to approach staff members for help: the fact that staff acted as a filter for such services could reduce their effectiveness.

In general, then, deaf people entered institutional settings primarily because secondary handicaps prevented them from living independently in their own homes in the absence of suitable domiciliary services – services often required as a substitute for family care no longer available, or as a supplement to those which remained. Once there, only a minority enjoyed the care of a therapeutic regime, despite the therapeutic objectives of care espoused by most staff. Indeed, lack of specialist training and the consequent difficulties experienced in communication with the deaf, largely precluded staff from providing anything more ambitious than shelter, food and warmth. Britain is not alone in failing to provide suitably trained people for the care of the deaf. It has been reported of psychiatric services for the deaf in the United States that most staff were 'practising without substantive knowledge of either deafness or deaf people . . . without the ability to communicate manually or to establish productive interpersonal relations with manual deaf subjects'.[40]

Furthermore, it must be remembered that in the general institutions deaf people were a minority of those receiving care: their problems were only an intensification of those faced by the hearing majority of residents and patients.

6 Living space

If the therapeutic role of institutions was at most muted, how far did they create a 'home from home' for deaf people, who, after all, often had their counterparts in terms of physical and mental health as well as degrees of incapacity for daily activities among those living in their own homes?

In the years immediately following the end of the Second World War, when the destruction of the Poor Law was a fundamental objective of social policy, the creation of 'a homelike atmosphere' was considered to be the primary requirement of 'promotional welfare' as it was applied to residential care. In practice, little consideration was given at the time to what constituted a homely atmosphere or how it might be achieved in an institutional setting. However, from the outset the number of persons in any one institution was considered to be important: large numbers necessitated the *regimentation* which had been the hallmark of the workhouse. Therefore in the late 1940s and 1950s the central concern of government policy in relation to residential care for the elderly was that homes should be small. The precise number of beds at which local authorities should aim in any one institution varied, according to the economic climate, between twenty and sixty. Furthermore, for most of that period, there was an emphasis on the importance of providing single bedded rooms. Thus at policy-making level the creation of a 'homely atmosphere' was assumed to involve a decrease in regimentation, relatively small numbers gathered into a single institution, and, ideally, single bedded rooms. By the end of the 1950s local authorities were urged by central government to allow those entering residential care to take with them a few possessions, including small items of furniture. Not only did the provision of single bedded rooms, which residents were allowed to furnish at least partially themselves, remain a largely unattained ideal, but the degree to which regimentation was to be abandoned was never spelt out.[1]

Much of the critical academic research concerned with institutional care in the 1950s and 1960s focused not on devising indices by which good care practice might be identified, but on describing and analysing the more extreme forms of closed institutions, and thereby developing models which denied the possibility of good institutional care.[2] Indeed, some argued not merely the negative effects of institutional life, but the positive, therapeutic benefits of life in 'the community'. In the case of residential care for the elderly, Townsend based his case against institutions largely on their failure to provide an opportunity for reciprocity between the generations and their segregating effects. However, he did indicate some criteria by which residential care could be judged a failure and which might be included in a measure of lack of 'homeliness' – for example, loss of privacy, of identity, and of the power of self-determination; isolation from family, friends and community; loss of occupation; loneliness; the weakness of relationships with other residents and staff; the restriction of those receiving care to a single generation, and the denial of opportunities for reciprocity. But the list is unsystematic, in the sense that it has no basis in any study of 'normal' life.[3] For example, there has been no comparison between privacy in ordinary households and in institutions, nor has there been any discussion of how a comparison might be made between the privacy of individuals in institutions, the privacy of households, and the privacy of individuals within households or families.

Perhaps because the focus of policy gradually shifted, during the 1960s, towards keeping people out of institutions and in their own homes, there has been little progress to date in devising systematic criteria by which the 'homeliness' of residential care might be assessed. Surprisingly, it is in relation to long-term hospital care, particularly for the mentally handicapped, that the advances on Townsend's work have been made. Tizzard's work on 'block treatment' is probably the most important example.[4] Recently, Dartington, Miller and Gwynne [5] have discussed experiments in the residential care of the severely physically handicapped which have emphasized autonomy and where practice is based on comparison, implied rather than explicit, with the lives of fit people in private households. But a 'homelike atmosphere' remains without definition, and as a consequence assessments of institutional life in this respect continue to be arbitrary.

A recent reappraisal of the anti-institutional literature has promoted growing criticism both of the methods of analysis and of the theories used by its major protagonists.[6] Furthermore, there has been evidence of growing scepticism about the practicability of a more extensive non-institutional response depending largely on unpaid or low paid care by women.[7] In the circumstances, it seems appropriate to return to the original objective of post-war institutional policy as a guide to good practice, namely the provision of a homelike atmosphere.

The nature of the present study precluded any attempt to devise a set of criteria by which the 'homeliness' of institutions involved in the study could be assessed. Instead, the works of Townsend and Tizzard were used to provide a framework for comparing deaf people living in institutions and in private households. But the basis for the comparison remains essentially arbitrary: it has no validity either as a reflection of what is generally considered to be desirable, or what is usual in the population at large, still less does it reflect what deaf people in general, or those living in institutions, perceive to be important in living arrangements.

Essentially Townsend and Tizzard were concerned to map out the degree of autonomy which people in institutions exercise over the way they use space and time. It might be argued that the hallmark of life lived in a home of one's own is the exercise of autonomy over the way life is lived and time disposed of, subject to modification by the demands of family, friends and society at large. Autonomy in this context is not synonymous with independence: it implies choice which may be exercised even by those who are heavily dependent on others. The purpose of this chapter is to explore the degree to which choice was exercised by deaf people in all settings – by those in residential and hospital care and by those who lived in their own homes – in the way living space was used. As such, discussion will focus on the degree to which deaf people enjoyed the freedom to come and go as they pleased, and to use facilities within their 'home' as they pleased, as well as the degree to which they could choose how the space around them was to be filled – for example, with furniture and other possessions.

Tenure

It is useful at the outset to consider the type of accommodation in which deaf people lived. By far the largest single category – almost two-fifths – lived in homes for the deaf run by voluntary organizations, and almost a fifth were in NHS hospitals. A tiny minority (3 per cent) lived in local authority homes for the elderly. Among those outside institutional care, the largest category (two-fifths) rented accommodation from the local authority (16 per cent of all deaf persons) though there were almost as many owner-occupiers (14 per cent and a third of those living in private households). In addition, a substantial minority (a tenth) lived in privately rented accommodation while 3 per cent were in housing association property. Among those living in private households, the distribution between the different types of tenure was unexpected: rather more were in council housing, substantially fewer were owner-occupiers, and substantially more were in privately rented accommodation that might have been expected from the distribution according to tenure of the general population.

Personal living space

How much space did deaf people have for themselves as individuals, and in
the case of those who lived in private households, for their families? To
have to share a room was a common experience: only a little less than
two-fifths had a room to themselves. Overall, sharing was considerably less
common among those in private households than in institutional settings.
Between two-fifths and a half of deaf people living in private households
had a room of their own, compared with only 16 per cent of those in
residential hostels, homes and in hospitals. However, there was a profound
difference between the nature of the sharing experienced by deaf people in
private households where sharing occurred from choice, mainly with
marital or cohabiting partners, and that elsewhere. Statutory overcrowding
was rare in private households, but conditions were often cramped, especially where the deaf person was young and a member of a large family, or
where deaf parents with a low income had young children.

Mr Rex, aged 34, lived with his wife and two children. They had only one
small bedroom, a small living room, a kitchen and bathroom. The children
were obliged to sleep downstairs in the living room, one of them on a sofa, and
the other on a lilo.

However, the vast majority of those living in their own homes either had a
room of their own or shared with a spouse.
  The only institutional setting in which all had rooms of their own was the
hostel for the young working deaf. Elsewhere, those with rooms to themselves were in a minority. For example, in the half-way psychiatric hospital, with one exception, rooms were shared by two people. In the homes
for the deaf, shared rooms were usual. Two-bedded rooms were the norm
in the south of England home, but in the London home and west of
England home, most deaf people were in three-bedded rooms, though in
the latter, a third were in a dormitory. Perhaps not surprisingly, deaf
hospital patients with their own rooms were a tiny minority (less than a
tenth), though single bedded rooms were more common in hospitals than
in homes for the deaf. For the most part the alternative to a single bedded
room for hospital patients was more dramatically communal than for the
residents of homes and hostels: those who attended the deaf unit of one of
the psychiatric hospitals were exceptional in that they were in two-bedded
rooms and not on wards.
  Among those in non-specialist accommodation, deaf people in homes for
the elderly were the most favoured in terms of personal living space, and
were at an advantage compared with residents of homes for the deaf. With

one exception they had rooms to themselves, and in one case a self-contained flatlet.

Thus only the residents of the hostel for the young working deaf were guaranteed the personal living space and privacy which was accepted as being normal by most of those in private households. How satisfied were deaf people with the amount of space at their disposal? Largely as a reflection of the crowded circumstances in which many young families lived, as many as a third of those in private households wanted at least one additional room. Only those in the hostel for the young working deaf made no complaint about the space available to them. Elsewhere, in residential accommodation, there was a strong desire among those who shared to have somewhere of their own. This was true of all the residents of the psychiatric half-way hostel and almost all of those in the homes for the deaf. In striking contrast there was no great demand among deaf hospital patients for a room of their own. Demand for single rooms was largely confined to those in settings where such an expectation was feasible: in the hospitals it was widely accepted that patients should live on wards.

Housing standards and facilities

However, personal space alone cannot be the sole indicator of 'a homelike atmosphere'. It seems reasonable to suppose that account should be taken of standard of accommodation and facilities as well.

Generally, in terms of the standard facilities, the accommodation of deaf people in private households was satisfactorily appointed. None of them shared facilities with other households, and all had an indoor sink, hot and cold water, a fixed bath or shower, and a cooker with two or more rings. However, one family had an outside WC and another living in a bed-sit had cooking rings but no oven. Among those living in institutional settings, the command over standard facilities enjoyed by people living in private households was most nearly matched by the residents of the hostel for the young working deaf. In every case they had their own amenities, except that baths were shared, usually with three others. In no other institutional setting was there anything like the same personal command over standard amenities, though among those living in local authority homes for the elderly, two had their own wash basin, while another had her own WC and cooking facilitities as well. In the homes for the deaf, the psychiatric half-way hostel and the hospitals, the amenities were present but in every case they were communal. Of course it is true that most of those in private households shared the standard amenities, but with members of the family.

No deaf person lived in seriously defective accommodation, but among those in private households, as many as two-fifths reported structural defects, usually damp, though three people complained of loose bricks and plaster, while another reported a leaking roof, and one showed us broken floorboards. Perhaps because they did not know, few of those in institutions reported structural defects in their accommodation. Residents of one home for the deaf complained that seven of the windows were hard to open or had broken sashes, and in the hostel for the young working deaf there were several complaints about broken window catches.

In most cases deaf people enjoyed, in addition to structurally sound accommodation with the standard amenities, the use of a garden, yard or balcony. All but a small minority – an eighth – of those in private households had their own space outside in which the whole household could sit. Of course, none of those in institutional settings had their own space outside but most of them had the opportunity to sit in a communal garden: all the homes and hostels for the deaf, and all but one of the homes for the elderly had gardens, while the hospitals were set in large grounds. Of course, communal gardens could be used for no more than sitting in. Most of those with access to an outside space considered its availability to be important, though none of those without such space wished to have it. For those with dependent children a garden was useful primarily as a safe play area, and in fact, all such people had a garden.

Few of those in institutional settings could assess their accommodation in terms of 'housing'. It was not surprising, then, that those who considered themselves to have a housing problem lived in private households – a seventh in all – usually because the property was damp or crowded. Perhaps it was a measure of the failure of most institutional settings to create a 'homelike atmosphere' that some residents and patients in considering housing conditions, recalled the homes which they had left. Yet this is not to say that attempts had not been made by those running institutions to allow deaf people to recreate some semblance of their own homes.

Private possessions

A 'homelike atmosphere' need not depend upon the availability of space which is private to a particular individual – the crowded nature of the accommodation of some of those who lived in private households was witness to that. To a considerable extent it is the use of space as much as its availability which creates a 'homelike atmosphere'. It has been argued in the literature and in government policy statements that the introduction of some personal possessions into institutional settings will help to create the atmosphere of the home that has been abandoned. But in addition, it has been suggested that such a practice may be therapeutic for long-stay patients in mental hospitals.[8] Most deaf people living in institutions had been allowed to keep some small personal possessions. Although almost all the residents of the homes for the deaf shared rooms, they had all been allowed to bring with them one or two small possessions and this was true of hostel residents and those in homes for the elderly as well. Of course, those who were in single-bedded rooms or flatlets had more opportunity than the majority in shared rooms to exercise choice in the utilization of their space, and to house more of their own possessions around them. It was in the hospitals that there was least opportunity to retain personal possessions. By no means all deaf patients interviewed even had a locker private to them-selves: some had only a share of communal locker space.[9] There was considerable variation between institutions in the extent of personal space allowed to individual deaf residents and patients, but little variation in the type and range of personal possessions which they were allowed to keep there. For example, in the homes for the deaf, residents were allowed to bring pictures, ornaments, toiletries, clocks and other small possessions: no furniture was allowed and residents had to share not only their rooms, but also the wardrobes and chests of drawers. Even though the residents of the hostel for the young working deaf lived in self-contained flatlets, these were already furnished and the only possessions to which no objection was made were small items including electrical equipment. In the psychiatric half-way hostel, bedrooms were shared, no personal furniture and no elec-trical appliances were allowed, although residents could bring in small objects such as ornaments and photographs. There was no homogeneity in the practice of the hospitals. Patients attending the deaf unit of a psy-chiatric hospital shared bedrooms and achieved privacy by the use of screens: within their personal space they were allowed to keep personal belongings such as photographs and ornaments. In another psychiatric hospital, however, patients had only their bed and locker area on the twenty-bedded wards: hoarding was actually discouraged, though clothes and a few small personal items were allowed. And in a mental handicap hospital, where deaf patients slept on wards with twenty or more beds, there was no personal space beyond the bed. Cupboards were communal, and storage space was minimal. As a consequence, personal possessions were discouraged.

Indeed, the space available to each resident or patient was so limited in most institutions that in only two – the London home for the deaf and the North Wales deaf unit – were there no written regulations determining the type of personal possessions allowed. However, it was not the case that institutions where the most personal space was available were the least likely to regulate the type and quantity of personal possessions: there were written regulations governing all personal possessions of the residents of the hostel for the young working deaf. Even though most institutions had some space for personal possessions, often there was nowhere private in which possessions could be locked away safely. In the homes and hostels, residents had space in wardrobes and either cupboards or chests of drawers, and though shared in most cases, these could be locked. Similar provision was made for patients attending the deaf unit of the psychiatric hospital, and in another psychiatric hospital, a drawer which could be locked as well as a locker was available to each patient. But in other hospitals keys were not available for lockers.

Despite the insistence in the literature and policy discussions on the importance of allowing residents and patients to retain small possessions and some furniture in the creation of a homelike atmosphere, it remained true that most of the personal possessions which deaf people had retained consisted of clothing. In all settings, residents and patients wore their own clothes, and it was these which filled the lockers, drawers and wardrobes. However, not all clothing was personal: patients who attended the deaf unit in a psychiatric hospital wore some hospital clothing, and in the west of England home for the deaf some clothing was provided by the home. There were settings in which the personal quality of clothing was emphasized by allowing at least part of the responsibility for its laundry to lie with patients or residents. Indeed in both of the hostels residents had sole responsibility for washing personal clothing. In the homes, the North Wales deaf unit and the deaf unit of the psychiatric hospital, responsibility for laundering personal clothing rested partly with the individual and partly with the institution. In hospitals, however, laundering clothes was largely or entirely an institutional responsibility. Furthermore, most patients and residents played some part at least in buying clothes, though the residents of the hostel for the young working deaf alone exercised complete freedom in this respect. Elsewhere, clothes were bought by the resident or patient acting on the advice of staff. However, in a mental handicap hospital, although clothes were exclusive to a particular individual, they were chosen and bought by staff. In all institutional settings, a high proportion of clothing was bought in local shops. Where homes and hospitals were isolated, shopping for clothes involved a trip to the nearest town. But there were other sources of clothing as well. Relatives often bought clothes for residents of the London home, while patients attending the deaf unit of a psychiatric hospital bought some clothes from the mobile shop which visited the hospital, and patients elsewhere bought them from the hospital. Thus, the sense of ownership over clothes tended to be weakened by the involvement of staff or relatives in their purchase, their supply by the institution or its shop, and to a large extent, their absorption into the institutional laundry system.

Use of personal space

The opportunity to use space without interference was the hallmark of normal home life. All of those who lived in private households used their own rooms whenever they wished to do so. In contrast, it was rare for those living in institutions to enjoy the same freedom, though the degree to which they did so was disputed by deaf people and staff. Only in the hostels for the young working deaf was it unequivocally agreed that the self-contained flatlets could be used entirely at the discretion of residents. Residents of the psychiatric hostel considered that they were discouraged from using their rooms during leisure periods of the day, except at weekends, but staff reported no such restrictions. And the same pattern of dispute emerged in the London home for the deaf. In contrast residents of the west of England home claimed complete freedom in their use of rooms, whereas staff considered their use to be restricted during the day. Only in the south of England home were both staff and residents clear that use of bedrooms for long periods during the day was discouraged. However in homes for the elderly, residents used their own living space whenever they wished to do so. On the other hand, hospital patients and staff agreed that the use of the bed areas during the day was not allowed, other than at weekends, except with the permission of the staff.

Use of household facilities

Beyond the ability to use personal space at will, it may be argued that a 'homelike atmosphere' depends as well upon the ability to use other household facilities, such as the kitchen, the bathroom and the lavatory, when required. All of those who lived in their own homes reported that they were able to use the kitchen whenever they wished to do so. But this freedom was rarely granted to deaf people living in institutions. Of those in institutional settings only the residents of the hostel for the young working deaf could use the kitchen at will. In the psychiatric hostel there were set periods during the week when residents were free to use the kitchen, but at weekends flexible arrangements for kitchen use were in operation. In general no access to the kitchen was available in homes for the elderly, but one resident had limited access while in the North Wales deaf unit, preparing and cooking meals in the unit's kitchen was encouraged for therapeutic reasons.

Nor were residents of the homes for the deaf given access to the kitchen. And this was true of the great majority of hospital patients as well.

Of course, for those living in private households much of the object of being able to use a kitchen was to have the freedom to make a cup of tea or a snack at will. Despite the general denial of access to the kitchen most institutions boasted tea and snack making facilities. The exceptions were the homes for the deaf, and one of the mental handicap hospitals. Even so, a few deaf people, even in these institutions, managed to retain the freedom of tea making.

Mr Johnstone who lived in the south of England home for the deaf had an electric water heater of the one cup type, which he kept locked in a suitcase. With this, he made a 'good strong cup of tea every morning', unknown to staff.

Hospital kitchen facilities though available were often kept locked up because staff shortages made the supervision of patients using them diffi-cult. Staff were obsessed by the possibility of accidents from the use of hot water, patients playing with the knobs on the cooker, or with the tea or the food. As a consequence deaf patients who could use facilities appropriately – the majority – were denied the chance to do so. Whether facilities were used or not depended on the type of ward and the attitude of the staff. The higher the assessed dependency of the patients, the less likely it was that access to facilities would be available. Thus patients on a high dependency ward of a mental handicap hospital were never allowed into the kitchen area. During the day they were confined to two areas – the main living room, and the corridor and adjoining lavatory area. The locked door between these areas was opened only to allow patients, escorted by a member of staff, to go to the lavatory. The entrance to the eating area was barricaded with rows of sofas and chairs two or three deep.

Despite the widely available facilities for tea making in institutions, few made regular use of them, in marked contrast to deaf people living in private households, where everyone was accustomed to make tea both for themselves and other people, and all but two had done so that day. Else-where, only in the hostels was tea making common. All of the residents of the hostel for the young working deaf where independence was assumed had made a pot of tea that day, and even in the half-way psychiatric hostel where no such assumption was made, only two residents were not in the habit of making tea regularly.

In contrast, those in other settings who made tea for themselves or other people were the exception rather than the rule. Thus only one of the residents in each of the homes for the deaf were accustomed to undertake the task and this was true of only one person in the homes for the elderly, and three hospital patients. In all, then, apart from hostel residents only a tenth of those living in institutions regularly made themselves or other people a cup of tea.

The making of snacks followed much the same pattern. Only hostel residents among the institutional population could match those in private households in the freedom they enjoyed to get a snack whenever they wished to do so. Most deaf people in private households were accustomed to prepare some food daily, while residents of the hostel for the young working deaf always did so. In the case of the half-way psychiatric hostel, bread, butter and tea were always available to be taken at will: residents always made themselves tea during the week, and prepared breakfast at weekends. In sharp contrast none of the residents of the homes for the deaf were allowed to get their own food. Although they were allowed to buy immediately consumable food none, apart from sweets – not even biscuits – could be kept in bedrooms. Indeed, the homes for the deaf were more restrictive in their attitude towards food than any other setting. Even in the hospitals kitchens were sometimes open to patients, though normally under supervision, especially on high dependency wards where staff reported that they were forced to keep kitchens locked by the activities of particularly disturbed patients – 'the flooders, burners, thieves and compulsive eaters'. The only deaf patient who was responsible for all her own food lived in a hospital house. Two pairs of patients attending the deaf unit of a psychiatric hospital were responsible for cooking the meal for the entire unit once a week; four others were allowed to cook, though one did so only with supervision. Thus a third of all hospital patients had been responsible for making at least one snack within the previous month. And the residents of homes for the elderly were allowed to make snacks, though only one prepared her own food daily.

Although the majority – four-fifths – of the deaf living in institutions were able to get a snack for themselves at least occasionally, it was only in the hostels that the freedom to do so matched that of those living at home. Nor did other institutional settings compensate by adopting flexible mealtimes. Apart from the hostel for the young working deaf, only in the psychiatric half-way hostel was any flexibility in the time of meals permitted during the week, or even at weekends. Rigid adherence to mealtimes was abandoned only occasionally in two other institutions – a mental handicap hospital, and the west of England home for the deaf.

The *manner* in which meals were conducted was an indicator of the degree to which a homelike atmosphere had been achieved in an institution. Only in half of the wards in one hospital for the mentally handicapped and one psychiatric hospital did a self-service system operate and create a canteen atmosphere, though in the half-way psychiatric hostel patients served themselves in the interest of autonomy. In the London home for the deaf an attempt was made to generate a sense of community at mealtimes by insisting on the observance of grace. Indeed, it was the communality, particularly of the main meal, which was so strikingly evident of those in private households: this was a time at which everyone sat down together. Some institutions (two homes for the deaf, the psychiatric hostel, the hospital deaf unit and two wards of a psychiatric hospital) attempted to create the communality of the family meal by insisting that staff ate with patients or residents. There was little attempt in most institutions to compensate for a lack of homeliness by the introduction of autonomy through the exercise of some choice within the menu. Indeed, it was striking that choice was largely restricted to institutions where mealtimes were most 'homely' – the London and south of England homes for the deaf, and the psychiatric half-way hostel, though choice was also available at the North Wales deaf unit and one of the psychiatric hospitals.

It was in some of the high dependency wards of the mental handicap hospitals, where block treatment was most apparent that mealtimes were least 'homely'. Indeed, they often appeared to be occasions for the destruction of all shreds of personal dignity. Those who were unable to feed themselves were often fed too fast. And on one ward, six patients of the most dependent type who required feeding, had incontinence pads, slit through the middle, placed around their necks as bibs.

Another important indicator of a 'homelike atmosphere' was the exercise of autonomy in the use of the bath and the lavatory. Studies of residential care carried out in the 1950s and 1960s emphasized as a factor in the creation of an 'institutional' atmosphere the block treatment and supervision of washing, bathing and toileting. In particular, attention was drawn to the needless invasion of privacy and autonomy by the supervision of bathing in many institutions regardless of the degree of dependence of residents. The practice was justified by the problem of accountability in the event of accidents. Criticism tended to be based on an assumption that those who remained in their own homes despite substantial incapacity were prepared to take the risks involved in unsupervised bathing and so on, and did so to preserve independence, autonomy and privacy – the constituents of normality. Therefore, in the interests of providing a regime which would approximate to normality, it was argued that those caring for people in residential establishments should also be prepared to risk the accidents which would attend privacy in the bathroom and lavatory.[10]

Such discussion was rarely conducted on the basis of a systematic comparison between practice in institutions and private households, particularly in respect of severely incapacitated people. Indeed, much of the force of the argument derived from the revelation that social factors other than incapacity forced people to seek refuge in residential institutions, and that as a consequence, only a small minority experienced severe incapacity in functional terms.

Studies conducted in the 1960s and 1970s of handicapped people living in private households indicated that a small minority of the very severely handicapped were dependent on others for toileting and/or bathing.[11] It is true that for the most part such help was given by relatives and therefore perhaps involved less of an invasion of privacy or a reduction of autonomy than where supervision was carried out professionally. But this was not always the case: some were aided by neighbours and friends as well as by home helps, district nurses and bathing attendants. Moreover, those who were dependent on the help of others found that their autonomy had largely disappeared with their privacy, for help was provided at a time and in a manner convenient to the giver rather than the recipient.

Thus the argument against supervision in terms of normality could not be sustained in the case of the severely incapacitated. However, it remains true that supervision of bathing and toileting is not 'normal' and is widely dreaded as a prospect by disabled people. Of all the day-to-day activities with which help might have to be received disabled people most dislike the prospect of, or the actual provision of help with going to the lavatory. Help with bathing or having an overall wash is disliked but not to anything like the same degree; the prospect of having to be fed is far more worrying.[12]

In fact, there are a number of ways in which normality may be considered in any reflection on institutional regimes. First, there is the comparison between life in an institution and life in 'normal' private households. It seems appropriate in such comparisons to make distinctions between people of different types and levels of incapacity. Thus the benchmark for determining normality of practice in institutions would be the level and type of incapacity at which supervision of toileting and bathing usually took place in private households. Normality, considered in this way, differs substantially from normality viewed in terms of loss of autonomy and privacy, which may have nothing to do with institutional life as such, but which may be a function of incapacity and consequently, occurs among those living in private households as well as among residents of institutions. A further dimension of normality is the manner in which needs arising from dependency are met. Normality may be seen in terms of the degree to which autonomy or choice is built into the provision of a service, whether in a private household or in an institution, to create an approximation to the autonomy or choice available to those who are not dependent.

In the case of the present study, there were few in institutions and even fewer in private households who were assessed as having severe and very severe levels of incapacity in addition to deafness. Therefore, precise comparisons could not be made of practice across the settings in terms of degree of incapacity. However, broad comparisons were possible since the full range of incapacity arising from additional handicaps was represented in all settings.

All deaf people living in private households were able to have a bath whenever they wanted one. None were supervised in the bath or received help when going to the lavatory. And this was true as well of all the hostel residents. The only restriction on baths in a half-way psychiatric hostel arose from the availability of hot water: residents complained that the water was hot only in the morning and late evening. In the homes for the deaf most staff reported that baths could be taken whenever residents wished to have them, but residents themselves insisted that a rota system was strictly enforced for baths, and in the west of England home, bathing was restricted to afternoons and evenings. The degree of supervision insisted on in bathrooms varied between the homes: only a minority of residents were supervised in the London and south of England homes, but in the west of England home, most were supervised. In contrast, there was no bathtime supervision in the homes for the elderly: in three of the homes, baths were not restricted in any way, but in one residents were rationed to only two baths and in another to only one bath a week.

The privacy allowed in bathrooms and lavatories in homes for the deaf was reflected in the state of door locks. Lavatory door locks invariably worked satisfactorily, but this was by no means the case with bathrooms. Indeed, in the west of England home for the deaf it was a rule that bathroom doors should not be locked.

In the hospitals much depended on the type of patient in question and therefore on the ward concerned. Infrequent access to baths was not invariably considered a deprivation: very few patients liked bathing. Those attending the rehabilitation unit of a hospital for the mentally handicapped and a deaf person living in a hospital house could bath whenever they wished to do so. But in the mental handicap hospitals generally, even on low dependency wards, bathroom doors were usually kept locked by hospital staff to prevent patients flooding the wards. Unfortunately wash basins were in bathroom areas, and as a consequence, although low dependency patients could use the lavatories at will, they were unable to wash their hands. Almost all baths were supervised: indeed, privacy was impossible because the inside locks on bathroom doors were usually broken. For a minority of patients, loss of autonomy lay both in the regulation of the number of baths to be taken and in the loss of privacy involved in supervision. Block treatment in the use of lavatories was adopted for most medium as well as high dependency patients in mental handicap hospitals, while patients on high dependency wards were supervised as well. The toileting of high dependency patients in one hospital took place on commodes kept in the corridors: whether moveable screens were used or not depended on the staff on duty.

Household tasks

For adults, much of the use made of living space in private households concerns the running of the home – in cleaning, cooking, washing up, and so on. To what extent was space used by deaf people in the different settings by engaging in household tasks? Among those living in private households it was common to help with the full range of household tasks, including the preparation and cooking of food, cleaning, making beds, laying tables, washing up, tidying, helping with laundry, gardening and maintenance jobs. In all institutional settings some or even all of these activities were undertaken by residents or patients. Hostel residents were expected to help with the full range of household tasks. Those in the hostel for the young working deaf were entirely responsible for looking after their own flatlets apart from gardening and maintenance jobs. Personal living space was more restricted in the half-way psychiatric hostel, but all residents were expected to contribute to the running of the hostel community and undertook all chores including gardening and maintenance. In this the hostel more nearly resembled the homes and hospitals than the hostel for the young working deaf and private households, where tasks were undertaken for the benefit of the individual deaf person or immediate members of the family. It is unclear how far tasks performed for an institutional community in this way may be regarded as therapeutic, whether because they create a role for dependent persons,[13] or because they offer an opportunity to maintain reciprocity and therefore reduce the necessity for compliance[14] and restore some degree of power to those who are dependent.[15]

Residents of the homes for the deaf helped with all domestic tasks except gardening and maintenance. The range of tasks undertaken by hospital patients was usually more restricted than in other settings. In the deaf unit of a psychiatric hospital help was expected with all household tasks other than laundry, gardening and maintenance. However, in another psychiatric hospital, patients were not involved in the preparation of food, though they did help with the laundry, and portering. There was wide variation in practice between the mental handicap hospitals. In one hospital, the full range of household tasks was undertaken by patients, including gardening and maintenance, whereas in another they helped only with the preparation of food and cleaning. In almost all institutional settings staff considered that patient and resident involvement in household chores was both therapeutic and a means of overcoming staff shortage. Only in the hostel for the young working deaf did residents behave and were expected to behave as they would have done in private households.

In most institutional settings household chores were carried out according to a rota – formally in the case of the homes for the deaf, the half-way psychiatric hostel and the North Wales deaf unit, informally elsewhere. In the homes for the deaf and the North Wales deaf unit, the 'normality' of engaging in household chores was emphasized by the absence of any system of payment. But in the hospitals and the psychiatric half-way hostel, perhaps because 'therapy' directed towards paid employment rather than the creation of a homely atmosphere was a preoccupation, payment was made to those who undertook household tasks.

However, to report that residents and patients were involved in carrying out household tasks, whether on a paid basis or not, provides no indication of the involvement of deaf people in such chores. In practice, none of those living in homes and hospitals undertook a range of chores on a regular basis as was customary for those living in private households and the hostel for the young working deaf. For example, everyone living in private households helped to get meals, while the residents of the hostel for the young working deaf were accustomed to cook for themselves. In the half-way psychiatric hostel, all except three older men helped to cook meals from time to time. But in the homes for the deaf, cooking was undertaken only by a minority: a quarter of those in the London home, none in the south of England home, and one resident in the west of England home, helped to get meals. And only two residents of the homes for the elderly cooked for themselves. Among hospital patients preparing and cooking meals was even more of a minority occupation: only two patients regularly cooked while another did so occasionally in the weekly cookery class.

Perhaps it was understandable that there was reluctance to involve residents and patients in the complex operation of large scale cooking. But the same consideration could not apply to a straightforward task such as laying the table, and, indeed, rather more deaf people in the larger institutions took part in this activity than in the preparation and cooking of food, though they remained a minority. All of those in private households and in the hostel for the young working deaf were accustomed to lay the table while all the residents of the psychiatric half-way hostel did so on a rota basis. But despite the emphasis on the creation of a homelike atmosphere in the homes, only a sixth of their residents were regularly involved in laying the table. In contrast, almost half of hospital patients reported that they regularly chose to undertake the task.

It might have been thought that the routine task of washing-up would be widely undertaken. All of the deaf in private households and the hostels were accustomed to wash-up regularly. And in some of the homes, too, it was common for residents to help with the washing-up. In the London home for the deaf, three-quarters of the residents were organized into a rota for the purpose and a quarter helped on a daily basis, while in the west of England home a quarter of the residents had their names on the washing-up rota. But none of the residents of the south of England home were involved in the task, and only two of those in homes for the elderly washed up. It was rare for deaf hospital patients to wash-up: only a sixth did so, half of them only occasionally.

Visitors

Thus involvement in household tasks concerned only a minority of the deaf outside private households and hostels, and in this sense the use of living space in institutional settings was not 'normal'. Normality and autonomy in the use of living space, however, are not necessarily related solely to the way in which an individual is able to operate within it: the ability to choose to invite others to share that space, if only for a short visit, is important. All deaf people in private households were able to have visitors overnight whenever they wished to do so. In all institutional settings deaf people were able to have visitors at any time, though few could have them to stay. Even in the hostel for the young working deaf, where in many respects the availability and use of living space most closely resembled conditions prevailing in private households, permission was required for overnight visits. But in other settings it was rare for facilities to be available to enable visitors to stay for more than a few hours.

The freedom to come and go

Autonomy and choice in the use of space also implies the freedom to come and go at will. Much of the criticism of institutional care in the 1950s and 1960s focused on the 'closed' nature of institutional life – the fact that for residents and patients there was neither the opportunity nor the need to venture from the institution, for example, to shop.[16] How far were people free to come and go at will? To what extent were they able to visit shops and exercise autonomy in the choice of, say, clothes? All deaf people in private households were free to shop for their own clothes, and all residents of the hostel for the young working deaf followed this 'normal' pattern; while in the half-way psychiatric hostel, a little more than two-thirds of the residents shopped for their own clothes. In other settings, however, it was far less usual for people to exercise such autonomy. Of the homes for the deaf, only in the London home did a majority of residents buy their own clothes unaided, while in the south of England home, half of the residents did so and in the west of England home this was true of only a quarter. For other residents, matron or relatives provided either assistance or the clothes, but overall, more were taken out and assisted than had clothes bought for them.

Far less autonomy in choosing and buying clothes was exercised by residents of the homes for the elderly: all but one of them had their clothes bought by someone else. And few hospital patients exercised any choice. Only one patient went shopping alone to buy clothes, while an eighth were assisted by a member of staff. The remainder – five-sixths in all – had their clothes bought for them by a member of staff, but in most cases the patient was included in a shopping expedition, though only in the role of a passive observer to the transaction.

However, the importance of autonomy in buying clothes may be diminished if facilities are not available to ensure that clothes remain private property and at the disposal of the owner. All of those living in private households and homes for the elderly had their own wardrobes, chests of drawers, and so on, in which to keep their clothes. But this was true for only one of the homes for the deaf: in the west and south of England homes, residents stored some of their clothes in shared cupboards. Even in the hospitals, most of the deaf patients had drawers and lockers in which to store clothes, but no possessions were safe because locks were faulty and locker doors insisted on swinging open. On the high dependency wards many clothes were kept communally. Although clothes were name-labelled, they often ended up on other patients, for which the laundry, the pressures arising from incontinence, and the short supply of linen were blamed.[17]

How far were deaf people accustomed to shop for other goods besides clothes? All of those who lived in private households were keen on domestic shopping, and none of them had any particular preference as to types of shops: supermarkets were used by everyone, but small local shops were also used for a few items. Hostel residents stated a preference for self-service shops because these reduced the likelihood of communication difficulties:

all were accustomed to buy food, but in the psychiatric hostel they pur-
chased a far more limited range of domestic goods. Residents and patients
in other settings shopped only for a small range of items, if at all. Most of
the residents of the homes for the deaf went shopping, usually for small
toiletries, confectionery, newspapers and stationery. However, residents
of the London home for the deaf were discouraged from buying toiletries: if
they did so, their pocket money was withheld. But there was no attempt in
other homes to exercise control over small purchases. In the west of
England home residents made a point of reporting that they were well
received in Woolworth's. In contrast, few of the residents of homes for the
elderly and hospital patients visited shops. Only one person living in a
home for the elderly went shopping:

'I go out most days – for the paper, to buy food. Occasionally I buy some
clothes, and I go to the pub.'

More typical was the resident who said, 'I haven't been out shopping since I
had a stroke and a series of falls two years ago.'

Physical infirmity and the distance of the homes from shopping centres
largely prevented residents from shopping. Only an eighth of hospital
patients ventured out of the hospital grounds to visit local shops to buy
sweets and newspapers. Others were confined to using the hospital shop if
they wished to buy anything. One of the mental handicap hospitals was too
remote for patients to shop outside hospital grounds, being more than half
a mile from the nearest village.

To indicate 'normality' in terms of whether or not deaf people felt free
to undertake 'normal' shopping activities is to use a minimal benchmark: it
could be argued that the *frequency* of visits to shops is a more realistic
indicator of normality. In practice, frequency of shopping expeditions
varied according to ease of access to shops and the necessity of the task. It
was among the deaf living in private households and hostels, particularly
the hostel for the young working deaf, who were dependent upon their own
efforts to acquire food, that shopping expeditions were most frequently
undertaken. All but five people in these settings had been out shopping in
the previous week. Most residents of homes for the deaf were also frequent
shoppers. There were variations between the homes in the frequency with
which residents went out: much depended upon ease of access to shops. In
two homes, the majority of residents had been shopping during the previous week. The substantially less frequent shopping expeditions undertaken by residents of the west of England home were at least in part
explained by the steep hill which had to be negotiated by mainly elderly
residents before they could board a bus to town. Few hospital patients

shopped regularly. Indeed, only a little more than a tenth of all patients had done so during the previous week, while less than a third had been shopping once in the course of the year. Indeed, none of the deaf patients in one of the hospitals for the mentally handicapped had visited a shop since their arrival at the hospital. The residents of homes for the elderly shopped frequently – usually daily – when they did so at all, but the frail majority had not shopped for more than a year.

In fact, few institutions claimed to be any more closed than a private household. With the exception of a mental handicap hospital, most of the staff insisted that residents and patients were free to come and go at will. However, unlike private households, most institutions locked their doors at a specific time each evening – at 10 p.m. in the west and south of England homes for the deaf, the North Wales deaf unit, and the homes for the elderly, and between 10.30 and 11 p.m. at the half-way psychiatric hostel. The London home for the deaf was more flexible than the others: there the doors were locked when everyone was home. In the hospitals it was assumed that patients would not go out in the evening, and the absence of an official closing time was more an indication of the degree to which hospitals were 'closed' rather than of their 'open' nature. Only in the hostel for the young working deaf were there no restrictions placed on the time by which residents had to be in. To emphasize their similarity with people living in private households, residents were alone among those in institutional settings in having their own keys.

The existence of a locking-up time raises the question of what happened when patients or residents failed to observe regulations. Within private households there were no explicit regulations, though there could be implicit assumptions about required behaviour. Reaction to the possibility of regulation-breaking by patients and residents varied widely among staff. In the London home for the deaf and the psychiatric hospital with a deaf unit, it was stressed that regulations had never been broken. But whereas the hospital Senior Nursing Officer said:

'We would never send anyone away from the Unit', a care assistant in the home said 'They would be told to do it or else: they would have to go if not.'

Others suggested that the primary method of achieving obedience to regulations was persuasion.

The matron of the west of England home for the deaf said 'I have a talk with them and they calm down.'

In the hostels, too, persuasion, was the main weapon.

In the half-way psychiatric hostel, the deputy warden said 'We have group discussion and verbal counselling for those who break the rules.'

However, persuasion was not always the first course thought of by staff. In the south of England home for the deaf the right of staff to exclude those who failed to keep the regulations was emphasized:

A care assistant said 'Anyone who doesn't obey gets shot out; they can be removed at twenty-four hours notice.'

Such a choice was not open to the hospitals, which varied in their approach to rule breakers. Whereas at one hospital for the mentally handicapped all staff declared that they would only employ persuasion in such cases, a sister in another reported that rule breakers would be the subject of behaviour modification by the staff, and in a psychiatric hospital, a charge nurse said:

'If gentle persuasion doesn't work, they get transferred to an acute ward.'

In fact, it appeared to be common in the hospitals for discipline to be achieved by threatening to send patients to a lower grade ward: two deaf patients had been transferred to the lowest grade wards not for reasons of their condition, but because they refused to 'behave'.

Most deaf people living in institutional settings, then, were more restricted than those in private households in the degree to which they were able to come and go at will. In part they were restricted by the location of institutions, in part by the expectations and assumptions of staff. Yet even among hospital patients there were a few who had achieved both a considerable measure of autonomy over their use of living space - communal as well as private - and the freedom to come and go.

Mr Francis reported: 'I was born in 1904 and I came to the hospital in June 1916. I have never been to school. I have never been taught to sign. I use hospital signs. I wash myself, I'm proud of my clothes. I always have a good shave and no one has to tell me to bath. I see the tables are laid right. I watch the little things - make sure they've remembered the jam. I'm the foreman of the ward. I do a lot of errands: I'll go up to town to get the evening news-paper. I know my money - I always bring back the right change. I do the same for other patients. I take the night report to the officer - I've always done that and I feel put out if anyone interferes. I watch the clock and tell people when it's late. The porters do this on the other wards. I take people down to the pub for a night out sometimes. The most difficult thing is making myself understood - I get upset if I can't talk.'

But such autonomy was exceptional in institutional settings. Most found their movements beyond the institution even more restricted than within it. Nor did they necessarily enjoy alternative means of communication with the outside world. In addition to their ready and frequent physical access to the world outside home, a substantial minority – almost a third – of deaf people in private households were able to maintain contact through the household telephone as well. In contrast, no public call boxes were available in any of the homes or hostels for the deaf though in every case the warden had an office telephone which could be used in an emergency. However, there were telephone boxes, though none had been adapted for use by the deaf, in all the general institutions – the hospitals and the homes for the elderly, and in one specialist facility, the North Wales deaf unit.

To what extent were mechanical aids available to help to overcome communication problems which restricted the degree to which deaf people successfully operated within their living space? All of the specialist facilities had flashing fire alarms, while the west of England home had also introduced vibrating pillows. In the specialist facilities, then, accountability in the event of fire was the sole consideration in the installation of mechanical aids. In the hostel for the young working deaf, the only addition to flashing fire alarms were flashing door bells – essential if deaf residents were to maintain themselves independently. In addition a number of residents in both of the hostels had bought a flashing alarm clock. The only hospital with mechanical aids was the psychiatric hospital with a deaf unit: there the loop system had been installed in the main occupational therapy unit, and a television adaptor had been installed, but both of these were broken though a communicator was said to be in working order. Only the North Wales deaf unit had installed and maintained in working order a television adaptor and the loop which were installed in the upstairs lounge. It was surprising to find that in one specialist facility – the half-way psychiatric hostel – the staff had never heard of the loop system. All of the homes for the elderly had shown more resourcefulness than some specialist facilities, by introducing both communicators and television adaptors.

Despite the crowded nature of the accommodation in which many of those in private households lived and the restrictions experienced by the majority of those living in institutional settings, most deaf people (four-fifths) declared themselves to be happy living where they were, though there was considerable variation between the different settings in this respect. Almost all of those living in private households and all the residents of the hostel for the young working deaf were happy with their present living arrangements, compared with three-quarters of those at the half-way psychiatric hostel, but only a tenth of residents of homes, and a third of hospital patients.

Symptomatic of the general satisfaction with which the deaf viewed their accommodation was their widespread acceptance of their lack of privacy. Despite the crowded nature of private households, and the communal life of most settings, only 5 per cent wanted to be alone more often, and most of these were residents of the psychiatric half-way hostel and homes for the deaf who would have liked a room to themselves. It seemed that only in settings where it was considered reasonable for the expectation of privacy to be held was the lack of privacy resented: hospital patients accepted ward and unit life. Indeed, perhaps surprisingly, more than a tenth of deaf people would have liked to be alone less often. Thus the vast majority – two-thirds in all – were clear that they enjoyed a satisfactory balance between privacy and companionship.

However, deaf people drew distinctions between their satisfaction with their present living space about which they had realistic expectations, and their personal happiness in their current 'home'. As a consequence happiness 'at home', whatever the setting, was less prevalent than satisfaction with current living arrangements. Rather less than three-quarters claimed to be happy at home, and again, there were substantial variations between the residents of the different settings. Unhappiness was negligible among those living in private households, hostels and homes for the deaf, but it was found among as many as half of the hospital patients.

Yet while satisfaction with living space and happiness at home was highest among those living in non-therapeutic settings, they were most likely to wish to live elsewhere. It seems likely that hospital patients, of whom only a seventh could think of somewhere they would prefer to be, were less in touch with the world beyond the institution than any other group, and therefore made comparisons less easily and were less aware of alternatives. Perhaps the paradox of deaf people who were satisfied with their living space and happy in their present home, who, nevertheless would have liked to live elsewhere is to be explained in terms of 'realistic' expectations. Most deaf people considered that there was little prospect of any change in their living situation.

7 Family, friends and neighbourhood

Much of the literature on life in institutions has explored the lack of its normality only implicitly with reference to what happens in private households. While much of the literature has concentrated on the loss of autonomy, particularly in the use of living space, another concern has been the degree to which residents of institutions are prevented by their setting from making links with the 'normal' community, and it is with this dimension of 'normality' that the present chapter is concerned.

The 'normal' community usually has been held to include relatives, friends, and other components of the 'informal' network. Comparisons in the anti-institutional literature between the isolation from friends, relatives and neighbours of those living in institutions and the normal networks of those living in private households have tended to be implicit rather than explicit. Townsend's work is unusual in that his institutional studies make direct reference to his work on elderly people living in private households. Indeed, it was because the focus of his early work was the *family* life of old people that Townsend initially conceived of normality as the three generational family, in which care relationships between the generations were cemented by reciprocity. At the outset, then, for Townsend, the centre of life from which individuals might be removed by age, infirmity or other cause, was essentially family life, and an independence within it guaranteed by reciprocity. While the early studies indicated reciprocity between the generations among females, largely to the exclusion of males, no such distinctions were applied in the later institutional work. And despite evidence that men suffered from a lack of role in retirement because family life revolved around women, the absence of role for *all* residents of institutions was argued to be a criterion by which the departure from 'normal' life was to be measured in institutional settings.

Furthermore, throughout the literature there was a widespread implicit assumption that family care for those who become dependent is 'normal' and therefore superior to any other, and that provided by neighbourhood and friends is a further dimension of 'informal' family care. The normality of informal systems of care – primarily family provision, but including that of neighbours and friends – was established in a series of studies of dependent people living in their own households; statutory services were overwhelmingly identified as operating mainly where the informal network was not available. The tensions created by dependency within the family were explored largely in terms of the failure of statutory services to offer the flexibility, amount, and type of supplementary care required. There was a widely shared assumption that with sufficient help of the right type and at the correct time, dependency would cease to create additional tensions within families. And the disadvantage of home care for those who lived alone, such as isolation, could be overcome by judicious statutory intervention.[1] No client groups were excluded from such assumptions – not even those, such as certain categories of mentally ill persons, identified by some researchers as becoming dependent *because* of the way in which family relationships operated.

Within the anti-institutional literature, a variety of themes emerge to indicate the means by which all dependent people are to achieve normality. For Townsend, nothing less than the total reorganization of society will suffice: in addition to the family, the broader network of neighbours should be mobilized and trained by professionals. The redistribution of power and resources involved was an expression of Townsend's socialism, egalitarianism being achieved by the return of dependent people to 'the centre of life'.[2] Recently Hadley and Hatch[3] have argued the case for a return to voluntaryism because they consider that the welfare state has failed to deliver through statutory agencies appropriate services to enable dependent people to remain in their own homes. They urge that 'community resources' should be exploited, and that informal networks should be organized and developed. Here it is the normality of the informal network of care which is stressed. In contrast, Dartington, Miller and Gwynne,[4] while arguing for a redistribution of power in favour of the dependent, without which they consider a normal life cannot be achieved, have perceived the change required in service provision in terms of the power of dependent people to command the help they require to lead a normal life.

In the Townsend studies, conflicts of interest between the dependent and able-bodied are alluded to but not explored: it is assumed that the political will exists, or will exist, for the reformation of society to ensure normality for the dependent. Dartington, Miller and Gwynne explore the conflicts of interest between the dependent and non-dependent but fail to identify the mechanism by which power will be redistributed to the dependent, except in terms of 'disabled power'. However, the anti-welfare arguments of Hadley and Hatch have much in common with those who seek to minimize state intervention in the interests of self-sufficiency, independence and economy. For them, the development of informal networks is crucial to the reduction in formal provision which is required for three reasons: first, that the family should not shirk its traditional caring role; second, that the cheap alternative of family and neighbourhood care should replace expensive institutional and, where possible, statutory domiciliary care; and finally, that the current open-ended demand for care services should be brought to a halt before dependency arising from demographic changes becomes overwhelming.

In recent years, practical expression has been given to a combination of the Hadley and Hatch and the self-sufficiency approaches to care most systematically in the Kent experiments. With the primary objective of economy and the secondary aim of avoiding the possibility of institutionalization, care by 'ordinary' members of the community has been encouraged as a major method of intervention: in some cases training is provided for and payment made to volunteers organized by professional social workers. The permitted cost of the system, though substantial, has to be less than a specified proportion of the cost of an institutional place.[5] It is important to recognize that the driving force of such schemes is neither egalitarianism, nor the pursuit of normality or integration. The volunteers supplement the more rigid statutorily provided services. Dependence, unmitigated by reciprocity, remains the central feature of the system for those cared for, and although flexibility is the aim there is no intention of restoring to those cared for the capacity to engage in all normal activities of daily life. In this sense, the scheme differs substantially from some pilot experiments in the care of severely disabled younger people which involve at least one-to-one care by volunteers, who often receive board and lodging in return, and who are entirely under the instruction of the disabled person to ensure his or her engagement in 'normal' activities. In some experiments, professional help, from social workers and nurses for example, is deliberately excluded: the disabled are considered to be professionals in their knowledge of their own needs and how they should be met. Here, normality is defined in terms of activities engaged in: reciprocity is deliberately denied. Small-scale experiments in such care systems are being mounted in both residential settings and private households, and economy is not a major consideration.

Such schemes raise questions about the nature of normality. Little has been said about the legitimate interests of the full range of carers, from professionals to volunteers, paid and unpaid, as well as families. The differential costs of the various care systems to particular groups of carers have rarely been explored. It has been usual for patterns of care to be discussed in terms of either the interests of those who are dependent, and/or the interests of the community which are defined narrowly in terms of the financial cost to the public purse.

There has been little dissent to date from the view that neighbourhood resources exist and may be exploited to reduce the burden of the costs of institutional care. Abrams is unusual in having argued that the informal networks of close-knit working-class neighbourhoods, which provide the pattern for the ideal to which so many wish to return, was a response to conditions which are vanishing and which few would wish to revive.[6]

It was partly in pursuit of normality defined in terms of contact with the informal neighbourhood network that RNID justified its decision in 1975 to begin to phase out its homes for the deaf. The advantages of care for the deaf in local authority homes for the handicapped which were advanced to directors of social services were focused on the failure of specialist homes, because they were few in number and therefore housed deaf people away from their own locality, to promote ties with the informal network of family and friends. But the change in policy was in no sense based upon a rejection of institutional care as such. RNID acknowledged that deaf people would continue to be 'placed' in residential care, but applied the notions of 'normality' and 'integration' developed in the anti-institutional literature to the advantage of general, as opposed to its own specialist residential provision:

. . . it would be a more natural community if the majority were hearing, and helped deaf people to feel that they were continuing to belong to the community as a whole. . . The fact that they would be among hearing people would mean that they would see, and often take part in, a wider range of activities than they would in an isolated unit.[7]

Thus, the normality sought by the Institute for its deaf residents was limited to the balance between hearing and deaf within institutions. Yet the pursuit of 'normality' in these terms, despite its justification theoretically in the anti-institution literature is open to challenge when applied to those with communication difficulties, particularly the deaf. Recent research has raised questions about the nature of community, integration and normality in the context of severe communication handicap. In the field of deaf studies, there is a growing awareness that the generalizations derived from the anti-institutional studies may require substantial modification in the case of specific types of dependency. It is by no means clear that assumptions about the superiority of informal networks of family and neighbours because they are normal, necessarily apply to the case of the deaf.

All the evidence supports the assertion that

the most striking feature in any description of deaf persons is the insoluble dilemma that they are forced to live in a hearing world where the major part of the cognitive communication takes place orally.[8]

However, it is becoming apparent that many deaf people solve the dilemma by becoming part of a separate deaf society which some now argue constitutes a deaf subculture within the general society of the hearing.[9] That it is a solution to the dilemma which is actively *sought* by deaf people has been emphasized by Higgins who has argued that membership of a deaf community is not an ascribed status, but has to be achieved through explicit identification with the deaf world, shared experiences which are the result of hearing impairment, and participation in the deaf community's activities.[10]

A separate community of the deaf?

In recent studies, systematic attempts have been made to identify a separate community and culture for the deaf. Whereas Schlessinger and Meadow[11] specified that the deaf community is defined essentially by language, Padden and Markowicz argued more broadly that the deaf community is 'an ethnic group with its own language and culture',[12] and sought to establish the existence of characteristics identified by Barth[13] as being essential for an ethnic group – that members identify themselves and are identified by others as members of the group, that members share the physical and cultural characteristics 'considered significant by members and outsiders'[14] which often include 'language. . .general style of life, and basic value orientation'.[15] While Padden and Markowicz agree that 'language acts as a powerful cohesive force for the deaf community',[16] they observed the interaction of oral and manual deaf students at Gallaudet College, and established that oral deaf students encountered differences not only of language but also of behaviour.[17] They found, too, that distinctions were made between members and non-members of the deaf community in terms of linguistic and social behaviour.[18] And part of the linguistic behaviour to be learnt was the *appropriate* use of sign.[19] The cultural separation of the deaf community from that of the general hearing society was exemplified by the role of oral deaf students as cultural brokers.[20]

How far did deaf people perceive themselves as different from members of the normal community? And how far did they identify with a specifically deaf community rather than with the predominantly hearing 'normal' community? What effect did communication difficulties, including reliance on BSL, have on contact with the 'normal' hearing community of relatives, friends and neighbourhood, and how did that pattern of interaction vary between those living in the different settings?

Recently, it has become clear that substantial numbers of the general public regard the deaf as constituting a definite group identified by characteristics other than hearing impairment, such as below average intelligence, more than the average number of other physical complaints, and odd behaviour, which set them apart from the normal community.[21] Although there is a widespread recognition of the deaf as a separate group within the community,[22] there is little appreciation of the degree to which they are isolated from the general community by communication difficulties. The majority of the general public over-estimate the abilities of the totally deaf to overcome communication difficulties, and assume an unimpaired capacity to acquire information.[23] Thus most people are curiously ambivalent about the status of deaf people within society: while the deaf are considered to be different from the rest of the community, there is great reluctance to concede that such differences may create barriers to their integration into society at large.

Yet difficulties of communication made it impossible for a third of deaf people (mainly hospital patients) even to comprehend the question of differences between their lives and those of the hearing. For a few, a failure of communication was not the only barrier to response: there were deaf people who had lived in hospitals for so long and without a systematic communication system that the question had no meaning for them. That there was no difference between their own lives and those of the hearing was held by only a small minority (9 per cent) of the deaf, mainly younger people and those with good lip-reading skills.

Miss Northiam, who lived at home with her parents, three brothers and three sisters, said 'I find there's no problem. I watch TV, go to the cinema, I can lip-read.'

Disproportionately, such people lived in the hostel for the young working deaf. It may be that because of the overtly integrationist policy of the hostel they wished to stress their normality, or perhaps the hostel's protective environment shielded them from some of the harsher experiences to which those living in their own homes had been exposed.

However, most (56 per cent) considered that their lives were different from those of hearing people, though some deaf people found it difficult to identify the nature of the difference.

Miss Ray, aged 41, who lived with her sister, said, 'There is a difference in that I can't hear – but I can't tell the level of impact this makes.'

Many encapsulated the nature of the difference in the phrase 'It's hard being deaf, it's difficult to understand.' Others itemised specific activities with which they had difficulty. The technical gadgetry which requires audiological perception and which has become central to daily life, was often invoked.

Mrs Gray, aged 68, who lived with her deaf 89-year old husband, said: 'You're used to being deaf all your life but I get embarrassed at hearing functions. Then there's the telephone, the TV, the record player, the news flash. I sometimes get irritated about not hearing.'

More often, deaf people expressed their differences with the hearing community in terms of being shut out of the larger society by the hearing majority.

Mrs Rostow, aged 43, who lived with her deaf husband and four hearing children, said 'The hearing avoid us. They like their music and talk with the hearing all the time and forget us.'

And the exclusion of the deaf by the hearing operated both at the level of social interchange and at that of finding out about the dominant hearing society.

Mr Frome, aged 60, who lived in the half-way psychiatric hostel, explained 'It's difficult to get information about different things. People don't say what this is for, why things are this way and not that.'

However, most deaf people agreed that despite the difficulties, they managed to copy the way of life of the hearing community, in certain essentials.

Mrs Frame, who lived with her deaf husband and brother, said 'I find it very difficult to understand the world of politics, which some deaf people understand very well. I try, try. But we manage the important things – a roof overhead, enough food.'

Mr Hunsworth, aged 50, who lived with his deaf wife, his mother, and two young children, said 'Some things are difficult – specific things – but our life-style is very similar, nearly the same.'

Others regarded outward appearance of similarity in the life-styles of the deaf and hearing as deceptive.

Miss Ray, aged 41, who lived with her deaf sister, said 'I seem to feel very withdrawn from society, as though I was living on the edge of a circle.'

Sometimes the feeling of separation and lack of involvement was expressed in a concrete way.

Miss Jenkins, aged 73, who lived with her hard-of-hearing sister, said 'If I had been hearing, I would have used more initiative – got involved, got married. My sister says her friends feel very awkward with me. I don't like to keep asking them to repeat, so I nod and smile, and pretend to understand.'

And it is true that most hearing people have been shown to conform to the misinformed and unhelpful stereotype reported by deaf people: most members of the general public would shout, talk loudly or raise their voices when talking to the hearing impaired. Yet some have shown an appreciation of the communication problems which beset the deaf, and a capacity to respond appropriately. Thus, more than a quarter of the general public would enunciate their words with greater care when conversing with the deaf, while as many as two-fifths would make sure they were facing the deaf person.[24]

However, apart from the fact that only a minority are disposed to be helpful, there is nothing to indicate a willingness to *persist* in the attempt to communicate, still less to sustain a relationship. And it is this uncertainty of response and ambiguity of attitude among the hearing which doubtless explains the uncertainty which many of the deaf felt regarding them. In all settings there were those whose experience of the hearing community's response to deafness ranged from interest, sympathy or help on the one hand, to embarrassment, lack of interest, and flight on the other. Indeed, it was striking that almost half the deaf people reported responses by the hearing which were both negative and positive, while the remainder were almost equally divided between those who reported solely positive and solely negative responses. In general, deaf people living in private households tended to experience rather less negative reaction than was true of those living in the homes for the deaf and the elderly, and hospital patients. Why this should be so is unclear. Perhaps the retreat of hospital patients and the residents of homes to institutional settings was in part at least determined by their greater vulnerability to insensitive responses or their greater incapacity for coping with the hearing world.

Whatever the reactions of the hearing in general, deaf people encountered far less ambiguity among their immediate circle of hearing relatives and friends. As many as half found the people around them generally patient, understanding and sympathetic compared with only 15 per cent who experienced impatience, lack of understanding or consideration. The remainder (about one-third) considered that those around them were as likely to be sympathetic as to fail to understand deafness. Again, it was among hostel residents that the most positive reaction was expected from their immediate circle. Thus, while there appeared to be a marked tendency to regard the hearing world as separate from that of the deaf community both in terms of differences between the lives of the two groups as well as the expected negative reaction of hearing people to deafness, the division between the two communities was modified to some extent by the sympathy which was widely experienced by deaf people from those among whom they lived.

Childhood

Family relationships and friends, then, were important not only in interpreting the wider community of the hearing to deaf people, but also in providing them with a framework within which responses to deafness were both predictable and more positive than in the hearing community at large. What range of family members did deaf people have to call on to perform these two important functions? In fact, the majority had at least one sibling: only 17 per cent were only children. Indeed, more than a third came from large families of four or more children.

Thus, most deaf people shared family life with at least one brother or sister who might be expected to interpret the hearing world to them. But it was by no means the case that such interpretation ensured that deaf people were satisfactorily integrated into family life. As many as a third reported that their deafness was a substantial problem when they were young, especially when playing with other children, including brothers and sisters. Almost a fifth had been brought up in households in which there was at least one other member of the immediate family – a parent or sibling – who was deaf, but this was no guarantee that there would be greater understanding of the deaf child's problem. Indeed, problems were as prevalent in such families as among those who were brought up in entirely hearing households. Those below the age of 40 were marginally less likely than older people to have experienced considerable problems through childhood deafness. Perhaps the slightly happier childhood experiences of the younger deaf could be attributed to the greater ease and earlier diagnosis of hearing impairment which has become possible in the last forty years, as well as the development of specialist services for and understanding of the deaf.

The nature of the problem for those who experienced difficulties in childhood was primarily one of being excluded from all the complicated interchanges of family life – a difficulty that was overcome only on entry to the deaf community.

Miss Gregson, aged 76, lived in a home for the deaf but had been a member of a hearing family of six children. Despite plenty of childhood company, she found little pleasure in it: 'I always felt left out when I was young.'

Often there was little interchange with other children even where there was a large number of siblings.

Miss Jackson, aged 74, had been lonely despite having four brothers: 'I used to get very upset. It was all talk, talk. I couldn't understand the conversation.'

And some deaf people appear to have been excluded in childhood from certain family activities.

Miss Elton, aged 75, now a resident in a home for the deaf, had been brought up in a hearing household with her three brothers: 'I was very shy when I was young. I got on best with my older brother. When I was little I never went on holiday with my mother and father. I spent the school holidays at home – for much of the time I collected firewood and broke it up. I never went shopping with my mother – I always stayed at home to watch my youngest brother.'

Few of those who lived in hearing households enjoyed the company of relatives who could sign, and as a consequence communication was only achieved laboriously.

Mr Owen, aged 60, now lived alone, but had been brought up with three sisters and a brother: 'It was very difficult when I was young. I could only communicate with my sisters by writing.'

Miss Ayers, aged 35, who lived in the half-way psychiatric hostel, said: 'My mother signs a little bit, but my father doesn't know any signs, and nor do my brother and sister. I find I can talk a little bit to my mother.'

As a consequence many deaf people felt that they had failed to achieve any real understanding of their immediate family.

Mrs Salisbury, a widow of 88, who was a patient in a hospital for the mentally ill: 'I had two brothers and a sister. But I didn't really get to know them or my parents.'

Where other members of the family were handicapped, the communication problem could be acute.

Miss Franks, aged 88, who was a resident in a home for the deaf, had been brought up in a hearing household with two sisters and a brother who was blind. 'As my brother was blind and I had poor speech because of my deafness we found it difficult to understand each other.'

The failure to communicate tended to mark deaf people off from others in childhood. And because they were marked out as being different many reported that they were tormented by other children.

Mr Brown, aged 52, who lived with his wife, and who had been brought up in a hearing household with two brothers and a sister, said 'My mother and father neglected me because I was deaf. And all the children teased me – they called me "deafie". And because I couldn't play because I couldn't talk, they thought I was snooty.'

Where relationships were congenial there was little incentive for some deaf people to stray beyond the family circle in childhood, especially when other members of the household were deaf as well.

Miss McClean, aged 58, lived in a home for the deaf: 'There were five of us – two boys and three girls – and we were all deaf. I never had any friends except my brothers.'

The presence of other deaf children in the neighbourhood similarly restricted the circle of childhood friends.

Miss Grimsby, aged 49, who lived in the hostel for the young working deaf, said 'My parents and my brother were hearing. But I had deaf friends living near, so I did not play much with hearing children. I suppose I was very protected.'

Mixing with hearing children outside the family circle could be daunting.

Miss Ray, aged 41, now lived with her deaf sister, but she had been brought up with three brothers and two other sisters, all of whom were hearing: 'I mostly played with my deaf sister. But my other sisters sign. So I played with all my brothers and sisters and the hearing children who came in to play with them. I used to get frightened and cry when I was little because the other children could hear with my brothers and sisters, and I got very upset.'

Fear in childhood arising from a failure to understand spoken communication between hearing children or loud shouting – the traditional mode of communication with the deaf – was common.

The misunderstanding and the isolation which many experienced in childhood frequently resulted in the development of a self-sufficient attitude to life.

Miss Watson, aged 84, who now lived alone, had been brought up with her brother, by her hearing father and deaf mother, who failed to understand her predicament: 'I attended a hearing school, so I got slapped a lot because it was thought I was being naughty when I didn't hear. Being deaf you are thrown on yourself. Even church is little help – I heard nothing there. You have to think for yourself and always make your own decisions. As a little girl they (the family) always said of me that there must be good blood at the bottom. No-one will ever know what it is to be deaf. It's surprising how I haven't got worse (nastier) than I am.'

Self-sufficiency was often accompanied in later life by a rejection of the hearing community.

Mr Rostow, aged 42, who now lived with his deaf wife and four hearing children, had been the only child of deaf parents: 'There were awful problems when I was young. In the end I turned away from hearing people to deaf friends. Even in the supposedly mixed club I belong to, the hearing are used to the deaf. They sign a bit and then run away and forget us, and speak, speak with the hearing. I continue to feel the same problems of isolation and frustration that I did when I was a kid.'

The sense of isolation was often profoundly and most poignantly evident in relation to close and loved members of the family.

Miss Rowlands, aged 62, who now lived in a home for the deaf, had been brought up with her brother in a hearing household: 'I'm very fond of my mother and father, and of my brother. But they have never understood me – they don't understand about deafness.'

The routine use of special educational provision sometimes reinforced feelings of rejection by and isolation from the family. Some deaf people blamed their early removal to a school for the deaf on the failure of their parents to comprehend the nature of deafness and deal with the problems to which it gave rise.

Miss Probert, aged 35, who now lived in the half-way psychiatric hostel, but who had been brought up in a hearing household with four brothers, said: 'My deafness caused such problems that I was sent away by my parents to school.'

Sometimes, rejection was associated with hospitalization, while other families devised their own internal strategies for expressing rejection.

Mr Johnson, who lived in a home for the deaf, recounted, at the age of 88, 'It was regarded as a dreadful thing. My father was a vicar on the Isle of Blank. I was kept out of normal society, while my brother grew up and went to live on the mainland, got married and so on.'

Far from being rejected, however, others suffered from overprotection.

Mrs Owen, a widow of 54 years, who now lived in a home for the elderly, said 'There were seven of us children altogether, and none of the others was deaf. There were awful problems because I was very spoiled. One brother was marvellous – he was my ears. But another brother was furiously jealous.'

For the majority (three-fifths) however deafness presented few difficulties in childhood.

Mr Nelson, aged 16, who lived with his parents and older sister, said 'I enjoyed mixing with children who could hear.'

Mrs Fulton, a 56-year old widow who now lived on her own, had been brought up as one of six children in a hearing household: 'Mum was very strict but she never raised a hand to any of us. We had a good family life. I was a bit of a tomboy.'

A few mentioned minor modifications to the communication system for playing with hearing chilren.

Mrs Brown, aged 52, who now lived with her husband, had been brought up with her brother in a hearing household. 'I didn't find any difficulty when I was young. I played with hearing children. Deaf children enjoyed frightening other children with their signs. The only difference for me was that the other children had to tap me on the shoulder sometimes.'

Others found that the intensity of play was such that little verbal communication was required. Sometimes integration with a hearing network of friends was achieved largely through the influence of hearing siblings.

Mrs Hunsworth, aged 43, who lived with her husband, two children and her mother-in-law, had been brought up in a hearing household with her sister and brother: 'I didn't find there were any difficulties. I went around with my sister all the time and played with her and her friends. It was fine.'

And a robust attitude could prevent difficulties materializing, especially with regard to taunting by other children.

Mrs Osborne, a 66-year old widow, who now lived with her daughter, but who had been brought up with two brothers and a sister in a hearing household, said 'I didn't have any real difficulties when I was young. When other children took the mickey, I stuck up for myself.'

To a substantial degree, however, integration into family and neighbourhood life was achieved largely through the development of a satisfactory system of communication. In some cases this depended entirely on the efforts of the deaf child.

Miss Northiam, a 19-year old, lived with her parents, three brothers and three sisters in a hearing household, said 'I lip-read well, so I understand my mother and father, and I was always able to play with my sister.'

But there were occasions on which hearing relatives made an effort to learn a mode of communication suitable for the deaf child.

Miss Spring, aged 59, now resident in a home for the deaf, had been brought up in a hearing household with her three brothers and a sister: 'I didn't have any problems as a child. My sister can sign and finger-spell. We were a happy family. We all tried to communicate.'

Others had found it an advantage to be brought up in a household containing at least one other deaf person.

Miss Patison, aged 23, who lived with her parents and a brother, said 'There were six of us children and the last three – myself and two of my brothers – were deaf. But I didn't have any problems. I find the hearing OK after they explain a bit and I get used to it. The others in the family – the hearing ones – don't sign, but they understand very well. My brothers who are deaf lip-read well. But my father is the hardest – he doesn't communicate very well with the deaf in the family. My mother is OK, though.'

Mrs Faulkner, an 88-year-old widow who was now a resident in a home for the deaf, said 'There were four of us – two boys and two girls. My mother was deaf. I really had no problems. Mother was always at home, and my sister and two brothers could sign. It was a happy childhood.'

Perhaps not surprisingly, the effort required of a deaf child to build up a friendship system was considerable, and, once that system was lost, it was difficult to re-establish.

Miss Grimsby, aged 49, who lived in the hostel for the young working deaf, explained; 'There were nine of us children altogether, and I was the only one who was deaf. I had no difficulties at all in early childhood. I had plenty of hearing friends. It was OK until we moved, and then I lost my friends, and I didn't have many after that.'

Friendly networks which were developed at school continued to be used in later life as an aid for withstanding the pressures and avoiding the difficulties resulting from deafness. A number of deaf people spoke of the reliance they placed on their network of school friends: although they wished to shrug off the protectiveness of parents, many nevertheless needed a source of advice on such subjects as changing jobs, setting up in business, the best time to start a family, and the way to ensure that buying a home or a car was a sound investment. Apart from the school network, some hard-of-hearing and hearing peers as well as siblings were much in demand as informal counsellors and as sources of new ideas.

Getting married

It might be expected that the difficulties experienced in childhood by a substantial minority of deaf people in establishing for themselves a place in the hearing community might cut them off from the adult hearing community. How far did deaf people enter the adult hearing community by adopting its norms? For instance, to what degree did deaf people enter upon marriage and establish families of their own? In fact, a substantial minority (36 per cent) of them were or had been married. However, only a fifth were currently married, while as many as a tenth were widowed and a tiny minority were separated or divorced – 3 per cent and 4 per cent respectively. Marriage was most common among those living in private households, where only a little more than a third had remained single, and among residents of homes for the elderly. In contrast, as many as three-quarters of the hostel residents and four-fifths of those living in the homes for the deaf had remained single, while only one hospital patient had had experience of married life. Perhaps it was their normality in this respect which determined the entry of residents of homes for the elderly into the type of residential care traditionally available to members of the hearing community in old age.

However, to adopt the norms of the hearing community was not necessarily to establish close relationships with hearing people. Indeed, as many as three-quarters of the marriages were between deaf people. Yet there was no indication that marriages with the hearing were less successful than those with the deaf. Most marriages had lasted for many years and gave every appearance of producing tranquillity and satisfaction. Indeed, a few of those who were widowed early in life were sufficiently encouraged by the first experience to embark upon a second marriage. In most cases, marriage to a hearing person was found to be stimulating to the deaf partner.

Mrs Finniston, aged 56, who now lived alone, said 'My husband died sixteen years ago. My husband was a good man. He helped me get the right words.'

Mr Patel, aged 52, who lived with his hearing wife and three sons in London, said 'Since we got married I keep talking all the time.'

But marriage to a deaf person was equally likely to produce companionship and comfort. For example:

Mrs Johnson, aged 61, who lived with her deaf husband and her half-brother, said 'I married three years ago when my mother died. I found he was good company so decided to get married. We were married at the Register Office. My husband is deaf and so is some of his family – they came too. Mr Swinton, the social worker, interpreted for us during the ceremony.'

It was clear, however, that some relationships whether with deaf or hearing people were stormy, and were of short duration. But not everyone who found their first attempt at married life unsuccessful lost hope in establishing a more permanent and satisfactory marital relationship: half of those who were divorced or separated had decided to try again. There was little evidence that, having failed with a deaf marriage partner, there was any tendency for a hearing alternative to be sought. Indeed, little attempt was made to ascribe the difficulties of married life to loss of hearing as such. However, despite the evidence of successful marriages with hearing people, a small minority of failures were attributed to the fact that the spouse could hear.

Mr Thornton, aged 38, who lived in the hostel for the young working deaf, said 'I divorced my wife two months ago. She was hearing. My friends are mainly deaf now because I find it easier with the deaf: it's too difficult to talk to the hearing.'

Yet single people were in the majority. How far was this because deafness restricted the range of friendships from which marriage might arise? In fact, as many as 90 per cent of the single claimed to have friends of the opposite sex, but deaf people differed in this respect according to settings. Whereas all single people in private households, homes for the elderly and hostels had such friends, this was true of only two-fifths of those living in homes for the deaf, half of the patients in psychiatric hospitals, and a tenth of the deaf in hospitals for the mentally handicapped. Thus, in settings where there were disproportionately high numbers of single people, deaf people were least likely to have friends from whom a marriage partner might be chosen. To a considerable extent, however, the pattern of friendship reflected the practice of, rather than integration into the 'normal' hearing community. As many as half the single people found their friends solely in the deaf community. Only 15 per cent sought to integrate into the wider hearing community by choosing their friends only from among the hearing. Occasionally there was no choice.

Miss Hughes, aged 57, who lived on the Isle of Blank, said 'There are no deaf men on the island though there are lots on the mainland. So I've got a hearing boy friend.'

But most of those who sought friendship only among the hearing did so in a determined and deliberate effort to achieve integration into the larger hearing community. This determination was most marked among the most 'normal' – those who lived in their own homes, among whom as many as a quarter had only hearing friends. In contrast, none of the hostel residents, who in other respects most closely resembled deaf people living in private households, sought to confine their friendships to members of the hearing community. Even among those living in private households, a quarter restricted their friendships to the deaf community. Elsewhere this was true of the majority, except the homes for the deaf. Thus, there was overwhelming identification with the deaf community, rather than the hearing, in all settings except private households and homes for the deaf.

Although only a small minority actively sought to identify with the hearing by excluding themselves entirely from the deaf community, a more substantial minority – a little more than a third of single deaf people – sought friendship in both communities. However, it was once more the case that those who attempted to attain some proximity to 'normality' by engaging with members of the hearing community in social terms rather than merely imitating within the deaf community the practices of the hearing came disproportionately from those living in private households. As many as half of the people living in private households had both hearing and deaf friends, but this was true of only a little less than a fifth of hostel residents and few of those living in other settings.

A restricted range of friends from which a marriage partner might be drawn was not necessarily the cause of a failure to marry. Almost a tenth of those who remained single reported that they had deliberately decided against marriage, usually because deafness seemed to impose a tremendous barrier to success. Such decisions were often taken reluctantly. Others were critical of the emphasis placed on the institution of marriage, partly because it posed problems for the deaf and thereby presented a barrier to their entry into normal society, and partly because they questioned the heedlessness with which so many people appeared to enter into matrimony.

Miss Watson, aged 84, lived alone, but enjoyed the company of both deaf and hearing friends: 'I never felt I wanted to marry, perhaps because of deafness. It would be better if people weren't so fascinated by the idea of marriage, as a sort of fairy tale. They'd be much better suited later. Some people are for marrying, some not. My friends told me I could have Bert, but I wouldn't let him have me!'

Among the tiny minority of single people who had decided that they were 'not for marrying' were a few who found it difficult to cope with members of the opposite sex whether deaf or hearing.

Mr Brown, aged 45, who lived in a home for the deaf and had no friends, said 'I didn't like the ladies much – they embarrassed me.'
74-year-old Miss Griffin, who lived in a home for the deaf said 'I never courted. Men made me feel upset.'

Others considered that, despite having suitable friendships, they did not earn enough to marry and establish a family, or they were too busy working to bother. Only a few blamed and resented the restricted nature of their circle of friends for their failure to marry.

Not all single people ruled out the possibility of marriage. A small minority – 7 per cent – were planning to marry or establish a marital-type relationship in the near future, in most cases with another deaf person.

Mr Morton, aged 22, lived in the half-way psychiatric hostel and restricted his friendship to members of the deaf community: 'There's a deaf girl friend. If I go to London I will live with my mother. My girl friend will come and eventually we will move out.'

However, there were exceptions who saw advantages in having a hearing spouse.

Mr Taunton, aged 46, who lived in the hostel for the young working deaf, said: 'I've got lots of deaf and hearing friends. I think it's better to have a hearing girl like you who can sign. Then there can be talk with the deaf and the hearing, and the telephone. There are no deaf women in Blankwich. My present girl friend is hearing. We will get married next year.'

Having children

Most marriages had been embarked upon with every expectation of raising a family. Only three couples had consciously decided not to have children. Yet a third of marriages were childless, and only two of the women concerned regretted not having a family.

Thus, the majority (two-thirds) of those who had been married, had succeeded in establishing families of their own, though it is true that a substantial minority (one-third) had sought to minimize their difficulties by having only one child. However, the majority, in their pursuit of normality, had sought no such concessions in the face of the difficulties involved in rearing a family in the hearing world, which most had anticipated to some degree. Indeed, a little more than a quarter of parents were so confident that they had three or four children. Whereas only a fifth of hostel residents and only one hospital patient had established a family of their own, half of those in private households had reinforced their normality by doing so.

The age range of deaf people was such that those with independent children were in the majority, though a little more than two-fifths had dependent children, and in all but two of these cases there were children under the age of 10 years. Not surprisingly, then, in most cases (three-fifths) deaf parents no longer lived with their children and it was understandable that those who did so lived in private households. But not all children separated from deaf parents were mature and seeking to establish an independent life. As many as a third of those with children under the age of 10 years had had them placed with adoptive parents, taken into care, or cared for by separated wives. The role of hearing impairment in splitting families in this way was unclear. Some parents were unwilling to talk about their absent children.

Mr Timpson, aged 58, who now lived with a deaf woman, said 'I separated from my wife three years ago. She was deaf, too. The child has been in care since she was 18 months old when my wife went into hospital with mental trouble. I have no regrets about the adoption. But it's best to forget it now.'

Others recalled the step with deep regret.

Mrs Court, aged 37, lived in the half-way psychiatric hostel: 'I left my boy-friend – he was hearing. I had my daughter adopted – she will be nine now. She is hearing. I'm very fond of babies.'

It seemed that deafness together with the absence of a stable partner rendered the problems of child-rearing overwhelmingly difficult.

Miss Robertson, aged 25, said 'I have never been married, though I have had both deaf and hearing boy friends. I've got two little girls. I haven't seen the first for six years. She's been adopted. The second daughter is in a home. I don't go to see her at all. I was very depressed having the second child. I couldn't cope with caring for the child. I last saw the first girl when she was nine months old, and haven't seen the second since she was six weeks old.'

However, the cases in which the difficulties involved in achieving normality by establishing a family became overwhelming constituted only a minority – about a seventh in all. But such parents experienced child-rearing problems at their most extreme. How widespread were difficulties at a less intense level? In fact, only an eighth of parents claimed that their deafness had caused no problems in child-rearing. In most cases, the absence of difficulties was attributed to the presence of a hearing parent or grandparent.

Mrs Rostow, aged 43, who lived with her deaf husband and four children, said 'My mother and father helped when they were little. It was easy really. If they were awake or sick we watched all the time. If they were asleep, I got on with the housework – no problem. Now they explain the television to their mother and father. The first boy started to sign at 9 months old. We sent him to a nursery from the age of $2\frac{1}{2}$ years. My parents visited frequently, and the children realized the difference between hearing and deaf. My parents don't sign, only lip-read, and they speak clearly to the children.'

Mrs Jackson, aged 55, who lived with her deaf husband, said 'I've got the one married son. There were no problems because we all lived together in this house with grandmother and grandfather who were both hearing. Now Gran has died and Grandfather is 82. He's out tonight with his sister who lives in Southend. My son signs very well – he picked it up easy, especially finger-spelling.'

However, in some instances deaf parents may have underestimated the difficulties involved in bringing up their children.

Mrs Hunsworth, said 'There was no difficulty in bringing up the children.'
But her daughter said: 'On the contrary, we had to shoulder responsibility earlier than other children.'

Mrs Fixton, aged 62, said 'My two were born clever girls. We were a perfectly happy family. Whenever school became difficult, the teachers were very good.'
But the eldest daughter said: 'My sister suffered badly with nerves because of my (deaf) father's harsh treatment. Neither of us liked my father until we were grown up.'

The child-rearing difficulties (experienced by two-fifths of deaf parents) were primarily associated with problems of communication. The most common difficulty (admitted by two-fifths of deaf parents) being their inability to help their children at school. Those with young children, who considered that they were managing well at present, anticipated difficulties once the children started school.

Another effect of parental deafness which was commonly perceived to have an impact on childhood (by as many as a fifth of parents) was that children were forced to undertake responsibilities earlier than other children, partly because deaf parents were less able to provide support than their hearing counterparts and partly because children soon became interpreters between their parents and the hearing community.

Mrs Brown, aged 57, lived with her deaf husband: 'My daughter is grown up and married now. Even when she was very little she acted as interpreter for her father and myself. There were no real difficulties. If there were problems at school, my husband and I would go to see the teachers and we helped her with reading, writing and so on.'

About a seventh of parents reported a wide range of other child-rearing difficulties most of which arose indirectly from communication problems such as those associated with low income resulting from restricted job opportunities, or reluctance to stray beyond the customary environment.

Miss Rose, aged 36, who lived with her two dependent children, a boy and a girl: 'They don't communicate with me. I have had trouble with my daughter and men; she takes money from strangers, plays truant, smokes. I'm frightened that she steals – I'm worried about my own reputation. A teacher came to see me, she said that my daughter plays too much at school, she has the wrong friends. When they were little I didn't know where to take them, and I couldn't afford much for them anyway.'

Did communication difficulties jeopardize the chances of deaf parents achieving the degree of understanding of their children customary among hearing parents? Only a sixth considered that they had failed in this respect.

Mrs Fixton remained puzzled by the attitudes of her youngest daughter, who had suffered from the harsh treatment of Mr Fixton: 'I don't understand my other daughter. When I visited her in Worcester I asked her why she wouldn't marry. Her boy friend had asked her, but she refuses, she says she feels too upset. I asked my other daughter if her sister would ever get better, but she said "No, same, same".'

Those who considered that they had achieved a good understanding of their children sought to substantiate their claim with evidence.

Mr Forster, aged 60, who lived with his deaf wife, said: 'We both feel very close to our son – he's an LEB electrician.'

Mr Rostow said: 'Although they're so young, the children already get help for us – repairs done, and so on. And the children bring in their friends and they seem to relate well to us – there's no problem.'

However some parents interpreted 'understanding' as the immediate comprehension of communication rather than a broad assessment of their relationship with their children and they were concerned to explain precisely how they communicated with their children.

Mr Patel, aged 52, who lived with his hearing wife and three young sons said 'My sons write on my hand or on a newspaper, and my wife uses some signs with her speech.'

Mrs Singh, aged 36, who lived with her hearing husband and two young children, said 'I don't think I have any problems. The children speak to their father in a normal voice, as they do to other children. And they speak to me in sign and particularly clear speech.' Her husband agreed with this assessment.

Some of those with very young children anticipated problems in the future.

Mrs Oxton, aged 29, who lived with her deaf husband and two young children, said 'At the moment we have no problem understanding them and they us, but I think there will be difficulties later.'

29-year-old Mrs Paxton, who lived with her deaf husband and young son said 'Everything is OK at present, but I have my doubts about what it will be like later.'

However most deaf parents were concerned to emphasize the limits of their failure to understand.

Mr Hunsworth, aged 59, who lived with his deaf wife and two of his three children, said 'Music is the only area where we cannot communicate fully – and rhymes and poetry.'

Even though the majority of parents considered that they had encountered few unusual child-rearing problems and that they had achieved a normal understanding of their children, it was nevertheless clear that a majority (two-thirds) thought that, as a result of their deafness, they had missed something of their children's growth process, usually because there were situations in which, not hearing, they felt helpless or in which they were forced into actions which they knew were not 'normal' in the hearing community.

A deaf wife with a hearing husband, Mrs Boseby, said 'They – my sons – spoke mostly to my husband who was hearing. I had to keep repeating myself, though they knew some signs.'

Mr Singh said 'The training and education of the children has been basically her job. But our son – the first child – started speaking like my wife, so I took him to a play-group to meet other (hearing) people. I took him early, so he grew out of it. There was no problem with the girl as my son spoke to her. My wife has great strengths: domestically she is very good and she takes great pride in their appearance.'

Mr Rostow, aged 42, had a deaf wife and they had decided at the outset that their children should be forced into the company of the hearing at an early age: 'It was nursery for them at the age of $2\frac{1}{2}$ and then they went to school. School was the major difference for us from a hearing family. We missed out on a lot of the training for the hearing world.'

Other parents felt a sense of loss arising from their own dependence on their hearing children.

Mrs Oxton said 'My husband is deaf too. I am sure we will never be able to do much for them and we already depend on the eldest for interpretation. My 2 years old son signs already. He can tell me when he's thirsty and so on. And he can tell me when my baby daughter is crying. He is already an interpreter.'

Still other parents considered that they missed much through their own inability to participate effectively in the activities of the 'normal' hearing community. Much disquiet was focused on the education and other social services.

Mr Hunsworth said 'I don't go to parents' evenings at school, and neither does my wife. She is usually working anyway. There are too many people there to expect the teachers to make a special effort to communicate with us. Parents

and teachers cannot get along with the deaf – I and my wife feel embarrassed.
But both girls do very well.' (He proudly showed his second daughter's
reports, which were full of praise.)

Miss Rose said 'I don't know how to get proper medical care for the
children – when to take them to the doctor. And I don't understand the other
services.'

Most of the parents who experienced no sense of having missed anything
in the development of their children stressed the 'normality' of their
children.

Mrs Rostow said 'The children realized very young that we were deaf – they
soon picked up how to get attention, when to be quiet. None of the children
have ever been a problem, though my husband thinks that maybe the boy is
less bright than the girls.'

Mr Exon, aged 62, who lived with his deaf wife and one of his three sons, said
'No, we didn't miss anything in their childhood. There were no problems –
they were always very helpful.'

Others described the communication methods by which they had
avoided missing anything during the childhood of their offspring.

Mr Ross, aged 81, whose deaf wife had died 22 years ago, said 'The children
could sign and finger-spell very well. We didn't rely on the interpreting skills
of the children at all. The two boys always talked to me. From the earliest
years they managed little signs, and then the alphabet.'

One of the prime tasks of parenthood, as part of the socializing process,
is to teach children to speak. Yet most deaf parents experienced profound
communication difficulties, and few of them had easily intelligible voices.
How did they fulfil this function? In a third of the families concerned, the
task was undertaken 'normally' in the sense that a hearing spouse was
present who took the primary responsibility for speech training, though
even in these households, the deaf parent was sometimes involved.

Mr Morris said 'My wife is hearing and she did most to teach them to speak.
But I helped, as I have quite a good voice.' (This was true.)

Where both parents were deaf, the task was sometimes handed over to
other hearing relatives with whom there was close contact. In as many as a
fifth of the families with children, hearing grandparents lived either in the
same household or in an adjacent household and undertook full responsibility for the development of the children's speech.

Mr Hunsworth said 'To start with Grandma helped the children to speak, and
that was a great help. Then the eldest girl helped the second, and the second

girl helped the boy. They've been very close. In addition, we have always talked to the children, and they have learnt a little sign.' (The parents have well pronounced deaf voices.)

But where there were no close hearing relatives living nearby deaf couples had two options open to them – to carry out the task themselves or leave it to the education services. In fact, deaf parents gave up their responsibility to the education authorities only with the greatest reluctance: a little more than a quarter struggled to complete the task unaided.

Mr Oxton, who had a boy and a girl both under the age of 5, said: 'We speak with good lip patterns, and we make a great effort to use voice all the time. We have hearing friends and relatives who look after the children quite a lot – this helps.'

Miss Rose, who did not speak very clearly, said 'I speak to them, but the girls only learned to speak slowly, though the boy has been quicker. Perhaps he learnt from his sister. The girl learnt from me. They did not go to school particularly early.'

Where husband and wife differed in the quality of their speech, inevitably the parent with the best speech skills trained the children to speak.

Mr Jones said 'Mother (his wife) taught our daughter to speak because she speaks well. In fact, our girl picked up speech early. All three of us understand each other well.'

In contrast, only a little less than a fifth of deaf parents left the teaching of speech to the education services.

Mr Rostow said 'We sent the eldest to school early – he learnt there. They all did, though the younger ones learnt from the eldest. The youngest son is very clever.'

Of course, it would be wrong to assume that the effects of deaf parenting are necessarily negative. And indeed, the majority of deaf parents (two-thirds) considered that in some respects their deafness had been beneficial to their children. They reported that their children, by having to come to terms with hearing impairments from the outset, were more understanding, tolerant or helpful than those of hearing parents.

Mrs Paxton said 'Although they are so young I can tell they are more understanding. They already understand deafness. Although my son is only 2 years old, he doesn't shout.'

Mrs Jones said 'I find they are more sensitive, more patient than other children.'

A number of parents considered that the acquisition of sign language by their children was a benefit which could be exercised to the advantage of the broader community.

Mrs Simpson said 'When they were growing up from very small, I was surprised how quickly they learnt sign. Now the eldest daughter signs like a deaf person, and my grandson is the same – he understands all deaf people very well.'

Some considered that the demands of communicating with deaf parents gave children an edge over the others when they first went to school.

Mr Hunsworth said 'Because of the finger-spelling, and having to write so much, they became literate more quickly than other children.'

Adult children of deaf parents

On the whole once they had left home children maintained contact with their parents. Of course, proximity encouraged contact and almost two-thirds of deaf parents had at least one child who lived nearby, within a fifteen minute journey. However, the more 'normal' the living setting, the more likely this was to be true. As many as a quarter of deaf people living in private households had children living nearby, but only an eighth of the residents of hostels and homes for the deaf, and only one of the hospital patients. In general deaf parents maintained frequent contact with their children in the vicinity. Although only a ninth saw a child daily, as many as a half maintained weekly contact and all but a sixth saw at least one child once a month.

In most cases children had been seen recently. As many as two-thirds of parents had been in contact with a child during the previous week, while only a seventh reported that they had not been visited for a month or more. Not only were parents living in private households most likely to have children living nearby, they were also most likely to receive frequent visits from those children and to have seen them within the previous week. Only parents living in hostels enjoyed anything like the same degree of contact. On the whole most parents (two-thirds) were satisfied with the frequency of the contacts, but the remainder would have liked to have seen more of their children. Not surprisingly, satisfaction was highest where contact was most frequent – among parents living in private households. The more closed the institutional setting, the less parents saw of their children and the less satisfactory that contact was seen to be.

Other relatives living nearby

As only a minority of deaf people were parents, the majority had to rely on relatives other than children to provide interpretation. But only a little more than a tenth had a sister, and even smaller minorities a brother, aunt, uncle or in-law in the vicinity, and nieces, nephews, and cousins living nearby were claimed by very few. The range of relatives available in the vicinity was greatest among deaf people living in private households closely followed by those living in hostels. Patients in hospitals for the mentally handicapped appeared to have no relatives living within a fifteen minute journey.

Despite the wide range of relatives living in the vicinity enjoyed by some deaf people, the vast majority – three-quarters – had none at all, and of those who did most (three-fifths) had only one or two relatives. For the most part, proximity ensured that relatives maintained regular and reasonably frequent contact. Daily contact was unusual, but a substantial minority reported seeing a relative at least weekly, while another third did so at least once a month. It tended to be the case that those living in private households or hostels were the most likely to have frequent and regular contact with their relatives who lived nearby.

The close relationship which a minority of deaf people had established with their relatives is illustrated by the fact that a tenth had seen a relative, other than a child, on the day of the interview or the previous day, and that another half had done so in the previous week. Recent contact with relatives was most marked among those living in private households, though weekly contact was also common among residents of the hostels and homes for the deaf.

Despite the regularity and frequency of contact which prevailed for the most part between deaf people and their relatives, such relationships were available only to a minority. Only a tenth of deaf people saw a relative other than a child at least once a week, while a little less than a fifth did so at least monthly. And such visits tended to take place instead of, rather than to supplement those of children: only 5 per cent of deaf people had children and other relatives living nearby with whom they were in regular contact, and those in private households and hostels were no more likely to be numbered among them than deaf people living elsewhere. In fact, the vast majority of deaf people – three-quarters – were in touch with neither children nor other relatives living in the vicinity.

However, the proximity of relatives may be less important to deaf people than to some other groups where physical dependence is the overriding concern. Perhaps interpretation is more compatible with geographic separation than the provision of physical help with daily activities. What part did relatives living beyond the neighbourhood play in the lives of deaf people?

Relatives outside the neighbourhood

The vast majority of deaf people (all but one sixth) had at least one relative living beyond the neighbourhood. But the availability of such relatives was far greater among those living in private households and hostels than among people living elsewhere. The opportunities for contact with relatives were most constrained for those living in large non-specialist facilities of the most closed kind.

Of course, the availability of relatives is no guarantee that they will play a prominent, or indeed any part, in one's life. And it was true for the majority of deaf people that relatives other than children and those who lived nearby, maintained little regular contact – only 8 per cent had at least weekly and another quarter monthly contact with them. For the vast majority (two-thirds) of those with relatives living beyond the neighbourhood, contact was infrequent, taking place several times a year at most. As might be expected, those living in private households, hostels, and homes for the deaf were the most likely to see such relatives frequently and regularly. Deaf people isolated in general institutions, especially hospitals, had little contact with relatives living beyond the neighbourhood, even where these existed.

Even so, some relatives who lived beyond the neighbourhood performed a useful task both in supplementing contacts with other relatives, and in maintaining family links, and those in large general facilities were disproportionately dependent upon them. Indeed, such visits accounted for almost half of the contacts reported and supplemented the regular contacts already maintained with children or other members of the family living nearby for 15 per cent of deaf people. It was striking that only those living in their own homes and the homes and hostels for the deaf enjoyed the luxury of at least monthly contact with both relatives living nearby and outside the neighbourhood.

The value of family contacts

What was the quality of the relationships which deaf people maintained with members of the family? How far was it true that even infrequent contact remained important for its promise of help in time of need, as well as the reaffirmation of bonds which create a sense of belonging? It was clear that for some deaf people even infrequent contact with relatives was of major importance in their lives.

Mrs Glending said 'I only see the family a few times a year: they're all in Ireland. My two brothers and sisters have never signed. But I go for holidays to my son and daughter-in-law. They're very good to me. They sign and so does my grand-daughter.'

Indeed it was common for even infrequent family contacts to be valued, especially when they involved the deaf person in 'ordinary' activities, such as holidays, or even though no more than a visit to reaffirm family ties took place.

Mrs Fulton said 'My brother and sister come a couple of times a year. They just visit. They don't sign – they never did. They speak and I lip-read – I understand.'

However, the value of family contacts was sometimes questioned, particularly by those who had maintained numerous and close family ties, largely because they considered that hearing relatives generally failed to make any effort either to communicate with the deaf or to ensure that the deaf felt 'included' in activities.

Mr Rossiter, a resident of the hostel for the young working deaf said 'I see my sister every two weeks, and my brother and father once a month. My sister came on bank holiday – a week ago. But I find it difficult to chat with the family. They talk quickly and it's hard lip-reading.'

Miss Probent said 'My hearing friends and family have no sympathy with the deaf. They talk, talk, talk to each other. Ask "What?" One word to explain all that talk.'

As a consequence, the attraction of hearing society for some was far from obvious, and there was little regret for the tenuous nature of family relationships. Some deliberately distanced themselves from hearing relatives.

Mr Wilcox, aged 43 said 'I get bitter and resentful because I feel left out at parties. The family doesn't help to make me feel comfortable. It's better to have deaf friends and hearing friends who sign. I've been invited to my nephew's wedding, but I'm not going.'

Indeed, a few deaf people had established a pattern of daily activities which excluded even those relatives who lived nearby.

Mr Lipp said 'I get up to the pub and luncheon clubs regularly but somehow I never get to see my sister and she only lives the same distance.'

It was more usual, however, despite the strains induced by communication difficulties, to wish to reaffirm the family bonds by family reunions at birthdays, weddings, funerals and so on.

Mrs Finniston said 'My brother came for my birthday this week but my sister rarely visits. We write letters to keep in touch.'

Often family links were more satisfactorily maintained through written correspondence than by meetings where communication difficulties were acute.

Mrs Canter, a resident of the psychiatric half-way hostel said 'We mainly keep in touch by letter. My brother and sister visit monthly – they came two weeks ago. We have to write everything down – there's not much speech.'

Indeed, many deaf people appeared to be comfortable with family relationships maintained over a distance through letters.

Miss Francis, who lived in a home for the deaf said 'I haven't seen my sister, brother or niece for three or four years. My sister doesn't sign but I'm fond of her. She writes regularly. I had a letter from her this morning. But I don't see my brother now.'

However, in cases where a satisfactory communication system had been established with relatives, contact which was reduced or broken was deeply mourned by the deaf person.

Miss Flynn described her dismay at the loss of her sister's company: 'I used to see a lot of my younger sister with whom I was very close before she moved out of London. We still meet monthly but I miss her frequent company. We used to go to the deaf club together – they all thought she was deaf too.'

The sense of isolation was particularly acute for those who lived outside their own neighbourhoods in institutional settings.

Miss French, who was a resident of the London home for the deaf said 'It's too long ago, I can't remember too many details. But I could do all the practical things around the house, and we had a very good relationship. Now they're all dead. Only one brother remains and he's been in hospital seven months with leukaemia.'

Many blamed hearing impairment for their tenuous relationships with other members of the family. And this was as true of those who lived 'integrated' lives in their own homes, as of those who had broken with the 'normal' community to enter residential or hospital care.

Mr Owen observed 'One of the effects of deafness is that the family doesn't often visit.'

Miss Grove said 'I haven't any relatives whom I see. My brother was never interested as a child and I haven't seen him since childhood.'

In a few cases relatives went to considerable lengths to maintain a formal contact, but also to prevent the development of a closer relationship.

Miss Rickmansworth, who lived in a home for the deaf, said 'I never see my sister. At Christmas she sends a card without an address via friends in Carisbrooke.'

Entry into residential care often occasioned a complete break with relatives.

Mr Browne, who lived in a home for the deaf, said 'Since coming here I've lost all touch with the family.'

Miss Grove, who lived in the same home, said 'I don't even know the address of my niece, nephews or sister. I don't see any of them. I haven't seen a relative since I was admitted here four years ago.'

Of course, the residents of homes and hostels for the deaf at least had the consolation of the company of other deaf people. But for those in the homes for the elderly and the hospitals, the isolation created by loss of familiar family contacts was reinforced by the absence of deaf companions.

Mr Butler, who was a patient in a hospital for the mentally handicapped, said 'I haven't had any visitors here. In 1975 the social worker visited my mother but she did not want to come here.'

Mr Levitt, another patient, said 'I've lost contact with my family since 1961.'

Yet despite the tenuous nature of many family relationships a substantial number of deaf people (a little more than half) said that they had a relative who helped them in some way. It was striking that those who were least likely to receive help were those in non-specialist institutions, particularly the hospitals. Surprisingly, residents of the homes for the deaf were most likely to receive such help, though help from relatives was almost as common among those living in private households, while almost half of hostel residents reported that they received help. Holidays were the most usual form of help provided by relatives; as many as a third of deaf people went on holiday with a relative.

Miss Hughes, aged 57, who lived on her own, said 'I go to see my brother and sister for holidays. They drive down and pick me up in turn.'

For those in residential and hospital care, the opportunity afforded by a holiday in the home of a relative offered a regular escape to 'normal' life.

Miss Johnson, aged 51, who was a patient in a hospital for the mentally ill, said 'I have weekends and holidays at home with my brother and his family.'

Indeed, for some deaf people the annual holiday was their sole contact with a member of the family.

Where a deaf person had access both to the normal hearing community as well as the deaf community, as was the case of those who lived in their own homes or in hostels, there was a greater readiness to be critical of the company provided by hearing relatives on holidays, than was true of other deaf people.

Miss Beynon, aged 20, said 'I see my aunt, my grandmother, and some cousins about once a month. I saw my grandmother last week. I went on holiday with my aunt to Athens this year. Sometimes I feel a little excluded from talk with the family.'

Mr Nelson, aged 16, said 'I sometimes go on holiday wth my mother and father. I see my grandparents, aunts and uncles about once a month. Sometimes the family talks and I feel left out. If they talk *to me* I can lip-read.'

Often reciprocity was the basis on which relatives were prepared to offer holidays and weekends: payment in kind was considered to be an essential reward for the inconvenience of a deaf relative in the house.

Mr Rossiter, aged 66, who lived in the hostel for the young working deaf, said of his relatives: 'I do things for them. I stay with them and do jobs. One son gets very impatient. I find all my family get irritable at my presence – after a couple of weeks, if I'm not giving them some form of practical help. But I don't think this has anything to do with deafness.'

For others, however, reciprocity comfortably cemented the family relationship, and where the deaf person lived in a private household, the provision of holidays could be within *their* gift.

Mr Selsby, aged 65, who lived on his own, said 'My sister comes and stays. She gives me much advice and help – she's very kind.'

Taking deaf people out was, next to taking them on holiday, the most common form of help provided by relatives. A little less than a quarter of the deaf who received family help (and a little more than a tenth of all deaf people interviewed) said that they were taken out by a relative. This was an activity which, with one exception, was confined to those living in private households or specialist institutions. The outing reaffirmed the deaf person as a member of the general community (by enabling them to go out in the company of the hearing and participate in the activities of the hearing community) and cemented relationships within the family. It was common for the outing to be one of a number of provisions made by relatives.

Miss Garnett, aged 54, who lived in a home for the deaf, said 'Each of my brothers visits me five or six times a year. They interpret for me at the hospital, they take me out and they have me for holidays.'

A wide variety of other types of help was received by as many as a fifth of deaf people, though once more it tended to be concentrated on those living in private households or specialist facilities for the deaf. Such help ranged from doing the shopping to releasing deaf people from their responsibilities for short periods: a number of deaf women had devised a way of life so 'normal' that they found their activities constrained not by deafness but by the care they provided for ageing parents.

Miss Angus, aged 47, said 'My brother comes monthly but he really comes to see Mum. He takes Mum when I go on holiday.'

In a minority of cases where relatives lived nearby, help was part of a neighbourhood pattern of life, but distance did not necessarily preclude even substantial help from relatives.

Mrs Boseley, aged 76, who had lived on her own for twenty-four years since the death of her husband, said 'I don't see my brother and sister-in-law much since they moved to Durham but they have me for holidays, and pay for things like the TV rental and licence, the decoration of the flat, and they help me with negotiations for things.'

Indeed, practical help was sometimes used as an alternative to contact, especially where long journeys were involved, or where visits were likely to occasion distress or guilt in hearing relatives.

Mr Crabbe, aged 28, who was a patient in a hospital for the mentally handicapped, said 'My brother came last month, but my parents and my other brother rarely come. They send presents.'

But the majority of the deaf living in institutional settings had neither contact with relatives, nor anything done for them by members of the family.

Mr Johnstone, aged 71, explained: 'They don't realize that I feel isolated in the home and they rarely contact me.'

Even among deaf people living in private households there was a substantial minority of all ages who enjoyed neither the company nor the help of relatives.

By no means all of those who were currently without the contact or help of relatives had always been so isolated. Time and distance had often severed what had been close relationships.

Miss Ayers said 'They don't do anything now, but when I was younger I used to go on holiday with my deaf cousins.'

73-year-old Mrs Ogmore said 'They can't do anything for me any more. They've all moved out of London – brother and sister, nephew, niece and child. My hard-of-hearing sister uses the phone and visits occasionally.'

Perhaps not surprisingly, admission to a home or hospital often reinforced the effect of distance and years.

Miss Cox, aged 72, who was a patient in a hospital for the mentally ill, said 'I grew up with my cousin and I used to go on holiday with her but I don't know her whereabouts now.'

And the death of a key family figure could effectively cut the deaf person from the companionship and help of the rest of the family network.

Miss Greene, aged 54, who lived in a home for the deaf, said 'My parents were very good but after they died, no relatives came to visit.'

Indeed, deaf people who were at the centre of a close-knit set of family relationships within which gifts were exchanged were in a small minority. More than half had neither regular contact on a monthly basis with a relative, nor help on even a few occasions a year. As might be expected, those living in their own homes were by far the most likely to be at the centre of a close-knit family network, while this was true of a large minority of hostel residents. Isolation from relatives was most marked among those living in institutional settings and especially non-specialist institutions, while the pattern of family relationships of hostel residents were those which most nearly resembled those of deaf people leading a 'normal' life in private households. Substantial numbers of the deaf, then, could not rely on family members for interpretation. Indeed more than half of the deaf people interviewed had not seen a member of the family from outside the household in the past two months.

Unhappily it was among those who were most in need of the services of a sympathetic interpreter that frequent contact with relatives was least likely. Only a fifth of those who were most in need of interpretation had seen a member of the family in the previous month. Indeed, the greater the communication difficulties of the deaf, the less likely they were to be in regular and frequent contact with relatives. It seemed as if problems of communication were themselves responsible for reducing or severing contact with the most trusted interpreters of the hearing world, members of the family. Whereas a little more than a tenth of those who were oralist, or used a combination of oral, written and signed communication at home had not seen a member of the family living outside the household for more than ten years, this was true of as many as a quarter of signers and those who relied on a combination of gesture and sign.

The degrees to which deaf people used methods of communication which were typical of the hearing community had a considerable effect on their degree of contact with relatives living outside the household. Use of voice appeared to be an important factor in encouraging relatives to maintain contact with a deaf person. More than nine-tenths of oralists had seen a relative, other than those in the household, within the previous three years, compared with rather less than two-thirds of those who never used voice. Indeed, the greater the reluctance or inability of deaf people to use voice the greater was the likelihood of complete loss of contact with relatives outside the home. Capacity to receive spoken communication also appeared to be important to maintaining contact between the deaf and their families. The better deaf people lip-read the more likely they were to maintain family contacts.

Despite the dearth of family contacts among deaf people living in institutional settings, staff in hostels, homes and hospitals insisted that visiting by relatives was actively encouraged.

The deputy matron of the south of England home for the deaf said 'We are glad to see relatives at any time.'

The charge nurse in a hospital for the mentally handicapped said 'We have open visiting – we encourage it.'

But with the exception of one establishment, staff admitted that the degree of contact maintained by residents or patients and their relatives was disappointing.

It was striking that the hostel for the young working deaf (where alone ties between deaf people and their families were even stronger than in the case of those living in private households), was the only institution which offered easily available facilities for relatives wishing to stay the night. There was confusion among staff in three other establishments as to whether such facilities were available, but whatever the truth, relatives had not stayed there for some years.

Neighbours

Of course, the role of neighbours and friends in maintaining the informal network becomes crucial when contact with relatives is slight, as was usually the case. Yet neighbours played only a minimal role if any in the lives of most deaf people: a little more than a third had no contact with neighbours at all. Predictably, those with fewest neighbourhood ties lived in the homes and hospitals. Whereas only a ninth of deaf people living in private households and the hostels had no neighbourhood contacts, this was true of well over half of the residents of the homes for the deaf and the elderly, and nine-tenths of hospital patients. The residents of hostels and homes often reflected on the close neighbourhood ties to which they had been accustomed at home: admission to a hostel or home had severed links with a network which proved to be difficult to recreate in another area, especially from an institutional base.

A resident in the psychiatric hostel, Mr Ringmer, aged 60, said 'At home in Manchester I spend all my time with the hearing neighbours – go for a drink, chat, talk, buy each other a drink. But not here.'

Mrs Faulkner, a widow aged 88, said 'We always used to have good relations with the neighbours in Ilford, but there's none of that here, now.'

Even where deaf people established a relationship with a neighbour, the contact tended to be minimal. Almost half reported that their involvement with neighbours amounted to no more than 'just saying "hullo" ' or 'standing for a chat'. Neighbourhood relationships established by those in institutional settings were predominantly of this minimal variety.

Miss Gregson, aged 18, who lived in the half-way psychiatric hostel, said 'The hearing people round here are all right. They say "Hullo Teresa" and thumbs up.'

Communication difficulties were often perceived as dictating the brevity of the contact with neighbours. The contrast in neighbourly treatment of the deaf and hearing or those who could operate the hearing communication system was stark: where they were present, all transactions were carried out through the hearing or oral spouse.

Mr Paxton, aged 35, said 'They are more frequently with my wife because she has better speech, so communication is easier. Through her they will telephone for us and watch the kids.'

Neighbourliness which went beyond the friendly salutation or a chat in the street or the shops was experienced by only a minority of deaf people: 13 per cent visited or invited home a neighbour for a chat, took things in for neighbours who were out and occasionally went out with a neighbour. Furthermore, all but three of those with such close neighbourhood ties lived in private households.

Typical of the deaf who enjoyed close neighbourhood ties was Mrs Simpson, aged 67, who lived with her deaf husband: 'We're very intimate. We have known our neighbours since 1940. She comes to the deaf club with me – she even signs a little. We are frequently in each other's houses, and we take things in for each other.'

Mrs Boseley, a 77-year-old widow, said 'I'm very friendly with next door. We go out together and they help me with negotiations. I'm going on holiday with them this year. They have a telephone and will get the doctor if I don't feel well.'

Some of those who had succeeded in establishing reciprocal relationships with their neighbours attributed their achievement to their own communication skills.

Mr Fox, aged 75, said 'The neighbours are very good, and the local shop-keepers. I'm a very good lip-reader and the hearing understand my speech – that's helpful. They telephone for me, help me with cut-price decorating, and the local shop gives me chocolates and flowers at Christmas.'

Where institutions were large and remote from the neighbourhood, as was the case with all but one of the hospitals, it was interesting to find deaf people identifying other patients and staff as neighbours, and thereby defining the hospital as their local community.

Mr Franks, a hospital patient, said 'People around the hospital always acknowledge me because I'm always cheerful and I help with the trolley.'

While neighbours on the whole were reluctant to go beyond the brief salutation and chat, some were disposed to be helpful in ways which involved no long-term or sustained commitment. Thus a tenth of deaf people reported that although in other respects their relationships with neighbours were minimal there was at least one neighbour who was willing to make telephone calls for them.

In view of the limited nature of neighbourhood contacts it was not surprising to find that neighbours did little to repair the failure of the family network to provide the crucial service of interpretation. Only a tenth of deaf people depended upon neighbours in any way to interpret for them. However, there appeared to be no necessary connection between familiarity with neighbours and reliance on their interpreting role. As many as a third of those who reported that they used neighbours as interpreters from time to time otherwise had only minimal contacts in the neighbourhood. But the nature of the interpreter's role differed substantially between that adopted by neighbours who were close to a deaf person, and whose interpretation of the hearing world was continuous and part of daily conversation, and that adopted by neighbours whose contact was normally minimal, but who were prepared to interpret occasionally when a specific and isolated problem arose.

Their minimal neighbourhood contacts were not considered to be normal by a fifth of deaf people, and were thought to be explained by the negative attitudes of neighbours towards deafness.

Mr Forrester said 'If I were hearing, people round here would talk to me more.'

Only a quarter of deaf people considered that the attitudes adopted by neighbours towards them were wholly positive, though their judgement in this respect appeared to be unaffected by the familiarity of their neighbourhood relationships.

Understandably, those with close neighbourhood ties were impressed with the friendliness of their neighbours.

Mrs Singh, aged 36, said 'Everyone round here is nice and friendly: they give company, we have chat, we give confidences. They have phoned to my husband's office when I have been ill.'

Others stressed the importance of opportunities for reciprocity in neighbourhood relationships.

Mrs Formby, aged 80, said 'I babysit for next door. They are sympathetic to me because I'm widowed.'

Mrs Jackson, aged 43, who lived with her deaf husband said 'We are great friends with next door. She's an elderly lady and I sometimes help her to shop or call the doctor for her.'

Some deaf people found no uniformity of response among their neighbours.

Mrs Smith, aged 62, who lived with her deaf husband said 'My neighbour across the road helps with any domestic problems. With that neighbour there's no difference because I'm deaf. Otherwise, the neighbours are awkward when they see me.'

Mr Jones, aged 52, who lived with his deaf wife said 'Most of the neighbours are funny, but we get on well with the ones on one side: they will help us in an emergency.'

A number of deaf people explained the lack of neighbourhood friendliness in terms of their neighbours' unfamiliarity with deafness:

Miss Beynon, aged 20, said 'Neighbours are usually understanding: it's only those who don't know me well who are awkward.'

But attitudes to deafness were not alone in determining neighbourhood relationships: some deaf people themselves had preferences based on 'normal' criteria.

Mrs Forster, aged 53, who lived with her deaf husband, said 'The neighbours next door but one are nice and friendly. But we never speak to the mucky ones next door: we have complained to the Council about them.'

Although many deaf people found their neighbours awkward, very few (4 per cent) reported that neighbours avoided them: it was more common for the deaf to admit to their own diffidence in neighbourhood encounters. Indeed as many as a tenth were fearful of, and in some cases deliberately avoided, contact with neighbours. To a large extent such attitudes appeared to reflect the uneasiness aroused by the unfamiliar:

Miss Blume, aged 39, who lived in a home for the deaf explained: 'It's very different here from the hospital. In the hospital, the nurse used to say "Take off your hearing aid." Here in the home they say: "you must wear your hearing aid". In the home people are interested in talking, but I'm a bit nervous talking to neighbours.'

Friends

Unlike relatives and neighbours, friends may be chosen. However, friendships have to be sought and their acquisition may prove to be difficult for those with severe communication problems, especially where there is a reluctance to move beyond the familiar. And it was their willingness to move beyond the familiar which determined the type of role played by friendship in deaf people's lives. For friendship may be considered at two levels in the present context. First, there is friendship as an indicator of normality: most of us assume that we will enjoy the companionship of friends. And at another level, friends may be regarded as an important part of the informal network of support. But in the case of the deaf support meant interpretation. The degree to which friendship offered interpretation of the hearing world as well as companionship depended upon the extent to which deaf people were prepared to seek and were successful in finding friends among the hearing.

In general few deaf people were willing to venture so far into the unfamiliar as to depend entirely on the hearing community for friendship: only 4 per cent reported that all of their friends were hearing. Most (51 per cent) balanced their need for interpretation with that for ease of communication by drawing their friends from both the hearing and the deaf communities, though in this respect there was a marked difference between the settings. Those with hearing and deaf friends were in a substantial majority among the deaf in private households and hostels, but comprised only a third of the residents of the homes for the deaf, and a tiny minority of hospital patients.

For the most part, such people found the two groups indistinguishable in terms of the degree of companionship they offered: as many as two-thirds said that they were equally relaxed with both sets of friends.

Miss Sweet, aged 37, said 'I've got both hearing and deaf friends living round here and they're all very good. I 've got a very good hearing friend I've known for many years. I used to stay with her until her mother and father moved to Tottenham to be nearer. She makes dresses for me.'

Mr Patel's wife, who was hearing, said of her husband's friends 'We have deaf and hearing friends. The hearing all respect him: there's no treating him as inferior.'

It was taken for granted by both deaf people and their hearing relatives that difficulties would be encountered in friendships within the hearing rather than the deaf community. In practice, however, the small number of determinedly oralist deaf sometimes found it easiest to establish a companionable relationship with hearing people. For others, however, it was true that the greatest difficulties, predominantly of communication, arose in establishing and maintaining friendships with the hearing:

Mrs Ogmore, aged 77, who lived with her deaf husband, said 'It's easier with the deaf – you have to explain everything to the hearing.'

Indeed, for some the hearing represented a separate and alien society, and this was particularly true for younger people, whose schooldays had been spent with other deaf children and who had yet to build up an understanding of the hearing world.

Miss Gosford, aged 23, said 'Friendship is easier with the deaf. The hearing are more like foreigners.'

For some, such feelings persisted in later life.

It emerged that in many cases hearing friends were primarily the friends of hearing relatives.

Miss Harris, aged 39, said 'My hearing friends are mostly friends of the family. They talk to me a little.'

In such cases, 'real friends' were deaf. Sometimes age reduced contact with deaf friends and forced reliance on hearing, family friends.

Mrs Nixon, aged 60, said 'I used to have a lot of deaf friends when I was able to get out more – to the Brixton (deaf) club. But I'm more wary now. Our hearing friends are the friends of my son's family, not my own friends.'

Not surprisingly, in such cases, deaf people found it difficult to establish an equal partnership with the hearing.

Mr Brown, aged 57, said 'I have deaf and hearing friends. I share my friends with my wife.' And his wife added: 'I tend to take command with the hearing friends now.'

In such circumstances, deaf people often found friendship with the hearing to be unsatisfactory.

Mrs Jackson, aged 55, explained 'I have to keep asking for explanations. The hearing talk, talk, but don't explain well. So the family help me to understand, but it is difficult because I am always asking.'

Moreover, the hearing involved in the friendship network often reinforced the unequal position of the deaf person.

Mrs Rose, aged 36, said 'My boy friend and the family and friends often neglect me in conversation. He says this is only natural, but I get bitter about it.'

A large minority of deaf people (between a quarter and a third) had established friendships solely within the deaf community: although they were a minority of hostel residents and those living in private households, they accounted for two-thirds of the residents of the homes for the deaf. Most deaf residents of specialist institutions had enjoyed the friendship of the hearing until admission to a hostel or home effectively severed the relationship.

Mrs Faulkner, an 88-year-old widow who lived in the London home for the deaf said 'I've no hearing friends, I used to have plenty but not now, not locally. I prefer the hearing: they're better informed, more interesting.'

However, many of the residents of specialist institutions preferred the company of deaf people, but had left them behind on admission to the home or hostel. Some found substitutes among fellow deaf residents, but these rarely acquired the status of 'real' friends. Often, the friendships of the past had been associated with the deaf community and its clubs.

Mr Browne, aged 45, said 'All my real friends are among the Coventry deaf. Before I came here I used to go every Saturday to watch football, have a drink. There would be 300 to 400 in the Coventry Deaf Club – a big club – it had a big house bar. I had many friends before. It was open every night – darts, dominoes, three snooker tables.'

Perhaps the largest homes for the deaf offered the best opportunity to replace the friendships previously enjoyed within the deaf community.

Mr Bey, aged 78, who lived in the west of England home for the deaf, said 'There are four of us men – Sam, Herb, Harry and myself – we're very close.

We always sit in the same part of the sitting room and talk and smoke together.'

Miss Spring, aged 59, a resident of the south of England home for the deaf, said 'I go with blind Albert to the shops nearly every day.'

Residents of homes and hostels were by no means alone in restricting their friendships to the deaf: almost a third of those living in private households had only deaf friends.

Mr Gregory, said 'We have good deaf friends. We go to functions together, and we like to go on holiday with other deaf couples and their children. We go out to tea together, as well.'

Nor was preference for deaf friends confined to the middle aged or elderly.

Miss Beynon, aged 20, said 'I have one good friend – deaf – I go to the cinema with, also discos and roller skating. At College there are seven girls and eight boys, all good friends and all deaf. We don't see the hearing much.'

Overall, then, friendships with the deaf were more common than with the hearing: while four-fifths of the deaf had deaf friends, little more than half had made friends within the hearing community. Thus a high proportion – more than four-fifths – had achieved the status of 'normality' in the sense that they had made friends with someone. But to what degree could the total reliance of some, and the heavy reliance of more on the deaf community for friendship be regarded as 'normal'? In terms of the interpretation of the hearing world to the deaf – an activity which undoubtedly aided 'integration' – friends played only a modest role. Only a minority of deaf people achieved a position of parity in their relationship with hearing friends: in many instances deaf people played a subordinate role to that of hearing relatives in the affections of hearing family friends, and often could secure little even in the way of explanation of a small part of the conversational exchanges between the hearing, still less much sustained interpretation of the hearing world. But at least they may be argued to have achieved through friendship some measure of 'normality' or 'integration'. What of those who were without any friends?

A substantial minority (17 per cent) of deaf people reported that they had no friends at all. It was striking that none of the friendless lived in private households or the hostels, and only a small minority of the residents of homes were without friends, but such people were the majority among hospital patients – four-fifths, in fact. Most hospital patients suffered the disadvantage of both removal from familiar friends at home, and of having little or no opportunity for establishing friendships with other deaf people within the institution.

Mr Green, aged 76, said 'I've no friends now, I don't know any deaf in the hospital.'

As none of the hospitals had more than six deaf patients, there was little opportunity for deaf patients to find substitutes within the institution for the friends with whom they could communicate at home.

Of course, the reported existence of friends in itself provides no indication of the degree to which friendship was a sustained and active relationship. In general, deaf friends were more likely to reside nearby than hearing friends: while all but a tenth of deaf friends lived locally, only two-thirds of hearing friends did so. Indeed only a minority of deaf people could take advantage of the interpreter's role of hearing friends on a regular basis: only a third had at least one hearing friend compared with almost three-quarters who had deaf friends living nearby. In most cases, then, friendship offered easier access to the deaf than the hearing community, and as a consequence, the companionship of those with similar modes of communication rather than integration into the wider, hearing community. Moreover to have deaf friends in the locality did not necessarily imply companionship within a community beyond the setting: most of those living in homes and the psychiatric half-way hostel identified as friends other deaf residents in the same institution.

Even so, going out with friends was widespread as an activity. As many as four-fifths of deaf people went out with friends, and all but a tenth did so regularly. But these outings by no means always 'integrated' the deaf into the 'normal' hearing community. The most popular outing undertaken by almost half of deaf people was to deaf clubs; and two-fifths regularly visited or received visits from friends who were usually deaf. However, almost as many – a little more than a third – enjoyed going to shops and pubs, while a fifth attended bingo sessions and a tenth went to football matches with friends. But another third were involved in a wide range of additional activities which included going to the cinema and the deaf theatre, whist drives, church, discos, as well as going out with friends for meals and coffee, on walks, watching or taking part in sport (including fishing, wrestling, boxing, karate) and membership of the Women's Institute. However, the more normal the setting, the greater the likelihood of outings with friends. Whereas everyone who lived in private households, and all but two of the hostel residents went out regularly with friends, this was true of two-thirds of the residents of homes, but only a minority of hospital patients.

Many deaf people enjoyed an active social life in the company of their friends.

Mr Rex, aged 34, said 'I go to the deaf club, pub, football matches, shopping and bingo, and I belong to a football team myself. In addition I play cricket and I go swimming – I'm a good swimmer.'

Most of those living in institutions explained that their activities had contracted substantially since their admission:

Miss Probent, aged 35, who lived in a half-way psychiatric hostel, said 'At home I go to pubs, but not here. The only place I go to here is the deaf club once a week.'

Miss Greene said 'I go out at home in Manchester, but not here. I go out shopping with a friend but apart from that I rarely go out. I stop in and do my washing and watch TV.'

Friendship, then, although widespread, was not a common means for integrating deaf people into the 'normal' hearing community. Not only were deaf friends more usual than hearing, friends were more abundant and indeed, tended to be concentrated among those whose way of life most nearly matched the normal – those in private households and hostel residents. Furthermore, although many of the deaf engaged in a wide variety of activities with their friends, often in the hearing community, the most popular activities were those which involved little interaction with the hearing community.

Furthermore, deaf people who were most likely to need interpretation and encouragement to engage in 'normal' activities were least likely to receive such help. Thus only those who never or only sometimes used voice had no friends, and the less frequently voice was used, the less likely were deaf people to have hearing friends. In addition, the greater the difficulty experienced in lip-reading non-signers, the fewer the friendships made, especially among hearing people.

Of course, integration into the deaf community may be a satisfactory substitute for integration into the broader hearing community, and in terms of the companionship with which it provides deaf people it can be viewed as preferable. But those whose living setting was least 'normal' were also least likely to have deaf friends outside the home. Thus the deaf who were already most isolated from the life of the community at large were also most likely to be denied the opportunity of integration even within the deaf community. Those living in specialist institutions, or specialist facilities within general institutions were driven back on the resources of the institution for the companionship of friends, but those in general institutions were effectively isolated from anyone with whom they could communicate.

Although most institutional staff acknowledged the importance and desirability of links with the outside world, they did little to promote such contacts. A telephone was available to residents and patients in all except the west of England and south of England homes for the deaf, but in no case had it been adapted in any way for use by deaf people. Nor were letters necessarily a reliable alternative to the telephone. Although help with letter writing was said to be available to those who asked for it for all except those in two mental handicap wards, in practice rather less than half of those in residential institutions and hospitals received help with letter writing. Indeed a little more than a quarter wrote no letters at all, and it appeared that little help and encouragement was given to them to maintain contact by this means with the world beyond the institution. Most of the residents of the homes and hostels received mail, and some were assisted by staff to understand their letters. But those who were least likely to find substitutes within the institution for the friends they would have made in the deaf community – the hospital patients – were also the least likely to maintain contact with the informal network of family, neighbours and friends by means of letters. Few deaf patients received mail, especially in the hospitals for the mentally handicapped, and staff were less likely than those elsewhere to encourage outside relationships through the mail. Indeed, some senior ward staff were unaware of whether or not their patients could understand the mail they received – or even, in one case, whether they received any.

8 The formal network of services

It became clear that the informal network of family, friends and neighbours was of doubtful effectiveness in providing interpretation, the provision most deaf people required. There appeared to be some support for the Abrams view that in so far as it still remains, the informal network now largely consists of families providing care for dependent members, generally in isolation from other sources of help. Of course, friends were important to deaf people, but on the whole, neighbourhood ties were weak. Those with more than minimal neighbourhood contacts were unusual, though neighbours were willing to be helpful provided that no sustained involvement was required: hence neighbours were well disposed in the matter of making the occasional telephone call, or helping in an emergency.

Weak though neighbourhood ties were in general, they were far stronger among deaf people living in private households and hostels, than elsewhere. However, in all specialist settings – homes and hostels, deaf people were more likely to remain in contact with their relatives than was true of those living in hospitals and the homes for the elderly. Regardless of type of institution, though, the severance of ties with friends and neighbours whose company had been enjoyed before admission to the institution was remarked upon by many deaf residents and patients, and all regretted their isolation from the modest informal network of the past.

It is important to note, however, that there was a widespread preference for the company of other deaf people – even over that of hearing relatives. Communication difficulties reduced the value of relatives as interpreters. Few felt entirely relaxed with hearing friends and neighbours. Thus, the value of the informal network was at its weakest in precisely the area of greatest dependence, namely, communication and interpretation. The preference for the deaf community was a force for integration in the sense that it ensured absorption into what has been termed the 'deaf subculture'.[1] While the deaf community provides for the companionship and friendship which are regarded as normal, it does so only by segregating the deaf from the hearing. Furthermore, it has been argued that it is unwise to assume that the norms of hearing society will be accurately transmitted within the deaf community.[2] Hence reliance on the deaf community both segregates from the hearing and reduces the likelihood of deaf people gaining an understanding of the values and patterns of behaviour regarded as normal in society at large.

Yet to operate effectively within the hearing world the primary requirement for the deaf person is reliable interpretation. In practice, the deaf rely heavily on the interpreting services of professional, specialist communicators, particularly the social workers for the deaf employed by local authority social services departments or specialist voluntary organizations, and the clergy – the descendents of the missionaries to the deaf. Warren has suggested that non-specialist professionals, from whom the hearing community seeks advice on problems – doctors, health visitors, and teachers, for example – are often unlikely to succeed in making themselves understood, even when they are aware of the scale of the communication problem.[3]

In the crucial area of communication and interpretation, therefore, a reliable service depends upon the formal, not the informal network. Furthermore, the role of the interpreter has emerged in recent years as pivotal, not only between the deaf and the hearing communities, but also between the deaf and non-specialist professional services.[4] As such, interpreters are being required to expand the range of what traditionally has been regarded as acceptable sign, particularly in relation to health services and the counselling services concerned with marriage guidance and sexual problems.[5] There are those who argue that the continuing involvement of the church in the interpreting service, and its missionary origin, creates a barrier of embarrassment to knowledge available from professional counselling services when personal topics are under discussion.[6] At the same time, the very origins of the interpreting service provide it with considerable authority in the eyes of many deaf people: social workers are ascribed expertise in the values and practices of hearing society, and have acquired the respect and authority traditionally associated with the chaplain interpreter.[7]

Despite the tradition of interpretation as a service to the deaf, there is widespread evidence that many professionals disregard and have no knowledge of the dimension of hearing impairment when treating the deaf.[8] Furthermore, the presence of deaf specialists, either in their own right, or as interpreters, as members of an interdisciplinary team, is far from common.[9] Yet in the United States, and increasingly in Britain as well, there is a growing demand both from within the deaf community and from specialists in hearing impairment, that interpreters be present in all situations involving the deaf. Indeed, Merrill has gone so far as to suggest that where professionals find that no interpretation is available, they should withdraw. Furthermore, he envisages an expanding role for the deaf within society in general, and particularly in relation to policies affecting the deaf – a move which, he considers, should have the full support of professionals.[10] Inevitably, the widespread use of interpreters would be a central requirement of such a development.

In view of the need for interpretation, the non-specialist voluntary sector was no more immediately accessible than the statutory services. Specialist services are both voluntary and statutory: indeed, many local authorities continue to operate their services for the deaf on an agency basis through voluntary organizations. And the deaf clubs, which have been the focus for much of the development of the deaf 'subculture' are largely the creation of the voluntary specialist societies. But there was no evidence to support the argument for the superiority of the voluntary over the statutory services which is becoming increasingly fashionable. Type of facility rather than method of financing is the most important factor in creating an ambience within which deaf people feel at ease in their relationships with the hearing community.

While it is true that the major experiments in residential living – the hostels – were in the voluntary sector, it must be remembered that most specialist residential care for the deaf, as for other groups of the disabled, has been provided largely through voluntary organizations. Furthermore, the homes for the deaf, all of which were voluntary, were far from innovative in their approach to residential care. And experimentation was to be found in residential provision within the statutory sector: the North Wales deaf unit held the promise of considerable potential. Furthermore, there was evidence elsewhere that local authorities were prepared to innovate in developing, for example, self-help groups to overcome the isolation of deaf wives and mothers, which were likely to reinforce the deaf community at least as much as to integrate deaf people into the hearing society.[11]

Yet it is noticeable that whether an experiment in residential living, or a community or self-help initiative is in question, the necessary liaison with the hearing community involved has to be undertaken by the interpreter, statutory or voluntary.

The objective of statutory services has received little direction from statute. The National Assistance Act 1948, in which local authority services have their origin, did no more than identify the object of services for the deaf – as for other groups of the handicapped as well as the elderly – as the promotion of welfare.[12] For all groups of the handicapped, the pattern of services which emerged in the 1950s was based ultimately on that established for the blind in 1920, with an emphasis on visiting and the creation of employment opportunities. As domiciliary provision for the elderly developed, these general services were gradually made available to younger handicapped people, including the deaf, where this was appropriate. For the deaf, the equivalent of the blind home visitor and teacher of braille and moon was the deaf specialist worker, with a knowledge of sign language, whose role included the provision of an interpreting and mediating service.

The hesitant development of the specialist deaf service during the 1960s, was brought into question in the enthusiasm for genericism in the wake of the Social Services Act 1970. And in the same year, the Chronically Sick and Disabled Persons Act provided, by implication, a particular definition of promotional welfare – the integration of the disabled into society at large. Statutory support was provided for services which would enable disabled people to avoid being pushed from the centre of life. In the case of the deaf, such an approach was not inconsistent with that identified in 1976 by Merrill, namely that the deaf should be provided with the opportunities generally available in society to make the decisions which affect their lives, to gain control over their own lives.[13] Within the new social services departments such an objective was assumed to involve the creation of access for deaf people to services generally available by the provision of interpreters. But the difficulties of doing so within a generic framework soon became apparent. As early as 1972 it was appreciated that the increasing emphasis on *social work* with the deaf in specialist training schemes was diluting the interpreting skills acquired by newly qualified specialist workers. Furthermore, it was already clear that while there appeared to be the promise of making general statutory services available to the deaf and the possibility of a basic training in the care of the deaf for generic family social workers, the need for a skilled interpreting service to ensure access for the deaf to the non-specialist formal system of care remained. And there was already disquiet lest specialist services suffer as a consequence of the emphasis on genericism.[14]

From the outset there appeared to be an assumption that the separate nature of specialist services would be reduced under the new regime. The needs which the deaf shared with other groups, for family support and so on would be emphasized, while the interpreting role of the deaf specialist would be utilized only where substantial problems of communication arose. But in practice, considerable ambivalence soon emerged about the role of specialists, and their relationships with area teams and with non-specialists generally. In recent years it has become clear that the effect of the emphasis on genericism and the focus on work with families, and particularly with children, has been to isolate the deaf specialist.[15]

The remainder of this chapter will be concerned with the use made by deaf people of local authority and voluntary general welfare services, and the role of specialist provision, particularly that of interpretation, in their lives. The focus here is on welfare services designed to ensure daily care: those aimed to extend the social lives of the deaf, such as the provision of clubs and holidays, will be considered later.

Identifying badges and letters

In previous chapters, variations in the degree to which deaf people were willing to commit themselves to the deaf community have been charted, but it has been clear that a majority preferred the company of the deaf to that of the hearing. However, few were willing to mark themselves out deliberately as being different to others in the community. In particular, there was a widespread reluctance to carry an identifying card or badge – only 5 per cent did so. Yet a badge, though discriminatory, could have the effect of integrating if it alerted hearing people to likely problems of communication and to behave appropriately. The badge of the deaf could be seen as analagous to the white stick of the blind.

Although few in number, badge or card carriers were to be found in all settings except hospitals. The absence of a card or badge did not necessarily imply hostility to the idea of owning one or the other: a tenth of the residents of the homes for the deaf reported having had badges or cards which they had lost since their admission. And there were others who, while they did not possess anything which identified them as *deaf*, were prepared to carry the green card which indicated disability in respect of work. Identification as disabled rather than deaf was also acceptable to those who held concessionary bus passes. But it remained the case that few were prepared to label themselves as deaf in any obvious way, though active hostility to the carrying of labels was rare, and was found solely among younger people living in private households.

Although they were unwilling to draw attention to their deafness, a substantial minority (one-third) were anxious about communication difficulties in the event of an emergency, and always took the precaution of carrying either their own address or the address or telephone number of next of kin. Understandably, hospital patients, most of whom rarely ventured beyond the hospital grounds, were least likely to take such precautions. Yet those who were most engaged with the hearing community – deaf people living in private households or hostels – were not disproportionately represented among the carriers of labels or home and next of kin addresses. Residents of the specialist homes were the most likely to carry such information. Why this should be so was not clear. Perhaps those who felt most vulnerable sought refuge in special homes. Even among them, however, a narrow majority had neither an identifying label nor an address for contact in an emergency.

Emergencies

An emergency was likely to be a crucial test of capacity to communicate with the hearing community at speed, and, perhaps, in a panic. To whom would deaf people turn? In fact, the informal network of family, friends and neighbours was most commonly regarded as a source of help in an emergency – by as many as two-fifths of deaf people. Indeed, more than a quarter considered that they would seek help in the first instance from the family and another 13 per cent from neighbours; only 3 per cent were confident that friends lived near enough to be relied upon in the event of an emergency.

Rather less reliance was placed on the formal network: in all, a little more than a third (37 per cent) said that they would call for help from such a source. However, reliance on the informal or formal network emerged as a function of setting, rather than the expression of choice. For those living in institutions staff represented the nearest authoritative members of the hearing community. Little reliance was placed on other aspects of the formal network: only three deaf people depended on the help of the social worker with the deaf, and two on the police.

Generally, the aim in an emergency was to contact the nearest hearing person. Although it was true in general that those living in institutional settings would seek help from the formal network, among hostel residents there was a substantial minority (two-fifths in all) who would depend on relatives and friends. And even among the residents of the homes about a fifth rejected the notion of seeking help from staff in an emergency in favour of contacting relatives or friends. However, neighbours as a source of help were not mentioned at all by the residents of hostels and homes. In so far as the informal network continued to function after admission to a residential home or hostel, the new neighbourhood had no role to play.

Even among those living in private households there were a few who preferred to seek help from the formal rather than the informal network, and there were two who considered that their only source of help would be their place of work. Even so, the formal network usually played a key role in emergencies only when it had taken over the day to day caring role and deaf people were removed from their informal network.

Not everyone considered that help would be available in an emergency: they were a small minority – 7 per cent – to be found predominantly among those living in private households and the hostels. All declared that they would have to shout and wait. Even where deaf people had someone to turn to in an emergency, there remained the problem of how they would attract attention. By far the most common method was to shout – resorted to by as many as two-fifths. A little more than a tenth, most of whom were oralists, reported that they would seek the help of a neighbour with a telephone. But oralists were in the minority, and not everyone could shout. It was not surprising, then, that a tenth said that they would have to go round and fetch the person on whom they relied in an emergency, while 5 per cent would run out and grab someone. However, not everyone was capable of such activity, especially in institutional settings. It was among such people that those who relied upon an emergency bell or cord (3 per cent) or upon clapping (6 per cent) were to be found. However, as many as a fifth of the deaf were unsure what they would do in an emergency.

Not all the systems for coping with an emergency had been tested in practice. Indeed, as many as two-fifths said that they had never experienced an emergency, and many of the proposals for dealing with such an event were hurriedly devised.

Mr Thornton, aged 38, who lived in the hostel for the young working deaf said: 'I look after myself; nothing like that has ever happened. I don't know what I would do. I suppose I would shout, fetch someone. The warden will telephone someone OK.'

Few of those living in institutional settings, and therefore heavily dependent upon the formal network for help in an emergency had experienced much difficulty in attracting attention.

Miss Jackson, aged 74, who lived in a home for the deaf said 'I can shout as I did when I fell: Matron came.' And Mr Johnson, aged 71, who lived in a home for the elderly said 'The warden would help. There's an emergency cord in the living room. The nurses call on the telephone and the doctor comes. That's what happened when I had a very bad pain. The Assistant came and helped.'

On the whole, those who lived with hearing relatives found that the informal support system of the family was reliable in an emergency.

Mr Jones, aged 55, said 'Not long ago my car was stolen: my daughter who lives with me went to the police.' Mr Robinson who lived in the hostel for the young working deaf said 'My car broke down – I rang my brother – he spoke to the AA – a long wait till the AA came.'

However, deaf people themselves proved to be capable of taking the initiative when required, despite the expectation that a hearing relative would bear responsibility.

Mr Newton, aged 33, said 'I would rely on my mother. Workmates would telephone a neighbour and ask her to give my mother a message. But last time there was an emergency, my mother had a bad accident. I had to get help. The ambulance came and took her to hospital.'

In general, neighbours had rallied effectively when required to do so.

Mr Gray, aged 89, said 'I would depend upon my neighbour. I haven't thought much about it – I would have to go out to them. What happened last time was I came home and found a flood. I got my neighbour over the road and he turned off the stopcock. Then I negotiated with number 33 for compensation because it was their fault.'

Sometimes, however, emergencies occurred at times when neighbours were not easily available.

Miss Gratton, aged 54, said 'Mother had a stroke. It was in the night. I had to shout, shout to my neighbour. I threw pebbles up to the windows. I couldn't lift my mother off the floor.'

In general there appeared to be little difference between the service provided by formal and informal networks for deaf people in emergencies: both those living in their own homes and those in institutional settings were confident of support. But it was unclear how easily deaf people with severe communication difficulties and living in non-specialist settings, were able to convey the *nature* of their problem to hearing people.

Daily care services

The dichotomy between those living in private households and persons resident in institutional settings in terms of their reliance on formal or informal networks in emergencies was maintained in respect of services providing daily care. For example, only 7 per cent of deaf people living in private households took advantage of at least one domiciliary local statutory service. The only substantial measure of support was that received by a woman in her eighties who had a home help and a bathing attendant, as well as a welfare visitor. In so far as others who lived in private households were in any way dependent, they relied entirely though not always happily on the informal network for help. As many as a sixth of those in private households would have preferred the help of statutory services – particularly of home help – to their dependence on relatives on whom they were reluctant to impose.

By definition, deaf people living in institutional settings with the exception of hostel residents were dependent on the provision of the formal network: the residents of the homes, and hospital patients were sometimes heavily dependent on the formal network for daily care. To some extent the greater dependence on help among the residents of homes for the deaf was a reflection of their frailty though the anxiety of managers of homes concerning accidents was crucial. Thus in only one of the homes for the deaf did all residents have regular access to a chiropodist, yet in all of the homes bathing attendance was regularly provided and forced on half the residents regardless of their wishes and degree of incapacity. And all residents of homes had their meals provided regardless of their capacity for cooking. Similarly in the homes for the elderly all residents had a bathing attendant, though all but one had regular chiropody as well.

In the hospitals, a minority of patients (rather less than a quarter) received no support services other than treatment and the meals and housecare generally available, but the remainder received bathing attendance. Only two patients received chiropody. Thus whereas few of those in private households actually received *any* domiciliary services, institutional living, other than in hostels where normality was an objective, ensured substantial home care support at a level which even the most generous domiciliary provision was unlikely to match in private households. Promotional welfare for deaf people living in their own homes and in hostels demonstrably did not mean domiciliary support by the formal network of care. In this, the contrast between such people and those in the homes and hospitals was stark, and was by no means always justified by differences between the two groups in their capacity for self-care.

Registration

However, the formal network of care was not absent from the lives of those in private households: all but one of them had contact with the specialist services through registration with the local authority as a deaf person. In contrast, only a fifth of hospital patients were known to be registered, and even in the homes for the deaf more than two-thirds were unsure about their registration. Hostel residents, almost two-thirds of whom were registered as deaf, once again appeared to represent a mid-way position between the institutional and 'normal' populations. The 'normality' of the residents of the homes for the elderly was underlined by their registration as deaf.

There were wide differences between the settings in the attitudes of staff towards registration which appeared to be determined by whether the setting was specialist or general. Staff in specialist institutions usually encouraged deaf people to register while those in general institutions either did not know of the existence of the register, or did not encourage registration. When working with those in private households, social workers with the deaf reported that they left the question of registration entirely up to the deaf themselves, though area teams, where they had responsibility for registration, often differed in their policies.

In contrast, staff in the specialist homes and hostels invariably notified the voluntary organizations of their residents, largely because these institutions were themselves voluntary. Similarly, social workers for the deaf employed by voluntary organizations which operated on an agency basis for local authorities encouraged the deaf to join their organizations. However, with one exception, those employed directly by local authorities did little to encourage membership. But of hospital staff, only those working in the deaf unit of a psychiatric hospital systematically made known to the local voluntary organization the names of deaf patients in their care. Indeed, in one hospital, staff admitted that they had no knowledge of the existence of such organizations. Thus, overall there was as much pressure on deaf people to join specialist voluntary organizations as to register with the local authority, but the source of pressure differed and was exerted on different populations. Overall the majority of deaf people (62 per cent) were registered, and indeed the proportion may well have been higher: some residents of the homes for the deaf were unsure about registration, and in the case of some hospital patients neither they nor staff could provide definite information about registration.

Social workers with the deaf

Even among the exceptional few who showed antipathy towards registration, the service provided by social workers with the deaf was appreciated.

Mrs Fox, aged 75, said 'I'm not registered. I don't want to be on any lists. I don't want to be associated with the local deaf. But my husband is registered. The social worker is a very good young man. Very understanding and helpful.' (This was said with tears in her eyes.) 'He uses sign and speech with us. We need two drains installed and he's helping us with a council grant.'

However, visits from a specialist social worker were not guaranteed by registration. Only a little more than half of those registered as deaf (and a third of all deaf people) had been visited within the previous twelve months by either a statutory or voluntary specialist social worker. For the most part, the absence of visits is to be explained by the failure of a London borough, where the majority of deaf people living in private households resided, to replace their specialist social worker when he resigned.

Did it matter that some registered deaf people were deprived of visits from their social worker? In fact, almost all of those who were visited found the relationship a helpful one. In a few cases, where deaf people interacted with the hearing community with some ease, the specialist social worker did no more than establish a friendly relationship and maintain a watchful contact.

Mrs Bosely, a widow aged 74, said 'The social worker comes, but I can manage on my own really. So we talk and chat. It's a social call rather than dealing with any problems. We use sign, finger-spelling, and speech together.'

In other cases, the social worker appeared to concentrate on family relationships and household problems.

Mr Oxton said 'The social worker talks to both of us, but he spends most of his time talking to my wife about the children. But he explains well – he uses good sign – total communication. We haven't any problems really, except that we're not very well off.'

But there were occasions when the social worker mediated in more formal circumstances between deaf people and the hearing community.

For example, 59-years-old Mr Jackson, who lived with his deaf wife, said 'The social worker only comes when we ask him to. He came about the accident last year. He interpreted for us at the police station and he helped us with the negotiations with the insurance. We use sign, speech and lip-reading when he comes.'

Mr Jones, aged 55, who lived with his deaf wife, explained 'The social worker with the deaf interpreted at our wedding in the Register Office, and of course, when I was charged with stealing newspapers.'

Not everyone realized the full potential of the help provided by the social worker.

Mr Kenton said 'I've seen the social worker two or three times – whenever I have asked to. I never thought to get him to help with that trouble with the police two years ago, or over my low salary. When he comes we talk about my problems, especially with work and so on. We communicate in speech with a few signs. I would be glad of advice on jobs, unemployment benefit and social security.'

Those who were suddenly left without the help of a social worker with the deaf found it difficult to replace a trusted service.

Miss Robertson, aged 25, said 'I'm used to having him as an interpreter. It's hard when there isn't one. I find it's better when Mr Estell (the social worker with the deaf) goes too – with the adoption people, supplementary benefits, DHSS, the employment people. I can't get a social worker now, so social security and the job situation are difficult to sort out. I've been to the law centre, my neighbour and deaf friends for help with letters.'

And Miss Rose, aged 36, said 'I need an interpreter all through – with work, the housing, the doctor, the children's school. But I haven't got any help now: I would be glad to have someone. No one is available at the moment. I wouldn't go to the ordinary social worker. I try to manage letters myself – I leave the ones I can't cope with.'

A few deaf people had found a replacement for a specific occasion.

Thus Mr Rostow said 'There's no social worker with the deaf in the borough now. I had to go outside the borough to get an interpreter when I was in court recently. The police tried to fool me – but you can't fool me.' (He tapped his nose.)

In the absence of a specialist social worker, many deaf people found that they had to deal with a range of different hearing people who acted as mediators between the deaf and service providers, none of whom appeared to be as effective as the social worker with the deaf.

For example, 58-year-old Mr Timpson said 'I needed help in court and with my housing problems as well as at work and with the adoption people. But now there is no one to help. The probation officer and the supplementary benefit lady came. I would have been glad of help. I had no money and there was a problem with the redundancy. I went to the ordinary social worker and the probation officer but they sent me to the law centre. I got the letters sent to the social worker like he asked me to: he had the letters for some time and did nothing even though he knew I had to act quickly.'

But others had been unable to find even ineffective substitutes.

Mr Nixon, aged 67, said 'I need help with employment and rebates. There's no help now and I do everything in sign. The problems are always the same – it's ask, phone, wait, wait. If something happened now I don't know how long it would take to get it sorted out.'

Indeed, the work of the specialist social worker was regarded as so valuable that as many as 43 per cent of deaf people wanted more frequent visits, and no one felt they could manage with fewer. In general, there was satisfaction both with the duration of the visits and the range of problems with which the special social worker dealt. Criticism of the service was largely confined to a demand for more visits, and this was true of all settings and every location.

That the demand for more frequent visits was not idle, was clear from the numbers of people (as many as half) most of whom lived in hostels, private houses and hospitals, who claimed to have problems with which they required help from the specialist services. The problems involved varied widely, and included finding nursery places, moving house, employment difficulties, ophthalmology appointments, negotiating with the council, obtaining unemployment benefit. Such dependence reflects the considerable trust placed by deaf persons in their specialist social worker.

Interpretation

Thus interpretation was the service most frequently required of the formal network of care by those living in their own homes. In other settings, care provided through the formal network was predominantly the non-specialist daily care of shelter, and in the case of the homes and hospitals the equivalent of home help, meals-on-wheels, and nursing services, though many received the specialist interpretation service as well. How crucial was interpretation as a service, and how reliant were deaf people on the formal network of provision for interpretation?

Reliance on interpretation was widespread. However, those living in private households, of whom a seventh had managed without the services of an interpreter, appeared to be rather less dependent than others in this respect. In contrast, there were few residents of homes for the deaf and hostels, and none among the hospital patients and residents of the homes for the elderly who had not used an interpreter at some time. By far the most common source of help with interpretation was the social worker with the deaf, whose services had been used by as many as half of deaf people. In comparison, only a quarter relied on relatives while 9 per cent had depended upon friends or neighbours, and 1 per cent always went to the police. Thus dependence on the formal, specialist services far outweighed that on the informal network for interpretation.

However, to concentrate on specialist provision is to understate the contribution of the formal network to the interpretation service. Almost a quarter of deaf people had depended at some stage upon the non-specialist formal network for an interpreter – mainly the residents of homes or hospital patients, who relied on their warden, matron or ward sister to provide interpretation. Yet in the hospitals and homes for the elderly staff with a knowledge of sign language were rare, and even in the homes for the deaf the interpretive skills of those in charge of the daily running of the homes were sometimes limited. And the absence of easy communication created substantial barriers to understanding in homes and hospitals. Where the informal network of relatives and friends did not exist, and the social worker with the deaf was not a regular visitor, deaf people preferred to keep their troubles to themselves. Although the interpreting skills of non-specialists within the formal network were similar to those of relatives and friends, it was evident that for those with the power of choice, the informal network was the preferred source of help. But by no means everyone was reluctant to entrust interpretation to the non-specialist formal network, though Mrs Hopkins was more typical in her preference for specialist help in the absence of aid from relatives:

Mr Kelly (the social worker with the deaf) handled the death of my husband very well. My husband handled all my affairs while he was living. Mr Kelly saw to all the funeral arrangements and so on. I regard having him to interpret as normal, but I don't know how to approach matron for help. I usually manage letters myself but it is becoming difficult because my eyes are deteriorating.'

It was in the specialist settings that the greatest use was made of the specialist interpreters. Almost all hostel residents, and more than half the residents of the homes for the deaf used the social worker with the deaf, while their use of the informal network was correspondingly limited. In contrast, although the residents of private households made consider-able use of the specialist formal network – two-fifths had used the social worker for the deaf at some time – the informal network was more popular, and almost two-thirds said that they relied predominantly on relatives, but also on neighbours or friends, for interpretation. Hospital patients made little use of either the informal network or specialist formal provision for interpretation. Although a fifth had used the specialist social worker, patients were otherwise dependent upon hospital staff for inter-pretation. In general, help with interpretation was drawn either from the formal or the informal network – only 8 per cent of deaf people used both networks.

By far the most common use made of interpreters was in encounters with medical services. In all, a little more than half reported that they had used an interpreter in such circumstances. Not everyone who required inter-pretation when dealing with health services actually received it, yet without it, hospitals for example, could be bewildering. Most of those who had the choice preferred the less expert services of a close relative to the specialist service when attending their general practitioner. And among those living in private households, a small minority preferred to 'manage' on their own, once no close relative such as a mother or sister, was available.

An example was Mrs Fixton, aged 62: 'I had the social worker with the deaf to interpret in court for the divorce, and in the business of getting maintenance from my husband. It's not really necessary at the doctor's, so I manage OK. But I don't always understand what's going on. The social worker with the deaf explains the council's letters.'

Next to the health services, employment was the area in which interpretation was most usually required. Almost a third of deaf people had used an interpreter either in obtaining employment or in sorting out difficulties which arose at work.

Mrs Nixon explained: 'I need an interpreter's help to get a job. I talked to the social worker with the deaf about it last July. I need to see him again. The man at the Labour doesn't seem to care and doesn't understand.'

Formal, legal situations, such as court appearances and encounters with the police created difficulties which only the intervention of a skilled interpreter could overcome. Almost a fifth of the deaf had appeared in court with the aid of an interpreter.

Mr Rex, who lived in the hostel for the young working deaf said 'I've only used the social worker with the deaf once and that was when I went to court for the divorce. Otherwise I manage on my own.'

And Mr Craig, who lived in a half-way psychiatric hostel said 'I had an interpreter to deal with the police when I had my accident. I was in court four times – no fine, no prison. Mr Gibbins (the social worker with the deaf) interpreted in court. I don't write – I telephone to my brother.' (Finger-spelling gave way and suggested literacy problems.)

A minority of those running specialist facilities had good BSL and sometimes adopted the role of a specialist interpreter.

Miss Phillips, who was a resident of the half-way psychiatric hostel said 'The warden helped me in court. It was a case of attempted rape a few years ago. A man banged me on the head and pushed me around. I couldn't shout because I have only a very small voice. I was nervous in court.'

Despite their lack of training in sign language, non-specialist staff sometimes found themselves in the role of interpreter even in difficult legal situations. In all, 11 per cent had received interpreting aid when dealing with the police – but such help was more commonly required by those who lived in close proximity to the hearing community, that is, in private households and hostels, than by those living more sheltered lives in homes and hospitals.

Negotiations with local authorities commonly required the services of an interpreter, and little more than a tenth had sought the aid of an interpreter for this purpose.

Mrs Thompson, aged 60, said 'Before, the social worker with the deaf helped me with my pension, and more recently he helped with the Town Hall person in the Housing Department to get rebates. But not now – he's left the borough.'

Help with such negotiations was predominantly a requirement of deaf people living in private households, as was interpretation at schools, though only 4 per cent of deaf people had used an interpreter in this context – a reflection not so much of need, as the extent to which deaf people were willing to parade their disability before their children's teachers as well as their anxiety that interpretation would take up teachers' valuable time.

Other situations in which an interpreter was used included negotiating with government officials across the full spectrum of income maintenance provisions, for sheltered care in homes and hostels, and attending to funeral arrangements. Indeed, many deaf people (half) had used an interpreter in more than one situation. Understandably, it was among hospital patients that dependence upon interpretation was most pronounced: almost three-quarters had used an interpreter in more than one situation, and many more were continuously dependent.

Miss Jones, aged 42, said 'All decisions seem to be made for me. The social worker with the deaf helps at the hospital, and with the social security people, and getting me admitted here. Mr Simon (the social worker with the deaf) will always turn out if I need him. Sister writes to mother for me.'

Residents of homes for the elderly almost matched hospital patients in their degree of dependence on interpretation. Substantial proportions of hostel residents, residents of the homes for the deaf and those living in private households (two-thirds) had used an interpreter in more than one situation.

It was not only in verbal exchanges that interpretation was required by the deaf. As many as a third needed help to read and write letters, and there was little variation in this proportion between settings. Typical of such people was Miss Jackson, who lived in a home for the deaf:

'Matron asks me what I want to say in letters, and she writes it and then posts it, I don't write myself.'

It was not always easy to acquire the service precisely when it was required. In all, 13 per cent had experienced difficulties in finding an interpreter when they needed one.

Miss Argus explained: 'I need an interpreter for the theatre, lectures, jobs, solicitors. A lot of people help – neighbours, friends, relatives, and the social worker with the deaf. Sometimes the supervisor at work explains what the others are saying. I needed a formal interpreter when I went to see the solicitor. How I feel about it depends on my relationship with the interpreter. Some are empathetic, others not so much. I had trouble at the hospital – the interpreter was unable to attend. And I have had difficulty in finding people to interpret written communication. At work I can ask in the office.'

Others commented on the length of time it could take for an interpreter to arrive.

Mr Taunton, a resident of the hostel for the young working deaf, said 'I need an interpreter for work, at the hospital and to sort out my social security problems. I usually get help from my family, the social worker with the deaf, and the voluntary social worker. It takes a long time to get a social worker to interpret – he didn't visit me in hospital. Mavis will help with letters but I usually manage. The warden will explain difficult letters or get the social worker with the deaf to help.' And Miss Probent, another hostel resident observed: 'You always have to wait, wait for an interpreter, but they come at last.'

Considerable difficulty could arise when an interpreter was required quickly or at 'unsocial hours'.

Mrs Owen said 'Generally there is no problem and I am used to having to do things through an interpreter. But I had a dreadful experience a little while ago. It took me a long time to get the doctor when my husband had a stroke. There was no interpreter and I had to make the chemist understand.'

Difficulties were arising in the London borough which had been deprived of its specialist social worker:

Miss Nixon said 'I need attention for my foot. I used to enjoy Francis Owen's and Mel Waley's visits. I used to forget that they were hearing. I need help to get my foot seen to. I don't want to contact the ordinary social worker – I need an interpreter.'

And Mr Rex said 'I want help to find a job. I need a signer: the Labour don't have one and Francis Owen has left.'

To consider only the problems experienced by those who had sought an interpreter's service, is to underestimate substantially the difficulties which arise in the absence of systematic cover by specialists. A number of those who had not so far required interpretation, considered that they might do so in the future, but were unsure of possible sources of help.

Mrs Gray said 'I don't know who I would go to for interpretation. We managed to claim compensation for the water drainage by ourselves, and we usually go to the Town Hall for advice. But what if something complicated arose?'

Second, there were deaf people living in hostels, homes and hospitals, far away from their accustomed neighbourhoods, who would have been more confident with access to the advice and interpreting skills of their 'old' specialist social worker.

Mr Reed who lived in the half-way psychiatric hostel, said 'I never see my social worker with the deaf from Manchester now. I would like to. I've got a lot of problems – moving, getting a flat, money. The warden is helping.'

Interpretation was most satisfactory when it was undertaken by a specialist with whom the deaf person was familiar and had established considerable empathy: in such circumstances there was less possibility of embarrassment.

Then there were hospital patients for whom no interpretation was available, and on whose behalf, as a consequence, staff made all decisions.

Miss Wheatley said 'The ward staff do the lot. I'm glad you've come to have someone who signs for a chat. I can write but I haven't any writing equipment.' Care staff made all Miss Wheatley's decisions.

There were some hospital patients for whom staff recognized that specialist advice, help and interpretation was required.

A nursing sister in a hospital for the mentally handicapped said of Mr Oliver 'In the past the social worker with the deaf from Durham was involved. We would like his advice now, especially regarding suitable occupational therapy, assessment of his hearing, and with obtaining a psychological and psychiatric report.'

Mr Butler had no one among his carers who could sign fluently. Staff made decisions on his behalf. It was open to speculation how he had been assessed by a non-signing psychologist without the aid of an interpreter. Indeed, staff found it impossible to make him understand the unacceptability of his behaviour when he caused a stir by exposing himself in Harrogate.

Finally, there were deaf people who because they had been treated solely as mentally handicapped had been given no opportunity to be taught a communication system by a deaf specialist; for them, no interpretation was possible.

The dearth of specialist communication skills and the failure to employ satisfactory interpreters for deaf people in general institutions or within general services is not restricted to Britain. In the United States, a survey carried out in 1971 of psychological services for the deaf concluded that the large majority of those providing care were practising without a knowledge of deafness or deaf persons; that they had received little or no specilaist preparation or training for their work, and that they were unable to communicate manually.[16]

Although there were some who had no need of the formal network either in terms of general service provision or for specialist care and interpretation, there was considerable demand for interpreting services. The provision of interpretation has become closely linked with social work, and in view of the role of registration and the history of the development of the specialist services, it is understandable that this should be so. But as the ACSHIP report points out, an interpretation service is not synonymous with social work. However, the report's only further observation on the subject is that 'very often a deaf person's communication needs can be met by a volunteer but these are in short supply. We are therefore particularly pleased to learn that DHSS has made a grant to the BDA to enable them to pilot courses in manual communication for volunteers'.[17] On the other hand there appears to be an irrefutable case for a specialist social work service for the deaf. It has been observed that 'work with the pre-lingually deaf is inevitably time-consuming since communication can never be speedy. Those most often in need of social services help may be those with acute communication difficulties. Where resources are very limited much of the help given tends to be crisis orientated and preventive work is almost negligible. Consideration therefore needs to be given to more concentrated social work intervention at particular life stages of the individual'.[18] However, the relationship between the interpreting and social work services remains a vexed question. Furthermore, the specialist, whether as social worker or interpreter, as Merrill has pointed out, has been drawn beyond the limits of the job description to work in the area of advocacy on behalf of the deaf population. And given their mediating role between the deaf and the hearing it is difficult to refute Merrill's contention that specialists should expand their advisory role.[19]

9 Education, training, employment and income

Education

The variety of experience so evident in other aspects of deafness was pronounced in relation to interpretation. While some deaf people required no more than direct translation on a few isolated occasions, others wanted an empathic person to interpret the intricacies of the hearing world, and a few needed social work support combined with substantial mediation. But it is not only in terms of who should do it that interpretation is a vexed question. There are also problems which arise from the question of the *nature* of British Sign Language, and which have implications for the education of the deaf.

Kyle *et al.*[1] have advanced the argument for BSL as a language in its own right on the basis of studies of variation in receptive and expressive skills of hearing and deaf users of BSL. They suggest that even in test situations which favour the hearing, deaf people achieve a higher level of sign comprehension than anyone except those with deaf parents. Furthermore, they have discovered substantial differences in the characteristics of the sign produced by hearing and deaf people: the hearing who learn sign as a direct translation of written English make substantial use of finger-spelling and speech following the grammatical idiom of written English, whereas deaf signers use little finger-spelling or speech, but when they do, follow the pattern of sign, not grammatical English. And hearing signers often do 'not use the basic features of BSL, like simultaneity, mimetic description, lip movement patterns characteristic of the deaf signer, and body movement'.[2]

These differences in the use of sign are attributed in part to the lack of contact hearing sign learners have with the deaf sub-culture – few deaf people are involved in teaching sign to the hearing – and in part to the consequent 'English-based' approach to the teaching of sign. These conclusions throw into doubt the level of communication achieved by hearing and deaf signers.[3] The implications for hearing teachers of the deaf are clear. Kluwin casts doubts even on the practice of representing English manually to aid deaf children who are learning to read and write: conventional manual systems are based on written English, which contribute to 'later problems in their use for simultaneous communication' within the classroom because written language is not the same as spoken language.[4] For the deaf, such conclusions pose problems not only within the classroom but also for the objectives of education itself. Studies which reinforce the status of BSL as a language in its own right inevitably reinforce the notion of the existence of a deaf sub-culture. Many have drawn attention to the inadequacies of the education system currently available to deaf children. Some Scottish parents of deaf children have argued that, frequently, on leaving the school the deaf child 'has not acquired the basic skills of reading, writing and arithmetic. Often he cannot communicate adequately even in sign language since in some schools signing is still frowned upon'.[5] They blame the variety of teaching methods which have operated in schools for a number of years without the benefit of evaluation, each of which succeeds with only a minority of children, and reflect the preconceptions of different factions. The parents argue for the adoption of total communication in schools, since it appears to suit oral as well as non-oral children,[6] a single sign language to provide the comprehensive language which is a necessary part of total communication,[7] and instruction for parents on the methods being used.[8]

Yet, despite their emphasis on sign language, the parents insist on evaluating the pattern, standard and achievement of education in terms of that for the hearing: schools for the deaf should 'provide an equivalent educational standard to that offered in hearing comprehensive schools, by lengthening the school day,[9] expanding the teaching on basics, and ensuring that deaf children are taught speech patterns, grammar, and general knowledge that hearing children pick up effortlessly from birth'.[10] The overall objective of the education system is perceived in terms of enabling deaf children to compete with hearing children in the hearing world.[11]

It is the duality of purpose in education to integrate the deaf into the deaf sub-culture and at the same time into the mainstream culture which is raised and explored by W.J. Watts, who points out that in their concentration in recent years on integrating the deaf into hearing society the efforts of teachers have met with only limited success.[12] However, judged by the criterion of integration into the deaf community, there has been considerable success. Probably the most successful deaf people are those who are integrated into and move freely between the two communities.[13] Unhappily, those who teach the deaf have little contact with the deaf sub-community, and yet, as Watts argues, 'It may well be that the best education for a large number of deaf children should be concerned with fitting them to take their place in their immediate sub-community and not so much into the total community.'

To what extent did formal education help deaf people to integrate either into hearing society or the deaf community? The importance of the formal education system for ensuring that deaf children acquire a grasp of the type of general knowledge which hearing children pick up automatically has long been recognized, and legislation encourages their early attendance at school. Yet as many as 7 per cent of the deaf had received no formal schooling at all. Although the majority of these were hospital patients, almost a third of whom had received no formal education, a minority were residents of homes for the deaf.

Miss Andrews, aged 57, lived in a home for the deaf. 'I never went to school – I don't know why. When I was little I could read and write a bit, then I forgot because it was work, work. My brother and sister went away to school, far away on a ship. I learned to make shoes and cleaning. I had to talk to my brother and sister, there was very little signing.

Those who were hospital patients either entered hospital at an early age, or were kept at home while they were of school age. All of those without schooling belonged to the older age-group: the youngest was aged 47, and three-quarters were over retirement age.

Despite the legislative encouragement to attend school early only a little more than a quarter of deaf people had started before the age of 5, while 3 per cent had done so as early as 3 years: indeed, almost as many had begun attending school late. Overall, the ages at which school attendance commenced ranged from 2 to 12 years. Early entries were most frequent among people living in private households and hostels, while those who entered at the age of 6 or later were to be found predominantly among the residents of homes for the deaf and hospitals for the mentally handicapped. It seemed as though the most vulnerable were denied both prolonged exposure to formal education and the security of a family home.

There was considerable variation, too, in the number of years for which deaf children were exposed to formal education. While some finished their schooling at the early age of 10 years, others remained at school until they were aged 19 years. One deaf person had only one year for formal education, while others had attended school for as many as seventeen years. It might be expected that deaf children would be exposed to the education system for longer than the minimum of eleven years experienced by most hearing children. Therefore it was all the more surprising to find that a quarter had been at school for ten years or less. Only 28 per cent of deaf people had attended school for longer than most hearing children and only a tenth had stayed for fourteen years or more. Not all the discrepancy between the duration of school attendance implied by statutory provision, and the reality, was explained by the great age of many of those involved.

It might be assumed that continuity would be an important element in the educational experience of deaf children and indeed, three-quarters had attended only one or two schools. There was no doubt that changing schools was a disruptive experience, and often unhelpful to the learning process, though a few had found a second or subsequent school more to their taste than the first. Often, the move involved changing between oral and signed communication as the predominant vehicle for education, or to a different system of sign.

Miss Jones said ' I was shocked when I lost signing with the speech when I changed schools. If speech is used alone I find it difficult – sometimes I think the wrong words. Signs help – they help lip-reading. The changes of school, and the different signs held me back from learning.'

Traditionally, much of the specialist educational provision for deaf children has taken the form of residential schooling, away from the influence of parents whose commitment to speech may be doubtful, to ensure the socialization of deaf children into the customs and habits of hearing society. Therefore it was not surprising that almost half of the deaf had received all their education in residential schools, and a further fifth in both day and residential schools, while only a fifth had been educated entirely at day schools. Thus a majority of deaf people had been removed in childhood from family and neighbourhood. Almost all were distraught at the separation from family and friends.

Miss Gratton, aged 47, said 'I went to a residential school for the deaf in the West Country. I never saw my mother for five years. I didn't like going over on the boat from Jersey – I cry, cry, cry. But there were very few other deaf on the island.'

A few found the experience too difficult.

Mr Johnstone said 'I ran away from school twice. I was picked up by soldiers, once on the Lewes road and once on the London road. When I got back I was whipped and given one week on bread and water. I never saw my mother and father for six years. I don't know how much I learned. In lip-reading I can understand if a wide mouth is used, but if a small mouth – no.'

In fact, short holidays of a few weeks at Christmas and in the summer appeared to be more common that total separation from the parental home. At least one small child did his best to remain at home.

Mr Morris, aged 74, said 'I went round and round to make myself giddy to avoid being sent off to boarding school. The doctor knew I was fixing it, so I was sent off to school the next year. I didn't know why I was going away to school.'

As well as enduring the terror of separation from the family most of those who had attended boarding schools appeared to have been educated in an atmosphere of considerable violence.

Mr Wilcox, aged 43, said 'I was taught one-handed sign at school which is useful if you're courting or drinking. They were very strict at school – we were often sent to bed with no supper. I believe it's much better now but then there was a lot of cruelty – flogging. Some of the mental children had very bad punishing.'

Mr Murdoch, aged 44, said 'They were very cruel at Blankton's. There were violent beatings.'

It was not only boys who were subjected to beatings.

Miss Britton, aged 42, said 'The staff were bad. They threw things at us and beat us. They hit us in the face with things. They were cruel. They all used signs. I was often sick.'

However, not all cruelty involved overt violence.

Mrs Perkins, aged 70, said 'The teachers were very cruel at my school. Their favourite punishment was to lock us up. I will never forget it. And I was treated as stupid by my parents. We only had one holiday a year. I was frightened and miserable. They never even tried to teach us to speak.'

Mrs Owen said 'Some were cruel. For the slightest thing you were sent to bed with no dinner. We were up at five in the morning doing the cooking and the cleaning.'

Only a tiny minority of those who had been to boarding school reported that they had enjoyed themselves there.

Mrs Simpson, aged 67, said 'I loved school, I never had a day away. The teachers signed, we all signed. I stayed at school in the holidays until I was 12 years old. My mother died when I was a baby, and my father was away in the armed forces. I was looked after by a neighbour.'

In general, deaf people felt deeply antagonistic towards their residential schools. It was striking that none of those who had experience only of day schools felt so deeply about their education. Presumably, the effects of punishments meted out in day schools were ameliorated by the knowledge that school would be over at the end of the afternoon. And however demanding parents were in the help they required, there was a qualitative difference between their demands and those of teachers.

The residential experience was by no means distributed evenly across the settings. Only among those living in private households were deaf people as likely to have been to a day as to a residential school: in all other settings the vast majority had experience only of residential education. Perhaps those who had attended day schools, even for part of their education, maintained closer links with family and neighbourhood than those whose education was entirely residential, and were more easily absorbed into the 'normal' community.

Of course, attendance at special schools whether day or residential may create a chasm between deaf people and the normal community. But it would be a mistake to suppose that all deaf people attended special schools. It is true that the vast majority – 69 per cent – had experience only of deaf schools or deaf units attached to hearing schools, but a substantial minority – 17 per cent – had attended hearing schools at some stage, while 4 per cent had been educated exclusively at such establishments. Those now living the most 'integrated' lives – in private households and hostels – were the most likely to have attended at least one hearing school. Indeed, almost a third of deaf people who lived at home had done so. Deaf people who had spent all their school days at hearing establishments were usually now elderly, and represented tremendous contrasts in educational experience. A few received totally unsympathetic treatment from both parents and teachers.

Miss Watson, aged 84 years, said 'I was pushed to the back of the class and slapped all the time. I often went home with welts on my arm, I didn't know what for. My parents said I'd got them so I must have deserved them. Deafness threw me into reading much more than was good for me. Life may be easier today, but it's not character forming.'

Miss Gregson, aged 76, said 'Mother realized I was deaf when I was 4 or 5. The teacher had to be very firm with me to get me through. I had to sit in front at school and must not sing! Well educated? Not that I know. I read books, books, books: *The Razor's Edge, Cakes and Ale*. Mother was a good talker and liked conversation about broader things and not tittle tattle. Politics? Yes, I loved to hear mother talk about politics.'

To the hazards of attendance at hearing schools were added, for some, the confusions arising from changing schools.

Mr Taunton, aged 46, said 'I liked school. I couldn't understand anything at first, because it was a hearing school. And there were problems because I always seemed to be changing schools.'

More usual and equally challenging were moves from hearing to deaf schools. It was evident that in some cases arrival at a deaf school created a sense of release as a systematic method of communication was made available.

Mr Rossiter, aged 66, said 'I went to a hearing day school first. I sat at the front of the class but I found I was unable to lip-read. The second school was residential, for the deaf. I was there from 11 to 16. There were only two holi-days a year, at Christmas and summer. I picked up finger-spelling and signing quickly. I had not been able to read at all at 11.'

Others, however, found the constraints of the special school where there were fewer opportunities to take public examinations and a narrower cur-riculum, greater than those of the hearing institution.

The majority of deaf people, then, found the continuity of their education broken in some way – by a move from one school to another of the same type, by moving between residential and day or hearing and deaf schools. In addition, a small minority (7 per cent) found their school careers disrupted by an absence of six months or more, caused by illness or accident.

What assumptions about the nature of integration underlay educational approaches? To what extent was integration viewed entirely in terms of absorption into the hearing community and education based, therefore, entirely on oral principles? And how far did schools acknowledge the existence of the deaf community and attempt to ensure entry into that community by teaching sign? On the face of it, there appeared to be evidence to suggest that in general, the schools attended by deaf people supported integration into the deaf community rather than into the total society. Almost half had attended only schools in which sign was used, while another tenth had been to both entirely oral schools as well as schools where some sign was allowed. Only 18 per cent of deaf people had experi-ence solely of oralist schools. Indeed, the evidence appeared to lend some support to the point of view of determined oralists who have argued that integration into the total society can be achieved only if schools exclude sign: whereas only half of those living in private households had been educated at schools where at least some sign was used this was true of a large preponderence of those living in all other settings.

However, in practice, few deaf people had been to schools in which sign had been used systematically as a major means of comunication, and those who had experience of such schools tended to be elderly.

Mrs Fox, aged 73, said 'I went to the Blankton residential school for the deaf. All the teachers were good signers: they taught me to read and write.'

Miss Franks, aged 88, said 'I went to Blankley day school for the deaf. They were good teachers. They used sign and speech together.'

Recollections such as these were a reflection of educational practice before the advent of determined oralism. Where younger people had used sign at school, it had generally been only as a minor communication tool within a largely oralist approach.

Mr Formby, aged 17, said 'I went to three day schools for the deaf. No one told us not to sign but it was very much an oral education. We didn't use sign much at school.'

Despite the apparently widespread use of sign at the schools attended by most deaf people there was little evidence, other than that from those educated before the introduction of thoroughgoing oralism, of an attempt to teach sign as a systematic method of communication. In many instances sign appeared to be used only to clarify the meaning of spoken and written English – in fact, as a tool to ensure entry into hearing society, rather than to promote an understanding of the language used by the adult deaf community. Yet sign for most deaf schoolchildren had been the preferred means of communication. As many as two-thirds had used sign openly with schoolfriends both in class and the playground, while another tenth did so surreptitiously.

Yet the use of sign was actively discouraged by many teachers. Almost a third (30 per cent) of deaf people had attended schools in which they had been forbidden to use sign.

Mr Craig, aged 23, said 'From the age of 3 until I was 16 I was at a school for the hard of hearing and deaf. It was very strict: you were caned if you signed.'

Mr Ross, aged 81, said 'The teachers didn't sign: they slapped our hands if we used it.'

Not all punishments for signing were conventional:

Mrs Frame, aged 61, said 'They pulled your ears if you signed.'

It is clear that even before oralism became dominant, there were schools where its adoption was thoroughgoing.

The failure to adopt a consistent policy in schools has been the subject of complaints by parents of deaf children in recent years. One of the hazards encountered by children as they move from one school to another is that a change of school may involve a change of policy on the use of sign. As many as 11 per cent of deaf people had experienced both oral and signing schools. But confusion arising from such differences was not confined to those who changed schools: some found that teachers within the same school differed in their attitudes towards manual communication.

Mr Rostow said 'There was some signing at both my schools. I liked one or two teachers: for instance in the second the class teacher's sign and expression was very good. There was no sign at all in the first class: that made me angry because it meant that I went to the bottom of the class. But when I went to a different class I went to the top because the teacher signed.'

Whether it was prohibited or not, most deaf people developed signed communication with their friends at school.

Miss Robertson, aged 25, said 'I never speak: I have never made voice. We used secret sign hiding from the teachers at school.'

It is not surprising, therefore, that 'schoolsigns', which are often peculiar to individual schools, have developed which differ from those used by the adult deaf community. As a consequence, for many deaf adolescents, leaving school involves not only attempting to grapple with an adult, hearing world, but also learning the signs of the adult deaf community.

Deaf people themselves were clear in their preferences for total communication to be adopted within the education system. The vast majority (all but eight) favoured the use of both speech and sign throughout education for the deaf, and many of them wished to see greater use made of deaf teachers who could introduce deaf children to the language and community of the adult deaf world.

Despite the insistence on oralism in schools there was little evidence that the importance attached to speech understanding and acquisition, was reflected in the achievement of educational qualifications. Only 6 per cent of deaf people had gained either a CSE, matriculation, school certificate or an O or A level. It was only among the younger deaf that those with education qualifications were to be found.

Mr Lipp, aged 71, explained 'In my day everyone was the same at school – reading, writing and no exams.'

Yet the absence of formal educational qualifications was not necessarily an indication of the failure of schools to prepare deaf children for the labour market. A little more than half had received some kind of training for work while at school, and they were found disproportionately among those living in private households, hostels, and homes for the deaf. There was a clear distinction between the type of training made available in schools for girls as compared with boys. Only a seventh of the women who had received a training had been taught a trade, the remainder having concentrated on domestic skills, mainly cooking, cleaning, laundry and sewing.

Miss Jackson, aged 74, said 'We were taught to sew, knit, clean, scrub, dust, iron and wash.'

In part, however, domestic duties were undertaken by pupils in residential establishments to reduce the necessity for paid domestic labour. But it was also hoped that training in domestic duties would fit girls for domestic service.

Mrs Gray, aged 65, said 'I was taught cleaning to be a servant.'

In contrast, only three boys had been expected to learn domestic skills, and then solely to reduce the cost of domestic help.

Mr Timpson, aged 58, said 'We did cleaning by a rota.'

Others had been taught manual skills, usually carpentry, shoe making or repairing, or tailoring. The value of the training was sometimes questioned.

Mr Fox said 'They taught me tailoring at school, but it was very different when I went to work.'

In many cases, more than one skill had been learnt.

Mr Ringmer said 'I did some baking, cobbling, tailoring and shopfitting – carpentry.'

Mr Selsby recalled 'We did sewing, building crafts, carpentry, shoes, gardening and cabinet work.'

Although sewing was widely taught to deaf girls, tailoring remained the preserve of the boys.

Even though a majority of deaf people were prepared at school in some way to meet the demands of the labour market, as many as 44 per cent left without training or educational qualifications. Most of these stressed the emphasis which had been placed on educational 'basics' by their teachers.

Miss Ray, aged 41, said 'I did well at school – good marks. There was not much sewing, drawing or cookery.'

In other schools, the focus appeared to have been on the production of speech.

Mrs Jenkins, aged 73, said 'No, the school was not in the business of teaching us a trade – it was teaching us to speak. There was no time for sport. I didn't play badminton, tennis or table tennis until I left school. They taught us some French, but I think it would have been better to concentrate on English.'

It was evident that schools varied in their approaches to integration. Whereas some had concentrated on success in the labour market either by providing training in manual skills or – more recently – commercial skills and the opportunity to acquire education qualifications, others had emphasized the importance of speech acquisition, and still others had focused on literacy.

Of course, evidence about education depended upon recollections of the sometimes distant past, and no doubt many memories were distortions of reality. Nevertheless, the recollections of any one deaf person were usually corroborated by a number of others. Most suggested that there was little formal discussion at school to prepare them for life when they left. Only about a third had attended any discussions about possible careers after leaving school, and it was striking that a disproportionate number of these lived in private households and hostels – the most 'normal' settings.

On leaving school, the vast majority (three-quarters) of deaf people returned to the family home: this was true disproportionately of those who currently lived in private households, hostels and homes for the elderly; it seemed as though even in adolescence, those who were to end up in homes for the deaf or hospitals had only tenuous contact with 'normal' life.

Training

Recent research has suggested that when compared with hearing children, the hearing-impaired exhibit a considerably depressed level of aspiration.[14] Furthermore, the greater the degree of hearing impairment, the lower the child's aspirations will be. As a consequence, 'The hearing-impaired appear to be less likely to use existing opportunities for part-time further education.'[15] Perhaps it is not surprising that this should be so, if it is true, as Conrad has argued, that deaf children achieve on average a substantially lower academic standard than their hearing counterparts on leaving school. The discrepancy in the levels of achievements of the two groups is compounded by the absence of specialist institutions of higher education for the deaf, and the scarcity of courses specifically designed for them. As D. Langley and J. Hatton Lane observe, 'For many hearing-impaired school leavers, integration is the norm'[16] because they have no choice. The Warnock Report[17] recognized that until the transition from school to work is accompanied by skilled help and advice to children and their parents, much of the effort of special education will be wasted. In practice, no rational system of provision for the hearing-impaired exists in further education. The post-school deaf child is faced with finding an appropriate course within a range of uncoordinated experiments in the field of further education,[18] or competing with hearing children for a place within the general available provision. R. Green has described some of the experiments which are taking place in the field,[19] which include teaching in schools for the deaf on how to write letters of application, handle interviews and complete employment forms, and the availability within the Open University of a tutor skilled in sign language, who has an understanding of deafness, and special help for deaf students on integrated courses studying for City and Guilds examinations in certain areas.

In view of the fragmentation of specialist provision in further education, it was not surprising to find that only one person had a degree, while two had City and Guilds qualifications. Of those who had, or were taking further education courses, one had done so on a hearing course without specialist help, though other types of help and support had been invaluable.

Miss Benson, aged 20, said 'I went to college for three years for a full time Diploma course in Graphic Design. I've got a large folder of my stuff here. I had a lot of help from an artist friend of the family. I had a hard time socially at college.'

Others were involved in experiments in further education provision for the deaf.

Mr Nelson, aged 16, said 'At the moment I'm at North London College with approximately twenty other deaf people, where I am studying Technical Drawing, Woodwork, Metalwork, Art, Maths and English – some of them at the City Lit. I also go out to work one day a week – work experience is on Thursday. And I have been going to the London College of Printing on Tuesday and Furniture on Friday.'

However, although only 5 per cent had completed an apprenticeship this was by far the most important source of training for deaf people. Indeed, the number of years in school rather than training as such, appeared to be the important factor in determining employability. Work appeared to be most secure among those who had been at school for ten or more years. In view of the importance of school and the types of training available there it was small wonder that Rodda *et al.* discovered that deaf girls are more likely to have part-time jobs in the 'social service' category and boys in the 'farming' and 'trades' categories.[20] The domestic activities in which so many girls were trained at school have ensured their employment within the social services, now that domestic service is no longer widespread.

Of course, those removed from the normal life of private households and hostels tended to be removed as well from the opportunities of the formal further education and training systems, though this was not always the case. One home for the deaf and more than half of the hospitals had educational facilities suitable for the deaf.

Employment

In recent years research has begun to document the employment problems of the deaf. Rodda has argued that from the outset of their working lives, deaf people are at a disadvantage in the labour market; on leaving school, 'significantly less of the hearing-impaired children are already placed in employment than are the normally hearing children'.[21] In Ireland, a disproportionate number of deaf people (11 per cent) never obtained paid work at all.[22] No comparable information exists for Britain, and it seems reasonable to suppose that, because there must be an over-representation of mentally handicapped and mentally ill persons, as well as those with additional physical handicaps, the present study overstates the failure to find paid employment among deaf people generally in this country. In fact, 13 per cent had never done work for which they had been paid the going rate for the job, though some of these had worked hard for small payment in institutions. Such people came disproportionately from hospitals and homes for the deaf, where they accounted for between a quarter and a third of deaf residents and patients. In contrast less than 4 per cent of those who lived in private households had never found a job.

Those with work experience had found a job soon after leaving school. Although there were few with apprenticeships, more than a quarter (26 per cent) had received some kind of training, usually on the job. The Irish study drew attention to the predominance of certain trades among first jobs – tailoring, shoe making and repairs, labouring and factory work, carpentry and agricultural work among the men, and textile work, clerical work and typing, service and factory work among the women.[23] The numbers involved in the present study were too small for comparison, and in any case were never intended to be representative. Even so, there were striking similarities between the two populations in the type of jobs acquired on leaving school, despite the differences between the structure of the British and Irish labour markets. Among those involved in the present study, service jobs predominated among school leavers, being undertaken mainly, though not entirely, by women working as cleaners or in laundries. The second largest group worked in trades associated with garment manufacture – tailoring and dressmaking, labouring and light factory work (32 per cent on leaving school). Upholstery and related trades provided first jobs for 12 per cent of those with work records, while 9 per cent entered the boot and shoe making and repairing industry; the same proportion worked as farm labourers or in market gardening; and 7 per cent became carpenters.

Thus the majority entered skilled, semi or unskilled manual jobs on leaving school. Few became clerks or typists (4 per cent) or entered jobs associated with the new technology, such as data processing (4 per cent). The type of job acquired after leaving school reflected the training provided by schools. As apprenticeships and on-the-job training were most common among those living in private houeholds, it was not surprising to find that it was among them that skilled and semi-skilled first jobs were most often to be found. To a considerable degree, first jobs were also a reflection of widely held beliefs in society about suitability of certain types of employment for the deaf.[24]

On the whole, deaf people appeared to have little difficulty in finding work. The vast majority – more than four-fifths – changed their jobs at least once in the course of their working lives; indeed a high proportion of all except patients in hospitals for the mentally handicapped had managed to change their jobs at least once. A number of deaf people commented upon the ease with which they could find jobs.

Mr Fox, aged 75, said 'I was trained as a tailor and I was always a tailor. Conditions at work were very good but small firms had a habit of closing down, especially after the First World War. The job before last finished after twelve years. I usually worked round Hackney or Kings Cross. I found all the jobs from the paper. It was always easy to find jobs – I made uniforms in war time. I had quite a number of jobs in my time – never any trouble. I never felt I'd been unfairly dealt with.'

Mrs Fixton described her work experience: '1931–9 I learned cleaning at the home for the deaf. Then I worked as a cleaner in a London hospital until 1961. In the meantime, I got married – that was in 1947, and my daughters were born in 1952 and 1953. I continued to work while I was bringing up the girls. When I left the hospital in 1961, I cleaned part time for a year in a deaf club, but the money was terrible. So in 1962 I went to work in another hospital and I stayed there until 1968, when I got a job in British Home Stores working up in the restaurant. I stayed there until I retired in 1977. While I was in the last job I also worked part time cleaning tables in a cafe.'

In fact nearly all who reported a change of job described moving between similar jobs, though a minority – a tenth – moved between manual and non-manual work.

There were few instances in which a job change involved promotion, and this appeared to be typical of the deaf in general:

where discrimination exists, it is as often amongst employees as employers. The problem is one of under-employment rather than unemployment. Deaf people can usually get a job, but it is often one that is not commensurate with their abilities, not one that offers chances of promotion.[25]

Recent research has indicated the widespread appreciation of the promotion problems of deaf people among the general public, among whom difficulties are attributed to employer prejudice and communication difficulties.[26]

How did deaf people manage to overcome their undeniable communication difficulties at work? By far the most common method of communication was a combination of speech, writing and lip-reading: as many as two-fifths communicated at work in this way; in comparison, only a tenth were sufficiently oral to rely entirely on speech and lip-reading. Writing was an important aid to communication: a little more than a tenth relied entirely on the written word when communicating at work, while the same proportion used a combination of writing and gesture, occasionally accompanied by speech and sign. Of course, the written word required a degree of literacy which by no means all deaf people had achieved: indeed not everyone who relied on the written word for communication at work could understand it.

Mr Brown, aged 52, who worked in a fibreglass boat factory, said 'When the boss writes down instructions, I say "yes", and put it in my pocket and take it home to my wife – she explains.'

Despite their influence on employment patterns by the expectations set, and the type and level of training provided, schools played little practical part in helping to secure the first job. In all, only 15 per cent of first jobs were obtained through the school, whereas as many as half had been obtained through a relative and another 8 per cent through friends, while as many as a tenth had been acquired with no help at all. Nor had the formal employment services been of much help – only 3 per cent of first jobs had been obtained through labour exchanges[27] compared with as many as 17 per cent through the social worker for the deaf. In general, family and neighbourhood help was most common among those whose current ties with the informal network were strongest, namely people living in private households. In contrast, help from social workers for the deaf was most common among those now living in other settings, where ties with the informal network were weakest.

However, the method by which first jobs were obtained by no means set the pattern for the subsequent use of the formal employment services. Almost half of the deaf had visited a labour exchange at least once, and as many had been registered as disabled by the Department of Employment. Among older people, the practice of visiting the labour exchange was restricted to the period of mass umemployment before the Second World War.

Mr Wiles, aged 78, said 'I went to the labour exchange several times between the wars, but never had a green card.'

Mr Frome, aged 60, explained 'I went before the war. It was always the same "No jobs, no jobs!" '

However, others had gone solely to register as a disabled person. Yet the majority of deaf people had neither visited a labour exchange nor registered.

The failure to use the formal employment services was largely attributable to the ease with which deaf people generally were able to find employment.

Mrs Osborne, aged 66, said 'I never bothered with the labour exchange or the green card because I worked right through.'

In part, however, the reluctance to rely on the official agencies stemmed from a lack of confidence in their efficiency.

Mr Green, aged 29, said 'I've never bothered because they're too slow. It's better to get your own job.'

Mrs Thompson, aged 60, said 'I never went because I've learned they're hopeless rubbish – no good. I didn't have a green card because I didn't think it would be any good. I relied on the newspaper, and friends told me about jobs.'

And Mrs Rostow, aged 42, explained 'It's no good going, or being registered because they always say "full up" when the Labour tells them you're a "deaf person". '

Attendance at a labour exchange failed to ensure that a deaf person would meet the Disablement Resettlement Officer. In fact, only a fifth (less than half of those who had visited the labour exchange), had seen the DRO. In the majority of cases, only two or three interviews with the DRO at most were reported. However, far more deaf people had visited than had received practical help in finding a job from the DRO: only 12 per cent reported that they had obtained work through the DRO. Satisfaction with the service was not high. Half of those who had visited the DRO considered that he had done all he could for them. Those who had made most use of the service tended to have the highest opinion of it. However, it was clear that few concessions were made to take account of the specific difficulties of deaf people. None had encountered a DRO who could sign well. Despite severe communication problems, only two people had been accompanied to a job interview by the DRO, and in only one case had a DRO arranged for an interpreter to be present at an interview. The failure of the DRO to sign and of most deaf people to produce intelligible speech resulted in discussions between them which were brief and conducted in writing.

Mr Johnstone, aged 71, said 'I saw the DRO many times. There was no speech. He gave me a piece of paper with a job written on it, I read it, then it was a matter of going away, getting the job.'

Mr Simpson said 'I knew him (the DRO) down Medliott Road. He
talked – no sign. I wrote what I wanted, and he gave me a piece of paper with
a job on it, and I went to work.

Others had been thrown back on their own resources.

Mr Exon said 'The DRO at the labour exchange couldn't sign. We had to
write everything down. He didn't get me a job so I used the paper.'

Mr Hunsworth reported 'I went to the DRO five or six times. But he's not
much help, it's quicker to use the newspaper.'

The experiences reported here appear to be typical. After a recent conference on employment for the hearing impaired, the RNID concluded
that there was a need for trained interpreters for the deaf, improved communication with the Manpower Services Commission, and a specialist
officer in the Department of Employment.[28]

Thus communication difficulties generally prevented deaf people from
offsetting their disadvantage in the labour market with the help of the
skilled placement services. Did this mean, then, that they were left to rely
entirely on their own resources when seeking work? In fact, between a
quarter and a third had relied entirely on their own initiative, while
another fifth had received help from the informal network of family and
friends.

Mr Selsby said 'I always found work for myself in the newspaper, or friends
put in a word for me.'

Mr Hunsworth, aged 52, said 'My daughter's husband helps me get my
jobs – I work with him at the moment.'

Mrs Nixon described how she was forced to use her own initiative. 'I went to
the Labour and asked, asked, asked for a job. They said, "Nothing because
the deaf don't try very hard." The man couldn't sign and couldn't be patient
to write anything down. It was just "come along tomorrow" – and nothing.
So I found jobs myself – walking, walking. There are a lot of deaf with no jobs
now. I know quite a few out of work in North London.'

Although the employment services were of little help, as many as half of
those who had worked had been helped to find a job by the social worker
with the deaf.

Miss Gosford said 'The social worker came with me to the interview for my
last job – we went together, and my sister as well. He interpreted and we
wrote it all down.'

Mr Browne, aged 45, said 'I've never been to the DRO section at the labour. I

take a walk every morning with the dog to get a paper to look for jobs. The
social worker helped me with the gas board job, and the last job I got myself.'

Mrs Jackson said 'I always see the social worker about a job. The social worker
came with me to the last interview and interpreted.'

The formal support system was responsible for actively discouraging a
minority of deaf people from seeking work. A little more than a tenth had
been told 'officially' – by teachers, medical personnel, or those working for
the employment services – that they would be unable to hold a job. But the
determination to be 'normal' was so decided, that as many as three-
quarters of them managed to find employment, though for a few, work was
a relatively fleeting or fragmented experience.

Mr Watson, aged 63, said 'In 1934 I worked as a farm labourer but the next
year I went to work for my father in a garage – not successful. I left there in
1938 and the following year I was admitted to hospital for the first time. I've
been in and out of hospital ever since. In 1948 one hospital let me work as a
carrier but in 1951 they declared me unemployable. In 1960, I began work in
the wood shop, and in 1967 I attended woodwork OT. This was here on the
ward until 1977. Now I've no occupation. I just wander about the grounds.'

However, others clung tenaciously and successfully to their employed
status by taking on a succession of poorly paid jobs.

Mr Goad, aged 55, said 'I had no work for two years after leaving school then
in 1943 I worked with my father as a carpenter and painting woodwork. In
1945 I moved to a private firm where I had a job as a labourer/painter. I
stayed there for seven and a half years. Then I had two years at
Remploy – from 1952-4. I slept there in the week, but I had to leave because
the pay was too low. So I got a job as a general handyman in a hotel on the Isle
of Wight. I stayed there for fourteen years. My last job – from 1968-72 was in
a nursery greenhouse where I worked with flowermen. But I had a stroke while
I was there, and another in 1976. I haven't worked since.'

Sometimes a suitable job was found early in working life.

Mrs Job said 'After I left school I stayed home for three years. In 1931 I went
to work at Chilprufe. I was 24 years old. I did the seaming and ribbing for the
combination vests and pants – children's. I had two deaf friends there but they
left to get married. I stayed on until 1971. They gave me a gold watch in 1968.
I hardly communicated there: if I did, it was by writing or gestures.'

Of those below retirement age rather more than half (56 per cent) were
employed, and of these the majority lived in private households and hostels. More than four-fifths of those living in private households, and more
than three-quarters of hostel residents were at work, though this was true of

only tiny minorities of those in hospitals or homes for the deaf. Despite the high number of women involved, most (three-quarters) were in full-time employment – indeed, a quarter had worked forty-two hours or more in the previous week. Furthermore, as many as three-quarters were in open employment, while the remainder worked in sheltered conditions in local authority, Remploy or voluntary workshops, or in hospitals. The hospital patients undertook considerable duties in the. laundry, gardens, and boilerhouse, and worked a substantial number of hours each week.

Mr Fready, aged 75, who lived in a hospital for the mentally ill, continued to work a twenty-hour week despite his age. He began to work in 1931 on the hospital farm, and in 1974 when the farm was finally phased out he transferred to the gardens. By staff he was regarded as 'energetic for his age and a very good worker in the hospital garden and social club'. He had been known to have only one friend, Sam. They never spoke but always worked together, the hearing Sam taking the initiative.

A number of hospital patients were now 'retired' after working hard for many years within the hospital.

Miss Cox was admitted to a hospital for the mentally ill at the age of 20 in 1936. She was employed in the laundry, where she worked well, until forced to transfer against her will to ward work at the age of 70. But she did not have the same feel for this, and now did very little.

Mr Levitt, aged 79, had worked on a farm where he had enjoyed looking after cows before his admission to a hospital for the mentally ill in 1924. Throughout his hospital life he had been a willing worker. In his younger days he had wheeled coal trolleys, and had helped on the wards in later years.

Although those in work clung tenaciously to their employed status, as many as two-fifths were dissatisfied at work. Of these, a sixth found the hours too long, an eighth complained about the unhelpful attitude of workmates, while a tenth considered that they earned less for the job or worked harder than the hearing. For more than a quarter of the employed, however, unhappiness was associated mainly with isolation from hearing workmates.

Mrs Ray who worked for an engineering company in the workshop said 'The people who work there are not friendly. Everyone enjoys themselves, but they're selfish, they don't include me.'

Mr Brown, who worked in a boatyard as a laminator, said 'My workmates are only fair. I'm left alone, there's not much talking.'

However, the majority (four-fifths) admitted to advantages at work. The largest category (half) identified the helpful attitude of the boss as a major advantage, and a factor which could be crucial when deaf people were isolated by communication difficulties.

Mrs Brown, who worked for a paintbox manufacturer, said 'The boss is very nice, and explains everything.'

Mr Forster said 'The supervisor explains what's going on when there's a lot of chat.'

Others (two-fifths) were attracted by the friendly attitudes of workmates.

Mr Oxton, who worked as a carpenter said 'They're good mates. We go to the pub and so on.'

Other factors which substantial minorities of deaf people found attractive included good working conditions (one-third) and hours (two-fifths). In addition as many as two-thirds of the employed appreciated their current job either because it offered independence or an escape from loneliness.

Mr Selsby said 'I should have retired last year, but I went part-time instead. I thoroughly enjoy my job. I feel lonely at home.'

Mr Morris said 'Before, I was working with other deaf people and there was a lot of trouble, but not now. I can suit myself. I enjoy working alone.'

Mr Fairfax, who worked as a welfare assistant for a voluntary organization for the deaf, said 'My job is problem solving for the deaf. I work at my own discretion with very little supervision. That's the big advantage.'

Of course, some (a third) considered their present job to have both advantages and disadvantages. Despite the repetitive nature of the work and the low pay which was the lot of most deaf workers, the majority of retired people looked back on their working lives with pleasure.

Miss Gregson, aged 76, said 'Those were happy times. I remember the names of all the girls. Mr Green used to bring a big box of chocolates for Christmas, and there was a party if someone got married, and leaving presents.'

Few reported that any concessions were made in the way in which they carried out their work, other than in the method of receiving instructions in writing. Exceptions were

Mr Thornton, a builder's mate: 'I do the same as everyone else, but I'm not allowed on the crane', and Mr Fairfax: 'Because I'm deaf I have a teleprinter and a video system.'

However, five observed sourly that they were differentiated from their hearing colleagues only in the rate at which they worked.

Mr Selsby, a shop fitter, said 'The boss knows that I know that I have to be a good worker: if I didn't work hard I would get the push because I'm deaf.'

Of course, communication difficulties usually prevented not only the establishment of relationships with workmates, but also effective engagement in the labour movement which might have offered reassurance to counteract the common feeling of insecurity and exploitation. In fact, a quarter of those at work were members of trade unions. At union meetings deaf workers relied on workmates or shop stewards to interpret – none were able to follow the details of procedures. Reliance on the interpretive skills which depended heavily on gesture, inevitably ensured for deaf people only a limited understanding of union affairs.

Communication difficulties at work created a strain: this was true for about three-fifths of those employed. On the whole receiving instructions was not a problem, but a sixth found some difficulty in both giving and receiving information, while rather more reported being isolated as a result of communication difficulties. Although the great majority of the employed used at least some speech at work, most found it necessary to resort to writing as well, despite generally poor literacy skills. Manual workers – the majority of the men – used gesture in day-to-day routine talk with workmates. In any complex situation writing, regarded as the swiftest and most certain means of ensuring comprehension on both sides, was always used. Many sought to limit work stress by minimizing the journey to work. Few deaf people sought work at a distance from home: as many as three-fifths travelled for no more than fifteen minutes to work, and none for more than an hour.

Understandably among a group with few formal skills or qualifications and overwhelmingly employed in low paid manual or service jobs, the constant search for work nearer home, or with slightly better pay and conditions, was reflected in frequent job changes. Almost three-fifths had been in their present job for no more than five years, and indeed, the majority of these for two years or less. However, there were deaf people who had clung to a job for many years. A little more than a fifth had worked in the same place for more than ten years, and half of these had not changed their jobs for twenty years or more. To some extent long years of loyal service in the same job were a tribute to satisfaction at work; but another important factor was fear lest another job could not be found. Many were apprehensive about the future.

Mr Patianou, aged 29, who worked as a cutter in the clothing trade said 'There were seven cutters in the firm but in April four were given their cards, so there are only three of us now. Maybe we will be made redundant too, and the factory close soon. I work very hard to keep my job.'

Indeed, there was a widespread reluctance to take sick leave even among those with secondary handicaps: only a tenth had had four weeks or more off sick in the previous five years, mainly for accidents. Most deaf workers were proud of their employment record.

Mr Hunsworth, aged 52, said 'I never had a day off school for sickness, and I haven't had a day off work.'

Mrs Johnson, aged 43, said 'I've only had one week off in the five years I've been with this firm.'

Mr Patel, aged 52, who worked as a compositor in the printing industry, said 'I've been off work for two weeks sickness in eighteen years.'

Initial experience ensured that few deaf people subsequently placed reliance on the formal employment services. None of those who had obtained their current job through the labour exchange had seen the DRO. Indeed, as many as a sixth had obtained work through newspaper advertisements or notice boards, while the same proportion had done so through the intervention of friends, relatives, or the social worker for the deaf. But most jobs (more than half) were obtained by a visit or writing to likely firms.

In contrast, heavy reliance was placed on the formal network – social workers for the deaf, or the DRO – in the search for jobs by a substantial minority (two-fifths) of the non-employed who were seeking work. Most wanted full-time work in areas where deaf people were already predominantly employed – light assembly factory work, laundries, and cleaning. Although those seeking work came from all settings, it was striking that only the hospital patients and residents of the homes for the deaf were receiving no help with their quest. Ironically, those living in private households and hostels, who were most likely to have help from the formal network, also retained the closest links with the informal network as well. In general the communication problems of those without work were far more profound than was true of employed people.

In looking back over their working lives most people could identify a particular job which they preferred above others. But only in a few cases were such jobs superior in terms of social or skill status: most were preferred for the friendly atmosphere, marginally better pay, a particularly benevolent boss. Difficulties arising from deafness had been experienced at work by only a minority – a fifth in all. A third of the reported difficulties concerned promotion and transfer to other jobs.

Miss Fanshaw, aged 26, who worked for the Area Health Authority, said 'I shan't get promotion, and it's difficult to get a transfer because I can't use the phone.'

Miss Argus said 'I work as a machine operator in the Civil Service. My promotion interview was conducted without an interpreter or any understanding of my deafness. I couldn't lip-read well enough. I'm bitter about it.'

But most difficulties were associated with unfair pay.

Mr Oxton, a carpenter, said 'I was exploited. I was a skilled man but others got more, so I complained.'

Mrs Fox had worked as an upholsterer: 'They were not paying me overtime. I had to be firm.'

Mr Selsby, a carpenter, said, 'I was exploited. I wasn't getting a bonus like the others so I left the job.'

Despite the low status and lack of skills involved in much of the work undertaken and the difficulties with which it was often retained, work remained important not only as an indicator of 'normality' but also as a source of income – a third of employed people were their household's sole earners.

Income

For the deaf as for other disabled people, financial independence may be seen as a reflection of the extent to which normality has been achieved in other respects. To a large extent both the level and source of personal income were influenced by the success with which deaf people were able to operate 'normally' in the hearing community. Occupation, the determinant of wage level, and indeed whether a paid occupation could be followed at all depended upon the degree to which deaf people mastered the communication system of the hearing and acquired the qualifications at school which gave access to skilled jobs and the professions.[29]

In all, only a third of deaf people reported employment to be their major source of personal income. Of course, to some extent, source of income was determined by age: a third of the deaf were above retirement age and dependent primarily upon state benefits. Yet a further third were both of working age and dependent upon social security for their personal income. It is true that about a quarter of these received payment for work undertaken in hospitals, but the sums involved were small. Most of those over retirement age received the state retirement pension and in only four cases was it augmented by a small employment pension. Invalidity Benefit was the most common source of income for the non-employed below retirement age, while another 14 per cent depended entirely upon Supplementary Benefit and 8 per cent did so in part. Few received short term or sickness benefit: on the whole, financial dependence was long term.

In all only half of those under retirement age, many of whom lived in hostels or private households, received a wage or salary. Of course, the prevalence of unskilled, manual and service jobs among deaf people determined that the group as a whole was low paid. In fact only a seventh of those at work earned above the average for male manual workers, all of whom lived in private households, while another seventh received earnings which were around the average; for the vast majority, earnings were below this level.

To compare earnings with the male manual wage offers little guidance as to the standard of living of deaf people. The demands made on earnings may vary widely between households, and whereas in some households they may be the main or only source of income, in others, they may be one of many. It has become customary, therefore, to compare total household income, including interest from savings and so on to the level of payment to which that household would have been entitled under the Supplementary Benefits scheme – to compare household income with the official poverty line. However, considerable difficulties arise in the case of those living in hostels, homes and hospitals where so much is found by the institution, and provided at a level regardless of the individual's income. Therefore the comparison between income and Supplementary Benefit levels was confined to deaf people living in private households. The vast majority (seven-tenths) lived within the margins of poverty defined as 140 per cent[30] of their entitlement on the Supplementary Benefits scale. In general deaf people who themselves depended on state benefits as their main source of income even though others in the household had earnings or other means of financial support were more likely to live in households assessed as poor, than were those who depended upon earned income. Whereas all but one of the households in which the deaf person was dependent upon social security benefits were in poverty, this was true of a quarter of those households where he or she was an earner.

While comparisons with average wages and supplementary benefits levels are useful to indicate the departure from the norm in terms of income, they are not necessarily helpful in determining the *adequacy* of an income. In recent years, increasing attention has been paid to 'the extra costs of disabled living'.[31] Considerable difficulties are attached to establishing the nature and scale of such costs. For example, if activities contract as a result of disability, it is possible for disabled people to find that they 'save' more after the onset of a disabling condition.[32] In the case of the deaf, Tumin has drawn attention to the financial and other costs borne by the parents of deaf children. As the emphasis on deaf education has shifted in recent years from a belief in the value of severing the links between children in boarding schools and their parents (the system experienced by so many of the deaf involved in the present study), to an insistence on the value to deaf children of parental ties, parents are faced with the costs of fetching their children home for the weekend, often over long distances, and returning them to school on Sunday every week during the term.[33] The additional costs of their handicap to deaf adults has been described by Loach in terms of the costs of aids to communication, such as flashing doorbells, and the batteries required to run them. The amounts involved are small, but must be assessed within the context of low wages or dependency on social security benefits.[34] In assessing the adequacy of income in relation to the extra costs arising from deafness, it proved impossible to include those living in residential hostels, homes and hospitals. Where aids were available in such settings, they were 'found' by the institution rather than bought by individual residents and patients.

In practice only a quarter of those living in private households reported that their condition resulted in extra expenditure – mainly on postage and travel arising from inability to use the telephone. It was normal for three letters to be sent to make an arrangement which a hearing person could have secured with a single telephone call. Delays in receiving replies to letters often necessitated travel to find out what had gone wrong. Social contacts, too, had to be maintained through the mail or by visits.

Mr Gray said 'You have to buy stamps to write to friends, or you travel to see them and they're out. It happens quite a lot because no phone.'

Furthermore, visits to deaf clubs, the focus of the deaf community, often entailed long journeys.

Miss Hughes said 'The nearest deaf club is on the mainland. That's a boat and a bus journey away. I do that once a fortnight.'

A quarter of those who reported additional expenditure pointed to the cost of batteries for hearing aids, and two people complained that car insurance was higher because they were deaf.

However, for almost a quarter of deaf people, expenditure was below normal: more than half of them were entitled to free bus travel, and in some cases, cheap rail travel as well. The remainder, however, considered that deafness so restricted their activities that they had little opportunity to spend money. Of course, had they insisted on leading a normal life, the costs would have been substantial. Furthermore, it was clear that there were substantial costs associated with deafness which did not involve financial expenditure: almost half of the deaf people interviewed reported that the costs involved time rather than money, though, of course, cash equivalents might be devised. The whole process of understanding the hearing, writing instead of using speech, making arrangements by letter instead of telephone, waiting for someone to translate or explain, the repeats which understanding on both sides required, trying to gain an understanding of the background to events, all took a long time. The following are typical comments.

Miss Hughes: 'I have to go to see people or write – no telephone.'

Mrs Thompson: 'The whole business of talking, of waiting for things to happen, takes a time.'

Mr Simpson: 'I talk quicker with the deaf. Lip reading (the hearing) is very slow.'

Mrs Habant: 'It takes a long time to write things down. It's quick to speak.'

Miss Ray: 'It's a business finding out about things: I wait, wait.'

Mrs Fulton: 'Making arrangements to see people takes a time. No phone, always no phone.'

Mrs Glending: 'It's repeat, repeat.'

Mr Paxton: 'Talking, getting things done – news comes through other people. The hearing talk, talk, it all takes a long time to get sorted out.'

Despite the difficulties involved, it is important not to exclude those living in institutional settings from consideration of their command over resources. Kramer and Piachaud have drawn attention to the dearth of knowledge about the disposal of the incomes of elderly people in residential homes.[35] They suggest that it is usual for such people to lose control of their pension books, while the personal allowance is often below the level of entitlement defined by the DHSS. Furthermore, the elderly in residential settings are largely denied the opportunity to exercise economic choices even with the little money they are allowed, by the restricted nature of the shopping facilities available to them. Yet financial decision making is both an indicator of 'normality' and a means by which integration into the mainstream of society may be maintained.

Except in the hostel for the young working deaf where residents had to budget for all their requirements, deaf people in residential and hospital settings were excluded from the major responsibility of providing basic shelter, warmth, light, an adequate diet, basic furnishings and facilities. Pension books, regardless of the wishes of the residents, were held by the matron, who handed out the personal allowance in the south of England home for the deaf. Although in other homes decisions on the control of the pension book were taken jointly by matron and each resident, the result was usually the administratively convenient arrangement of matron holding the book and handing out the personal allowance. In practice, few residents held their books. In the case of the half-way psychiatric hostel no attempt appeared to be made to camouflage the control by staff of residents' incomes. In the hospitals, the full range of attitudes towards the control of patients' incomes was displayed, but though patient control never extended to the benefit book, some patients were allowed to exercise complete control over the disposal of the personal allowance.

Abdication of control over income was not confined to pension books. It was startling to find that in most cases in the half-way psychiatric hostel, the disposal even of income from full-time employment was in the hands of the superintendent. And in the hospitals control was often exercised by staff over the small amounts of money (usually amounting to no more than £2 per week) earned by patients in occupational therapy, or for work in the wards, boiler room, gardens, laundry and so on.

It would be wrong to think, however, that hospitals were alone in controlling more than the benefit book. As long ago as 1962 Townsend[36] drew attention to the widespread failure to pay residents of homes for the elderly the full personal allowance: the decision to withhold part of the allowance and the amount which was deducted appeared to be largely arbitrary and entirely within the discretion of the matron/superintendent, and the practice continues on a wide scale.[37]

Among the deaf, a little more than two-fifths of those in hostels, homes and hospitals received less than the personal allowance determined by the DHSS. Hostel residents of whom a quarter (all of them in the psychiatric hostel) failed to receive the full allowance were least likely to be denied their full entitlement. In most cases the allowance was reduced to around £1.25 per week, though one resident was allowed fifty pence plus his fares, and another received seventy-five pence. In the homes for the elderly and the deaf, about a third of the residents received less than the full amount, while one resident was not allowed to handle money at all.

Matron said 'Don't let her have any more money because she spends it on more and more cosmetics and toiletries she doesn't use up. I thought it was reasonable to stop her buying them.'

Miss Blume said 'I get twenty-five pence a week pocket money which I give to the lady who does my hair. Matron gives me cigarettes which she says are better than sweets, but I don't smoke.'

Hospital patients were the most likely to receive a reduced personal allowance – two-thirds did so, in fact. Half of these were paid for work in the hospital, and one patient worked hard in the laundry for no payment. While it was usual for the payments received to have a value of about a third of the standard allowance, more than half of the patients who worked handled no money at all. They were generally on the 'shopping list' for comforts such as sweets, though there was often little control by patients over the nature of the comforts bought on their behalf.

Most of the balance between the full personal allowance and that actually received went into compulsory savings either in the personal accounts or were held to pay for holidays and so on. In a few cases the balance was kept by relatives. Where the money was saved it could amount to a substantial sum.

In the case of Miss Redde, aged 57, there was well over £1000 in the bank, £124 in the hospital bank, and £44 in the Post Office: she handled no money herself and was on the ward shopping list for sweets.

Of course, it may be argued that those who received less than the personal allowance were not capable of spending the full amount responsibly. To some extent the variation between the settings in the control exercised by staff over the income of residents and patients reflected differences in the difficulties experienced by deaf people in the management of money. Thus almost all hospital patients and as many as two-fifths of the residents of homes for the deaf and the elderly reported difficulties in managing money – groups whose income was subjected to considerable control by staff. Even among those living in hostels two-thirds experienced difficulties in handling money yet hostel residents were the most likely to retain control over personal income. Furthermore, those who lived in their own homes could also find the management of money difficult – indeed, as many as two-fifths did so, yet none were deprived of the right of disposing of their income; indeed, they were responsible for making the full range of economic choices – from paying the rent and the fuel bills to budgeting for clothes, holidays, and outings. And, where there were children, they exercised those economic choices on behalf of others as well.

Difficulties in handling money were widespread in all settings: how did the deaf manage to obtain social security benefits to which they were entitled? To illustrate the problems encountered by deaf people in their attempts to understand the complexities of the social security system, let us consider claims for Supplementary Benefit. Although some of those who lived in institutions were in receipt of Supplementary Benefit payments, the problem of acquiring the full entitlement was largely confined to those who lived in private households. In the homes and hospitals financial questions were handled by the management while hostel residents were almost always assisted by members of staff when making claims. But no such help from the formal network was immediately available to deaf people living in private households.

Understandably, there was much confusion about the nature of Supplementary Benefits, but a substantial minority (a little more than a third) of those living in private households had applied for Supplementary Benefit at some time. To acquire the full entitlement the scheme requires of claimants the capacity to explain their circumstances fully. How did deaf people whose speech was usually limited and unclear and who were unskilled in lip-reading manage to convey their needs and understand the type of information required? Rather more than half of those who had claimed Supplementary Benefit had done so without the help of an intercessionary. Of these, the majority attempted to make their needs known by means of speech, though a small minority (an eighth) had communicated in writing. In two cases, people had been overjoyed to receive a visit from an officer who signed to a high standard.

Mr Timpson explained 'I wrote to the officer, and then a lady came who signed very well.'

Those who were entirely reliant on speech or the written word when communicating with officers tended to be bemused by the outcome of the negotiations.

Mrs Frinton, aged 80, said 'A man came to see me, but I didn't understand the details.'

Mrs Ray said 'I went to see them eight years ago with my (deaf) sister. We used a few signs, but mostly it was writing. We found the forms very confusing, but they gave me £3 per week on top of my £8 social security.'

Most claimants, however, found an intermediary, usually the social worker for the deaf, through whom they could negotiate. In all a quarter of claimants saw the Supplementary Benefit officer in the company of the social worker for the deaf. General practitioners, too, occasionally helped to make the initial contact with officers. Although it is true that the formal network provided most help and perhaps it was understandable that this should be so in view of the complexity of the social security system, a small minority particularly of younger persons (an eighth of all claimants), who lived with hearing relatives relied entirely upon them to negotiate. Help from the formal or informal networks usually cushioned deaf people from the necessity to understand their financial position.

Mrs Habant said 'I don't know anything about it. Harry (the social worker for the deaf) saw to everything. I know I got some of the furnishings through them. My husband dealt with all this at the time.'

Furthermore, help from an intermediary appeared to speed up the response of Supplementary Benefit officers. Those who were self-reliant often complained of the delayed response which followed their initial application.

Mr Timpson said 'I went to the local office, but I got no help until I asked the social worker for the deaf to intervene as a matter of urgency: he sent a letter and telephoned.'

Miss Robertson, aged 25, said, 'I went to the office five weeks ago. It was the first time I'd been. I tried to make them understand in sign and writing. But I haven't had any money from them yet.'

The protection afforded by the availability of help from the formal and informal networks, and the problems encountered by people with acute communication difficulties in grasping a complex system, combined to ensure that few claimants realized the existence of an appeals system. Only three claims had been refused outright, and others considered that they were in no position to challenge what they had been given. Only one appeal had been made to a tribunal:

Miss Oxton, aged 33, said 'I went to the office myself: we communicated in speech. They refused me an allowance so I appealed, but I lost it. I had a supporter from a welfare office who did most of the talking.'

10 Leisure

So far we have been concerned to trace the degree of normality achieved by deaf people in terms of the mode and extent of their interaction with the hearing community, their family life and relationships within the family and neighbourhood, the degree of autonomy and choice they exercise over their day-to-day lives, their capacity to maintain a financial independence and the role of their educational and financial experiences in determining the level of that independence. Throughout, normality has been viewed in terms of how far the deaf engage in the activities which it is assumed most hearing people undertake and essentially how far they do so within the hearing world. Allusion has been made to the strength of the deaf community, but apart from an assessment of the reliance placed by deaf people on others who are deaf for friendship, there has been little consideration of the degree of dependence on the deaf rather than the hearing community at a more general level.

An analysis of leisure activities offers the opportunity not only to explore how far deaf people's social activities are normal in the sense of reflecting those of the hearing community, but also the relative strength of the hearing and deaf communities in their lives. To what extent did deaf people seek and achieve normality in their leisure time only by segregating themselves from the hearing community?

Mobility

Mobility is essential, and the mobility afforded by transport is an advantage, for the enjoyment of social activity outside the home. Car ownership, which ensures maximum choice in mobility, was not widespread: only 13 per cent owned a car or lived in households in which someone else did so. The low incidence of access to private cars is largely explained by the presence of institutional populations: cars were available only to those living in private households and hostels. Although it was understandable that there should be no car owners among hospital patients, there was no reason in principle for there to be none among the residents of the homes, especially those for the deaf. As it was, even hostel residents were less likely than those in private households to have access to a car – only a sixth compared with two-fifths did so.

The greater access to private cars among those living in private households could not be explained by reliance on the presence of others to drive, for the skill to drive was more common among deaf people than car ownership: more than two-fifths currently held, or had held a licence. Deaf drivers were proud of their skill.

Mr Vincent, aged 60, said 'I'm the only one in the family who can drive. I started late – when I was 45.'

Mr Morris, aged 74, said 'I passed the driving test first time, at 69 years old.'

It was important to be seen to drive well, to counteract hostility to deaf drivers among the hearing community, and accidents appeared to be rare.

Ability to drive was less disproportionately concentrated in private households than was car ownership: a fifth of hostel residents held a driving licence, as did two of those in homes for the deaf. Entering an institution often involved giving up the ownership of a car, but as many as two-fifths of licence holders in private households had done so as well. Usually car ownership was abandoned either because of its cost or the hazards associated with driving.

Mr Bey, aged 78, said 'I had an Austin 7 in 1929, and I've had motorcycles as well. But I gave up driving nine or ten years ago. It's not worth it – too expensive. The family has transport and the train services to London are good. Buses are difficult – I'd sooner walk for the exercise.'

Mr Johnstone, aged 71, said 'I drove for years, I was always very careful because of being deaf – no accidents. But it costs too much.'

But not everyone had been careful.

Mr Craig, aged 23, said 'I've had plenty of accidents with bikes and cars. Last time I was breathalized and fined £100. My brother gave me a black eye when he found out. I was disqualified for one year, but I haven't driven since.'

For a small minority (4 per cent), a bicycle was or had been a satisfactory and cheap alternative to a car.

Mr Butler, who lived in a hospital for the mentally handicapped, said 'I've got a bike – saved up and bought it myself. I get the bus into Harrogate, but I use the bike a lot.'

Mr Gray, aged 89 years, had remained an enthusiastic cyclist into old age. 'I used to go everywhere by bike. I gave up the tandem two years ago.'

There was no widespread desire to possess a car – only a fifth wished to do so and were to be found mainly among hostel residents. It was the cost or anticipated dangers involved which prevented most of those who would have liked a car from owning one.

Mr Simpson said 'I'd like a car, but I can't have one because I'm not working at the moment – no money. There's no problem on public transport: I don't have to say anything because I've got a free bus pass.'

The attraction of a car was that it freed people from the embarrassment of communication which was an essential part of travel on public transport. Others, while they were aware of the freedom in mobility afforded by cars were discouraged by the potential danger which they considered the deaf driver inevitably represented.

Mr Ringmer said 'I would like a car but I can't drive – too dangerous. I've never been on public transport by myself –. I'm OK on the train with my sister. Taxis are too expensive.'

Such people were adamant in their views, whatever their difficulties in using public transport.

Mrs Fixton said 'I'm deaf and dumb. The traffic is too fast and there are all those noisy lorries. I don't want to drive a car and I'm not bothered about having one – it's too much responsibility. I sometimes get a taxi at night if it's raining.'

Mr Patel said 'Twenty years ago in Kampala I used to drive but not now, there's too much traffic. The family phone for a taxi sometimes if I'm late for work.'

The objection to cars was maintained despite poor public transport.

Mrs Gray said 'No, I don't want a car because I'm deaf and dumb. I rely on the bus, but there are long waits. I often walk long distances rather than wait for a bus.'

Mr Owen said 'I'm not bothered about cars: I lip-read well on the bus.'

In fact, however, only two deaf people had been formally assessed as being incapable of driving, and another two were cheerfully learning to drive with every expectation of owning a car in the near future.

Not all could compensate for their lack of access to a private car by using public transport. As many as a third said that they experienced difficulty in using public transport and only one of these had access to a private car. The more closed the setting, the greater the likelihood that difficulty would be experienced in using public transport. The variation between settings appeared to be a reflection in part of the distribution of those with additional physical handicaps and mental disorder, and in part of the lack of practice in using public transport which gradually robbed those in homes and hospitals, where there was no compelling reason to go out, of the confidence to board vehicles and communicate with those operating the system.

Miss Gregson, aged 76, who lived in a home for the deaf said 'I don't ever use public transport now. I used to go to church on the bus, but not now.'

Mr Douglas, aged 45, who was a hospital patient, said 'I don't use public transport except with an escort. I used to go to the deaf club on the bus, but not now.'

A few people who had entered hospital early in their lives, had never discovered whether they could use public transport.

Miss Muldoon, aged 35, said 'I've never been on a pay bus.'

   Additional handicaps, then, were an important cause of difficulties in negotiating the public transport system.

Mr Thompson, aged 70, said 'I get very breathless these days, so I can't use buses and I'm frightened of the tube.'

Mrs Watson, aged 84, explained 'It's my gammy hip, I find buses very difficult these days.'

But a low income was almost as frequently blamed as additional handicaps for lack of access to public transport.

Miss Gree, aged 54, who lived in a home for the deaf said 'I don't use public transport now. I used to go on the train to Worcester, but not any more because it's so expensive.'

Furthermore, there was increasing apprehension about using buses and trains at night: many felt that, being deaf, they were particularly vulnerable to street violence. As a consequence, there was a tendency to reduce evening social activities including attendance at deaf clubs and restrict the use of public transport to daylight hours.

   However, the majority were happy and able to use public transport. Communication problems had been dramatically reduced by the introduction of the bus pass.

Mrs Gray, aged 65, said 'I don't want a car now, I'm happy to go out by train. I have a train and bus pass.'

Even among hospital patients there were a few who enjoyed using public transport.

Miss Heathcote, aged 26, who was a patient in a hospital for the mentally ill, said 'I can get home easily by bus on my own. I find taxis frightening. I only go in them with my mother and father.'

Mr Watson, aged 73, lived in a hospital for the mentally handicapped 'I go to York on my own by bus and train. I drove a tractor in my youth but no car.'

Many were frustrated by the inadequacies of the transport system, but only a few were able to supplement it by taking taxis.

Mrs Fixton said 'There is no problem with public transport except the terrible waiting for the bus. Sometimes in cold weather I take a taxi to the station.'

But travel by taxi posed communication difficulties.

Miss Ray, aged 41, said 'I have a bus pass but travel by bus takes so long. I get a taxi back from the club. I have to write the address down.'

Miss Rose, aged 35, said 'I always go to the hospital by taxi – it's a tradition. I never use public transport when I go there, though I don't have any problems with it. I've been to the hospital many times this year. Mostly when I'm in a taxi I use a note for the address, but not always.'

Going out

Much of the literature which has sought to describe the segregating nature of institutional care has focused on the dearth of contacts between residents or patients and those living in the outside community. To move about outside the institution ensures the possibility of such contact. Yet it is clear that the autonomy in mobility achieved by private or public transport was much less in evidence among hospital patients and residents of homes than among those living in other settings. To what extent did deaf people in institutional settings engage in activities outside the home, and how did they compare in this respect with those who lead 'normal' lives in private households?

In general, deaf people appeared to enjoy frequent outings. As many as four-fifths had been out socially during the previous week: only a little more than a tenth had not been out for two months or more. However, important differences emerged between hospital patients and others in this respect. It was strikingly evident that those who lived in private households and hostels were actively engaged in moving about the neighbourhood for social purposes: all had been out socially during the previous week. Even among the residents of homes outings were frequent: more than five-sixths had been out within the preceding fortnight. But only a sixth of hospital patients had been out in that period, while as many as half had not been out for two months or more.

Furthermore, hospital patients were far more likely to go out only when accompanied. While it is true that some patients had been accompanied by a relative or another patient, most had been on trips organized by staff who acted as escorts. In contrast deaf people living in private households and the hostels tended to be accompanied by a friend (usually deaf) or a relative, while the residents of homes were often accompanied by another resident and only occasionally by a relative or a member of staff. Thus hospital patients tended to be dependent upon staff for outings. Whatever the setting, though, there was a marked similarity in the object of the outings – to visit friends or relatives, to go to shops, parties, pubs or clubs and (less frequently) to visit a cinema or church.

By no means everyone was satisfied either with the frequency with which they went out or the range of places to which they were able to go. In all, a little more than a third of deaf people, to be found in all settings, wished to go out more often, though this desire appeared to bear little relationship to the frequency of outings already enjoyed. There were even those who went out daily who craved for more frequent outings. However, dissatisfaction was aroused more by the limited range of places available to visit rather than the frequency of outings. Many of those who lived in private households found themselves constrained by a combination of the daily routine and a low income.

Mrs Glending said 'It's mostly the house and the shops, I'd like to go really out – to tea, have a weekend away.'

Mr Gray said 'I've got expensive tastes. I'd like to go out to dinner.'

Cinemas were now beyond the pockets of a number of keen filmgoers.

Mr Frame said 'I'd like to go to the films. But cinemas are too expensive now. And I have to travel in to Portsmouth and South Hampshire: travel is too expensive – it should be cheaper.'

Not everyone was seeking a wider range of places to visit: some merely found that there were increasing barriers to continuing with their customary activities.

Mr Robinson found his activities curtailed by increasing handicap: 'I'd like to see more of my friends. I'm not mobile enough now. It's too far on the bus to see friends now.

Those in institutions who were dependent on the staff to arrange outings found the range and nature of their activities determined by others.

Mrs Morrison, who lived in a home for the deaf, said 'I'd like to go to Church. I miss communion. I'm very hurt that it isn't arranged.'

Others, who lived outside city centres, where there was no concentration of deaf people, and therefore no provision of special activities, found little compensation in the activities of the hearing.

Miss Garnett said 'There's nothing much to do around here. I could do things if I could have more deaf friends. I need more company.'

Mrs Frame also found her activities restricted by the absence of a local deaf community: 'I keep busy around the house: it's a long day. If there were more deaf and a club on the island I would probably attend more often than at present – the nearest club is at Portsmouth.'

Residents of homes in small towns found little opportunity for entertainment, and were almost entirely dependent upon their fellow residents for companionship.

Miss McClean said 'I sometimes walk up and down, up and down, same, same, if Margaret doesn't go. I walk at the top of the town, not at the bottom. I like going for coach drives. Margaret and her mother have just come back from a drive. I'm very interested in where they've been.'

Although the presence of a deaf community in the locality ensured opportunities for friendship and a range of specialist facilities such as clubs, additional physical handicaps and a low income often restricted outings. The constraints were greatest on hospital patients, particularly those in hospitals for the mentally handicapped who were entirely dependent on staff to arrange social activities. They could rarely meet other deaf people with whom they could communicate, far less enjoy the opportunities for companionship offered by even the smallest deaf community. Most patients were dependent upon busy staff even for walks around the grounds, and few had been taken beyond the hospital boundary since their admission. Communication difficulties alone rarely created a barrier to getting outside: only two people admitted that they restricted their outings because they found it difficult to understand the hearing.

Active in the hearing world

The deaf community was seen to be important to a satisfactory social life by many deaf people, yet most also stressed the value they placed on making friendships within the hearing community. Indeed, only a small minority (a tenth) had not attended some social occasion within the hearing world in the previous month. Eating out was by far the most popular social activity undertaken with the hearing: rather more than half had been out to a café or a restaurant in the past month. Going to the pub and to church were also activities which appealed to substantial numbers of deaf people. As many as a third had visited a pub and as many had been to church at least once in the previous month. Bingo was frequented by a fifth while almost as many had been on an outing to the country or the seaside. Few had been to a theatre, exhibition or museum but rather more than a tenth (13 per cent) had been to a cinema.

There were marked discrepancies between settings in the degree to which such activities were engaged in. While all of those in private house-holds and hostels and all but one of the residents of the homes for the deaf had been involved in some form of social activity in the hearing community within the previous month, this was true of only half of hospital patients. It is true that for a deaf person to visit a pub, say, in the course of a month represents little in the way of integration or normality. But the range of activities engaged in could reflect in some measure the degree of confidence with which they moved within the hearing world. Most had participated in a wide range of social activities with hearing people: more than a third had engaged in three or four different types of social activity within the previous month, while two-fifths had been involved in five or more.

Mr Fairfax aged 49, led an active social life, much of it within the hearing community: 'In the past month I've been to the pub a couple of times each week, I went to the theatre this week, and I've eaten out in a cafe several times. I've got a theatre company of my own which uses deaf and hearing. I'm also keen on billiards, darts and ping-pong which I play with deaf and hearing.'

Mr Kenton, aged 19, was typical in the range of his social life: 'I've been out to the pub this month, and the cinema, and I've been out to the country with my parents in the car.'

Even within the week preceding the interview, the majority of people had been out socially to a place of entertainment frequented predominantly by the hearing. Almost two-thirds had done so on at least one or two occasions. Most deaf people in all settings could expect to go somewhere socially in the course of a month, but hospital patients did so less fre-quently. Patients who were able to arrange their spare-time social activities independently went out as frequently as those living in other settings, but where they were dependent upon others to make the arrangements, outings were more likely to be monthly rather than weekly and in some cases never took place beyond the hospital grounds. However, dependence on others restricted the social outings of other deaf people too: the more infirm residents of homes (a sixth) reported that they were unable to go out more than once a month.

Of course, although deaf people were taking part in a range of social activities of the same kind as those engaged in by and often alongside hearing persons, this did not necessarily involve them in much interaction with the hearing beyond the family circle. Traditionally the church has played a prominent role in the care of the deaf, and it was not surprising, therefore, to find that as many as two-fifths belonged to a church or chapel. Membership was highest among residents of homes for the deaf (four-fifths), who to some extent provided a 'captive audience' for local religious activities. Yet this should have been true of hospital patients, of whom only a seventh belonged. Membership was high even among hostel residents and those in private households, one third of whom belonged to a church or chapel.

In most cases, church membership was more than nominal: only a little more than a tenth of those who claimed to be members attended services less than once a month. Indeed a substantial minority (more than two-fifths) attended weekly. However, church attendance did not necessarily involve interaction with the hearing: rather more than half of those who attended regularly went to a church for the deaf. Reliance on the 'deaf' church was highest in the specialist homes, where only a quarter of those in membership attended a 'hearing' church. And even among those living in private households, the majority (two-thirds) of church members attended a 'deaf' church. Only in hostels and hospitals did most members attend a 'hearing' church. Many members did no more than attend services regularly, but a fifth were involved in group activities associated with their church.

Despite the long tradition of missionary work among the deaf, only a little more than a tenth of deaf people received a regular visitor from a church. Ironically, almost all church visits were paid to homes for the deaf, where the majority were already in regular attendance at church. In contrast, no visits were received by hospital patients, for whom little provision was made to meet spiritual needs. But even where regular attendance at church was possible it was usually the case that deaf people had to follow a service in speech: only a third of church members reported that an interpreter was regularly available at the service or that the officiating clergy used sign. And again, it was the residents of the homes for the deaf who were the most likely to benefit from specialist provision.

Some residents of homes for the deaf who were regular churchgoers attended services more because it was expected than out of conviction.

Miss Evans, aged 57, said 'My parents never went to church, and I went for the first time last year when I came here. I attended harvest festival at Worcester. I'm not bothered about it. I don't go if it's cold.'

Even where deaf people were committed churchgoers, they often found themselves unable to understand the service.

Mrs Frinton, aged 80, said 'I can't lip-read the Rev. Owen very well. He gives long boring sermons. He never announces any news about the deaf, and he never visits.'

Good interpretation created enthusiasm for church attendance: in the psychiatric hospital with a deaf unit, interpretation was provided by a nurse fluent in sign language and some of those who lived in private households reported that good interpretation was provided at services by a specialist social worker. For some, church attendance provided the opportunity for socializing.

Miss Garnett, aged 54, said 'We all meet and have coffee after the service in Worcester.'

Miss Elsom said 'I go the local Church of England. I've got friends at the church.'

But others found nothing beyond the service at church.

Miss Heathcote, aged 26, said 'Everything is in speech. The priest just says "hullo".'

Miss Harris, aged 39, said 'I don't talk to the vicar or anyone. We just shake hands and I go home on the ship.'

However, not everyone was seeking a social dimension to church attendance, and keen members were usually disappointed by the alternatives available to them when they were no longer able to get to church.

Mrs Frances, aged 76, said: 'I used to go to St Peter's over the road, but it's too far for me now. There's a chapel here in the home and there used to be a service every week or fortnight, but they've cut it down to only once a month. An interpreting priest comes to the chapel, but there's no local deaf church.'

Churchgoing, then, often represented a normal activity in the sense that churches were part of the hearing world, but it involved little or no interaction with the hearing. Although many deaf people engaged in the same kind of activities as the hearing, they did so parallel to, and often separately organized from the hearing. Where interaction with the hearing was essential or the likely involvement of the deaf too small to warrant specialist provision, few deaf people were active: thus only two were members of a political party. Similarly, although membership of deaf clubs was high, few (4 per cent) belonged to clubs in which the hearing predominated.

Reading

In so far as the deaf made use of parallel specialist provision their attempts at normality had the effect of reinforcing their segregation from the hearing. It could be argued, however, that it is not necessary to participate directly in activities with the hearing in order to be an integrated member of that wider community. Integration at a certain level may also be achieved by having some knowledge of that society from books, news-papers and television.

The practice of reading books was not widespread among deaf people. Only a little more than a tenth belonged to a library, and those who did so were drawn almost entirely from private households and, though less disproportionately, from the homes for the deaf. All of the hospitals had libraries of their own, and in some hospitals there was a ward (trolley) library service as well, but this did not reach the 'back wards'. In the specialist homes, few books were available to residents. There was one bookcase in the London home, and two in the south of England and west of England homes. The books available were regarded as 'old fashioned' by residents, that is, they were not colourful books with large print, an easy text and plenty of pictures. However, in all homes, the staff brought in a variety of popular women's magazines. Most library members were suffi-ciently keen on reading to change their books at least once a month though the infirm (two-fifths) were dependent upon the choice offered by the mobile library.

There were few voracious readers: only three reported that they had read three or more books in the course of the month.

Mr Sutton, aged 78, a resident of the hostel for the young working deaf, was unusual in his reading habits: 'I go to the library at least once a week and I get out three or four books. I also exchange books with another resident.'

Most library members (two-thirds) borrowed no more than one book at a time which took at least two weeks to read. In fact, books presented enor-mous problems as sources of information about the wider hearing society. To begin with, a large minority (a tenth of deaf people) of keen readers had sight problems and required books in large print, though for only half of them were these available. A far more pervasive difficulty, however, was reading itself, especially in a sustained way. Indeed, between a quarter and a third of those who were not members of a library admitted that they found the task of reading so difficult that they were unable to finish, and in some cases to begin to read a book. Even among library members there were some who needed all their enthusiasm to complete a book within two to four weeks.

Miss Thorpe, aged 23, said 'I go to the library once a month. I generally get through one book in that time, though it depends on the book.'

In view of Conrad's assessment that most deaf children leave school with a reading age of 7 years, perhaps it is surprising that so many belonged to a library. A small proportion of those who were unable to read adult books tried to read those brought home by children.

Mrs Hunsworth, aged 43, said 'I don't read anything other than magazines or papers and the deaf news because there's no time. I look at the children's books when they bring them home but they're difficult to understand.'

Mr Valery, aged 39, a resident of the hostel for the young working deaf, said 'Books are too hard; I sometimes try the ones brought home by the second child.'

But most of those with reading difficulties were completely defeated by books.

Miss Pattison, aged 23, explained: 'There are so many long words – I have to keep looking them up.'

Mr Root, aged 55, said 'I'm not interested in books – reading is too hard.'

A few who were not library members bought books, usually thrillers or those associated with a hobby. But book readers were generally confined to library members. However, newspapers and magazines present neither the problem of great length nor that of a wide vocabulary. But a minority (13 per cent) were unable to read even these, while as many did so only with difficulty. Nevertheless, newspapers and magazines offered a more promising means than books for keeping deaf people in touch with the hearing world. In all, almost a quarter read at least one newspaper regularly while two-fifths read magazines. Although hostel residents did not read books, all but a tenth of them as well as those in private households read at least one newspaper. But it seemed to be the case that the more closed their settings, the less likely deaf people were to keep in touch with the community in general by reading newspapers. Only half of the residents of homes, and a third of hospital patients, read a newspaper. Magazines, too, were most commonly read by the deaf living in private households. However, not all the magazines read reflected the hearing world: a quarter of magazine readers confined their attention to the publications of the British Deaf Association.

To some extent, then, the magazines reinforced their segregation from the hearing society, and integration into the deaf community. And it was difficult to assess how successfully newspapers conveyed an impression of the hearing world to those who found them difficult to read. It was rare for such people to attempt to read a paper on a daily basis.

Miss Hughes, aged 57, who lived alone, was typical in her reading habits: 'I read papers and magazines a little sometimes, I'm not bothered about books.'

Indeed, most of those who reported difficulty in reading newspapers could read very little.

Mr Paxton, aged 35, who lived with his deaf wife and young son, said 'I find even the papers are too hard to read. I often want to read, and I get frustrated.'

Some men reported that all the energy devoted to reading was absorbed by their efforts to understand the sport reports. But most of those with reading difficulties bought newspapers and magazines only to look at the pictures.

Miss Wheatley, aged 60, who lived in a home for the mentally ill, said 'I try papers and magazines but I don't understand them very well. I like the pictures. I've never looked for large print books: I do need glasses.'

Viewing

A visual and pervasively available medium such as television would seem to offer deaf people greater opportunities than the written word for understanding the wider, hearing community. And indeed, all but one deaf person had access to a television set, while as many as nine-tenths made a practice of watching regularly. For the most part, they were able to watch as much television as they wished, though a tenth of those in the homes for the deaf and the hospitals complained of the early hour at which the set was switched off by staff.

Mrs Inelton, aged 60, who lived in the south of England home for the deaf, said 'Even if you are in the middle of watching something nice it's switched off at 10 p.m. It's early to bed, every day, same on Saturday and Sunday.'

But more than a sixth of those living in residential and hospital settings regretted that television dominated the evenings.

Miss Jackson, aged 74, who lived in the west of England home, said 'There's too much television these days – I go to sleep. No one seems to want to play cards any more.'

It became clear, however, that the visual element in television was not strong enough to ensure that deaf people generally understood the programmes. Only a little more than a fifth claimed to be able to understand most of the programmes they saw, while under a fifth understood most of the dialogue. Where deaf people lived with hearing relatives, a member of the family was sometimes prepared to help with explanations.

Miss Friston, aged 80, said 'I want more subtitles; sometimes my niece explains what's happening.'

Only a small minority of deaf people could lip-read well enough to ensure that they understood most of the dialogue, and for them lip-reading required considerable concentration.

Miss Ray, aged 41, said 'I read the newspaper in the morning so that I can understand the news and pick up a bit extra lip-reading.'

Some found that colour was easier to lip-read than monochrome, and much criticism was levelled at those newscasters who failed to 'open their teeth properly'. Despite the fact that newsreaders often face the audience directly, deaf people found the news particularly difficult to lip-read.

Miss Jones, aged 51, who lived in a home for the deaf, said 'I can understand much of the television quite well but the news is hard. The Irish problem seems bad, but it's difficult to lip-read.'

Of course, where speakers were off screen or at an angle, lip-reading was impossible. The Deaf Broadcasting Campaign has recently drawn attention to the difficulties of lip-reading television programmes:

Lip-reading is an ambiguous and tedious form of receiving information . . . to a large percentage of deaf people, the speed of normal speech makes it impossible to lip-read.[1]'

Subtitles presented a more desirable alternative to lip-reading, and most deaf viewers watched subtitled programmes, though they were critical of their short supply.

Mr Newton, aged 33, said 'There should be more programmes with subtitles. They have them in Germany. And the deaf don't have to pay for a licence there: they shouldn't have to here.'

But even subtitles were not without their difficulties: they changed too quickly for most deaf viewers to comprehend them. It must be remembered that most deaf people found reading difficult, and there were some who could not read at all. The Deaf Broadcasting Campaign has suggested that the only satisfactory solution for most of those who are born deaf is to use 'sign language interpreters on selected programmes',[2] and special programmes for the deaf employing total communication – sign language, speech, and subtitles. In part, such programmes would reinforce the deaf community and its separate identity: '(they) would. . .act as a focal point for deaf children. Many deaf children have little contact with deaf adults and lack adult "models" who provide a necessary source of identity'.[3] The cost of Ceefax put it beyond the resources of most and only 9 per cent used the RNID programme synopsis, though all who did so found it helpful.

Most viewers admitted that their understanding of programmes was partial.

Mr Wright, aged 20, who lived in the hostel for the young working deaf, said 'I understand a little – enough to have an idea of what's happening.'

Mr Rossiter, age 68, another hostel resident, said 'I concentrate very hard, so I understand some of it.'

The full range of programmes was watched, though news, nature films and sport appeared to be particular favourites. However, there was one type of programme which was universally disliked:

Mr Frome explained: 'I get fed up with too much singing.'

Most of the minority who failed to watch television did so consciously.

Miss Watson, aged 84, who lived on her own, said proudly: 'I can't hear the wireless and there's no television. There's nothing here you didn't have in 1910. I just read.'

Deaf clubs

In view of the difficulties faced by deaf people when they attempted to participate in social activities with the hearing or sought to benefit from the entertainment and information systems designed for a largely hearing public, it was not surprising that many of them sought friendship, entertainment and information from within their own community, where they could enjoy most of the pastimes of the hearing, but in a largely segregated setting.

Despite the long-standing involvement of voluntary organizations in making provisions for the deaf, knowledge of them was not widespread. Only a quarter could name a voluntary body, local or national, which worked on behalf of the deaf. But such knowledge was by no means synonymous with participation in the deaf community or even in activities organized by voluntary bodies. Deaf clubs are generally considered to be the pride of the deaf community. As many as half of deaf people belonged to a deaf club, and about another tenth were accustomed to visit them casually from time to time in the company of friends who were members. Club membership was highest among hostel residents, and those living in private households – three-quarters compared with only an eighth of the residents of the homes for the deaf and none of those in homes for the elderly and the hospitals.

It was ironic that those who lived in the most 'normal' settings were the most likely to take the opportunity of participating in segregated social activities. But membership would have been high in other settings if there had been a club nearby. Admission to homes for the deaf severed previously strong connections with clubs.

Mrs Jackson, aged 74, said 'There are no clubs here locally. Before I came here I used to go every week.'

Mr Root, aged 53, said 'There are no local clubs and there is no transport to take us to the nearest one. I would go weekly if transport were available.'

Even the London home gave access only to a deaf–blind club. Most of the home's residents attended to benefit the deaf–blind members rather than themselves, and craved for an opportunity to talk to a wider circle of signers.

Miss Elton, aged 75, explained: 'We talk, watch the television, knit, and talk to the deaf–blind. I would like to talk more to the non–blind deaf.'

Furthermore, there were communication problems between the deaf and the deaf–blind.

Mrs Faulkner, aged 88, said 'We play bowls and dominoes. But I can't do deaf–blind manual, so I'm stumped. Before I came here I belonged to a deaf club and we went on outings – you see more people. We went to watch them Changing the Guard, and to the West End in a minibus.'

The residents of the homes for the elderly and some of the hospital patients had likewise been deprived of membership on admission to localities where there were no deaf clubs, and because they were in non-specialist facilities, little attempt was made to accommodate their special needs. Indeed, only the staff of the specialist homes were aware of activities outside their institution organized specifically for the deaf. In stark contrast, many of those with access to deaf clubs attended a number of clubs: as many as two-thirds of club members (and a third of all deaf people) had visited more than one club in the previous twelve months. The more 'normal' their living setting, the more likely were club members to have attended two or more of the segregating deaf clubs in the course of the year.

In many ways the deaf clubs existed on the overlap between the formal support network and the self-help of the deaf community itself. Although the majority were run by voluntary organizations, a quarter were organized by the deaf themselves, mainly in conjunction with the British Deaf Association. Some deaf people were involved in administration, an activity which was demanding of time and energy.

Mr Rex said 'I'm on the sports and social committee. Ours is an independent club. I'm getting fed up with it now – it's very demanding year after year.'

Mr Taunton said 'We're independent. I'm on the sports committee. I go all over the place in the car for them.'

Others were involved in the administration of clubs run by voluntary organizations.

Mr Glossop said: 'The County Association for the Deaf runs the club. I'm on the sports committee. It's all sports and games at the club.'

And whoever had ultimate responsibility for the clubs, most members made a contribution through their subscriptions, though residence in specialist institutions guaranteed the automatic payment of club subscriptions.

The main purpose of the clubs was to provide a meeting place for the deaf people of the locality. And indeed, a few people attended clubs which offered no more than the opportunity to chat and to watch television in the company of friends. But in most cases, clubs provided a wide range of activities commonly available to the hearing, but in a segregated setting. Quizzes, bingo, card games, snooker, football, dances, lectures, darts were among those commonly on offer. One activity aroused controversy – the consumption of alcohol. Some clubs already sold alcohol but in others the membership appeared to be divided on the advisability of such a move. Most members of unlicensed clubs appeared to wish to maintain a distinction between their club and a pub.

Miss Ray, aged 41, said 'I talk with the others, play bingo, have a dance. There's no bar – I wouldn't want one. But we go to the pub after, we always go to Brady's pub.'

Despite the wide range of activities in clubs, a substantial minority of members (a quarter) wanted changes in club activities, mainly the introduction of active pastimes and less emphasis on clubs as places where the elderly deaf talked and played cards together. It was among this group that the demand for the introduction of a bar was strongest.

There was a small minority of deaf people who, having once been members, rejected deaf clubs. Some younger people found the clubs dull.

Mr Gregg, aged 39, said 'The nearest club is full of old people. There's not much to do: it's very boring.'

But most of those who had given up membership had done so because they found there the deaf community at its most closely-knit and oppressive.

Mr Foy said 'There's chat at the club. But I don't like the atmosphere. We prefer to make our own amusements at home. Thank God for our situation – it's so much better than that of many hearing people. We love each other – we're very close.'

Mrs Glending said: 'I never go now as I used to with friends. There's too much gossip and so on.'

Only those living in private households and hostels enjoyed the luxury of an opportunity to reject the deaf community of the clubs. Elsewhere, deaf people were largely dependent on those running institutions for social activities. And with the exception of one of the homes for the deaf no arrangements were made to ensure that they met other deaf people socially. Although group activities were arranged for between a quarter and a third of those in other institutions, these were predominantly in hearing settings. For example, the residents of a home for the deaf were taken for one afternoon each week to a local authority day centre where they spent their time sewing. The keen embroiderers among them loved it, but others were less enthusiastic. Whatever the benefits occupational therapy or visits to day centres conferred, these did not include the opportunity to chat to a wider range of deaf people and engage in the social activities common among the hearing.

The strength of the deaf community and its importance in the lives of deaf people cannot be assessed solely in terms of club memberships. It is to be seen, too, in the friendships made by deaf people, especially where they were in a position to exercise choice. Other deaf people were over-whelmingly the preferred companions for an evening out. In all, between half and three-fifths were accustomed to going out in the evening. Perhaps not surprisingly, those who did so were drawn primarily from private households and the hostels. Outside the hospitals, where patients had to choose their companions solely from among the hearing, no one went out in the evening solely with hearing companions. The majority were accustomed to going out either with the deaf only (a little more than a third) or with both deaf and hearing people.

Holidays

The strength of the deaf community can be seen in holiday patterns. The vast majority of people emulated the habits of the hearing by taking a regular holiday. As many as two-thirds had been on holiday within the previous twelve months and another fifth had been at some time within the previous five years. Cost was the major deterrent for most of those who had failed to take a holiday recently, though among deaf people living in homes and hospitals, lack of mobility and a dependence on others to make the arrangements were more important. Most arranged their own holidays and stayed at hotels, camping sites and so on, patronized by the hearing, or with relatives. Only a third went on holidays specially arranged for the deaf, and they were drawn disproportionately from people living in hostels, homes and hospitals. Most specialist homes and hostels had their holidays arranged by voluntary organizations for the deaf, whereas holidays for those in the general institutions were organized by the institutions and involved hearing residents and patients as well. Therefore, while specially organized holidays were usually segregating in the sense that they often involved deaf people travelling and staying with similarly organized persons in groups, they reinforced the deaf community only in so far as they were organized by specialist voluntary organizations or institutions. But the deaf community relies on the informal as well as the formal network. And almost all of those who went on holiday independently did so in the company of at least one other deaf person.

Mrs Forster said 'We had a holiday grant from the Council. We went in a caravan with deaf friends and their family.'

Mrs Elsen said 'I went with deaf friends and their family. I like touring with other deaf people.'

Mrs Fulton, aged 56, said 'I prefer to go with other deaf like I did last year: I went with my deaf friend aged 80. We had a nice bedroom.'

In general, those who managed to arrange their own holidays insulated themselves to some extent from the hearing by going in the company of other deaf people and/or a relative who understood their communication problems. Holidays with family and friends were enjoyed primarily by those living in private households and the hostels. All of those who relied upon others to organize holidays and who were obliged to go in company not of their own choosing identified a family holiday as their ideal, whereas those who were in a position to exercise choice, insisted that an ideal holiday was one taken with the family in the company of other deaf people. Holidays arranged by others were far more likely to cause dissatisfaction than were self-arranged holidays.

Miss Garnett, who lived in a home for the deaf, said 'I've been on the same holiday for the last four years. Llandudno. I'd like something different. The food is good though. I go with other deaf residents. I have to save, save and pay Matron.

Holidays arranged by others, but not on an institutional basis, appeared to give greater satisfaction.

Mrs Roberts said 'My son paid for me to go to Canada to see him. I didn't want to come back: I loved the company.'

Miss Greeson said: 'I enjoy going to my deaf friends in Hampshire: they arrange it.'

But the self-arranged holiday remained the ideal.

Mr Taunton said 'I go on holiday every year with my sister and my deaf friends. The best was last year – Majorca. The sun, the sea, the food – perfect.'

That within the protective framework of the family and the deaf community deaf people achieved a considerable measure of 'normality' in the way they took their holidays is suggested by the fact that rather more than half had stayed in a hotel recently, while a little less than a third had stayed with relatives, and a seventh had gone camping. Only 7 per cent of deaf holiday makers had been obliged to spend their time away in an institutional holiday home. However, although in most cases holidays had the appearance of normality, in reality they were to a large extent dependent upon the support of the formal network: only a third of holidays were not subsidized either by a local authority or a voluntary organization. This was true of the vast majority of those living in institutional settings, but only a third of those in private households. Perhaps surprisingly, in view of the communication difficulties generally admitted by deaf people, only 14 per cent (most of them from private households) experienced problems of communication on holiday. To a large extent, the presence of understanding members of the family and other deaf people acted as protection against the hearing world. Those in institutional settings were effectively shielded from such problems by others who organized their holidays.

In general, then, most deaf people led active social lives. However, it was usual for social activities to take place in segregated settings or in settings which were insulated from the hearing world. Thus only a minority (one-fifth) had not been out in the afternoon or evening in the past fortnight, and most of these were residents of homes and hospital patients. In contrast, as many as a quarter had been out on between three and five occasions, while a third had been out six or more times in the past fortnight. Furthermore, the factors which might have been thought to be important in restricting the social life of the deaf – communication difficulties and lack of money – were dismissed as unimportant by the overwhelming majority.

As a consequence of their success in maintaining a social life which closely resembled that of members of the hearing community, most deaf people concluded that they had achieved a normal way of life. And this was true even in respect of income, despite the fact that many grumbled about low wages. For example, the majority (three-fifths) were confident that they were as well off as the average person in the country, while another seventh considered that they were better off: only a little more than a quarter would countenance the idea that they were worse off than the average person. Furthermore, most adopted a generally optimistic view about their current situation. As many as a third considered their situation to be better than ever, while more than a third declared their situation much the same as it had always been. Only a seventh thought that for them things were now worse than ever. Of course, it is undoubtedly true that communication difficulties prevented deaf people from acquiring the knowledge of the wider community which would enable them to arrive at a more 'realistic' assessment of their position. To a considerable extent, their very insulation from the hearing world may be blamed for their largely optimistic view of their own position. Nevertheless that optimism is an indication of the degree to which deaf people considered that they had achieved normality.

11 Conclusion

The aim of the study was to consider a number of different systems of care currently provided for profoundly deaf adults, focusing particularly upon problems of communication. Among the issues explored were concepts of normality and disability in the context of acute problems of communication; the degree to which current services promote segregation or integration; the overlap in care provision between the NHS, voluntary bodies and local authorities; the degree to which substitutability in care provision is possible.

Because of the dearth of information about the dispersal of profoundly prelingually deaf people, the study was based on interviews with those in a number of settings where the prelingually deaf were known to exist in reasonable numbers – specialist homes, psychiatric hospitals, mental handicap hospitals, specialist hostels, homes for the elderly, and private households. In all, 171 profoundly prelingually deaf people were interviewed: sixty-eight living in private households; five in local authority homes for the elderly (one in each of five homes); thirty-three in two hostels for the deaf; thirty-three in three homes for the deaf; twenty-two in four psychiatric hospitals; and ten in two mental handicap hospitals. Originally 175 persons were approached for interviews, but there were three non-contacts among those living in private households and one refusal in a hostel. In addition, interviews were carried out with forty-two care staff across the range of settings, including social workers with the deaf employed by local authorities.

Some difficulty attaches to the definition of prelingual deafness: in the event those interviewed were known to have been born deaf, or to have become deaf before the age of 2 years, or were dependent upon sign language.

The central issue explored in the present study has been the relationship between segregation and integration on the one hand and the pursuit and achievement of normality on the other. How do those with no useful hearing, and little (usually unintelligible), or no speech, make themselves understood in a verbal, hearing world, and find out about that world in which they have to live?

In general, the level of literacy attained by most deaf people was low, and as a consequence, books were largely excluded as a source of information, though it is true that a few deaf people with great application and continuous use of the dictionary, were voracious readers of thrillers and specialist journals. Newspapers appeared to be a more promising source of information since they did not require the sustained effort necessary to read a book. But even the tabloids were beyond the reading skills of most, and in this respect the deaf appeared to be typical of members of their community: other research had indicated that on average deaf children leave school with a reading age below that required to understand the least demanding newspapers currently available. Newspapers and magazines, where they played any part in the lives of deaf people, with a few exceptions, were bought for their pictures.

Television might appear to offer more hope of success than the written word as a medium of information about the hearing world for the deaf. But despite the emphasis on the visual, television relies on the verbal to a far greater extent than is commonly appreciated by the hearing. And in general, deaf people are little better than the hearing at lip-reading. So far, few programmes are subtitled, and deaf people, who usually depended either on low wages or on social security benefits, were unable to afford to take advantage of Ceefax. Everyone appreciated the current limited provision of subtitles and were anxious that it should be increased, but although subtitles improve the understanding of the deaf, they do not render television a reliable source of information because deaf people tended to be slow readers, and there were some whose level of literacy was so low that they were able to understand subtitles only partially, if at all.

On the whole, relatives were the preferred source of information about the wider, hearing society, and the preferred intermediary between the deaf person and that society. But even with members of the family, communication was usually imperfect and often dependent upon the written word. Furthermore, not all relatives were patient and sympathetic, and few had the forebearance to resist the temptation of acting on behalf of a deaf member of the family rather than enabling that person to retain control over day-to-day living. And relatives were not always available. All deaf people stressed the difficulties they faced in attempting to understand what was happening, and the protracted delays they experienced in achieving understanding because they were dependent upon the written word, or working through someone else.

The effects of severe communication difficulties on the lives of deaf people raised the question of what is meant by integration. Since the 1960s integration has become the objective of much service provision, but the term has been variously interpreted. In education, integration has been assumed to mean either the education in ordinary schools of those who had been taught previously in special schools, or the maintenance of some specialist teaching, but in special units within ordinary schools. In the field of personal social services, integration has been assumed to be achieved by non-hospital care and by non-institutional care for those groups who, in the past, had been sheltered in long-stay hospitals or residential homes. For the groups for whom specialist facilities have been made available in the past, such as the deaf and the blind, integration has been sought by abandoning specialist provision: it has been argued, for example, that homes for the deaf should be rejected in favour of mixing deaf people who need sheltered or residential accommodation with 'normal' people who have the same needs – for example, in homes for the elderly. Others have considered that integration can only be achieved by abandoning all residential care, and enabling the deaf and others to live in private households, with the help available where necessary of the formal and informal networks of care. In the present study, an attempt has been made to explore these different interpretations of the term integration, by talking to deaf people in a wide range of living settings – in integrated institutional settings such as homes for the elderly and hospitals for the mentally disordered, in specialist residential settings, such as homes and hostels for the deaf, and in integrated, non-institutional settings, namely private households. It must be stressed that the conclusions drawn are necessarily tentative: only a case study was attempted, and the numbers involved were relatively small. Nevertheless, this is the first study to provide systematic evidence about how deaf adults live, and what their experiences are of growing up and living in a predominantly hearing society.

At one level, integration may be equated with a life which in essentials follows a pattern considered usual to society. Thus normality may be assumed to be achieved if a person growing up in a family in a private household, subsequently inhabits a dwelling which does not depart substantially from the average in terms of amenities; exercises a reasonable amount of autonomy in and responsibility for the way he or she lives, subject to the pressures of the autonomy and responsibility of others; as an adult has a family, rears children to an acceptable standard, and maintains an economic independence by working; engages in a range of activities which are considered to be usual in the pursuit of a social life; is cared for in old age by the family. According to these criteria, deafness alone did not inhibit the achievement of normality, or integration. It was the type of living setting which determined the degree of integration. In general, deaf people living in private households lived lives which closely resembled those of the hearing. Of the institutional settings, only the hostels for the deaf encouraged residents to lead normal lives. Elsewhere, whether it was in the general facilities such as the hospitals for the mentally disordered and the homes for the elderly, or the specialist homes for the deaf, little attempt was made to re-create in sheltered circumstances the opportunities for the exercise of autonomy and responsibility, and the maintenance of links with family, friends and neighbours outside the institution which may be considered an essential part of normal life.

Evidence that this was so was not surprising: studies of specific types of institutions, and studies of specific categories of people in private households had suggested that such a pattern would emerge. But the present study was unusual because in itself it encompassed such a wide range of living settings in a consideration of the lives of a single category of people. It was an approach which allowed us, within a single study, to attempt to determine the effects of deafness on the possibility of achieving a normal life. That deafness alone did not determine the degree to which persons achieved normality in their daily lives raised the question of why some deaf people found themselves in living settings which placed considerable limitations on their capacity to live life normally. And here again, other studies prepared us for the explanation which emerged. Those who lived in hospitals and homes did not do so because their sensory impairment was greater than those living in private households: the degree of sensory impairment suffered by the people interviewed was broadly similar throughout the living settings. Nor was the presence of additional physical handicaps or mental disorders usually the sole direct cause for admittance to an institution: there were those with such handicaps and disorders among the deaf living in private households, while some of those living in hospitals and homes were only deaf. Far more important was the existence of a relative who was available and willing to provide care where it was necessary, and to adopt the role of intermediary with the hearing community for those who lacked the confidence to interact with the hearing unaided.

Yet even for those who had the confidence to operate in the hearing community and relatives who were prepared to act as intermediaries between the deaf and hearing worlds, a normal pattern of life was maintained only with great difficulty. While most of those living in private households were married, a minority of married people rejected the possibility of bringing up a family of their own. For the majority who became parents, communication enormously increased the problems of child-rearing. Where both parents were deaf the close proximity of dependable

hearing relatives was essential to ensure that the children acquired acceptable speech. And as the children grew and went to school few deaf people
were confident enough to communicate with teachers. Indeed, hearing
children themselves often became intermediaries between a deaf parent
and the hearing world from an early age. Again, although most of those
living in private households worked, or had worked when below pension-
able age, their limited education and training had ensured their employment only in low-paid routine clerical and manual jobs. Communication
with colleagues at work was minimal and despite the low level of literacy
achieved by most deaf people heavily dependent upon the written word.
Problems of communication created acute difficulties for deaf people
attempting to deal with the formal network of service provision – health,
education, housing, social security, employment and personal social services. For example, many found it difficult to know when they should visit
the doctor, and if a visit was made on a matter considered too personal for
the presence of an interpreter, deaf people were often confused about the
outcome of the consultation. Where no interpreter was available, a stay in
hospital could be terrifying. In the case of other services, letters had to be
written and replies awaited and then interpreted, or visits made in the
company of an interpreter because the time-saving telephone was not
available as a means of communication for the deaf. Yet because most deaf
people had an income which was at or below that officially determined as
the poverty level according to the Supplementary Benefit scales, they
belonged to a group who are generally expected to have above average
contact with the social services.

However, it became apparent that the existence of the deaf community
added another dimension to the question of what constituted integration,
and what was meant by segregation. For while deaf people usually engage
in normal activity, they do not do so with the hearing. Most appeared to be
effectively insulated from the hearing society by the deaf community. On
the whole, they had little contact with the hearing: those they identified as
hearing friends tended to be neighbours who were willing to give help in
emergencies. Otherwise, relatives were the only hearing persons with
whom the deaf had sustained contact, and this was so, because necessity
had forced both sides to establish at least a partial system of communication. Yet the family, too, insulated the deaf from the hearing by offering
a mediating service between the two. Thus, the deaf lived lives which had
much of the appearance of those of the hearing, but in practice, they were
not part of the hearing community: the deaf lived lives which were parallel
to those of the hearing. And in terms of social activities they were enabled
to do so by the existence of the deaf community, which in large measure,

was sustained and reinforced by the existence of the deaf clubs.

The importance of the deaf community in sustaining deaf people in their attempt to achieve a way of life which closely resembled that of the hearing, raises the question of the role of specialist provision. In the recent past there has been a tendency to denigrate specialist provision in the interests of normalization and integration. Yet it is the logic of this study that there is a need to reinforce and extend specialist provision. Those least integrated into the parallel deaf community were those in non-specialist institutions – the homes for the elderly, and the hospitals without specialist provision. But institutions were not alone in isolating the deaf, either among the hearing or from the deaf community. There were some in private households who, because infirmity or distance prevented access to a deaf community, were denied the consolation of communication in their own medium. In such 'integrated' settings deaf people were no more likely than those in the homes for the deaf to acquire normal patterns of living. Moreover, the specialist institutions, however isolated and closed, had the advantage over general institutions of ensuring that the deaf resident had the opportunity to communicate easily with others. Furthermore, where deaf people lived in institutions which existed formally to provide treatment for mental disorders, the likelihood of them receiving satisfactory treatment was remote in the absence of staff with specialist skills in the care of the deaf. Indeed, there was evidence to suggest that there was a dearth of properly trained specialist staff even in most of the specialist institutions; while in all specialist institutions deaf people communicated freely with each other, there was only minimal communication between them and staff: staff found it more convenient to take decisions on behalf of the deaf people in their care than to act as mediators between them and the hearing. Trained specialist staff who adopt the mediating role and enable deaf people to retain substantial control over their own lives are not enough: the maintenance of the links with the deaf community outside the institutions is essential if the deaf are to take advantage of the possibilities offered by that community for pursuing an integrated life in parallel to that of the hearing.

However, the deaf community cannot provide effective support for its members without the active intervention of the social worker for the deaf. Indeed, the specialist social workers play a key role in helping to maintain the deaf community both at the individual and the group level. They are indeed intermediaries between the deaf and the hearing because they are experts on the ramifications of the formal network. As such, their help is a vital addition to that of the family where family knowledge of the formal network is limited, and they replace the family as intermediaries where suitable relatives do not exist. Moreover, they alone fulfil the role of enabler: they have the patience and the skill to interpret and explain and to help deaf people to control their own lives, whereas others, including relatives, find it easier to make decisions on behalf of deaf people. And because they mediate between the deaf and hearing worlds across the full range of activities, including, for example, employment, their role is much wider than that normally associated with social work.

The evidence supporting the contention that British Sign Language is a language in its own right was impressive though not conclusive. If its status as a language is admitted, there are important consequences for the training of interpreters: they can no longer be trained by hearing persons who understand manual communication solely as signed English, but by skilled users of the language of the deaf community. It has clear implications too, for the education of deaf children. Increasingly, manual communication is allowed in the schools for the deaf, where total communication is beginning to be seen as essential if the conceptual, literacy and social skills of the deaf are to be developed. Although our evidence suggests that the exclusion of sign was never as rigorous even in the hey-day of oralism as has sometimes been implied, for many years speech was the dominant mode of communication in the education of the deaf, a dominance which is only now being eroded.

The importance of sign language and the deaf community in the lives of deaf people, and the role played by the deaf community and specialist social workers in helping deaf people acquire normal patterns of life, mean that in the case of the deaf, at least, little reliance can be placed on the informal network within the community to offer a cheap system of support as a satisfactory alternative to more expensive, trained workers. If deaf people are to achieve financial independence by finding jobs, if they are to receive appropriate medical treatment at the right time, if they are to rear and educate their children satisfactorily, they will require the services of the trained deaf specialist. Outside the family, only the deaf community operates effectively at the informal level, because of the central problems of communication. Yet the deaf community itself is dependent to a considerable degree on the formal network – on statutory and voluntary agencies – for help in financing and running clubs, in arranging and helping to pay for holidays, as well as for the provision of social workers for the deaf.

Notes and references

Chapter 2   Method

1 See DHSS, Advisory Committee on Services for Hearing-Impaired People, *Report of the Sub-Committee appointed to consider the role of social services in the care of the deaf of all ages* (1977), para. 11, p. 4.
2 National Assistance Act 1948, Section 29.
3 Department of Health and Social Security, *Health and Personal Social Services Statistics for England 1978* (HMSO 1980), p. 162.
4 ibid.
5 See Chartered Institute of Public Finance and Accountancy, *Periodical Social Services Statistics, 1978–79 Actual*, pp. 4–27.
6 DHSS, Advisory Committee on Services for Hearing-Impaired People, ibid., p. 4.
7 ibid., June 1977, p. 5.
8 ibid., p. 5.
9 ibid., p. 5.
10 In Autumn 1970, the Royal Association for the Deaf and Dumb carried out a survey of six hospitals for the mentally ill in London and the south-east and identified 280 patients as being profoundly prelingually deaf. This was followed in 1971 by a postal survey of NHS hospitals for the mentally ill and mentally handicapped carried out by the Royal National Institute for the Deaf. Eleven Regional Hospital Boards responded to the survey, and of the hearing impaired identified, there were 1004 patients who were assessed as being profoundly deaf. (We are indebted to RADD and RNID for the results of this unpublished research.)
11 ibid.
12 For a discussion of definitions of disability see Sainsbury, S., *Measuring Disability* (Bell 1973), chs. 2 and 3.
13 See Bolderson, H., *Compensation, Maintenance and Rehabilitation* (unpublished PhD thesis, University of London 1980), and Blaxter, M., *The Meaning of Disability* (Heinemann Education Books 1976), p. 6.
14 See Di Carlo, L.M., *The Deaf* (Prentice Hall 1964).
15 Risberg, A., and Mantony, J., 'A method of classification of audiograms', in Fant, G. (ed.), *International Symposium on Speech Communication Ability and Profound Deafness* Stockholm, 1970 (A.G. Bell Association, Washington 1971).
16 Townsend, P., Introduction to Morris, P., *Put Away* (Routledge and Kegan Paul 1969).

17 See, for example, Abel, A., *An Investigation into some aspects of Visual Handicap*, Statistical and Research Report, Series no. 14 (HMSO 1976).

18 *First Annual Report of the Chief Medical Officer of the Board of Education* (1908), p. 64.

19 *Annual Report of the Chief Medical Officer of the Board of Education 1910*, p. 195.

20 Eicholz, A., *A Study of the Deaf in England and Wales, 1930-2* (HMSO 1932).

21 Board of Education, *Report of the Committee of Inquiry into the Problems relating to children with defective hearing* (HMSO 1938).

22 Board of Education, *Annual Report for 1927 of the Chief Medical Officer* (HMSO 1928), p. 153.

23 Department of Psychiatry, Whittington Hospital, and DHSS, *A Word in Deaf Ears* (RNID 1979).

24 Goodhill, V., 'Pathology, diagnosis and therapy of deafness', in Travis, L., *Handbook of Speech Pathology* (Appleton Century-Crofts Inc., New York 1957).

25 Kyle, J.G., 'Audiometric analysis as a predictor of speech intelligibility', *British Journal of Audiometry*, **11** (1977), pp. 51-7. See also Ling, D., *Speech and the Hearing Impaired Child* (A.G. Bell Association, Washington DC 1976), and Smith, C.R., 'Residual hearing and speech production in deaf children', *Journal of Speech and Hearing Research*, **18** (1975).

26 Scott, R.A., *The Making of Blind Men* (Russell Sage Foundation 1969), p. 13. For a discussion of the differences between congenitally and adventitiously blinded persons, see Carroll, T.J., *Blindness, what it is, what it does, and how to live with it* (Brown and Company, Boston 1961). For the impact of blindness on child development, see Scott, R.A., *The Handbook of Socialisation Theory and Research* (Rand, McNally and Company, Chicago 1969).

27 Scott, R.A., ibid.

28 Von der Lieth, L., 'Social psychological aspects of the use of sign language', in Schlesinger, L.M., and Namir, L. (eds.), *The Sign Language of the Deaf* (Academic Press, New York 1978).

29 Di Vasiliu, *International Audiology*, **7** (1968), pp. 181-5.

30 Hetherington, E.M., and Panke, R.D., *Child Psychology* (McGraw Hill, New York 1975), referred to in Meadows, K.P., *The Natural History of a Research Project*.

31 Goodnow (1970), quoted in Kennedy, A.E.C., 'Effects of deafness on personality', *Journal of Rehabilitation of the Deaf* (1973), pp. 22-3.

32 Lenneberg, E.H., *Biological Foundations of Language*, (Wiley, New York 1967).

33 Fry, D.B., 'The development of the phonological system in the normal and deaf child', in Smith F., and Miller, G.A. (eds.) *The Genesis of Language*, (MIT Press, London 1966).

34 Lenneberg, *Biological Foundations of Language*.

35 Brunner J., 'The ontogenesis of speech arts', *Journal of Child Language*, **2**, (1975), pp. 1-19.

36 Weir, R.H., in Smith, F. and Miller, G.A. (eds.), *The Genesis of Language*, (MIT Press, London 1966).

37 Mavilya, M., in the paper, 'Language development in children', in *Proceedings of the International Congress on the Education of the Deaf*, (Stockholm 1970), p. 73.

38 Lenneberg, *Biological Foundations of Language*, p. 134.

39 Di Carlo, *The Deaf*, ch. 8.

40 Ling, D., *Speech and the Hearing Impaired Child: theory and practice* (A.G. Bell Association, Washington DC 1976); and Smith, C.R., *Residual Hearing and Speech Production in Deaf Children*, Communication Science Lab. Report no. 4. (UNY Graduate Center, New York 1973).

41 *The Health of the School Child*, 1962-3, *The Health of the School Child* 1969-70.

42 Conrad, R., *The Deaf Schoolchild* (Harper & Row, 1979).

43 Conrad, R., *Towards a definition of oral success*, paper given at RNID/NCTD Education meeting at Harrogate 1976.

44 Rodda, M., *The Hearing Impaired School Leaver* (University of London Press 1970).

45 See also Conrad, R., 'Reading ability of deaf school leavers', *British Journal of Educational Psychology* (1977), pp. 144-5.

46 Ahlgren, I., *Early linguistic cognitive development in the deaf and severely hard of hearing*, National Symposium on Sign Language, Research and Teaching, (Chicago 1977).

47 Conrad, *The Deaf Schoolchild*, p. 283.

48 Belling, U., Klima, E.S., and Siple, P., 'Remembering in Signs', *Cognition, 3* (1974).

49 Wundt, W., 'Volkerpsychologie' (1) *Die Sprache* (Wilheim Engelmann, Leipzig 1900).

50 Pinter, R., and Petterson, R.D., *Journal of Experimental Psychology* 2 (1916).

51 Conrad, *The Deaf Schoolchild*.

52 Erber, N.P., 'Auditory-visual perceptions of speech', *Journal of Speech and Hearing Disorders*, **40** (1975), pp. 481-92.

53 Conrad, *The Deaf Schoolchild*.

54 See, for example, Gerber, S.E., *Audiometry in Infancy* (Grune and Stratton 1977).

55 National Census of the Deaf Population in the US was conducted in 1970, described in Schein, J.D., and Delk, M.T., *The Deaf Population in the United States* (National Association of the Deaf, 1974).

56 US Bureau of Census, 1928, 1930.

57 Denmark, J., 'Early profound deafness and mental retardation', *British Journal of Mental Subnormal* (December 1978).

58 Fundudis, T., Kolvin, I., and Garside, R.F., *Speech retarded and deaf children: their psychological development* (Academic Press 1979).

59 Denmark, J.C., *et al.*, *A Word in Deaf Ears* (RNID 1979).

60 Meadows, K.P., in Liben, L.S. (ed.), *Deaf Children: Developmental Perspectives* (Academic Press, New York 1978).

61 Kropka, B., *A study of the deaf and partially hearing population in the mental handicap hospitals of Devon* (Dept of Psych. Royal Western Counties Hospital, 1980).

62 *The Young Adult Hearing Impaired Population of Ireland* (National Association for the Deaf of the Republic 1973).

63 Rawlings, B.W., *Summary of Selected Characteristics of Hearing Impaired Students*, United States, 1968–9, Series D., no. 5, (Gallaudet College, Office of Demographic Studies, Washington DC 1971).

64 Myklebust, H.R., *Auditory Disorders in Children* (Grune & Stratton, New York 1964).

65 See Liben, L.S. (ed.), *Deaf Children: developmental perspectives* (Academic Press, New York 1978).

66 Schein, J.D., Gentile, A., and Hasse, K.W., 'Development and evaluation of an expanding hearing loss scale', Questionnaire, *Vital Health Statistics*, **2** (1970), p. 37.

67 Some students have shown that the hearing impaired children of parents who use sign language in their communication may not be as retarded in cognitive development as the children of non-signing parents, though their acquisition of speech is retarded. See, for example, Schlesinger, H.S., 'The acquisition of signed and spoken language', in Liben, L.S. (ed.), *Deaf Children: developmental perspectives* (Academic Press, New York 1978).

68 Lenneberg, E.H., *Biological Foundations of Language* (Wiley, New York 1967).

69 RNID and RADD unpubl. research 1970 and 1971: 'Survey of hospitals for the mentally ill and mentally handicapped'.

70 Denmark, J.C., *et al.*, *A Word in Deaf Ears* (RNID 1979), p. 15.

71 National Association for the Deaf, *The Young Adult Hearing Impaired Population of Ireland* (1973), p. 22.

Chapter 3   Personal characteristics

1 See, for example, Townsend, P., *The Last Refuge* (Routledge & Kegan Paul 1962).

2 *The Young Adult Hearing Impaired Population of Ireland* (National Association for the Deaf of the Republic 1973).

3 Eicholz, A., *A Study of the Deaf in England and Wales 1930–32* (HMSO 1932), p. 21.

4 Conrad, R., *The Deaf Schoolchild* (Harper & Row 1979).

5 Gentile, A., and Rambin, J.B., *Reported Causes of Hearing Loss for Hearing Impaired Students, US, 1970–71,* Series D, no. 12, (Gallaudet College, Office of Demographic Studies, Washington DC 1973).

6 Conrad, *The Deaf Schoolchild.*

7 Conrad, ibid.

8 Fisch, 'Sex ratio and congenital deafness', in Stephens, S.D.G. (ed.), *Disorders of Auditory Function* (Academic Press 1976).

9 Jeffreys, M. *et al.*, 'A set of tests for measuring motor impairment in prevalence studies', *The Journal of Chronic Diseases*, **22,** no. 5 (November 1969), pp. 314–15.

10 Meadow, K.B., 'Early manual communication in relation to the deaf child's

intellectual, social and communicative functioning', *American Annals of the Deaf*, **113** (1968), pp. 29–41.

11 Other studies have drawn attention to the predominance of manual workers among the disabled at large. See, for example, Harris, A., *Handicapped and Impaired in Great Britain* (HMSO 1971).

12 Census 1971, Economic Activity Tables Part IV, p. 96 (10 per cent sample).

Chapter 4   Communication

1 See, for example, Plato's *Gratylus*.

2 Stain, J.H., *Inquiries in the origins of language: the fate of the question* (Harper & Row, New York 1975).

3 See, for example, Stokoe, W.C., *Semiotics and human sign language* (Mouton, The Hague 1972); Stokoe, W.C., 'Classification and description of sign language', T.A. Sebeok (ed.), *Current Trends in Linguistics*, **12** (Mouton, The Hague 1966); Stokoe, W.C., *Sign Language Structure – Studies in Linguistics*, Occasional Paper 9, 1960 (reproduced Linstock Press, Silver Spring, Maryland); Stokoe, W.C., Casterline, D.C., and Croneberg, C.G., *A Dictionary of American Sign Language on Linguistic Principles* (Gallaudet College Press, Washington DC 1965).

4 Hewes, G.W., 'The phylogeny of sign language', in Schlesinger, L.M., and Namir, L. (eds.), *Sign Language of the Deaf: the grammar of sign language* (Academic Press, New York 1978).

5 Wundt, W., 'The language of gestures', *Approaches to Semiotics*, **6** (Mouton, The Hague 1971).

6 Jousse, M., 'Le mimisme humain et l'anthropolgie du langage', *Revue Anthropologique*, **46** (1936).

7 Gourlain, Le Roi, 'Les mains de Gargas', *Bulletin de la Société Prehistorique Francaise* (1967).

8 Critchley, E.M.R., *Speech Origins and Development* (Thomas, Springfield, Illinois 1967).

9 Boese, R.J., *Mature Sign Language and the Problem of Meaning* (PhD thesis, University of California, Santa Barbara 1971).

10 See Bellugi, I., and Fischer, S., 'Comparison of Sign and Spoken Language', *Cognition*, **73** no. 1 (1972), pp. 173–200; and Klima, E., and Bellugi, L., *The Signs of Language* (Harvard University Press 1979); and Dutrenne, M., *Language and Philosophy* (Indiana University Press, Bloomington, Indiana, 1963).

11 Hockett, C.F., 'The origin of speech', *Scientific American*, **203** (1960), pp. 88–96.

12 For further discussion see Schlesinger, H.M., 'The acquisition of bimodal language', in Schlesinger and Namir (eds.), *Sign Language of the Deaf*.

13 Ferguson, C.A., 'Diglossia', *Words*, **15** (1959), pp. 325–49.

14 Stokoe, W.C., 'Sign Language Diglossia', *Studies in Linguistics*, **21** (1969–70), pp. 27–40.

15 Deuchar, M., *Diglossia in British Sign Language*, (PhD Dissertation, Stanford University, 1978).

16 Cicourel, A.V., 'Sociolinguistic aspects of the use of sign language', in Schlesinger and Namir (eds.), *Sign Language of the Deaf.*

17 See Stokoe, Casterline and Croneberg, *A Dictionary of American Sign on Linguistic Principles.*

18 Tervoort, B.J., 'Bilingual interference', in Schlesinger and Namir (eds.) *Sign Language of the Deaf,* p. 269.

19 Conrad, R., *The Deaf Schoolchild* (Harper & Row 1979).

20 For example, Stokoe, W.C., Casterline, D.C. and Croneberg, C.G., *A Dictionary of American Sign Language on Linguistic Principles* (revised edn), (Linstock Press 1974), Silver Spring MD; Madsen, W., *Conventional Sign Language: an intermediate manual* (Gallaudet College Press, Washington DC 1972); and O'Rourke, Y. (ed.), *A basic course in manual communication* (National Association of the Deaf, Silver Spring, Maryland 1973).

21 Sutcliffe, T.H., *Communication with the Deaf* (Royal National Institute for the Deaf 1971); Jones, H.E., *Talking Hands* (Stanley Park 1972); and British Deaf Association, *The Language of the Silent World* (BDA 1960). The recent publication of an analysis of the signs of British Sign Language begins to remedy the situation by describing the structure of individual signs and suggesting means of coding them. See Brennan, M., Colville, M.D. and Lawson L.K., *Words in Hand* (British Sign Language Project, Edinburgh 1980).

22 The publication of *Sign-It*, the first substantial attempt at a dictionary which is intended to include 2000 native British signs and has been in preparation for several years, is still awaited.

23 Battison, R. and Jordan, I.K., 'Cross-cultural communication with foreign signers, fact and fancy', *Sign Language Studies,* **10** (1976), pp. 53–8.

24 Brennan, M. and Hayhurst, A., 'The Renaissance of BSL', in Baker, C. and Battison, R. (eds.), *Sign Language and the Deaf Community* (National Association of the Deaf, USA 1980).

25 Conrad, R., *The Deaf Schoolchild.* (Harper and Row 1979).

26 Brennan, M., 'Can deaf children acquire language? An evaluation of linguistic principles in deaf education', *American Annals of the Deaf,* **120** (1975), pp. 463–79.

27 Lewis M.M., *The Education of Deaf Children: the possible place of Finger Spelling and Signing,* (HMSO 1968).

28 Where teachers of the deaf are trained.

29 Brennan, M., and Hayhurst, A., 'The Renaissance of BSL', in Baker and Battison (eds.), *Sign Language and the Deaf Community.*

30 A substantial proportion of these people used speech rarely, or not at all.

31 Markides, A., 'Methods of assessing speech intelligibility of hearing impaired children', *The Teacher of the Deaf,* **74** (1970), pp. 307–47.

32 For a discussion of the particular circumstances in which interpretation was used, see pp. 104–6, 140, 223–4, 231–40.

33 Conrad, *The Deaf Schoolchild*, ch. 7, especially pp. 186–91.

34 Conrad, R., 'Lip reading by deaf and hearing children', *British Journal of Educational Psychology*, **47** (1977), pp. 60–5.

35 Denmark, J.C. *et al., A Word in Deaf Ears* (RNID 1980).

36 The problems of lip reading are discussed briefly in Evans, L., 'Psycholinguistic perspectives on visual communication', in Woll, B., Kyle, J.G. and Deuchar, M. (eds.), *Perspectives on BSL and Deafness* (Croom Helm 1981).

37 Llewellyn Jones, P., Kyle, J.G., Woll, B., Paper presented at the International Conference on Social Psychology and Language (Bristol July 1979) (unpublished).

38 For a full discussion, see Baker, C. and Padden, C., 'Focussing on the non-manual components of ASL', in L. Friedman (ed.), *On the other hand – new perspectives on American Sign Language* (Academic Press, New York 1978). A recent English publication has made a start in dealing similarly with British Sign Language. See, British School of Education Research Unit, 'Research in Deafness and BSL', in Kyle, J.G., Woll B. and Cantor, M., (eds.), *Coding British Sign Language* (Bristol Sign Language Group 1979).

39 Stokoe, W.C., 'Sign Language Structure: An outline of the visual communication systems of the American deaf', *Studies in Linguistics*, Occasional Papers no. 8 Buffalo, (Buffalo University Press, Buffalo, New York 1960).

40 See Stokoe, W.C., *The Language of gestures: approaches to semiotics 6*, (Mouton, The Hague 1972).

41 Wundt, W., *Volke psychologie* (1), Die Sprache, pp. 1–2 (Leipzig, Wilhelm Engelman 1900).

42 Private communication from Bristol and Edinburgh.

43 See Schlesinger, L.M. and Namir, L., in Schlesinger and Namir (eds.), *Sign Language of the Deaf*.

44 Hockett, C.F. and Altman, S.A., 'A note on design features', in Sebeok, T.A. (ed.), *Animal Communication* (Indiana University Press, Bloomington 1968).

45 Schlesinger and Namir (eds.), *The Sign Language of the Deaf*, pp. 97–141.

46 Baker and Padden, 'Focussing on the non-manual components of ASL'.

47 See, Walker, M., 'The Makaton Vocabulary', in Tebbs, T. (ed.), *Ways and Means* (Globe Education 1978).

48 Kiernan, C., Reid, B. and Jones, L., 'Signs and Symbols: who uses what?', *Special Education Forward Trends* **6** no. 4 (1979).

49 Kiernan, C., Reid, B. and Jones L., *Routes to Communication* (Costello Education Trust 1981).

50 Kyle, J.G. and Woll, B., 'Sign Language of Deaf People – the other English Language', *Special Education Forward Trends*, **8,** no. 3 (1981).

51 Conrad, R., 'Deafness and Reading', in *The Deaf Schoolchild*.

52 Conrad, R., 'The Reading Ability of Deaf School Leavers', *British Journal of Educational Psychology*, **47** (1979), pp. 138–48.

53 For example, Di Francesca, 'Academic achievement test results of a national testing program for hearing impaired students', Series D, no. 11, (Gallaudet

College, Office of Demographic Studies, US, Washington DC spring 1971); and Wrightstone, J.W., Arrow, M.S. and Moskowitz, S., 'Developing reading test norms for deaf children', *Annals of the Deaf*, **108** (1963), pp. 311–16.

54 Conrad, 'Deafness and Reading'.

55 See also, Montgomery, G.W.G., 'A factional study of communication and ability in deaf school leavers', *British Journal of Educational Psychology*, **38** (1968), pp. 27–37; and Hamp, N.W., 'Reading attainment and some associated factors in deaf and physically handicapped children', *Teacher of the Deaf*, **70** (1972), pp. 203–15.

56 Newsom, J. and E., 'Intersubjectivity and the transmission of culture: on the social origins of symbolic functioning, *Bulletin of the British Psychological Society*, **28** (1975).

57 Schlesinger, H.M., 'The Acquisition of Bimodal Language', in Schlesinger and Namir (eds.) *Sign Language of the Deaf* pp. 66–7. Wood, D., 'Some developmental aspects of prelingual deafness', in Woll, Kyle and Deuchar (eds.) *Perspectives of BSL and Deafness*.

58 Denmark, J. *et al.*, *A Word in Deaf Ears* (RNID 1979).

59 Russell, W.K., Quigley, S.P. and Power, D.J., *Linguistics and Deaf Children: Transformation Syntax and its application?* (Alexander Graham Bell Association for the Deaf, Washington DC 1976).

60 Denmark, *A Word in Deaf Ears*.

61 See Colville, M., 'Correct procedure for taking statements and interpreting in court for a deaf person', paper in *Soundbase* (1975), the NCSWD Conference Papers (copy in RNID Library).

62 Jones, P., 'Simultaneous interpreting', in Woll, B. Kyle Deuchar (eds.), *Perspectives on BSL and Deafness*.

63 Moser, B., 'Simultaneous Interpretation', in Gerver, D. and Sinaiko, H.W. (eds.), *Language Interpretation and Communication* (Plenum Press, New York 1978).

64 Kyle, J.G. and Jones, P., 'Signing the News: some comments on the experiment by HTV on Sign Language Interpreting', *Research on Deafness and BSL* (Bristol University School of Education Research Unit 1980).

65 DHSS, *Report of a Sub-Committee appointed to consider the Role of Social Services in the care of the Deaf of all Ages* (June 1977).

Chapter 5   Health, handicaps and the care setting

1 See, for example, Morris, P., *Put Away* (Routledge & Kegan Paul 1969); Townsend, P., *The Last Refuge* (Routledge & Kegan Paul 1962); Droller, H., 'Does community care really reach the elderly sick?', *Geront. Clin.* **11**, (1969), pp. 169–82; Evans, G., 'Current issues in the UK, in Exton-Smith, A.N. and Grimley Evans, J. (eds.), *Care of the Elderly* (Academic Press 1977); Hughes, B., and Wilkin, D., *Residential Care of the Elderly: A Review of the Literature*, Univ. Hospital. S. Manchester Research Report, no. 2 (1980); Marshall, M., and

Boaden, N., 'Residential Care: how can we make admission less haphazard?', *Modern Geriatrics*, **8**. no. 1. (January 1978), pp. 30–3.

2 Townsend, *The Last Refuge.*

3 Tempowski, I., Felstead, H., Simon, G.B., 'Deafness and the mentally retarded', *Apex*, **2** no. 2, (1974).

4 Williams, C., 'The forgotten few', unpublished paper, 1980 (Psychology Department, Royal Western Counties Hospital, Starcross).

5 ibid. pp. 1–2.

6 Denmark, J.C., 'Early profound deafness and mental retardation', *British Journal of Mental Subnormality*, **24** (1978).

7 Kropka, B.I., 'Towards the definition of the variables in a study of the hearing impaired mentally handicapped', unpublished paper presented to the London Conference of the EPS, December 1980).

8 Myklebust, H.R., *Psychology of deafness* (Grune and Stratton, reprinted 1971).

9 Kennedy, A.E.C., 'The effects of deafness on personality', *Journal of Rehabilitation of the Deaf*, **6** no. 3 (1973), pp. 24–6.

10 Montgomery, G.W.G., *Technical and Welfare Services for the Deaf in Scotland* (Churchill-Livingstone 1972).

11 Basilier, T., 'A socio-medical evaluation of hearing loss as a disabling factor', *Surdophrenia Norvagica*, pt 1, *Scandinavian Audiology* (1972), pp. 55–63.

12 Denmark, J.C. and Warren, F.S., 'A psychiatric unit for the deaf, *British Journal of Psychiatry*, **120** (1972), pp. 425–6.

13 For a discussion of the measurement, see Sainsbury, S., *Measuring Disability* (Bell 1973). For further discussion of measurements in general, see Duckworth, D., *The Classification and Measurement of Disablement* (HMSO, Research Report no. 10, 1983).

14 See, Sainsbury, S., *Disability and Social Policy* (forthcoming).

15 For a discussion of the criteria by which 'trouble with nerves' was identified, see Sainsbury, *Measuring Disability* ch. 4.

16 See, for example, Morris, P., *Put Away* (Routledge & Kegan Paul 1969).

17 See, for example, Townsend, *The Last Refuge.*

18 See, for example, King, R.D., Raynes, N.V. and Tizzard, J., *Patterns of Residential Care* (Routledge & Kegan Paul 1971); Miller, E.J. and Gwyne, G.V., *A Life Apart* (Tavistock Publications 1972); Dartington, T., Miller, E.J., and Gwyne, G.V., *A Life Together* (Tavistock Publications 1981).

19 Bunting, C., *Public Attitudes to Deafness* (OPCS, HMSO 1981), p. 1.

20 Denmark, J.C., 'Early profound deafness and mental retardation', *British Journal of Mental Subnormality*, **24** no. 2 (1978), pp. 81–9.

21 Denmark, J.C. and Warren, F., 'A psychiatric unit for the deaf', *British Journal of Psychiatry*, **120** (1972), p. 423.

22 ibid., p. 427.

23 ibid., p. 425.

24 ibid., p. 427.

25 ibid., p. 427. See also Cornforth, A.R.T. and Woods, M.M., 'Subnormal

and Deaf', *Nursing Times*, (10 February 1972), p. 179.

26 Kropka, B., 'Towards a definition of the variables in a study of the hearing impaired mentally handicapped', unpublished paper presented to the London Conference of the BPS (December 1980).

27 Cornforth, A.R.Y. and Woods, M.M., 'Disturbed and Deaf', *Nursing Times*, (3 February 1972), p. 139.

28 ibid., pp. 140-1.

29 Denmark and Warren, 'A psychiatric unit for the deaf', p. 427.

30 Cornforth and Woods 'Disturbed and Deaf', p. 140.

31 ibid., p. 139.

32 For example, ibid., p. 139.

33 Denmark and Warren 'A psychiatric unit for the deaf', p. 425.

34 Cornforth and Woods 'Disturbed and Deaf', p. 139.

35 Moones and Grant (1976), quoted in Kropka, 'Towards a definition of the variables. . .'.

36 See, for example, Kropka, B.I., *A Study of the Deaf and Partially Hearing Population in the Mental Hospitals of Devon* (Royal Western Counties Hospital, Starcross, Devon, 1979), p. 43.

37 Kyle, J. and Woll, B., 'Sign Language of Deaf People: the other English Language', in *Research on Deafness and British Sign Language* (1979-80), pp. 1-4.

38 See Townsend, *The Last Refuge*, p. 211.

39 For a discussion of the merits of intrinsic over extrinsic motivation in rehabilitation, see Adams, J., 'A Change of Scene: 1. Ridgehill, a home not a ward: Features of a bungalow', *Nursing Times*, **75** no. 39 (27 September 1979), pp. 1659-61; Davies, J.E., 'A change of scene 2. Effects of the new home on patients and nurses', *Nursing Times*, **75** no. 40 (4 October 1979), pp. 1725-6; Mouthwood, J., 'A change of scene 3. The progress of two patients after moving to Ridge Hill', *Nursing Times*, **75** no. 41 (11 October 1979), pp. 1769-70.

40 Reviewed in, Lavine, E.S. (ed.), *The Preparation of Psychological Services Provided to the Deaf* (Professional Rehabilitation Workers with the Adult Deaf Inc., 814, Thayer Avenue, Silver Spring, Maryland 2090, Monograph no. 4 July 1977).

Chapter 6   Living space

1 For a discussion of policy development during the period, see Townsend, P., *The Last Refuge* (Routledge & Kegan Paul 1962).

2 See, for example, Goffman, E., *Asylums: essays on the social situation of mental patients and other inmates* (Anchor books, Doubleday, New York 1961); Barton, W.R., *Institutional Neuroses* (John Wright & Sons 1959); Foucault, M., *Madness and Civilisation*, translated Richard Howard (Pantheon, New York 1965 and Tavistock 1967).

3 Townsend, *The Last Refuge*.

4 King, R., Raynes, N. and Tizzard, I., *Patterns of Residential Care* (Routledge & Kegan Paul 1971).

5 Dartington, T., Miller, E. and Gwynne, G., *A Life Together* (Tavistock 1981).

6 Sedgewick, P., *Psycho Politics* (Pluto Press 1982); Jones, K. and Fowles, A.J., *Ideas on Institutions* (Routledge & Kegan Paul 1984).

7 Finch, J. and Groves, D. (eds.), *A Labour of Love* (Routledge & Kegan Paul 1983); Abrams, P., 'Social change, social networks and neighbourhood care', *Social Work Services*, **22** (February 1980).

8 See, for example, Morgan, R. and Cushing, D., 'The personal possessions of long-stay patients in mental hospitals', *Social Psychiatry*, **1** no. 3 (1966), pp. 151–7.

9 According to the DHSS, *Schedule of Minimum Standards in Hospitals for the Mentally Ill*, DS 95/72 (1972), 'All patients should have personal enclosed cupboard space at the bedside or elsewhere.'

10 For a sustained discussion, see for example, Townsend, *The Last Refuge,* pp. 98, 135, 165, 246, 264, 422.

11 See, for example, Sainsbury, S., *Registered As Disabled* (Bell 1970); Blaxter, M., *The Meaning of Disability* (Heinemann 1976).

12 Sainsbury, S., *Social Policy and Disability* (forthcoming).

13 Camp, F.M., 'Urban life style and life cycle factors', in Lawton, M.P., Hewcomer, R.J. and Byents, C.T. (eds.) *Community Planning for an Ageing Society: designing services and facilities* (Dowden, Hutchinson and Ross, Stroudsburg, Pa. 1976).

14 Blau, P., *Exchange and Power in Social Life* (Wiley, New York 1964).

15 Cantor, M., 'Effects of Ethnicity on life styles of the inner city elderly', in Lawton *et al.* (eds.), *Community Planning for an Ageing Society*.

16 See, for example, Morris, P., *Put Away* (Routledge & Kegan Paul 1969).

17 In 1972, DHSS issued a *Schedule of Minimum Standards in Hospitals for the Mentally Ill*, DS 95/72 which specified that 'all patients should be encouraged to purchase and wear their own clothes'.

Chapter 7   Family, friends and neighbourhood

1 Typical of such studies were Bayley, M., *Mental Handicap and Community Care* (Routledge & Kegan Paul 1973); and Sainsbury, S., *Registered as Disabled* (Bell 1970).

2 See Townsend, P., in Morris, P., *Put Away* (Routledge & Kegan Paul 1969), Introduction.

3 Hadley, R. and Hatch, S., *Social Welfare and the Failure of the State* (George Allen & Unwin 1981).

4 Dartington, T., Miller, E. J., and Gwynne, G.V., *A Life Together* (Tavistock 1981).

5 See, for example, Davies, B. and Challis, D., 'Experimenting with new roles in domiciliary services: the Kent Community Care Project', *The Gerontologist*, **20** no. 3 (1980).

6 Abrams, P., 'Social Change, social networks and neighbourhood care', *Social Work Services,* no. 22 (February 1980).

7 Letter from the Secretary General, Royal National Institute for the Deaf, to Directors of Social Services in England and Wales (24 July 1975).

8 Von der Leith, L., 'Social Psychological aspects of the use of Sign Language', in Schlesinger, L.M., and Namir. L. (eds.), *Sign Language of the Deaf* (Academic Press, New York 1978).

9 Cicourel, A.V. and Boese, R.I., 'The acquisition of manual sign language and generative semantics', *Semiotica,* 3 (1972), pp. 22–256; Vernon, M., 'Sociological and psychological factors associated with hearing loss', *Journal of Speech and Hearing Research,* 12 (1969), pp. 541–63; Markowicz, H., 'Sign Languages and the Maintenance of the Deaf Community', Paper presented at NATO Symposium on Sign Language Research (Copenhagen 1979).

10 Higgins, P.C., *Outsiders in a Hearing World* (Sage 1980).

11 Schlessinger, S.H. and Meadow, P., *Sound and Sign – Childhood Deafness and Mental Health* (University of California Press 1972).

12 Padden, C. and Markowicz, H., *Cultural Conflicts between Hearing and Deaf Communities* (Linguistics Research Laboratory, Gallaudet College, Washington, DC March 1975), p. 6.

13 Barth, quoted in Padden and Markowicz, *Cultural Conflicts.* . . .

14 Padden and Markowicz, ibid.

15 Barth, see Padden & Markowicz, ibid.

16 ibid., p. 6.

17 ibid., p. 8.

18 ibid., p. 9.

19 ibid., p. 13.

20 ibid., p. 10.

21 Bunting, C., OPCS, *Public Attitudes to Deafness* (HMSO 1981).

22 ibid., p. 12.

23 ibid., p. 21.

24 ibid., p. 10.

Chapter 8   The formal network of services

1 Warren, R., *Marital Counselling* (Dept of Psychiatry for the Deaf, Whittingham Hospital, Preston, Paper for Day Conference of the National Council of Social Workers with the Deaf, 29 October 1977), p. 7.

2 ibid., p. 10.

3 ibid., p. 2.

4 ibid., p. 4.

5 See, for example, Colville, M., 'The Use of Sexual Signs in an interpreting situation' (unpublished paper for Day Conference of the National Council of Social Workers for the Deaf 29 October 1977).

6 ibid., p. 3.

7 Warren, R., *Marital Counselling* (Dept of Psychiatry for the Deaf,

Whittingham Hospital, Preston, Paper for Day Conference of the National Council of Social Workers with the Deaf, 29 October 1977), p. 7.

8 See, for example, *Parents as Partners* (The National Deaf Children's Society 1979).

9 Warren, F., 'Young deaf people with severe behaviour problems', *Hearing, RNID*, **35** no. 5 (September/October 1980), p. 223.

10 Merrill, E.C., 'The Responsibilities of Professionals to the Deaf Consumer', *Supplement to the British Deaf News* (December 1976), The British Deaf Association, p. 4.

11 Walker, P., 'Where I am least alone', *Community Care,* no. 368 (9 July 1981).

12 National Assistance Act 1948, pt III, ch. 29.

13 Merrill, 'The Responsibilities of Professionals'.

14 See, for example, Burton, D., 'Services for Deaf People in the New Social Services Departments' (unpublished paper given at the biennial conference of the Royal Institute for the Deaf at Harrogate October 1972).

15 Department of Health and Social Security, *Social Service Teams: the practitioner's view* (HMSO 1978), pp. 186–7.

16 1971, First national survey of psychological services for deaf individuals, reviewed in Lavine, E.S. (ed.), *The Preparation of Psychological Service Providers to the Deaf* (Professional Rehabilitation Workers with the Adult Deaf, Inc., 814 Thayer Avenue, Silver Springs, Maryland 2090, Monograph No. 4 July 1977).

17 Department of Health and Social Security, Advisory Committee on Services for Hearing–Impaired People, *Report of a Sub-Committee appointed to consider the role of social services in the care of the deaf of all ages* (June 1977).

18 ibid., para 64, p. 19.

19 Merrill, 'The Responsibilities of Professionals'.

Chapter 9   Education, training, employment and income

1 Kyle, J.G., Woll, B., Llewellyn-Jones, P., 'Learning and using British Sign Language: Current Skills and Training of Learning Professions', *Sign Language Studies*, **31** (summer 1981), p. 165.

2 Kyle *et al.,* 'Learning and using British Sign Language', p. 172.

3 Kyle *et al.,* 'Learning and using British Sign Language', p. 176.

4 Kluwin, T.H., 'A Rationale for Modifying Classroom Signing Systems', *Sign Language Studies*, **31** (summer 1981), p. 179.

5 *Education of Deaf Children: A Report*, prepared by a Sub-Committee of Parents of the National Deaf Children's Society, West of Scotland Region (January 1981), p. 1.

6 ibid., p. 2.

7 ibid., p. 3.

8 ibid., p. 8.

9 ibid., p. 4.

10 ibid., p. 5.

11 ibid., p. 6.

12 Watts, W.J., 'Education, Integration and Society', *Hearing*, The Royal National Institute for the Deaf (January–February 1981), p. 16.

13 ibid., p. 17.

14 Rodda, M., *The Hearing-Impaired School Leaver* (University of London Press Ltd 1975), p. 132.

15 ibid., p. 137.

16 Langley, D. and Hatton, J., 'Post-16 Education for the Hearing-Impaired', *The International Congress on Education of the Deaf* (Hamburg 4–8 August 1980) (unpublished) (May 1978), p. 2.

17 ibid.

18 ibid.

19 Green, R., *A Study of Careers Education and Job Placement Programs for the Deaf and Partially Hearing in England* (League for the Hard of Hearing, New York December 1979).

20 Rodda, *The Hearing-Impaired School Leaver*, p. 136.

21 Rodda, *The Hearing-Impaired School Leaver*, p. 137.

22 *Report Commissioned by the National Association for the Deaf and National Rehabilitation Board* (1970).

23 ibid.

24 Bunting, C., *Public Attitudes to Deafness* (Office of Population Census and Surveys, Social Survey Division, HMSO 1980), pp. 23–4.

25 ibid., p. 33. Appendix A. Comments on the Survey from Panel of Four.

26 ibid., p. 24.

27 The title has changed over the years: for consistency the terminology of those interviewed has been adopted.

28 Reported in Green, *A Study of Careers Education. . .*, p. 14.

29 For evidence which suggests that the educational, training and employment experiences recorded here are typical of deaf persons generally, see Rawson, A., *Deafness: Report of a Departmental Enquiry into the Promotion of Research* (DHSS Reports on Health and Social Service Subjects, no. 4, HMSO 1973), and DES, *External Examinations in Schools for the Deaf and Partially Hearing and Opportunities for Further Education*, SS41/65/03 (1972).

30 For the case for adopting 140 per cent of Supplementary Benefit as the 'official' poverty line see Abel-Smith, B. and Townsend, P., *The Poor and the Poorest* (Occasional Papers in Social Administration 1965). For further discussion see Townsend, P., *Poverty in the United Kingdom* (Penguin 1979), especially pp. 241–7. Of course, this is not to prejudice the issue of the nature of poverty and Townsend's concept of relative deprivation, for the difficulties of which see Piachaud, D., 'Peter Townsend and the Holy Grail', *New Society* (10 September 1981), pp. 419–21.

31 See, for example, Hyman, M., *The Extra Costs of Disabled Living* (National Fund for Research into Crippling Diseases, 1977).

32 See Sainsbury, S., *Social Policy and Disability* (forthcoming).
33 Tumin, W., *Weekly Boarding: Why and How* (National Deaf Children's Society 1974).
34 Loach, I., *The Price of Deafness,* The Disability Alliance (RNID 1976), pp. 24–5.
35 Kramer, J. and Piachaud, D., 'The Micro-Economics of Old People's Homes', *British Journal of Social Work*, **12** (1982), pp. 171–87.
36 Townsend, P., *The Last Refuge* (Routledge & Kegan Paul 1962).
37 Kramer and Piachaud, 'The Micro-Economics of Old People's Homes'.

Chapter 10   Leisure

1 The Deaf Broadcasting Campaign, *Does TV reach the Deaf?* (1981), p. 2.
2 ibid., p. 3.
3 ibid., p. 4.

Index